Readings in

PROPAGANDA *and*
PERSUASION
New and Classic Essays

To Adam
    —Garth Jowett

To Paul
    —Victoria O'Donnell

Readings in

PROPAGANDA *and*
PERSUASION
New and Classic Essays

Garth S. Jowett • Victoria O'Donnell

University of Houston   Montana State University

SAGE Publications
Thousand Oaks ▪ London ▪ New Delhi

For information:

Sage Publications, Inc.
2455 Teller Road
Thousand Oaks, California 91320
E-mail: order@sagepub.com

Sage Publications Ltd.
1 Oliver's Yard
55 City Road
London EC1Y 1SP
United Kingdom

Sage Publications India Pvt. Ltd.
B-42, Panchsheel Enclave
Post Box 4109
New Delhi 110 017 India

Printed in the United States of America.

Library of Congress Cataloging-in-Publication Data

Readings in propaganda and persuasion: new and classic essays / edited by Garth S. Jowett and Victoria O'Donnell.
    p. cm.
Includes bibliographical references and index.
ISBN 1–4129–0900–7 (pbk.)
    1. Propaganda. 2. Persuasion (Psychology) I. Jowett, Garth S. II. O'Donnell, Victoria. III. Jowett, Garth S. Propaganda and persuasion.

HM1231.R43 2006

                        2005018313

Printed on acid-free paper.

06   07   08   09   10   10 9 8 7 6 5 4 3 2 1

Acquisitions Editor:	Margaret H. Seawell
Editorial Assistant:	Sarah K. Quesenberry
Project Editor:	Astrid Virding
Typesetter:	C&M Digitals (P) Ltd.
Cover Designer:	Michelle Lee

Contents

Acknowledgments

We would like to acknowledge the authors of the new works in the volume: Beth S. Bennett and Sean O'Rourke, Margaret Cavin, Stuart J. Kaplan, and Nancy Snow for their original and scholarly work in the field; Margaret Seawell for her editorial guidance and patience; Sarah Quesenberry for her cheerful helpfulness; and Kenneth Burke for his scholarly and imaginative work in the field of rhetoric.

Introduction

Garth S. Jowett and Victoria O'Donnell

The 20th century saw an unprecedented interest in the concept of *propaganda,* however broadly and loosely that elusive term may have been defined. Precipitated by the growth of new communication systems and media in the late 18th and 19th centuries, it became increasingly obvious that new methods of disseminating messages over a wide geographic range with increasingly greater speeds would fundamentally alter the nature of human interaction. Since the beginning of recorded history, philosophers, politicians, historians, religious leaders, and others examining the human condition have voiced concern about the potential for "the few" to control the destiny of "the many." In Western civilization, the works of Plato, Aristotle, and Quintilian serve as our starting points for the study of rhetoric and its potential for good or evil, but in the past 2,000 years, many others have also signaled a concern about this possibility. Whether discussing the centralization of power and ideology by Julius Caesar in the ancient world or the establishment of a well-orchestrated cult personality and dramatic iconography by Napoleon Bonaparte or the horrors stemming from the psychologically based Nazi propaganda strategies of Josef Goebbels, critics and analysts have all evinced a fear that the general public can, under the right circumstances, be dangerously susceptible to manipulative communication techniques. These techniques may range over a wide array of symbolic or physical acts, but the central and simple purpose is to alter and manipulate public attitudes, perceptions, and ultimately behavior in such a way as to benefit those employing such techniques.

In particular, since the emergence of what is termed *mass media* in the early 19th century, we have seen an increasing articulation of the concern that these new media forms could be used for nefarious purposes by unscrupulous politicians and others wishing to manipulate public opinion. When combined with the political upheaval creating the democratic nation-states, offering the potential for political participation by previously disenfranchised classes, the so-called power of the media was often given greater weight than was its due. The growth in importance of advertising and its offshoot, public relations, seems to give credence to the emergent power of communications media to influence vast publics in a seemingly homogeneous manner. The final brush strokes to this growing canvas of concern about public manipulation were the two major world conflicts of the 20th century. In both World War I and World War II, the use of propaganda was widely acknowledged and even hailed as being an essential tool of any unified effort to win the war. The public on both sides of the conflict eagerly embraced such activities even when it was obvious that their emotions had been manipulated. Subsequent revelations about the extent of such propaganda activities seem to have little effect on the general public, although a small number of academics, politicians, and social activists used these findings as a basis for further condemnation and concern about propaganda.

Since the end of World War II, the dynamic growth and increased sophistication of communication systems of all types has provided an unparalleled opportunity for the development of new methods to influence public opinion on a wide range of activities and behaviors. The Cold War conflict between the competing ideologies of capitalism and communism precipitated the development and implementation of a long-lasting and worldwide series of propaganda strategies aimed at winning "the hearts and minds" of the world's population. This ideological conflict raged for more than 50 years and, perhaps of greater importance, created a global market for the production and selling of goods and ideas. Most experts agree that the end of the Cold War was as much attributable to the success at marketing the capitalist culture of consumption as it was a demonstration of military superiority. Two startling developments at the end of the 20th century served as a fitting cap to the ever-rising curve of human communication potential. First, there was the development of communications satellites, and the second was the unexpected emergence of the Internet as an international force for the dissemination of information. Both indicated great promise for fostering the development of truly democratic communication systems, but both also allowed the dangerous possibility for domination by centralized commercial or political entities. We have already witnessed major governments such as the People's Republic of China exert constrictive control over both media. We have also seen widespread use of the Internet by terrorists as a means of communicating with one another. The 21st century is an age of a mass technological and global society bombarded with information. More than ever, it is essential to understand and evaluate the nature of communication and its delivery.

In today's world, the interest in, and concern about, the manipulation of public opinion, attitude formation and/or change, and influencing behavior has reached unprecedented heights. This concern extends way beyond the political dimension that preoccupied 19th-century observers but now encompasses not only politics but also the realm of consumerism and the role that advertising plays in shaping our increasing desire and reliance on material goods for satisfying our social needs. In very recent years, the increasingly salient work of public relations agencies in deliberately manipulating and shaping public opinion has come under intense public scrutiny, revealing a hidden world of corporate activity previously not clearly understood by the general public. The Internet has proved to be invaluable in providing a public forum for the disclosure and discussion of these issues, and such public revelations have had an obvious effect on both of these industries.

It is very clear that there is a growing interest in the world of what has been loosely called "propaganda studies." When we wrote the first edition of our book *Propaganda and Persuasion* in 1986, we indicated our belief that public and academic interest in this subject was just then beginning to reemerge after a lengthy hiatus; since then, we have been gratified to see that our prediction has proven to be true. The issue of *propaganda* (using a variety of synonyms such as *spin* and *media bias*) is now widely discussed on television, in popular magazines and academic journals, in a remarkable number of books, and, most notably, in the hundreds, possibly thousands, of online sites in the form of professional media analysis organizations (such as the liberal www.Mediamatters.com and the conservative www.Mediaresearch.org) or personal "blogs." In the long run, such public interest can only be a positive development, although the current chaotic state of this new media analysis activity can be extremely confusing for those looking for accurate information.

The Scope of This Book

When we formulated the idea for this book, we had three objectives in mind. First, we wished to pull together a variety of salient readings that would complement and enrich the chapters in our book *Propaganda and Persuasion*; second, we hoped that it would also serve as a stand-alone volume, for use in a variety of contexts, of important readings indicative of the wide variety of subject matter that could be subsumed under the heading "propaganda studies"; and finally, by including a significant number of original essays by current authors as well as major historical pieces, it would serve as an encouragement to others to engage in similar analysis. We believe that we have achieved the first two of our objectives, and we will trust that we have encouraged others to consider the exciting intellectual challenges that propaganda studies offers at this time.

Although the book is loosely structured to follow the chapter sequence in *Propaganda and Persuasion,* it does not require the use of this textbook to be useful in its own right. The essays have been carefully chosen to guide the reader both vertically along an historical dimension as well as laterally to indicate the breadth of the subject matter. The opening essay by the French philosopher Jacques Ellul is an edited version from his book *Propaganda: The Formation of Men's Attitudes.* This essay sets the tone for what is to follow by indicating the ubiquity of propaganda activities as an integral function of modern society. Ellul was unique in his time in making a case for considering propaganda as a neutral, even necessary, activity for the functioning of the institutions of our modern society. He believed that propaganda is not made up of techniques but is technique itself, inseparable from ideology and seamlessly connected to all other technical phenomena. Ellul regarded propaganda as sociological phenomena but not as something produced by people of intentions. He also said that people need propaganda because we live in mass society, and it enables us to participate in important events such as elections and celebrations. Ellul's views are not universally held, in that propaganda is still most commonly considered to be a dysfunctional and negative activity. However, many modern scholars and analysts are moving toward a perspective closer to that of Ellul (a view also held by the editors of this volume) that propaganda can be either positive or negative depending on its purpose. This issue over the confusion of the meaning of the word *propaganda* is the subject of the essay by Beth S. Bennett and Sean Patrick O'Rourke, who review the role of rhetoricians who have analyzed propaganda together with an overview of the history of rhetoric that relates to the uses and abuses of persuasion. They have developed a lexicon that delineates the distinctions among true rhetoric, popular rhetoric, and manipulative rhetoric, depositing propaganda under the latter heading and recognizing that propaganda is rhetorical. Their progress toward theoretical development is an important contribution to the understanding of the place of propaganda in rhetorical theory, and their distinctions of terms go a long way to clarify confusion about definitions.

There is no confusion in the way that Gladys and Marcella Thum examine the so-called Boston "Massacre" and how it was used as a very successful propaganda symbol during the American Revolution. The American Revolution stands as a benchmark in the development of propaganda strategies, indicating that the judicious use of all available media—in this case, small newspapers and pamphlets—combined with a well-articulated, emotionally charged cause can be enormously effective in achieving objectives.

This theme is carried over in the next essay by Thomas C. Sorenson, in his detailed examination of the emergence of official propaganda activities in the United States in the early part of the 20th century. Sorenson describes the continuing conflict between the necessity to maintain an official propaganda agency and the natural suspicion of such activities inherent in a political democracy. These are conflicts that have not yet resolved themselves in the United States. There have been many changes in international relationships since Sorenson wrote his essay in 1968, and it is interesting to compare his observations about American "public diplomacy" with the current comments of Nancy Snow in her essay later in this book.

The 20th century also witnessed the emergence of the true totalitarian state, when citizens are required to sacrifice a wide range of their own personal liberties for "the good of the state." Philip Taylor's examination of the Bolshevik revolution and the emergence of the world's first propaganda state details how a totally controlled media system was used to disseminate an ideology that fundamentally altered the structure of Soviet society and set in motion the events that would culminate in the Cold War. David Welsh picks up the corollary theme in his analysis of Nazi propaganda, examining the vast extent of the Nazi propaganda apparatus that controlled virtually every aspect of German life from early education to death. Even today, whenever the word *propaganda* is used, images from the iconography of Nazi propaganda tend to spring to mind, indicating the inherent symbolic power of the legacy left by this evil regime. In the next essay, Kenneth Burke, one of the 20th century's most esteemed rhetorical-literary critics, turns his attention to an intensive analysis of Adolf Hitler's book *Mein Kampf*. Burke believed that rhetoric must investigate the symbolic means of ideological identification capable of creating cohesion and/or division. His premise was that language is a strategic response to a situation. Burke's brilliant perspective on the significance of *Mein Kampf* serves to underscore the damage done when many in the West chose not to take the contents of the book seriously upon its first publication. This essay also serves to demonstrate the potential that can be achieved by such an in-depth analysis of a propaganda activity.

The propaganda activities of World War II continue to provide a rich source for both case studies and social scientific analysis of various forms of persuasive techniques. The historian David Culbert examines the famous *Why We Fight* series of orientation films made by Hollywood director Frank Capra for the U.S. Army and provides us with the context within which to understand the role that these films were required to play and the political machinations that ultimately dictated their content. Some of the *Why We Fight* films were extensively analyzed by social scientists at the time to determine their effectiveness as training vehicles, and this body of work served as a significant underpinning to modern research in the field of persuasion studies. This theme of psychological warfare is continued in Paul M. A. Linebarger's essay, which is taken from his seminal work in this field. It is important to know that this essay was written in 1954 and reflects thinking on the subject based on the experiences of World War II. It is surprising to note that 50 years later, human nature being as consistent as it is, there would not be much to add to the strategies outlined in Linebarger's chapter, other than the use of more sophisticated analytical techniques. The final essay dealing with the use of propaganda during wartime is Garth Jowett's examination of one of the most painful and mysterious episodes in American military history, that of forced indoctrination or, as it was commonly called, the "brainwashing" of POWs during the Korean War. At the conclusion of hostilities in 1953, 21 American servicemen elected to remain with the enemy in North Korea, a situation unprecedented in any previous conflict and one that caused the military to reevaluate its training procedures regarding capture by the enemy. The word *brainwashing* subsequently entered the language, and this overview puts into context the complexity of a subject that has been much misunderstood and misinterpreted.

Of course, propaganda appears in a wide variety of forms and activities and can be found in seemingly benign objects. Victoria O'Donnell examines the influence of the built environment and demonstrates that architecture and various design elements can be an important source of both persuasive and propaganda messages for an unsuspecting public. Architectural design can influence both attitudes and behavior, depending on individual perception. Architecture is also a symbol of national ideology as well as a persuasive force that perpetuates ideology. Stuart J. Kaplan specifically extends this theme in his examination of the visual metaphor associated with the tragic events of September 11, 2001, and the decision to select a design for the memorial to those who lost their lives when the World Trade Center was attacked. Kaplan also provides a comprehensive background of metaphor studies and evaluates the role that visual metaphors have come to play in our society.

The last segment of essays deals with propaganda issues precipitated by the turmoil found in the Middle East and the role of the United States in world affairs. Margaret Cavin presents a fascinating case study about how fame gleaned from the entertainment world can be used to successfully launch a propaganda campaign. Using television programs and celebrity interviews, Cavin explains how context influenced Mavis Leno's campaign to help the women of Afghanistan as well as how it affected public responses. Nancy Snow, using her extensive personal experience in government service, offers a detailed evaluation of current U.S. activities in the field of international public diplomacy during this time, when many nations are opposed to American policies. She finds these activities severely deficient and lacking in both substance and a coherent strategy for success.

These essays, taken as a whole, not only provide the reader with information about the utilization of propaganda at specific points in history but also offer an opportunity to consider the broad field of human activity within which propaganda operates. In conclusion, we must consider Jacques Ellul's initial thesis that propaganda is an integral and essential part of the function of modern society. As such, and because it will not disappear, we do well to study and understand it.

1

The Characteristics
of Propaganda

Jacques Ellul

T rue modern propaganda can only function within the context of the
modern scientific system. But what is it? Many observers look upon
propaganda as a collection of "gimmicks" and of more or less serious practices.[1] And psychologists and sociologists very often reject the scientific character of these practices. For our part, we completely agree that propaganda
is a technique rather than a science.[2] But it is a *modern* technique—that is, it
is based on one or more branches of science. Propaganda is the expression of
these branches of science; it moves with them, shares in their successes, and
bears witness to their failures. The time is past when propaganda was a matter of individual inspiration, personal subtlety, or the use of unsophisticated
tricks. Now science has entered propaganda, as we shall reveal from four
different points of view.

First of all, modern propaganda is based on scientific analyses of psychology and sociology. Step by step, the propagandist builds his techniques on the
basis of his knowledge of man, his tendencies, his desires, his needs, his psychic mechanisms, his conditioning—and as much on social psychology as on
depth psychology. He shapes his procedures on the basis of our knowledge of

SOURCE: Excerpted from J. Ellul, *Propaganda: The Formation of Men's Attitudes,*
copyright © 1965. Reprinted with permission by Alfred A. Knopf, an imprint of
Random House, Inc.

groups and their laws of formation and dissolution, of mass influences, and of environmental limitations. Without the scientific research of modern psychology and sociology there would be no propaganda, or rather we still would be in the primitive stages of propaganda that existed in the time of Pericles or Augustus. Of course, propagandists may be insufficiently versed in these branches of science; they may misunderstand them, go beyond the cautious conclusions of the psychologists, or claim to apply certain psychological discoveries that, in fact, do not apply at all. But all this only shows efforts to find new ways: only for the past fifty years have men sought to apply the psychological and sociological sciences. The important thing is that propaganda has decided to submit itself to science and to make use of it. Of course, psychologists may be scandalized and say that this is a misuse of their science. But this argument carries no weight; the same applies to our physicists and the atomic bomb. The scientist should know that he lives in a world in which his discoveries will be utilized. Propagandists inevitably will have a better understanding of sociology and psychology, use them with increasing precision, and as a result become more effective.

Second, propaganda is scientific in that it tends to establish a set of rules, rigorous, precise, and tested, that are not merely recipes but impose themselves on every propagandist, who is less and less free to follow his own impulses. He must apply, increasingly and exactly, certain precise formulas that can be applied by anybody with the proper training—clearly a characteristic of a technique based on science.

Third, what is needed nowadays is an exact analysis of both the environment and the individual to be subjected to propaganda. No longer does the man of talent determine the method, the approach, or the subject; all that is now being calculated (or must be calculated). Therefore, one type of propaganda will be found suitable in one situation and completely useless in another. To undertake an active propaganda operation, it is necessary to make a scientific, sociological, and psychological analysis first, and then utilize those branches of science, which are becoming increasingly well known. But, here again, proper training is necessary for those who want to use them with their full effectiveness.

Finally, one last trait reveals the scientific character of modern propaganda: the increasing attempt to control its use, measure its results, define its effects. This is very difficult, but the propagandist is no longer content to have obtained, or to believe he has obtained, a certain result; he seeks precise evidence. Even successful political results do not completely satisfy him. He wants to understand the how and why of them and measure their exact effect. He is prompted by a certain spirit of experimentation and a desire to ponder the results. From this point on, one can see the beginning of scientific method. Admittedly, it is not yet very widespread, and those who analyze results are not active propagandists but philosophers. Granted, that reveals a certain division of labor, nothing more. It indicates that propaganda is no longer a self-contained action, covering up for evil deeds. It is an object of serious thought, and proceeds along scientific channels.

Some people object to this. One frequently hears psychologists ridicule the claim to a scientific basis advanced by the propagandist and reject the latter's claims of having employed scientific techniques. "The psychology he uses is not scientific psychology; the sociology he uses is not scientific sociology." But after a careful look at the controversy one comes to this conclusion: Stalinist propaganda was in great measure founded on Pavlov's theory of the conditioned reflex. Hitlerian propaganda was in great measure founded on Freud's theory of repression and libido. American propaganda is founded in great measure on Dewey's theory of teaching. Now, if a psychologist does not accept the idea of the conditioned reflex and doubts that it can be created in man, he then rejects Pavlov's interpretation of psychological phenomena and concludes that all propaganda based on it is pseudo-scientific. It is obviously the same for those who question the findings of Freud, Dewey, or anybody else.

What does this mean, then? That propaganda does *not* rest on a scientific base? Certainly not. Rather, that scientists are not agreed among themselves on the domains, methods, or conclusions of psychology and sociology. A psychologist who rejects the theory of one of his colleagues rejects a scientific theory and not merely the inferences that a technician may draw from it. One cannot blame the propagandist if he has confidence in a particular sociologist or psychologist whose theory is generally accepted and who is, at a given time and in a given country, considered a scientist. Moreover, let us not forget that if this theory, put to use by the propagandist, brings results and proves to be effective, it thereby receives additional confirmation and that simple doctrinal criticism can then no longer demonstrate its inaccuracy.

1. External Characteristics

The Individual and the Masses

Any modern propaganda will, first of all, address itself at one and the same time to the individual and to the masses. It cannot separate the two elements. For propaganda to address itself to the individual, in his isolation, apart from the crowd, is impossible. The individual is of no interest to the propagandist; as an isolated unit he presents much too much resistance to external action. To be effective, propaganda cannot be concerned with detail, not only because to win men over one by one takes much too long, but also because to create certain convictions in an isolated individual is much too difficult. Propaganda ceases where simple dialogue begins. And that is why, in particular, experiments undertaken in the United States to gauge the effectiveness of certain propaganda methods or arguments on isolated individuals are not conclusive: they do not reproduce the real propaganda situation. Conversely, propaganda does not aim simply at the mass, the crowd. A propaganda that functioned only where individuals are gathered together would be incomplete and insufficient. Also, any propaganda aimed only at groups as such—as if a mass were a specific body having a soul and reactions and feelings entirely different from individuals' souls, reactions, and feelings—would be an abstract propaganda that likewise would have no effectiveness. Modern propaganda reaches individuals enclosed in the mass and as participants in that mass, yet it also aims at a crowd, but only as a body composed of individuals.

What does this mean? First of all, that the individual never is considered as an individual, but always in terms of what he has in common with others, such as his motivations, his feelings, or his myths. He is reduced to an average; and, except for a small percentage, action based on averages will be effectual. Moreover, the individual is considered part of the mass and included in it (and so far as possible systematically integrated into it), because in that way his psychic defenses are weakened, his reactions are easier to provoke, and the propagandist profits from the process of diffusion of emotions through the mass, and, at the same time, from the pressure felt by an individual when in a group. Emotionalism, impulsiveness, excess, etc.—all these characteristics of the individual caught up in a mass are well known and very helpful to propaganda. Therefore, the individual must never be considered as being alone; the listener to a radio broadcast, though actually alone, is nevertheless part of a large group, and he is aware of it. Radio listeners have been found to exhibit a mass mentality. All are tied together and constitute a sort of society in which all individuals are accomplices and influence each other without knowing it. The same holds true for propaganda that is carried on by door-to-door visits (direct contacts, petitions for signatures); although apparently one deals here with a single individual, one deals in reality with a unit submerged into an invisible crowd composed of all those who have been interviewed, who are being interviewed, and who will be interviewed, because they hold similar ideas and live by the same myths, and especially because they are targets of the same organism. Being the target of a party or an administration is enough to immerse the individual in that sector of the population which the propagandist has in his sights; this simple fact makes the individual part of the mass. He is no longer Mr. X, but part of a current flowing in a particular direction. The current flows through the canvasser (who is not a person speaking in his own name with his own arguments, but one segment of an administration, an organization, a collective movement); when he enters a room to canvass a person, the mass, and moreover the organized, leveled mass, enters with him. No relationship exists here between man and man; the organization is what exerts its attraction on an individual already part of a mass because he is in the same sights as all the others being canvassed.

Conversely, when propaganda is addressed to a crowd, it must touch each individual in that crowd, in that whole group. To be effective, it must give the impression of being personal, for we must never forget that the mass is composed of individuals, and is in fact nothing but assembled individuals. Actually, just because men are in a group, and therefore weakened, receptive, and in a state of psychological regression, they pretend all the more to be "strong individuals." The mass man is clearly subhuman, but pretends to be superman. He is more suggestible, but insists he is more forceful; he is more unstable, but thinks he is firm in his convictions. If one openly treats the mass as a mass, the individuals who form it will feel themselves belittled and will refuse to participate. If one treats these individuals as children (and they are children because they are in a group), they will not accept their leader's projections or identify with him. They will withdraw and we will not be able to get anything out of them. On the contrary, each one must feel individualized, each must have the impression that *he* is being looked at, that *he* is being addressed personally. Only then will he respond and cease to be anonymous (although in reality remaining anonymous).

Thus all modern propaganda profits from the structure of the mass, but exploits the individual's need for self-affirmation; and the two actions must be conducted jointly, simultaneously. Of course this operation is greatly facilitated by the existence of the modern mass media of communication, which have precisely this remarkable effect of reaching the whole crowd all at once, and yet reaching each one in that crowd. Readers of the evening paper, radio listeners, movie or TV viewers certainly constitute a mass that has an organic existence, although it is diffused and not assembled at one point. These individuals are moved by the same motives, receive the same impulses and impressions, find themselves focused on the same centers of interest, experience the same feelings, have generally the same order of reactions and ideas, participate in the same myths—and all this at the same time: what we have here is really a psychological, if not a biological mass. And the individuals in it are modified by this existence, even if they do not know it. Yet each one is alone—the newspaper reader, the radio listener. He therefore feels himself individually concerned as a person, as a participant. The movie spectator also is alone; though elbow to elbow with his neighbors, he still is, because of the darkness and the hypnotic attraction of the screen, perfectly alone. This is the situation of the "lonely crowd," or of isolation in the mass, which is a natural product of present-day society and which is both used and deepened by the mass media. The most favorable moment to seize a man and influence him is when he is alone in the mass: it is at this point that propaganda can be most effective.

We must emphasize this circle which we shall meet again and again: the structure of present-day society places the individual where he is most easily reached by propaganda. The media of mass communication, which are part of the technical evolution of this society, deepen this situation while making it possible to reach the individual man, integrated in the mass; and what these media do is exactly what propaganda must do in order to attain its objectives. In reality propaganda cannot exist without using these mass media. If, by chance, propaganda is addressed to an organized group, it can have practically no effect on individuals before that group has been fragmented.[3] Such fragmentation can be achieved through action, but it is equally possible to fragment a group by psychological means. The transformation of very small groups by purely psychological means is one of the most important techniques of propaganda. Only when very small groups are thus annihilated, when the individual finds no more defenses, no equilibrium, no resistance exercised by the group to which he belongs, does total action by propaganda become possible.[4]

Total Propaganda

Propaganda must be total. The propagandist must utilize all of the technical means at his disposal—the press, radio, TV, movies, posters, meetings, door-to-door canvassing. Modern propaganda must utilize *all* of these media. There is no propaganda as long as one makes use, in sporadic fashion and at random, of a newspaper article here, a poster or a radio program there, organizes a few meetings and lectures, writes a few slogans on walls; that is not propaganda. Each usable medium has its own particular way of penetration—specific, but at the same time localized and limited; by itself it cannot attack the individual, break down his resistance, make his decisions for him. A movie does not play on the same motives, does not produce the same feelings, does not provoke the same reactions as a newspaper. The very fact that the effectiveness of each medium is limited to one particular area clearly shows the necessity of complementing it with other media. A word spoken on the radio is not the same, does not produce the same effect, does not have the same impact as the identical word spoken in private conversation or in a public speech before a large crowd. To draw the individual into the net of propaganda, each technique must be utilized in its own specific way, directed toward producing the effect it can best produce, and fused with all the other media, each of them reaching the individual in a specific fashion and making him react anew to the same theme—in the same direction, but *differently.*

It is a matter of reaching and encircling the whole man and all men. Propaganda tries to surround man by all possible routes, in the realm of feelings as well as ideas, by playing on his will or on his needs, through his conscious and his unconscious, assailing him in both his private and his public life. It furnishes him with a complete system for explaining the world, and provides immediate incentives to action. We are here in the presence of an organized myth that tries to take hold of the entire person. Through the myth it creates, propaganda imposes a complete range of intuitive knowledge, susceptible of only one interpretation, unique and one-sided, and precluding any divergence. This myth becomes so powerful that it invades every area of consciousness, leaving no faculty or motivation intact. It stimulates in the individual a feeling of exclusiveness, and produces a biased attitude. The myth has such motive force that, once accepted, it controls the whole of the individual, who becomes immune to any other influence. This explains the totalitarian attitude that the individual adopts—wherever a myth has been successfully created—and that simply reflects the totalitarian action of propaganda on him.

Not only does propaganda seek to invade the whole man, to lead him to adopt a mystical attitude and reach him through all possible psychological channels, but, more, it speaks to all men. Propaganda cannot be satisfied with partial successes, for it does not tolerate discussion; by its very nature, it excludes contradiction and discussion. As long as a noticeable or expressed tension or a conflict of action remains, propaganda cannot be said to have accomplished its aim. It must produce quasi-unanimity, and the opposing faction must become negligible, or in any case cease to be vocal. Extreme propaganda must win over the adversary and at least use him by integrating him into its own frame of reference. That is why it was so important to have an Englishman speak on the Nazi radio or a General Paulus on the Soviet radio; why it was so important for the propaganda of the *fellagha* to make use of articles in *L'Observateur* and *L'Express* and for French propaganda to obtain statements from repentant *fellagha.*

Clearly, the ultimate was achieved by Soviet propaganda in the self-criticism of its opponents. That the enemy of a regime (or of the faction in power) can be made to declare, *while he is still the enemy,* that this regime was right, that his opposition was criminal, and that his condemnation is just—that is the ultimate result of totalitarian propaganda. The enemy (while still remaining the enemy, and because he is the enemy) is converted into a supporter of the regime. This is not simply a very useful and effective means of propaganda. Let us also note that, under the Khrushchev regime, the propaganda of self-criticism continued to function just as before (Marshal Bulganin's self-criticism was the most characteristic example). Here we are seeing the total, all-devouring propaganda mechanism in action: it cannot leave *any* segment of opinion outside its sphere; it cannot tolerate any sort of independence. Everything must be brought back into this unique sphere of action, which is an end in itself and can be justified only if virtually every man ends up by participating in it.

This brings us to another aspect of total propaganda. The propagandist must combine the elements of propaganda as in a real orchestration. On the one hand he must keep in mind the stimuli that can be utilized at a given moment, and must organize them. This results in a propaganda "campaign."[5] On the other hand, the propagandist must use various instruments, each in relation to all the others. Alongside the mass media of communication propaganda employs censorship, legal texts, proposed legislation, international conferences, and so forth—thus introducing elements seemingly alien to propaganda. We should not only consider the mass media: personal contacts are considered increasingly effective. Educational methods play an immense role in political indoctrination (Lenin, Mao). A conference on Lenin's Doctrine of the State *is* propaganda. Information is extremely helpful to propaganda, as we shall demonstrate. "To explain correctly the present state of affairs is the great task of the agitator." Mao emphasizes that in 1928 an effective form of propaganda was the release of prisoners *after* they had been indoctrinated. The same was true of the care given to the enemy wounded; all this was to show the good will of the Communists. Everything can serve as a means of propaganda and everything must be utilized.

In this way diplomacy becomes inseparable from propaganda. Education and training are inevitably taken over, as the Napoleonic Empire demonstrated for the first time. No contrast can be tolerated between teaching and propaganda, between the critical spirit formed by higher education and the exclusion of independent thought. One must utilize the education of the young to condition them to what comes later. The schools and all methods of instruction are transformed under such conditions, with the child integrated into the conformist group in such a way that the individualist is tolerated not by the authorities but by his peers. Religion and the churches are constrained to hold on to their own places in the orchestra if they want to survive.[6] Napoleon expressly formulated the doctrine of propaganda by the Church. The judicial apparatus is also utilized.[7] Of course, a trial can be an admirable springboard of propaganda for the accused, who can spread his ideas in his defense and exert an influence by the way he suffers his punishment. This holds true in the democracies. But the situation is reversed where a totalitarian state makes propaganda. During a trial there, the judge is forced to demonstrate a lesson for the education of the public: verdicts are educational. And, we know the importance of confessions in the great show trials (e.g., the

Reichstag fire, the Moscow trials of 1936, the Nuremberg trials, and innumerable trials in the People's Democracies after 1945).

Finally, propaganda will take over literature (present *and* past) and history, which must be rewritten according to propaganda's needs. We must not say: this is done by tyrannical, autocratic, totalitarian governments. In fact, it is the result of propaganda *itself*. Propaganda carries within itself, of intrinsic necessity, the power to take over everything that can serve it. Let us remember the innocent example of democratic, liberal, republican propaganda, which without hesitation took over many things in the nineteenth century (perhaps without realizing it and in good faith, but that is not an excuse). Let us remember the Athenian democracy, the Roman Republic, the movement of the medieval Communes, the Renaissance, and the Reformation. History was hardly less modified then than Russian history was by the Bolsheviks. We know, on the other hand, how propaganda takes over the literature of the past, furnishing it with contexts and explanations designed to re-integrate it into the present. From a thousand examples, we will choose just one.

In an article in *Pravda* in May 1957, the Chinese writer Mao Dun wrote that the ancient poets of China used the following words to express the striving of the people toward a better life: "The flowers perfume the air, the moon shines, man has a long life." And he added: "Allow me to give a new explanation of these poetic terms. The flowers perfume the air—this means that the flowers of the art of socialist realism are incomparably beautiful. The moon shines—this means that the sputnik has opened a new era in the conquest of space. Man has a long life—this means that the great Soviet Union will live tens and tens of thousands of years."

When one reads this once, one smiles. If one reads it a thousand times, and no longer reads anything else, one must undergo a change. And we must reflect on the transformation of perspective already suffered by a whole society in which texts like this (published by the thousands) can be distributed and taken seriously not only by the authorities but by the intellectuals. This complete change of perspective of the *Weltanschauung* is the primary totalitarian element of propaganda.

Finally, the propagandist must use not only all of the instruments, but also different forms of propaganda. There are many types of propaganda, though there is a present tendency to combine them. Direct propaganda, aimed at modifying opinions and attitudes, must be preceded by propaganda that is sociological in character, slow, general, seeking to create a climate, an atmosphere of favorable preliminary attitudes. No direct propaganda can be effective without pre-propaganda, which, without direct or noticeable aggression, is limited to creating ambiguities, reducing prejudices, and spreading images, apparently without purpose. The spectator will be much more disposed to believe in the grandeur of France when he has seen a dozen films on French petroleum, railroads, or jetliners. The ground must be sociologically prepared before one can proceed to direct prompting. Sociological propaganda can be compared to plowing, direct propaganda to sowing; you cannot do the one without doing the other first. Both techniques must be used. For sociological propaganda alone will never induce an individual to change his actions. It leaves him at the level of his everyday life, and will not lead him to make decisions. Propaganda of the word and propaganda of the deed are complementary. Talk must correspond to something visible; the visible, active element must be explained by talk. Oral or written propaganda, which plays on opinions or sentiments, must be reinforced by propaganda of action, which produces new attitudes and thus joins the individual firmly to a certain movement. Here again, you cannot have one without the other.

We must also distinguish between covert propaganda and overt propaganda. The former tends to hide its aims, identity, significance, and source. The people are not aware that someone is trying to influence them, and do not feel that they are being pushed in a certain direction. This is often called "black propaganda." It also makes use of mystery and silence. The other kind, "white propaganda," is open and aboveboard. There is a Ministry of Propaganda; one admits that propaganda is being made; its source is known; its aims and intentions are identified. The public knows that an attempt is being made to influence it.

The propagandist is forced to use both kinds, to combine them, for they pursue different objectives. Overt propaganda is necessary for attacking enemies; it alone is capable of reassuring one's own forces; it is a manifestation of strength and good organization. A token of victory. But covert propaganda is more effective if the aim is to push one's supporters in a certain direction without their being aware of it. Also, it is necessary to use sometimes one, sometimes the other on the same group; the Nazis knew very well how to alternate long silences, mystery, the secret revealed, the waiting period that raises anxiety levels, and then, suddenly, the explosive decision, the tempest, the *Sturm* that seems all the more violent because it breaks into the silence. Finally, we well know that the combination of covert propaganda and overt propaganda is increasingly conducted so that white propaganda actually becomes a cover and mask for black propaganda—that is, one openly admits the existence of one kind of propaganda and of its organization, means, and objectives, but all this is only a façade to capture the attention of individuals and neutralize their instinct to resist, while other individuals, behind the scenes, work on public opinion in a totally different direction, seeking to arouse very different reactions, utilizing even existing resistance to overt propaganda.[8]

Let us give one last example of this combination of differing types of propaganda. Lasswell divides propaganda into two main streams according to whether it produces direct incitement or indirect incitement. Direct incitement is that by which the propagandist himself acts, becomes involved, demonstrates his conviction, his belief, his good faith. He commits himself to the course of action that he proposes and supports, and in order to obtain a similar action, he solicits a corresponding response from the propagandee. Democratic propaganda—in which the politician extends a hand to the citizen—is of this type. Indirect incitement is that which rests on a difference between the statesman, who takes action, and the public, which is limited to passive acceptance and compliance. There is a coercive influence and there is obedience; this is one of the characteristics of authoritarian propaganda.

Although this distinction is not altogether useless, we must again point out that every modern propagandist combines the two types of propaganda because each responds to different sectors of action. These two types no longer belong to different political regimes, but are differing needs of the same propaganda and of the various levels on which propaganda is organized. Propaganda of action presupposes positive incitement; propaganda through mass media will generally be contrasted incitement. Similarly, on the level of the performer in direct contact with the crowd, there must be positive incitement (it is better if the radio speaker *believes* in his cause); on the level of the organizer, that of propaganda strategy, there must be separation from the public. (We shall return to this point below.) These examples suffice to show that propaganda must be total.

Continuity and Duration of Propaganda

Propaganda must be continuous and lasting—continuous in that it must not leave any gaps, but must fill the citizen's whole day and all his days; lasting in that it must function over a very long period of time.[9] Propaganda tends to make the individual live in a separate world; he must not have outside points of reference. He must not be allowed a moment of meditation or reflection in which to see himself vis-à-vis the propagandist, as happens when the propaganda is not continuous. At that moment the individual emerges from the grip of propaganda. Instead, successful propaganda will occupy every moment of the individual's life: through posters and loudspeakers when he is out walking, through radio and newspapers at home, through meetings and movies in the evening. The individual must not be allowed to recover, to collect himself, to remain untouched by propaganda during any relatively long period, for propaganda is not the touch of the magic wand. It is based on slow, constant impregnation. It creates convictions and compliance through imperceptible influences that are effective only by continuous repetition. It must create a complete environment for the individual, one from which he never emerges. And to prevent him from finding external points of reference, it protects him by censoring everything that might come in from the outside. The slow building up of reflexes and myths, of psychological environment and prejudices, requires propaganda of very long duration. Propaganda is not a stimulus that disappears quickly; it consists of successive impulses and shocks aimed at various feelings or thoughts by means of the many instruments previously mentioned. A relay system is thus established. Propaganda is a continuous action, without failure or interruption: as soon as the effect of one impulse is weakened, it is renewed by another. At no point does it fail to subject its recipient to its influence. As soon as one effect wears off, it is followed by a new shock.

Continuous propaganda exceeds the individual's capacities for attention or adaptation and thus his capabilities of resistance. This trait of continuity explains why propaganda can indulge in sudden twists and turns.[10] It is always surprising that the content of propaganda can be so inconsistent that it can approve today what it condemned yesterday.

Having no more relation to real propaganda are the experiments often undertaken to discover whether some propaganda method is effective on a group of individuals being used as guinea pigs. Such experiments are basically vitiated by the fact that they are of short duration. Moreover, the individual can clearly discern any propaganda when it suddenly appears in a social environment normally not subject to this type of influence; if one isolated item of propaganda or one campaign appears without a massive effort, the contrast is so strong that the individual can recognize it clearly as propaganda and begin to be wary. That is precisely what happens in an election campaign; the individual can defend himself when left to himself in his everyday situation. This is why it is fatal to the effectiveness of propaganda to proceed in spurts, with big noisy campaigns separated by long gaps. In such circumstances the individual will always find his bearings again; he will know how to distinguish propaganda from the rest of what the press carries in normal times. Moreover, the more intense the propaganda campaign, the more alert he will become—comparing this sudden intensity with the great calm that reigned before.

What is needed, then, is continuous agitation produced artificially even when nothing in the events of the day justifies or arouses excitement. Therefore, continuing propaganda must slowly create a climate first, and then prevent the individual from noticing a particular propaganda operation in contrast to ordinary daily events.

Organization of Propaganda

To begin with, propaganda must be organized in several ways. To give it the above-mentioned characteristics (continuity, duration, combination of different media), an organization is required that controls the mass media, is capable of using them correctly, of calculating the effect of one or another slogan or of replacing one campaign with another. There must be an *administrative* organization; every modern state is expected to have a Ministry of Propaganda, whatever its actual name may be. Just as technicians are needed to make films and radio broadcasts, so one needs "technicians of influence"—sociologists and psychologists. But this indispensable administrative organization is not what we are speaking of here. What we mean is that propaganda is always institutionalized to the extent of the existence of an *"Apparat"* in the German sense of the term—a machine. It is tied to realities. A great error, which interferes with propaganda analysis, is to believe that propaganda is solely a psychological affair, a manipulation of symbols, an abstract influence on opinions. A large number of American studies on propaganda are not valid for that reason. These studies are concerned only with means of psychological influence and regard only such means as propaganda, whereas all great modern practitioners of propaganda have rigorously tied together psychological and physical action as inseparable elements. No propaganda is possible unless psychological influence rests on reality,[11] and the recruiting of individuals into cadres or movements goes hand in hand with psychological manipulation.

As long as no physical influence is exerted by an organization on the individual, there is no propaganda. This is decidedly not an invention of Mao Tse-tung, or merely an accessory of propaganda, or the expression of a particular type of propaganda. Separation of the psychological and physical elements is an arbitrary simplification that prevents all understanding of exactly what propaganda is. Of course, the physical organization can be of various types. It can be a party organization (Nazi, Fascist, Communist) in which those who are won over are absorbed and made to participate in action; such an organization, moreover, uses force and fear in the form of *Macht Propaganda*. Or such physical organization can be the integration of an entire population into cells by agents in each block of residences; in that case, it operates inside a society by integrating the whole social body. (Of course, this is accompanied by all the psychological work needed to press people into cells.) Or an effective transformation can be made in the economic, political, or social domain. We know that the propagandist is also a psychological consultant to governments; he indicates what measures should or should not be taken to facilitate certain psychological manipulations. It is too often believed that propaganda serves the purpose of sugar-coating bitter pills, of making people accept policies they would not accept spontaneously. But in most cases propaganda seeks to point out courses of action desirable in themselves, such as helpful reforms. Propaganda then becomes this mixture of the actual satisfaction given to the people by the reforms and subsequent exploitation of that satisfaction.

Propaganda cannot operate in a vacuum. It must be rooted in action, in a reality that is part of it. Some positive and welcome measure may be only a means of propaganda; conversely, coercive propaganda must be tied to physical coercion. For example, a big blow to the propaganda of the *Forces de Libération Nationale* (F.L.N.) in France in 1958 was the noisy threat of the referendum that the roads leading to the polls would be mined and booby-trapped; that voters would be massacred and their corpses displayed; that there would be a check in each *douar* of those who had dared to go to the polls. But none of these threats was carried out. Failure to take action is in itself counter-propaganda.

Because propaganda enterprises are limited by the necessity for physical organization and action—without which propaganda is practically non-existent—effective propaganda can work only inside a group, principally inside a nation. Propaganda outside the group—toward other nations for example, or toward an enemy—is necessarily weak.[12] The principal reason for this is undoubtedly the absence of physical organization and of encirclement of the individual. One cannot reach another nation except by way of symbols, through press or radio, and even then only in sporadic fashion. Such an effort may at best raise some doubts, plant some sense of ambiguity, make people ask themselves questions, influence them by suggestion. In case of war, the enemy will not be demoralized by such abstract propaganda unless he is at the same time beaten by armies and pounded by bombers. We can hardly expect great results from a simple dissemination of words unless we prepare for it by education (pre-propaganda) and sustain it by organization and action.

We must not, however, conclude from the decisive importance of organization that psychological action is futile. It is one—but not the only one—indispensable piece of the propaganda mechanism. The manipulation of symbols is necessary for three reasons. First of all, it persuades the individual to enter the framework of an organization. Second, it furnishes him with reasons, justifications, motivations for action. Third, it obtains his total allegiance. More and more we are learning that genuine compliance is essential if action is to be effective. The worker, the soldier, and the partisan must believe in what they are doing, must put all their heart and their good will into it; they must also find their equilibrium, their satisfactions, in their actions. All this is the result of psychological influence, which cannot attain great results alone, but which can attempt anything when combined with organization.

Finally, the presence of organization creates one more phenomenon: the propagandist is always separated from the propagandee, he remains a stranger to him.[15] Even in the actual contact of human relations, at meetings, in door-to-door visits, the propagandist is of a different order; he is nothing else and nothing more than the representative of the organization—or, rather, a delegated fraction of it. He remains a manipulator, in the shadow of the machine. He knows why he speaks certain words and what effect they should have. His words are no longer human words but technically calculated words; they no longer express a feeling or a spontaneous idea, but reflect an organization even when they seem entirely spontaneous. Thus the propagandist is never asked to be involved in what he is saying, for, if it becomes necessary, he may be asked to say the exact opposite with similar conviction. He must, of course, believe in the *cause* he serves, but not in his particular argument. On the other hand, the propagandee hears the word spoken to him here and now and the argument presented to him in which he is asked to believe. He must take them to be human words, spontaneous and carried by conviction. Obviously, if the propagandist were left to himself, if it were only a matter of psychological action, he would end up by being taken in by his own trick, by believing it. He would then be the prisoner of his own formulas and would lose all effectiveness as a propagandist. What protects him from this is precisely the organization to which he belongs, which rigidly maintains a line. The propagandist thus becomes more and more the technician who treats his patients in various ways but keeps himself cold and aloof, selecting his words and actions for purely technical reasons. The patient is an object to be saved or sacrificed according to the necessities of the cause.

Orthopraxy

We now come to an absolutely decisive fact. Propaganda is very frequently described as a manipulation for the purpose of changing ideas or opinions, of making individuals "believe" some idea or fact, and finally of making them adhere to some doctrine—all matters of mind. Or, to put it differently, propaganda is described as dealing with beliefs or ideas. If the individual is a Marxist, it tries to destroy his conviction and turn him into an anti-Marxist, and so on. It calls on all the psychological mechanisms, but appeals to reason as well. It tries to convince, to bring about a decision, to create a firm adherence to some truth. Then, obviously, if the conviction is sufficiently strong, after some soul searching, the individual is ready for action.

This line of reasoning is completely wrong. To view propaganda as still being what it was in 1850 is to cling to an obsolete concept of man and of the means to influence him; it is to condemn oneself to understand nothing about modern propaganda. The aim of modern propaganda is no longer to modify ideas, but to provoke action. It is no longer to change adherence to a doctrine, but to make the individual cling irrationally to a process of action. It is no longer to lead to a choice, but to loosen the reflexes. It is no longer to transform an opinion, but to arouse an active and mythical belief.

Let us note here in passing how badly equipped opinion surveys are to gauge propaganda. We will have to come back to this point in the study of propaganda effects. Simply to ask an individual if he believes this or that, or if he has this or that idea, gives absolutely no indication of what behavior he will adopt or what action he will take; only *action* is of concern to modern propaganda, for its aim is to precipitate an individual's action, with maximum effectiveness and economy.[16] The propagandist therefore does not normally address himself to the individual's intelligence, for the process of intellectual persuasion is long and uncertain, and the road from such intellectual conviction to action even more so. The individual rarely acts purely on the basis of an idea. Moreover, to place propaganda efforts on the intellectual level would require that the propagandist engage in individual debate with each person— an unthinkable method. It is necessary to obtain at least a minimum of participation from everybody.[17] It can be active or passive, but in any case it is not simply a matter of public opinion. To see propaganda only as something related to public opinion implies a great intellectual independence on the part of the propagandee, who is, after all, only a third party in any political action, and who is asked only one opinion. This obviously coincides with a conception of liberal democracy, which assumes that the most one can do with a citizen is to change his opinion in such fashion as to win his vote at election time. The concept of a close relationship between public opinion and propaganda rests on the presumption of an independent popular will. If this concept were right, the role of propaganda would be to modify that popular will which, of course, expresses itself in votes. But what this concept does not take into consideration is that the injection of propaganda into the mechanism of popular action actually *suppresses* liberal democracy, after which we are no longer dealing with votes or the people's sovereignty; propaganda therefore aims solely at *participation*. The participation may be active or passive: active, if propaganda has been able to mobilize the individual for action; passive, if the individual does not act directly but psychologically supports that action.

But, one may ask, does this not bring us right back to public opinion? Certainly not, for opinion leaves the individual a mere spectator who may eventually, but not necessarily, resort to action. Therefore, the idea of participation is much stronger. The supporter of a football team, though not physically in the game, makes his presence felt psychologically by rooting for the players, exciting them, and pushing them to outdo themselves. Similarly the faithful who attend Mass do not interfere physically, but their communicant participation is positive and changes the nature of the phenomenon. These two examples illustrate what we mean by passive participation obtained through propaganda.

Such an action cannot be obtained by the process of choice and deliberation. To be effective, propaganda must constantly short-circuit all thought and decision.[18] It must operate on the individual at the level of the unconscious. He must not know that he is being shaped by outside forces (this is one of the conditions for the success of propaganda), but some central core in him must be reached in order to release the mechanism in the unconscious which will provide the appropriate—and expected—action.

But we may properly ask how propaganda can achieve such a result, a type of reflex action, by short-circuiting the intellectual process. The claim that such results are indeed obtained by propaganda will beget skepticism from the average observer, strenuous denial from the psychologist, and the accusation that this is mere fantasy contradicted by experience. We must, however, qualify our statement. We do not say that *any* man can be made to obey *any* incitement to action in *any* way whatever from one day to the next. We do not say that in each individual prior elementary mechanisms exist on which it is easy to play and which will unfailingly produce a certain effect. We do not hold with a mechanistic view of man. But we must divide propaganda into two phases. There is pre-propaganda (or sub-propaganda) and there is active propaganda. This follows from what we have said earlier about the continuous and permanent nature of propaganda. Obviously, what must be continuous is not the active, intense propaganda of crisis but the sub-propaganda that aims at mobilizing individuals, or, in the etymological sense, to make them mobile[22] and mobilizable in order to thrust them into action at the appropriate moment. It is obvious that we cannot simply throw a man into action without any preparation, without having mobilized him psychologically and made him responsive, not to mention physically ready.

The essential objective of pre-propaganda is to prepare man for a particular action, to make him sensitive to some influence, to get him into condition for the time when he will effectively, and without delay or hesitation, participate in an action. Seen from this angle, pre-propaganda does not have a precise ideological objective; it has nothing to do with an opinion, an idea, a doctrine. It proceeds by psychological manipulations, by character modifications, by the creation of feelings or stereotypes useful when the time comes. It must be continuous, slow, imperceptible. Man must be penetrated in order to shape such tendencies. He must be made to live in a certain psychological climate.

The two great routes that this sub-propaganda takes are the conditioned reflex and the myth. Propaganda tries first of all to create conditioned reflexes in the individual by training him so that certain words, signs, or symbols, even certain persons or facts, provoke unfailing reactions. Despite many protests from psychologists, creating such conditioned reflexes, collectively as well as individually, is definitely possible. But of course in order for such a procedure to succeed, a certain amount of time must elapse, a period of training and repetition. One cannot hope to obtain automatic reactions after only a few weeks' repetition of the same formulas. A real psychic re-formation must be undertaken, so that after months of patient work a crowd will react automatically in the hoped-for direction to some image. But this preparatory work is not yet propaganda, for it is not yet immediately applicable to a concrete case. What is visible in propaganda, what is spectacular and seems to us often incomprehensible or unbelievable, is possible only because of such slow and not very explicit preparation; without it nothing would be possible.

On the other hand, the propagandist tries to create myths by which man will live, which respond to his sense of the sacred. By "myth" we mean an all-encompassing, activating image: a sort of vision of desirable objectives that have lost their material, practical character and have become strongly colored, overwhelming, all-encompassing, and which displace from the conscious all that is not related to it. Such an image pushes man to action precisely because it includes all that he feels is good, just, and true. Without giving a metaphysical analysis of the myth, we will mention the great myths that have been created by various propagandas: the myth of race, of the proletariat, of the Führer, of Communist society, of productivity. Eventually the myth takes possession of a man's mind so completely that his life is consecrated to it. But that effect can be created only by slow, patient work by all the methods of propaganda, not by any immediate propaganda operation. Only when conditioned reflexes have been created in a man and he lives in a collective myth can he be readily mobilized.

Although the two methods of myth and conditioned reflex can be used in combination, each has separate advantages. The United States prefers to utilize the myth; the Soviet Union has for a long time preferred the reflex. The important thing is that when the time is ripe, the individual can be thrown into action by active propaganda, by the utilization of the psychological levers that have been set up, and by the evocation of the myth. No connection necessarily exists between his action and the reflex or the content of the myth. The action is not necessarily psychologically conditioned by some aspect of the myth. For the most surprising thing is that the preparatory work leads only to man's *readiness*. Once he is ready, he can be mobilized effectively in very different directions—but of course the myth and the reflex must be continually rejuvenated and revived or they will atrophy. That is why prepropaganda must be constant, whereas active propaganda can be sporadic when the goal is a particular action or involvement.[23]

2. Internal Characteristics

Knowledge of the Psychological Terrain

The propagandist must first of all know as precisely as possible the terrain on which he is operating. He must know the sentiments and opinions, the current tendencies and the stereotypes among the public he is trying to reach.[24] An obvious point of departure is the analysis of the characteristics of the group and its current myths, opinions, and sociological structure. One cannot make just any propaganda any place for anybody. Methods and arguments must be tailored to the type of man to be reached. Propaganda is definitely not an arsenal of ready-made, valid techniques and arguments, suitable for use anywhere.[25] Obvious errors in this direction have been made in the recent course of propaganda's history.[26] The technique of propaganda consists in precisely calculating the desired action in terms of the individual who is to be made to act.

The second conclusion seems to us embodied in the following rule: never make a direct attack on an established, reasoned, durable opinion or an accepted cliché, a fixed pattern. The propagandist wears himself out to no avail in such a contest. A propagandist who tries to change mass opinion on a precise and well-established point is a bad propagandist. But that does not mean that he must then leave things as they are and conclude that nothing can be done. He need only understand two subtle aspects of this problem.

First of all, we recall that there is not necessarily any continuity between opinion or fixed patterns and action. There is neither consistency nor logic, and a man can perfectly well hold on to his property, his business, and his factory, and still vote Communist—or he can be enthusiastic about social justice and peace as described by the Communists, and still vote for a conservative party. Attacking an established opinion or stereotype head on would make the propagandee aware of basic inconsistencies and would produce unexpected results.[27] The skillful propagandist will seek to obtain action without demanding consistency, without fighting prejudices and images, by taking his stance deliberately on inconsistencies.

Second, the propagandist can alter opinions by diverting them from their accepted course, by changing them, or by placing them in an ambiguous context.[28] Starting from apparently fixed and immovable positions, we can lead a man where he does not want to go, without his being aware of it, over paths that he will not notice. In this way propaganda against German rearmament, organized by the "partisans of peace" and ultimately favorable to the Soviet Union, utilized the anti-German sentiment of the French Right.

Thus, existing opinion is not to be contradicted, but utilized. Each individual harbors a large number of stereotypes and established tendencies; from this arsenal the propagandist must select those easiest to mobilize, those which will give the greatest strength to the action he wants to precipitate. Writers who insist that propaganda against established opinion is ineffective would be right if man were a simple being, having only one opinion with fixed limits. This is rarely the case among those who have not yet been propagandized, although it is frequently the case among individuals who have been subjected to propaganda for a long time. But the ordinary man in our democracies has a wide range of feelings and ideas.[29] Propaganda need only determine which opinions must not be attacked head on, and be content to undermine them gradually and to weaken them by cloaking them in ambiguity.[30]

The third important conclusion, drawn from experiments made chiefly in the United States, is that propaganda cannot create something out of nothing. It must attach itself to a feeling, an idea; it must build on a foundation already present in the individual. The conditioned reflex can be established only on an innate reflex or a prior conditioned reflex. The myth does not expand helter-skelter; it must respond to a group of spontaneous beliefs. Action cannot be obtained unless it responds to a group of already established tendencies or attitudes stemming from the schools, the environment, the regime, the churches, and so on. Propaganda is confined to utilizing existing material; it does not create it.

This material falls into four categories. First there are the psychological "mechanisms" that permit the propagandist to know more or less precisely that the individual will respond in a certain way to a certain stimulus. Here the psychologists are far from agreement; behaviorism, depth psychology, and the psychology of instincts postulate very different psychic mechanisms and see essentially different connections and motivations. Here the propagandist is at the mercy of these interpretations. Second, opinions, conventional patterns and stereotypes exist concretely in a particular milieu or individual. Third, ideologies exist which are more or less consciously shared, accepted, and disseminated, and which form the only intellectual, or rather para-intellectual, element that must be reckoned with in propaganda.

Fourth and finally, the propagandist must concern himself above all with the needs of those whom he wishes to reach.[31] All propaganda must respond to a need, whether it be a concrete need (bread, peace, security, work) or a psychological need.[32] (We shall discuss this last point at length later on.) Propaganda cannot be gratuitous. The propagandist cannot simply decide to make propaganda in such and such a direction on this or that group. The group must need something, and the propaganda must respond to that need. (One weakness of tests made in the United States is that far too often the experimental propaganda used did not correspond to a single need of the persons tested.) A frequent error on the part of propagandists "pushing" something is the failure to take into account whether or not the propagandee needs it.

Finally, it is obvious that propaganda must not concern itself with what is best in man—the highest goals humanity sets for itself, its noblest and most precious feelings. Propaganda does not aim to elevate man, but to make him *serve*. It must therefore utilize the most common feelings, the most widespread ideas, the crudest patterns, and in so doing place itself on a very low level with regard to what it wants man to do and to what end.[33] Hate, hunger, and pride make better levers of propaganda than do love or impartiality.

Fundamental Currents in Society

Propaganda must not only attach itself to what already exists in the individual, but also express the fundamental currents of the society it seeks to influence. Propaganda must be familiar with collective sociological presuppositions, spontaneous myths, and broad ideologies. By this we do not mean political currents or temporary opinions that will change in a few months, but the fundamental psycho-sociological bases on which a whole society rests, the presuppositions and myths not just of individuals or of particular groups but those shared by all individuals in a society, including men of opposite political inclinations and class loyalties.

A propaganda pitting itself against this fundamental and accepted structure would have no chance of success. Rather, all effective propaganda is based on these fundamental currents and expresses them.[34] Only if its rests on the proper collective beliefs will it be understood and accepted. It is part of a complex of civilization, consisting of material elements, beliefs, ideas, and institutions, and it cannot be separated from them. No propaganda could succeed by going against these structural elements of society. But propaganda's main task clearly is the psychological reflection of these structures.

It seems to us that this reflection is found in two essential forms: the collective sociological presuppositions and the social myths. By presuppositions we mean a collection of feelings, beliefs, and images by which one unconsciously judges events and things without questioning them, or even noticing them. This collection is shared by all who belong to the same society or group. It draws its strength from the fact that it rests on general tacit agreement. Whatever the differences of opinion are among people, one can discover beneath the differences the same beliefs—in Americans and in Russians, in Communists and in Christians. These presuppositions are sociological in that they are provided for us by the surrounding milieu and carry us along in the sociological current. They are what keeps us in harmony with our environment.

It seems to us that there are four great collective sociological presuppositions in the modern world. By this we mean not only the Western world, but all the world that shares a modern technology and is structured into nations, including the Communist world, though not yet the African or Asian worlds. These common presuppositions of bourgeois and proletarian are that man's aim in life is happiness, that man is naturally good, that history develops in endless progress, and that everything is matter.[35]

The other great psychological reflection of social reality is the myth. The myth expresses the deep inclinations of a society. Without it, the masses would not cling to a certain civilization or its process of development and crisis. It is a vigorous impulse, strongly colored, irrational, and charged with all of man's power to believe. It contains a religious element. In our society the two great fundamental myths on which all other myths rest are Science and History. And based on them are the collective myths that are man's principal orientations: the myth of Work, the myth of Happiness (which is not the same thing as the presupposition of happiness), the myth of the Nation, the myth of Youth, the myth of the Hero.

Propaganda is forced to build on these presuppositions and to express these myths, for without them nobody would listen to it. And in so building it must always go in the same direction as society; it can only reinforce society. A propaganda that stresses virtue over happiness and presents man's future as one dominated by austerity and contemplation would have no audience at all. A propaganda that questions progress or work would arouse disdain and reach nobody; it would immediately be branded as an ideology of the intellectuals, since most people feel that the serious things are material things because they are related to labor, and so on.

It is remarkable how the various presuppositions and aspects of myths complement each other, support each other, mutually defend each other; if the propagandist attacks the network at one point, all myths react to the attack. Propaganda must be based on current beliefs and symbols to reach man and win him over. On the other hand, propaganda must also follow the general direction of evolution, which includes the belief in progress. A normal, spontaneous evolution is more or less expected, even if man is completely unaware of it, and in order to succeed, propaganda must move in the direction of that evolution.

The progress of technology is continuous; propaganda must voice this reality, which is one of man's convictions. All propaganda must play on the fact that the nation will be industrialized, more will be produced, greater progress is imminent, and so on. No propaganda can succeed if it defends outdated production methods or obsolete social or administrative institutions. Though occasionally advertising may profitably evoke the good old days, political propaganda may not. Rather, it must evoke the future, the tomorrows that beckon, precisely because such visions impel the individual to act.[36] Propaganda is carried along on this current and cannot oppose it; it must confirm it and reinforce it. Thus, propaganda will turn a normal feeling of patriotism into a raging nationalism. It not only reflects myths and presuppositions, it hardens them, sharpens them, invests them with the power of shock and action.

Of course, when we analyze this necessary subordination of propaganda to presuppositions and myths, we do not mean that propaganda must express them clearly all the time; it need not speak constantly of progress and happiness (although these are always profitable themes), but in its general line and its infrastructure it must allow for the same presuppositions and follow the same myths as those prevalent in its audience. There is some tacit agreement: for example, a speaker does not have to say that he believes "man is good": this is clear from his behavior, language, and attitudes, and each man unconsciously feels that the others share the same presuppositions and myths. It is the same with propaganda: a person listens to a particular propaganda because it reflects his deepest unconscious convictions without expressing them directly. Similarly, because of the myth of progress, it is much easier to sell a man an electric razor than a straight-edged one.

Finally, alongside the fundamental currents reflected in presuppositions and myths, we must consider two other elements. Obviously the material character of a society and its evolution, its fundamental sociological currents, are linked to its very structure. Propaganda must operate in line with those material currents and at the level of material progress. It must be associated with all economic, administrative, political, and educational development, otherwise it is nothing. It must also reflect local and national idiosyncrasies.

But a conflict is possible between a local milieu and the national society. The tendencies of the group may be contrary to those of the broader society; in that case one cannot lay down general rules. Sometimes the tendencies of the local group win out because of the group's solidarity; sometimes the general society wins out because it represents the mass and, therefore, unanimity. In any case, propaganda must always choose the trend that normally will triumph because it agrees with the great myths of the time, common to all men.

To sum up, propaganda must express the fundamental currents of society.[37]

Timeliness

Propaganda in its explicit form must relate solely to what is timely.[38] Man can be captured and mobilized only if there is consonance between his own deep social beliefs and those underlying the propaganda directed at him, and he will be aroused and moved to action only if the propaganda pushes him toward a *timely* action. These two elements are not contradictory but complementary, for the only interesting and enticing news is that which presents a timely, spectacular aspect of society's profound reality. A man will become excited over a new automobile because it is immediate evidence of his deep belief in progress and technology. Between *news* that can be utilized by propaganda and *fundamental currents* of society the same relationship exists as between waves and the sea. The waves exist only because the underlying mass supports them; without it there would be nothing. But man sees only the waves; they are what attracts, entices, and fascinates him. Through them he grasps the grandeur and majesty of the sea, though this grandeur exists only in the immense mass of water. Similarly, propaganda can have solid *reality* and *power* over man only because of its rapport with fundamental currents, but it has seductive excitement and a capacity to move him only by its ties to the most volatile immediacy.[39] And the timely event that man considers worth retaining, preserving, and disseminating is always an event related to the expression of the myths and presuppositions of a given time and place.

Besides, the public is sensitive only to contemporary events. They alone concern and challenge it. Obviously, propaganda can succeed only when man feels challenged. It can have no influence when the individual is stabilized, relaxing in his slippers in the midst of total security. Neither past events nor great metaphysical problems challenge the average individual, the ordinary man of our times. He is not sensitive to what is tragic in life; he is not anguished by a question that God might put to him; he does not feel challenged except by current events, political or economic. Therefore, propaganda must start with current events; it would not reach anybody if it tried to base itself on historical facts. We have seen Vichy propaganda fail when it tried to evoke the images of Napoleon and Joan of Arc in hopes of arousing the French to turn against England. Even facts so basic and deeply rooted in the French consciousness are not a good springboard for propaganda; they pass quickly into the realm of history, and consequently into neutrality and indifference.

Actually, the public is prodigiously sensitive to current news. Its attention is focused immediately on any spectacular event that fits in with its myths. At the same time, the public will fix its interest and its passion on one point, to the exclusion of all the rest. Besides, people have already become accustomed to, and have accommodated themselves to "the rest" (yesterday's news or that of the day before yesterday). We are dealing here not just with forgetfulness, but also with plain loss of interest.

The terms, the words, the subjects that propaganda utilizes must have in themselves the power to break the barrier of the individual's indifference. They must penetrate like bullets; they must spontaneously evoke a set of images and have a certain grandeur of their own. To circulate outdated words or pick new ones that can penetrate only by force is unavailing, for timeliness furnishes the "operational words" with their explosive and affective power. Part of the power of propaganda is due to its use of the mass media, but this power will be dissipated if propaganda relies on operational words that have lost their force. In Western Europe, the word *Bolshevik* in 1925, the word *Fascist* in 1936, the word *Collaborator* in 1944, the word *Peace* in 1948, the word *Integration* in 1958, were all strong operational terms; they lost their shock value when their immediacy passed.

To the extent that propaganda is based on current news, it cannot permit time for thought or reflection. A man caught up in the news must remain on the surface of the event; he is carried along in the current, and can at no time take a respite to judge and appreciate; he can never stop to reflect. There is never any awareness—of himself, of his condition, of his society—for the man who lives by current events. Such a man never stops to investigate any one point, any more than he will tie together a series of news events. We already have mentioned man's inability to consider several facts or events simultaneously and to make a synthesis of them in order to face or to oppose them. One thought drives away another; old facts are chased by new ones. Under these conditions there can be no thought. And, in fact, modern man does not think about current problems; he feels them. He reacts, but he does not understand them any more than he takes responsibility for them. He is even less capable of spotting any inconsistency between successive facts; man's capacity to forget is unlimited. This is one of the most important and useful points for the propagandist, who can always be sure that a particular propaganda theme, statement, or event will be forgotten within a few weeks. Moreover, there is a spontaneous defensive reaction in the individual against an excess of information and—to the extent that he clings (unconsciously) to the unity of his own person—against inconsistencies. The best defense here is to forget the preceding event. In so doing, man denies his own continuity; to the same extent that he lives on the surface of events and makes today's events his life by obliterating yesterday's news, he refuses to see the contradictions in his own life and condemns himself to a life of successive moments, discontinuous and fragmented.[42]

This situation makes the "current-events man" a ready target for propaganda. Indeed, such a man is highly sensitive to the influence of present-day currents; lacking landmarks, he follows all currents. He is unstable because he runs after what happened today; he relates to the event, and therefore cannot resist any impulse coming from that event. Because he is immersed in current affairs, this man has a psychological weakness that puts him at the mercy of the propagandist. No confrontation ever occurs between the event and the truth; no relationship ever exists between the event and the person. Real information never concerns such a person. What could be more striking, more distressing, more decisive than the splitting of the atom, apart from the bomb itself? And yet this great development is kept in the background, behind the fleeting and spectacular result of some catastrophe or sports event because that is the superficial news the average man wants. Propaganda addresses itself to that man; like him, it can relate only to the most superficial aspect of a spectacular event, which alone can interest man and lead him to make a certain decision or adopt a certain attitude.

Propaganda and the Undecided

All of the foregoing can be clarified by a brief examination of a question familiar to political scientists, that of the Undecided—those people whose opinions are vague, who form the great mass of citizens, and who constitute the most fertile public for the propagandist. The Undecided are not the Indifferent—those who say they are apolitical, or without opinion and who constitute no more than 10 percent of the population. The Undecided, far from being outside the group, are participants in the life of the group, but do not know what decision to make on problems that seem urgent to them. They are susceptible to the control of public opinion or attitudes, and the role of propaganda is to bring them under this control, transforming their potential into real effect. But that is possible only if an undecided man is "concerned" about the group he lives in. How is this revealed? What is the true situation of the Undecided?

One strong factor here is the individual's degree of integration in the collective life. Propaganda can play only on individuals more or less intensely involved in social currents. The isolated mountaineer or forester, having only occasional contact with society at the village market, is hardly sensitive to propaganda. For him it does not even exist. He will begin to notice it only when a strict regulation imposed on his activities changes his way of life, or when economic problems prevent him from selling his products in the usual way. This clash with society may open the doors to propaganda, but it will soon lose its effect again in the silence of the mountain or the forest.

Conversely, propaganda acts on the person embroiled in the conflicts of his time, who shares the "foci of interest" of his society. If I read a good newspaper advertisement for a particular automobile, I will not have the slightest interest in it if I am indifferent to automobiles. This advertisement can affect me only to the extent that I share, with my contemporaries, the mania for automobiles. A prior general interest must exist for propaganda to be effective. Propaganda is effective not when based on an *individual* prejudice, but when based on a *collective* center of interest, shared by the crowds.

We now take up another basic trait of the social psychology of propaganda: the more intense the life of a group to which an individual belongs, the more active and effective propaganda is. A group in which feelings of belonging are weak, in which common objectives are imprecise or the structure is in the process of changing, in which conflicts are rare, and which is not tied to a collective focus of interest, cannot make valid propaganda either to its members or to those outside. But where the vitality of a group finds expression in the forms mentioned, it not only can make effective propaganda but also can make its members increasingly sensitive to propaganda in general. The more active and alive a group, the more its members will listen to propaganda and believe it.[43]

Furthermore, it matters little whether the intensity of such collective life is spontaneous or artificial. It can result from a striving, a restlessness, or a conviction deriving directly from social or political conditions, as in France in 1848, or in the medieval city-states. It can result from manipulation of the group, as in Fascist Italy or Nazi Germany. In all such cases the result is the same: the individual who is part of an intense collective life is prone to submit to the influence of propaganda. And anyone who succeeds in keeping aloof from the intense collective life is generally outside the influence of propaganda, because of his ability to escape that intensity.

Of course, the intensity is connected with the centers of interest; it is not an unformed or indeterminate current without direction. It is not just a haphazard explosion. Rather, it is a force for which the focus of interest is the compass needle. Social relations in the group are often very active because of its focus of interest: for example, the interest in politics invigorated social relations in all Europe during the nineteenth century. In any case, intensity will be greatest around such an interest. For example, an important center of interest today is one's profession; an individual who cares little for the social life of his group, his family life, or books reacts vigorously on the subject of his profession. And his reaction is not individual; it is the result of his participation in the group.

Thus we can present the following three principles:

(1) The propagandist must place his propaganda inside the limits of the foci of interest.

(2) The propagandist must understand that his propaganda has the greatest chance for success where the collective life of the individuals he seeks to influence is most intense.

(3) The propagandist must remember that collective life is most intense where it revolves around a focus of interest.

On the basis of these principles the propagandist can reach the Undecided and act on the majority of 93 percent;[44] and only in connection with this mass of Undecided can one truly speak of ambiguity, majority effect, tension, frustration, and so on.

Propaganda and Truth

We have not yet considered a problem, familiar but too often ignored: the relationship between propaganda and truth or, rather, between propaganda and accuracy of facts. We shall speak henceforth of accuracy or reality, and not of "truth," which is an inappropriate term here.

The most generally held concept of propaganda is that it is a series of *tall stories,* a tissue of lies, and that lies are necessary for effective propaganda. Hitler himself apparently confirmed this point of view when he said that the bigger the lie, the more its chance of being believed. This concept leads to two attitudes among the public. The first is: "Of course we shall not be victims of propaganda because we are capable of distinguishing truth from falsehood." Anyone holding that conviction is extremely susceptible to propaganda, because when propaganda does tell the "truth," he is then convinced that it is no longer propaganda; moreover, his self-confidence makes him all the more vulnerable to attacks of which he is unaware.

The second attitude is: "We believe *nothing* that the enemy says because *everything* he says is necessarily untrue." But if the enemy can demonstrate that he has told the truth, a sudden turn in his favor will result. Much of the success of Communist propaganda in 1945–48 stemmed from the fact that as long as Communism was presented as the enemy, both in the Balkans and in the West, everything the Soviet Union said about its economic progress or its military strength was declared false. But after 1943, the visible military and economic strength of the Soviet Union led to a complete turnabout: "What the Soviet Union said in 1937 was true; therefore it always speaks the truth."

"In propaganda, truth pays off"—this formula has been increasingly accepted. Lenin proclaimed it. And alongside Hitler's statement on lying one must place Goebbels's insistence that facts to be disseminated must be accurate.[47] How can we explain this contradiction? It seems that in propaganda we must make a radical distinction between a fact on the one hand and intentions or interpretations on the other; in brief, between the material and the moral elements. The truth that pays off is in the realm of *facts.* The necessary falsehoods, which also pay off, are in the realm of *intentions* and *interpretations.* This is a fundamental rule for propaganda analysis.

The Problem of Factuality

Finally, there is the use of accurate facts by propaganda. Based on them, the mechanism of suggestion can work best. Americans call this technique innuendo. Facts are treated in such a fashion that they draw their listener into an irresistible sociological current. The public is left to draw obvious conclusions from a cleverly presented truth,[52] and the great majority comes to the same conclusions. To obtain this result, propaganda must be based on some truth that can be said in few words and is able to linger in the collective consciousness. In such cases the enemy cannot go against the tide, which he might do if the basis of the propaganda were a lie or the sort of truth requiring a proof to make it stick. On the contrary, the enemy now must provide proof, but it no longer changes the conclusions that the propagandee already has drawn from the suggestions.

Intentions and Interpretations. This is the real realm of the lie; but it is exactly here that it cannot be detected. If one falsifies a fact, one may be confronted with unquestionable proof to the contrary. (To deny that torture was used in Algeria became increasingly difficult.) But no proof can be furnished where motivations or intentions are concerned or interpretation of a fact is involved. A fact has different significance, depending on whether it is analyzed by a bourgeois economist or a Soviet economist, a liberal historian, a Christian historian, or a Marxist historian. The difference is even greater when a phenomenon created deliberately by propaganda is involved. How can one suspect a man who talks peace of having the opposite intent—without incurring the wrath of public opinion? And if the same man starts a war, he can always say that the others forced it on him, that events proved stronger than his intentions. We forget that between 1936 and 1939 Hitler made many speeches about his desire for peace, for the peaceful settlement of all problems, for conferences. He never expressed an explicit desire for war. Naturally, he was arming because of "encirclement." And, in fact, he did manage to get a declaration of war from France and England; so *he* was not the one who started the war.[53]

Propaganda by its very nature is an enterprise for perverting the significance of events and of insinuating false intentions. There are two salient aspects of this fact. First of all, the propagandist must insist on the purity of his own intentions and, at the same time, hurl accusations at his enemy. But the accusation is never made haphazardly or groundlessly.[54] The propagandist will not accuse the enemy of just any misdeed; he will accuse him of the very intention that he himself has and of trying to commit the very crime that he himself is about to commit. He who wants to provoke a war not only proclaims his own peaceful intentions but also accuses the other party of provocation. He who uses concentration camps accuses his neighbor of doing so. He who intends to establish a dictatorship always insists that his adversaries are bent on dictatorship. The accusation aimed at the other's intention clearly reveals the intention of the accuser. But the public cannot see this because the revelation is interwoven with facts.

The mechanism used here is to slip from the facts, which would demand factual judgment, to moral terrain and to ethical judgment.

The second element of falsehood is that the propagandist naturally cannot reveal the true intentions of the principal for whom he acts: government, party chief, general, company director. Propaganda never can reveal its true projects and plans or divulge government secrets. That would be to submit the projects to public discussion, to the scrutiny of public opinion, and thus to prevent their success. More serious, it would make the projects vulnerable to enemy action by forewarning him so that he could take all the proper precautions to make them fail. Propaganda must serve instead as a veil for such projects, masking true intentions.[55] It must be in effect a smokescreen. Maneuvers take place behind protective screens of words on which public attention is fixed. Propaganda is necessarily a declaration of one's intentions. It is a declaration of purity that will never be realized, a declaration of peace, of truth, of social justice. Of course, one must not be too precise at the top level, or promise short-term reforms, for it would be risky to invite a comparison between what was promised and what was done. Such comparison would be possible if propaganda operated in the realm of future fact. Therefore, it should be confined to intentions, to the moral realm, to values, to generalities. And if some angry man were to point out the contradictions, in the end his argument would carry no weight with the public.

Propaganda is necessarily false when it speaks of values, of *truth,* of *good,* of *justice,* of *happiness*—and when it interprets and colors facts and imputes meaning to them. It is true when it serves up the plain fact, but does so only for the sake of establishing a pretense and only as an example of the interpretation that it supports with that fact.

Propaganda feeds, develops, and spreads the system of false claims— lies aimed at the complete transformation of minds, judgments, values, and actions (and constituting a frame of reference for systematic falsification). When the eyeglasses are out of focus, everything one sees through them is distorted. This was not always so in the past. The difference today lies in the voluntary and deliberate character of inaccurate representation circulated by propaganda. While we credit the United States and the Soviet Union with some good faith in their beliefs, as soon as a system of propaganda is organized around false claims, all good faith disappears, the entire operation becomes self-conscious, and the falsified values are recognized for what they are. The lie reveals itself to the liar. One cannot make propaganda in pretended good faith. Propaganda reveals our hoaxes even as it encloses and hardens us into this system of hoaxes from which we can no longer escape.

Having analyzed these traits, we can now advance a definition of propaganda—not an exhaustive definition, unique and exclusive of all others, but at least a partial one: *Propaganda is a set of methods employed by an organized group that wants to bring about the active or passive participation in its actions of a mass of individuals, psychologically unified through psychological manipulations and incorporated in an organization.*

3. Categories of Propaganda

Despite a general belief, propaganda is not a simple phenomenon, and one cannot lump together all of its forms. Types of propaganda can be distinguished by the regimes that employ them. Soviet propaganda and American propaganda do not resemble each other either in method or in psychological technique. Hitler's propaganda was very different from present-day Chinese propaganda, but it substantially resembled Stalinist propaganda. The propaganda of the F.L.N. in Algeria cannot be compared to French propaganda. Even within the same regime completely different conceptions can co-exist; the Soviet Union is the most striking example of this. The propagandas of Lenin, Stalin, and Khrushchev offer three types which differ in their techniques, in their themes, and in their symbolism; so much so that when we set up too narrow a frame for the definition of propaganda, part of the phenomenon eludes us. Those who think of Soviet propaganda only as it was under Stalin are inclined to say that Khrushchev does not make propaganda. But Khrushchev's propaganda was as extensive as Stalin's and perhaps more so; he carried certain propaganda techniques to their very limits. But aside from these political and external categories of propaganda, one must define other differences that rest on certain internal traits of propaganda.

Political Propaganda and Sociological Propaganda

First we must distinguish between political propaganda and sociological propaganda. We shall not dwell long on the former because it is the type called immediately to mind by the word propaganda itself. It involves techniques of influence employed by a government, a party, an administration, a pressure group, with a view to changing the behavior of the public. The choice of methods used is deliberate and calculated; the desired goals are clearly distinguished and quite precise, though generally limited. Most often the themes and the objectives are political, as for example with Hitler's or Stalin's propaganda. This is the type of propaganda that can be most clearly distinguished from advertising: the latter has economic ends, the former political ends. Political propaganda can be either strategic or tactical. The former establishes the general line, the array of arguments, the staggering of the campaigns; the latter seeks to obtain immediate results within that framework (such as wartime pamphlets and loudspeakers to obtain the immediate surrender of the enemy).

But this does not cover all propaganda, which also encompasses phenomena much more vast and less certain: the group of manifestations by which any society seeks to integrate the maximum number of individuals into itself, to unify its members' behavior according to a pattern, to spread its style of life abroad, and thus to impose itself on other groups. We call this phenomenon "sociological" propaganda, to show, first of all, that the entire group, consciously or not, expresses itself in this fashion; and to indicate, secondly, that its influence aims much more at an entire style of life than at opinions or even one particular course of behavior.[58]

Of course, within the compass of sociological propaganda itself one or more political propagandas can be expressed. The propaganda of Christianity in the middle ages is an example of this type of sociological propaganda; Benjamin Constant meant just this when he said of France, in 1793: "The entire nation was a vast propaganda operation." And in present times certainly the most accomplished models of this type are American and Chinese propaganda. Although we do not include here the more or less effective campaigns and methods employed by governments, but rather the over-all phenomenon, we find that sociological propaganda combines extremely diverse forms within itself. At this level, advertising as the spreading of a certain style of life can be said to be included in such propaganda, and in the United States this is also true of public relations, human relations, human engineering, the motion pictures, and so on. It is characteristic of a nation living by sociological propaganda that all these influences converge toward the same point, whereas in a society such as France in 1960, they are divergent in their objectives and their intentions.

Sociological propaganda is a phenomenon much more difficult to grasp than political propaganda, and is rarely discussed. *Basically it is the penetration of an ideology by means of its sociological context.* This phenomenon is the reverse of what we have been studying up to now. Propaganda as it is traditionally known implies an attempt to spread an ideology through the mass media of communication in order to lead the public to accept some political or economic structure or to participate in some action. That is the one element common to all the propaganda we have studied. Ideology is disseminated for the purpose of making various political acts acceptable to the people.

But in sociological propaganda the movement is reversed. The existing economic, political, and sociological factors progressively allow an ideology to penetrate individuals or masses. Through the medium of economic and political structures a certain ideology is established, which leads to the active participation of the masses and the adaptation of individuals. The important thing is to make the individual participate actively and to adapt him as much as possible to a specific sociological context.

Such propaganda is essentially diffuse. It is rarely conveyed by catchwords or expressed intentions. Instead it is based on a general climate, an atmosphere that influences people imperceptibly without having the appearance of propaganda; it gets to man through his customs, through his most unconscious habits. It creates new habits in him; it is a sort of persuasion from within. As a result, man adopts new criteria of judgment and choice, adopts them spontaneously, as if he had chosen them himself. But all these criteria are in conformity with the environment and are essentially of a collective nature. Sociological propaganda produces a progressive adaptation to a certain order of things, a certain concept of human relations, which unconsciously molds individuals and makes them conform to society.

Sociological propaganda springs up spontaneously; it is not the result of deliberate propaganda action. No propagandists deliberately use this method, though many practice it unwittingly, and tend in this direction without realizing it. For example, when an American producer makes a film, he has certain definite ideas he wants to express, which are not intended to be propaganda. Rather, the propaganda element is in the American way of life with which he is permeated and which he expresses in his film without realizing it. We see here the force of expansion of a vigorous society, which is totalitarian in the sense of the integration of the individual, and which leads to involuntary behavior.

Sociological propaganda expresses itself in many different ways—in advertising, in the movies (commercial and non-political films), in technology in general, in education, in the *Reader's Digest;* and in social service, case work, and settlement houses. All these influences are in basic accord with each other and lead spontaneously in the same direction; one hesitates to call all this propaganda. Such influences, which mold behavior, seem a far cry from Hitler's great propaganda setup. Unintentional (at least in the first stage), non-political, organized along spontaneous patterns and rhythms, the activities we have lumped together (from a concept that might be judged arbitrary or artificial) are not considered propaganda by either sociologists or the average public.

And yet with deeper and more objective analysis, what does one find? These influences are expressed through the same media as propaganda. They are *really directed* by those who make propaganda. To me this fact seems essential. A government, for example, will have its own public relations, and will also make propaganda. Most of the activities described in this chapter have identical purposes. Besides, these influences follow the same stereotypes and prejudices as propaganda; they stir the same feelings and act on the individual in the same fashion. These are the similarities, which bring these two aspects of propaganda closer together, more than the differences, noted earlier, separate them.

But there is more. Such activities are propaganda to the extent that the combination of advertising, public relations, social welfare, and so on produces a certain general conception of society, a particular way of life. We have not grouped these activities together arbitrarily—they express the same basic notions and interact to make man adopt this particular way of life. From then on, the individual in the clutches of such sociological propaganda believes that those who live this way are on the side of the angels, and those who don't are bad; those who have this conception of society are right, and those who have another conception are in error. Consequently, just as with ordinary propaganda, it is a matter of propagating behavior and myths both good and bad. Furthermore, such propaganda becomes increasingly effective when those subjected to it accept its doctrines on what is *good or bad* (for example, the American Way of Life). There, a whole society actually expresses itself through this propaganda by advertising its kind of life.

By doing that, a society engages in propaganda on the deepest level. Sociologists have recognized that, above all, propaganda must change a person's environment.

Sociological propaganda must act gently. It conditions; it introduces a truth, an ethic in various benign forms, which, although sporadic, end by creating a fully established personality structure. It acts slowly, by penetration, and is most effective in a relatively stable and active society, or in the tensions between an expanding society and one that is disintegrating (or in an expanding group within a disintegrating society). Under these conditions it is sufficient in itself; it is not merely a preliminary sub-propaganda. But sociological propaganda is inadequate in a moment of crisis. Nor is it able to move the masses to action in exceptional circumstances. Therefore, it must sometimes be strengthened by the classic kind of propaganda, which leads to action.

All this obviously constitutes an ideal framework for organized propaganda.

We encounter such organized propaganda on many levels: on the government level, for one. Then there are the different pressure groups: the Political Action Committee, the American Medical Association, the American Bar Association, the National Small Business Men's Association—all have as their aim the defense of the private interests of the Big Three: Big Business, Big Labor, and Big Agriculture. Other groups aim at social and political reforms: the American Legion, the League of Women Voters, and the like. These groups employ lobbying to influence the government and the classic forms of propaganda to influence the public; through films, meetings, and radio, they try to make the public aware of their ideological aims.

Propaganda of Agitation and Propaganda of Integration

The second great distinction within the general phenomenon of propaganda is the distinction between propaganda of agitation and propaganda of integration. Here we find such a *summa divisio* that we may ask ourselves: if the methods, themes, characteristics, publics, and objectives are so different, are we not really dealing with two separate entities rather than two aspects of the same phenomenon?

This distinction corresponds in part to the well-known distinction of Lenin between "agitation" and "propaganda"—but here the meaning of these terms is reversed. It is also somewhat similar to the distinction between propaganda of subversion (with regard to an enemy) and propaganda of collaboration (with the same enemy).

Propaganda of agitation, being the most visible and widespread, generally attracts all the attention. It is most often subversive propaganda and has the stamp of opposition. It is led by a party seeking to destroy the government or the established order. It seeks rebellion or war. It has always had a place in the course of history. All revolutionary movements, all popular wars have been nourished by such propaganda of agitation. Spartacus relied on this kind of propaganda, as did the communes, the Crusades, the French movement of 1973, and so on. But it reached its height with Lenin, which leads us to note that, though it is most often an opposition's propaganda, the propaganda of agitation can also be made by government. For example, when a government wants to galvanize energies to mobilize the entire nation for war, it will use a propaganda of agitation. At that moment the subversion is aimed at the enemy, whose strength must be destroyed by psychological as well as physical means, and whose force must be overcome by the vigor of one's own nation.

Governments also employ this propaganda of agitation when, after having been installed in power, they want to pursue a revolutionary course of action. Thus Lenin, having installed the Soviets, organized the agitprops and developed the long campaign of agitation in Russia to conquer resistance and crush the kulaks. In such a case, subversion aims at the resistance of a segment or a class, and an internal enemy is chosen for attack. Similarly, most of Hitler's propaganda was propaganda of agitation. Hitler could work his sweeping social and economic transformations only by constant agitation, by over-excitement, by straining energies to the utmost. Nazism grew by successive waves of feverish enthusiasm and thus attained its revolutionary objectives. Finally, the great campaigns in Communist China were precisely propaganda of agitation. Only such propaganda could produce those "great leaps forward." The system of the communes was accepted only because of propaganda of agitation which unleashed simultaneously physical action by the population and a change in their behavior, by subverting habits, customs, and beliefs that were obstacles to the "great leap forward." This was internal propaganda. And Mao was perfectly right in saying that the enemy is found within each person.[59] Propaganda of agitation addresses itself, then, to internal elements in each of us, but it is always translated into reality by physical involvement in a tense and overexcited activity. By making the individual participate in this activity, the propagandist releases the internal brakes, the psychological barriers of habit, belief, and judgment.

As a whole these are appeals to simple, elementary sentiments requiring no refinement, and thanks to which the propagandist can gain acceptance for the biggest lies, the worst delusions—sentiments that act immediately, provoke violent reactions, and awaken such passions that they justify all sacrifices. Such sentiments correspond to the primary needs of all men: the need to eat, to be one's own master, to hate. Given the ease of releasing such sentiments, the material and psychological means employed can be simple: the pamphlet, the speech, the poster, the rumor. In order to make propaganda of agitation, it is not necessary to have the mass media of communication at one's disposal, for such propaganda feeds on itself, and each person seized by it becomes in turn a propagandist. Just because it does not need a large technical apparatus, it is extremely useful as subversive propaganda. Nor is it necessary to be concerned with probability or veracity. Any statement whatever, no matter how stupid, any "tall tale" will be believed once it enters into the passionate current of hatred. A characteristic example occurred in July 1960, when Patrice Lumumba claimed that the Belgians had provoked the revolt of the Congolese soldiers in the camp at Thysville.

Finally, the less educated and informed the people to whom propaganda of agitation is addressed, the easier it is to make such propaganda. That is why it is particularly suited for use among the so-called lower classes (the proletariat) and among African peoples. There it can rely on some key words of magical import, which are believed without question even though the hearers cannot attribute any real content to them and do not fully understand them. Among colonized peoples, one of these words is *Independence,* an extremely profitable word from the point of view of effective subversion. It is useless to try to explain to people that national independence is not at all the same as individual liberty; that the black peoples generally have not developed to the point at which they can live in political independence in the Western manner; that the economy of their countries permits them merely to change masters. But no reason can prevail against the magic of the word. And it is the least

Vertical and Horizontal Propaganda

Classic propaganda, as one usually thinks of it, is a vertical propaganda—in the sense that it is made by a leader, a technician, a political or religious head who acts from the superior position of his authority and seeks to influence the crowd below. Such propaganda comes from above. It is conceived in the secret recesses of political enclaves; it uses all technical methods of centralized mass communication; it envelops a mass of individuals; but those who practice it are on the outside. Let us recall here the distinction, cited above, made by Lasswell between direct propaganda and effect propaganda, though both are forms of vertical propaganda.

One trait of vertical propaganda is that the propagandee remains alone even though he is part of a crowd. His shouts of enthusiasm or hatred, though part of the shouts of the crowd, do not put him in communication with others; his shouts are only a response to the leader. Finally, this kind of propaganda requires a passive attitude from those subjected to it. They are seized, they are manipulated, they are committed; they experience what they are asked to experience; they are really transformed into objects. Consider, for instance, the quasi-hypnotic condition of those propagandized at a meeting. There, the individual is depersonalized; his decisions are no longer his own but those suggested by the leader, imposed by a conditioned reflex. When we say that this is a passive attitude, we do not mean that the propagandee does not act; on the contrary, he acts with vigor and passion. But, as we shall see, his action is not his own, though he believes it is. Throughout, it is conceived and willed outside of him; the propagandist is acting through him, reducing him to the condition of a passive instrument. He is mechanized, dominated, hence passive. This is all the more so because he often is plunged into a mass of propagandees in which he loses his individuality and becomes one element among others, inseparable from the crowd and inconceivable without it.

In any case, vertical propaganda is by far the most widespread—whether Hitler's or Stalin's, that of the French government since 1950, or that of the United States. It is in one sense the easiest to make, but its direct effects are extremely perishable, and it must be renewed constantly. It is primarily useful for agitation propaganda.

Horizontal propaganda is a much more recent development. We know it in two forms: Chinese propaganda and group dynamics in human relations. The first is political propaganda; the second is sociological propaganda; both are integration propaganda. Their characteristics are identical, surprising as that may seem when we consider their totally different origins—in context, research methods, and perspective.

This propaganda can be called horizontal because it is made *inside* the group (not from the top), where, in principle, all individuals are equal and there is no leader. The individual makes contact with others at his own level rather than with a leader; such propaganda therefore always seeks "conscious adherence." Its content is presented in didactic fashion and addressed to the intelligence. The leader, the propagandist, is there only as a sort of *animator* or discussion leader; sometimes his presence and his identity are not even known—for example, the "ghost writer" in certain American groups, or the "police spy" in Chinese groups. The individual's adherence to his group is "conscious" because he is aware of it and recognizes it, but it is ultimately involuntary because he is trapped in a dialectic and in a group that leads him unfailingly to this adherence. His adherence is also "intellectual" because he can express his conviction clearly and logically, but it is not *genuine* because the information, the data, the reasoning that have led him to adhere to the group were themselves deliberately falsified in order to lead him there.

But the most remarkable characteristic of horizontal propaganda is the small group. The individual participates actively in the life of this group, in a genuine and lively dialogue. In China the group is watched carefully to see that each member speaks, expresses himself, gives his opinions. Only in speaking will the individual gradually discover his own convictions (which also will be those of the group), become irrevocably involved, and help others to form their opinions (which are identical). Each individual helps to form the opinion of the group, but the group helps each individual to discover the correct line. For, miraculously, it is always the correct line, the anticipated solution, the "proper" convictions, which are eventually discovered. All the participants are placed on an equal footing, meetings are intimate, discussion is informal, and no leader presides. Progress is slow; there must be many meetings, each recalling events of the preceding one, so that a common experience can be shared. To produce "voluntary" rather than mechanical adherence, and to create a solution that is "found" by the individual rather than imposed from above, is indeed a very advanced method, much more effective and binding than the mechanical action of vertical propaganda. When the individual is mechanized, he can be manipulated easily. But to put the individual in a position where he apparently has a freedom of choice and still obtain from him what one expects, is much more subtle and risky.

Vertical propaganda needs the huge apparatus of the mass media of communication; horizontal propaganda needs a huge organization of people. Each individual must be inserted into a group, if possible into several groups with convergent actions. The groups must be homogeneous, specialized, and small: fifteen to twenty is the optimum figure to permit active participation by each person. The group must comprise individuals of the same sex, class, age, and environment. Most friction between individuals can then be ironed out and all factors eliminated which might distract attention, splinter motivations, and prevent the establishment of the proper line.

This form of propaganda needs two conditions: first of all, a lack of contact between groups. A member of a small group must not belong to other groups in which he would be subjected to other influences; that would give him a chance to find himself again and, with it, the strength to resist. This is why the Chinese Communists insisted on breaking up traditional groups, such as the family. A private and heterogeneous group (with different ages, sexes, and occupations), the family is a tremendous obstacle to such propaganda. In China, where the family was still very powerful, it had to be broken up. The problem is very different in the United States and in the Western societies; there the social structures are sufficiently flexible and disintegrated to be no obstacle. It is not necessary to break up the family in order to make the group dynamic and fully effective: the family already is broken up. It no longer has the power to envelop the individual; it is no longer the place where the individual is formed and has his roots. The field is clear for the influence of small groups.

The other condition for horizontal propaganda is identity between propaganda and education. The small group is a center of total moral, intellectual, psychological, and civic education (information, documentation, catechization), but it is primarily a political group, and everything it does is related to politics. Education has no meaning there except in relation to politics.

These groups are a means of education, but such education is only one of the elements of propaganda aimed at obtaining adherence to a society, its principles, its ideology, and its myths—and to the behavior required by the authorities. The small groups are the chosen place for this active education, and the regime employing horizontal propaganda can permit no other style or form of instruction and education than these. We have already seen that the importance of these small groups requires the breaking up of other groups, such as the family. Now we must understand that the education given in the political small groups requires either the disappearance of academic education, or its integration into the system.

Rational and Irrational Propaganda

That propaganda has an irrational character is still a well-established and well-recognized truth. The distinction between propaganda and information is often made: information is addressed to reason and experience—it furnishes facts; propaganda is addressed to feelings and passions—it is irrational. There is, of course, some truth in this, but the reality is not so simple. For there is such a thing as rational propaganda, just as there is rational advertising. Advertisements for automobiles or electrical appliances are generally based on technical descriptions or proved performance—rational elements used for advertising purposes. Similarly there is a propaganda based exclusively on facts, statistics, economic ideas. Soviet propaganda, especially since 1950, has been based on the undeniable scientific progress and economic development of the Soviet Union; but it is still propaganda, for it uses these *facts* to *demonstrate, rationally,* the superiority of its system and to demand everybody's support.

The problem is to create an irrational response on the basis of rational and factual elements. That response must be fed with facts, those frenzies must be provoked by rigorously logical proofs. Thus propaganda in itself becomes honest, strict, exact, but its effect remains irrational because of the spontaneous transformation of all its contents by the individual.

We emphasize that this is true not just for propaganda but also for information. Except for the specialist, information, even when it is very well presented, gives people only a broad image of the world. And much of the information disseminated nowadays—research findings, facts, statistics, explanations, analyses—*eliminate* personal judgment and the capacity to form one's own opinion even more surely than the most extravagant propaganda. This claim may seem shocking; but it is a fact that excessive data do not enlighten the reader or the listener; they drown him. He cannot remember them all, or coordinate them, or understand them; if he does not want to risk losing his mind, he will merely draw a general picture from them. And the more facts supplied, the more simplistic the image. If a man is given *one* item of information, he will retain it; if he is given a hundred data in *one* field, on *one* question, he will have only a general idea of that question. But if he is given a hundred items of information on all the political and economic aspects of a nation, he will arrive at a summary judgment—"The Russians are terrific!" and so on.

A surfeit of data, far from permitting people to make judgments and form opinions, prevents them from doing so and actually paralyzes them. They are caught in a web of facts and must remain at the level of the facts they have been given. They cannot even form a choice or a judgment in other areas or on other subjects. Thus the mechanisms of modern information induce a sort of hypnosis in the individual, who cannot get out of the field that has been laid out for him by the information. His opinion will ultimately be formed solely on the basis of the facts transmitted to him, and not on the basis of his choice and his personal experience. The more the techniques of distributing information develop, the more the individual is shaped by such information. It is not true that he can choose freely with regard to what is presented to him as the truth. And because rational propaganda thus creates an irrational situation, it remains, above all, propaganda—that is, an inner control over the individual by a social force, which means that it deprives him of himself.

Notes

1. Most French psychologists and psycho-sociologists do not regard propaganda as a serious practice or as having much influence.

2. In this connection Albig is right to stress that propaganda cannot be a science because in the field in which it applies there can be neither valid generalizations nor constant factors.

3. Edward A. Shils and Morris Janowitz have demonstrated the importance of the group in the face of propaganda; the Germans, they claim, did not yield earlier in World War II because the various groups of their military structure held fast. Propaganda cannot do much when the social group has not disintegrated: the play of opinions has relatively little importance.

4. [Refers to Appendix II in the original text.]

5. Many analyses of various possible topics, of "gimmicks," have been made often. The most elementary was made in 1942 by the Institute for Propaganda Analysis (see Eugene L. Hartley: *Fundamentals of Social Psychology* [New York: Alfred A. Knopf; 1952]). A more profound analysis is that of Lenin's strategy of propaganda: first stage—the creation in each organization of solid cores of well-indoctrinated men; second stage—cooperation with allies in political tasks that can compromise them; third stage—when the maximum advantage is reached—propaganda to demoralize the adversaries (inevitability of the Communist victory, injustice of the adversary's cause, failure of his means, etc.). The analysis of the type of campaign conducted by Hitler has been well done (Curt Riess: *Joseph Goebbels: A Biography* [New York: Doubleday & Company; 1948]), demonstrating the precise timing of the moment when a campaign should start and when it should stop, the silences and the verbal assaults; a schedule of the use of rumors, neutral information, commentaries, monumental mass meetings. Crowning all, and aiming at "concentrating the fire" of all media on one particular point—a single theme, a single enemy, a single idea—the campaign uses this concentration of all media, but progressively, for the public will take better to gradual attacks. (A good analysis of a Hitlerian campaign has been made by Jerome S. Bruner, in Katz et al.: *Public Opinion and Propaganda* [New York: Dryden Press; 1954], and on propaganda campaigns in general by Leonard W. Doob: *Propaganda: Its Psychology and Technique* [New York: Henry Holt & Company; 1935].)

6. This was the case in the Orthodox Church in the U.S.S.R. during the war.

7. In France, an example is the trial of the Jeanson network (September 1960), which aided the propaganda against insubordination and aid to the F.L.N. It is interesting to find this same idea of "educational" trials in Goebbels and Soviet jurists. The law itself in the U.S.S.R. is an instrument of propaganda intended to

make people *like* the Soviet order. The tribunal is a means of preaching to the public. Finally, Mao has shown how the army can become a most effective propaganda instrument for those who are in it *and* for the occupied peoples. The French army tried to do the same in Algeria, but with less success. It is evident that information itself becomes propaganda, or rather, wherever propaganda appears, there follows an inextricable confusion between propaganda and information. Amusements, distractions, or games can be instruments of propaganda, as well as films for children (in the U.S.S.R.) and the games used in American social group work.

8. The secret element can be a theoretically independent "faction," a network of rumors, and so on. The same effect is obtained by contrasting the real methods of action, which are never acknowledged, with totally different overt propaganda proclamations. This is the most frequently used system in the Soviet Union. In this case it is necessary to have an overt propaganda, in accordance with Goebbels: "We openly admit that we wish to influence our people. To admit this is the best method of attaining it." Hence the creation of an official Ministry of Propaganda. In any case, as Goebbels also said, when the news to be disseminated is unbelievable it must be disseminated by secret, black propaganda. As for censorship, it should be as hidden and secret as possible. Moreover, all serious propagandists know that censorship should be used as little as possible.

9. The famous principle of repetition, which is not in itself significant, plays a part only in this situation. Hitler was undoubtedly right when he said that the masses take a long time to understand and remember, thus it is necessary to repeat; but the emphasis must be placed on "a long time": the public must be conditioned to accept the claims that are made. In any case, repetition must be discontinued when the public has been conditioned, for at that point repetition will begin to irritate and provoke fresh doubts with respect to former certainties.

10. The propagandist does not necessarily have to worry about coherence and unity in his claims. Claims can be varied and even contradictory, depending on the setting (for example, Goebbels promised an increase in the price of grain in the country and, at the same time, a decrease in the price of bread in the city); and the occasion (for example, Hitler's propaganda *against* democracy in 1936 and *for* democracy in 1943).

11. Obviously propaganda directed at the enemy succeeds when it is coupled with victories. German propaganda in France during the Occupation failed because of the presence in France of German soldiers. (Thus the more victories, the more necessary propaganda becomes, said Goebbels.)

12. [Refers to Appendix I in the original text.] . . .

15. A note that appeared in *Le Monde* (August 2, 1961) criticizing the psychological campaign in Algeria shows clearly that its ineffectiveness was due in part to the "self-intoxication" of the propagandists, who came to believe so much in their system that they were no longer capable of considering reality; they were caught in their own trap.

16. When one analyzes the great modern systems of propaganda one always finds this primary aim of producing action, of mobilizing the individual.

Occasionally it is expressly stated, as when Goebbels distinguished between *Haltung* (behavior) and *Stimmung* (morale). But the former is of greater importance. After a bloody raid Goebbels could state: "The *Stimmung* is quite low but that means little; the *Haltung* holds well." The *Stimmung* is volatile and varies readily; therefore, above all, the right action must be obtained, the right behavior maintained. In the analysis of propaganda, specialists have especially noted this desire to obtain immediate action rather than a change of opinion. The same idea is held by Mao Tse-tung: propaganda aims at mobilizing the masses, thus it is not necessary to change their opinions but to make all individuals jointly attack a task. Even political education, so important with Mao, aims essentially at mobilization. And in the Soviet Union political education has occasionally been criticized for taking some intellectual and purely domestic turn to secure action, and then failing in its aim; the task of agitation is not to educate but to mobilize people. And there is always the matter of actual involvement in precise tasks defined by the party, for example to obtain increased productivity.

17. This passive participation is what Goebbels meant when he said: "I conceive of a radio program that will make each listener participate in the events of the nation." But at the same time the listener is forced into passivity by the dictator.

18. The application of "motivational research studies" to advertising also leads to this. . . .

22. The term "to mobilize" is constantly applied by Lenin, Stalin, Mao, Goebbels, and others to the work that precedes propaganda itself.

23. Political education, in Lenin and Mao's sense, corresponds exactly to our idea of sub-propaganda, or basic propaganda, as Goebbels would say. For this education is in no way objective or disinterested. Its only goal is to create in the individual a new *Weltanschauung*, inside which each of the propositions of propaganda will become logical; each of its demands will be indisputable. It is a matter of forming new presuppositions, new stereotypes that are prior justifications for the reasons and objectives which propaganda will give to the individual. But while the prejudices and stereotypes in our societies are created in a somewhat incoherent fashion—singly and haphazardly—in political education we have the systematic and deliberate creation of a coherent set of presuppositions that are above challenge. Probably, at the beginning of the Soviet revolution such political education did not have precise objectives or practical aims; indoctrination was an end in itself. But since 1930 this concept has changed, and political education has become the foundation of propaganda. Mao has done this even earlier. In the Soviet Union ideological indoctrination is now the means of achieving an end; it is the foundation on which propaganda can convince the individual *hic et nunc* of whatever it wants to convince him.

To make this clear we will use the classic terms of propaganda and agitation, taken in a new sense. Propaganda is the elucidation of the Marxist-Leninist doctrine (and corresponds to pre-propaganda); agitation's goal is to make individuals act *hic et nunc*, as a function of their political education and also in terms of this "education" (which corresponds to what we call propaganda). Active experience, in effect, makes further education easier. The different elements are easily mixed: the radio network is given the task to increase "political knowledge" and "political awareness" (pre-propaganda) and to rally the population to support the policy of the party and the government (propaganda). The film industry is given orders that even comedies "must organize the thoughts and feelings of the audience in the required proletarian direction." The effects of such political education are often described by Mao: it creates class-consciousness; it destroys the individualist and petit-bourgeois spirit while assimilating the individual in a collectivity of thought; it creates ideological conformity in a new framework; it leads to understanding the necessity for the sharing of property, obedience to the state, creation of authority and hierarchy; it leads the comrade to vote for suitable representatives, and to withstand the weariness and the difficulties of the battle for increased production. This describes perfectly the role of infrastructure assigned to political education in the process of propaganda.

24. The propagandist must know the principal symbols of the culture he wishes to attack and the symbols which express each attitude if he is to be effective. The Communists always make a thorough study of the content of opinion before launching their propaganda. A person is not sufficient unto himself; he belongs to that whole called culture by the Americans. Each person's psychology is shaped by that culture. He is conditioned by the symbols of that culture, and is also a transmitter of that culture; each time its symbols are changed he is deeply affected. Thus, one can change him by changing these symbols. The propagandist will act on this, keeping in mind that the most important man to be reached is the so-called marginal man: that is, the man who does not believe what the propagandist says, but who is interested because he does not believe the opposition either; the man who in battle has good reason to lay down his arms.

25. Beyond this, propaganda must vary according to circumstances. The propagandist must constantly readjust it according to changes in the situation and also according to changes made by his opponent; the content of propaganda has special reference to the opponent and must therefore change if he changes.

26. Here one can see the famous boomerang: When he is wrong in his analysis of a milieu, the propagandist may create the reverse effect of what he expected, and his propaganda can turn against him. There are innumerable examples of this. For instance, during the Korean War the Americans, who wanted to show that prisoners were well treated, distributed in China and Korea pictures of war prisoners at play, engaging is sports, and so forth. So that the prisoners should not be recognized and persecuted by the Communists after the war, their eyes were blacked out in the pictures. These photos were interpreted by the Chinese to mean "the Americans gouge out the eyes of their prisoners," an interpretation which stemmed from their prior belief that it is impossible to treat prisoners well, and normal to gouge out their eyes.

27. The most frequent response is that of flight. In the face of direct propaganda against a prejudice the propagandee flees: he rejects (often unconsciously) what he is told; he wants no part of it; he justifies himself by dissociating himself from what is attacked, projecting the attack onto another person, and so on—but he does not change.

28. Other methods of altering opinion are to offer forms of action, or to provoke rifts in a group, or to turn a feeling of aggression toward some specified object.

29. This is true of individuals and groups. It has been said quite accurately, for example, that if public opinion were really unanimous there would be no way for propaganda to work. It is only because in any body of public opinion there are groups of private opinions that propaganda can use these as seeds with which to reverse the trend of opinion.

30. It goes without saying that propaganda must also change *its* character according to the results it wishes to attain in given circumstances. For example, propaganda must be strongly personalized when it seeks to create a feeling of guilt in the adversary (e.g., "the French are colonialists"). On the other hand it must be impersonal when it seeks to create confidence and exaltation (e.g., "France is great").

31. At the most elementary level, propaganda will play on the need for physical survival (in time of war). This can be further utilized, either to weaken resistance or to stiffen it. For example, Goebbels used this theme in 1945 to prolong resistance: "By fighting you have a chance for survival."

32. Propaganda must also consider the image that the propagandee has of the ways in which his needs can be satisfied (*structure of expectation*). Propaganda also aims at modifying this image of what people expect.

33. Propaganda must stay at the human level. It must not propose aims so lofty that they will seem inaccessible; this creates the risk of a boomerang effect. Propaganda must confine itself to simple, elementary messages (Have confidence in our leader, our party. . . . Hate our enemies, etc.) without fear of being ridiculous. It must speak the most simple, everyday language, familiar, individualized—the language of the group that is being addressed, and the language with which a person is familiar.

34. It must be associated with the dominant cultural values of the entire society.

35. Formulated in this way, they seem to be philosophical notions but are not. We certainly do not see here any of the philosophical schools, hedonism or materialism, but only the instinctive popular belief marking our epoch and shared by all, expressing itself in very concrete forms.

36. But in this straining toward the future the propagandist must always beware of making precise promises, assurances, commitments. Goebbels constantly protested the affirmations of victory emanating from the Führer's headquarters. The pull toward the future should refer to general currents of society rather than to precise events. Nevertheless, the promise made by Khrushchev that Communism would be achieved by 1980 leaves enough margin; for though the desired effect is obtained in 1961, the promise will be forgotten in 1980 if it has not been fulfilled.

37. In this respect, a high-ranking officer made a completely valid criticism of the psychological campaign in Algeria (*Le Monde*, August 2, 1961) when he pointed out that the weakness of the Lacheroy system was to stress the material environment of the Algerian population without taking into account its instincts and myths, its nationalism, and its adherence to Western ideologies.

38. The history of Soviet propaganda is full of such reminders of the necessity for a propaganda of timeliness, relating to practical problems, and it rejects vague

and dogmatic propaganda. For example, public acceptance must be obtained for new work norms, salary reforms, and so on.

39. Propaganda must remember: "Goebbels said that the face of politics changes each day, but the lines of propaganda must change only imperceptibly." . . .

42. All this is also true of those who claim to be "informed" because they read some weekly periodical filled with political revelations.

43. The more the individual is integrated into a group, the more he is apt to participate in the political life of his group. The group does not even have to be solidly structured; thus, in a group of friends, when almost all vote the same way, there is little chance of any of them going astray. The friendly group involuntarily exerts pressure.

44. On the subject of this 93 percent, it is often stated—and opinion surveys tend to confirm this—that between 7 and 10 percent of all individuals consciously and voluntarily adhere to a trend, to a grouping, whereas about 90 percent fluctuate according to the circumstances. The first correct estimate of this apparently was made by Napoleon. It was revived by Hitler. . . .

47. This idea is now generally accepted. In the United States it is the Number One rule in propaganda manuals, except for unbelievable and harmful truths, about which it is better to be silent. SHAEF said in its manual: "When there is no compelling reason to suppress a fact, tell it . . . Aside from considerations of military security, the only reason to suppress a piece of news is if it is unbelievable. . . . When the listener catches you in a lie, your power diminishes . . . For this reason, never tell a lie which can be discovered." As far back as 1940 the American psychological services already had orders to tell the truth; in carrying them out, for example, they distributed the same newspapers to American and German soldiers. In the Communist bloc we find exactly the same attitude: Mao has always been very careful to state the facts exactly, including bad news. On the basis of Lenin's general theory of information, it is incorrect that the dissemination of false news does not create problems. French propagandists also have discovered that truthfulness is effective, and that it is better to spread a piece of bad news oneself than to wait until it is revealed by others.

There remains the problem of Goebbels's reputation. He wore the title of Big Liar (bestowed by Anglo-Saxon propaganda) and yet he never stopped battling for propaganda to be as accurate as possible. He preferred being cynical and brutal to being caught in a lie. He used to say: "Everybody must know what the situation is." He was always the first to announce disastrous events or difficult situations, without hiding anything. The result was a general belief, between 1939 and 1942, that German communiqués not only were more concise, clearer, and less cluttered, but were more truthful than Allied communiqués (American and neutral opinion)—and, furthermore, that the Germans published all the news two or three days before the Allies. All this is so true that pinning the title of Big Liar on Goebbels must be considered quite a propaganda success. . . .

52. The only element in the publication of a fact which one must scrupulously take into account is its probability or credibility. Much news was suppressed

during the war because it would not have been believed by the public; it would have been branded as pure propaganda. A 1942 incident is an excellent example of this. At the moment of Montgomery's decisive victory in North Africa, Rommel was absent. The Nazis had not expected an attack at that time and had called Rommel back to Germany. But Goebbels gave the order not to reveal this fact because everybody would have considered it a lie to explain the defeat and prove that Rommel had not really been beaten. Truth was not probable enough to be told.

53. The confusion between judgment of fact and judgment of value occurs at the level of these qualifications of fact and interpretation. For example: All bombings by the enemy are acts of savagery aimed only at civilian objectives, whereas all bombings by one's own planes are proof of one's superiority, and they never destroy anything but military objectives. Similarly, when another government shows good will, it is a sign of weakness; when it shows authority, it wants war or dictatorship.

54. Because political problems are difficult and often confusing, and their significance and their import not obvious, the propagandist can easily present them in *moral* language—and here we leave the realm of fact, to enter into that of passion. Facts, then, come to be discussed in the language of *indignation,* a tone which is almost always the mark of propaganda.

55. Many authors have stressed this role of covert propaganda. Speier says that the role of the propagandist is to hide political reality by talking about it. Sauvy says that the propagandist administers the anesthetic so the surgeon can operate without public interference. This is why, in many cases, according to Mégret, complete secrecy is a handicap to the propagandist; he must be free to speak, for only then can he sufficiently confuse things, reveal elements too disconnected to be put together, and so on. He must keep the public from understanding reality, while giving the public the opposite impression, that it understands everything clearly. Riess says he must give the public distorted news and intentions, knowing clearly beforehand what conclusions the public will draw from them. . . .

58. This notion is a little broader than that of Doob on unintentional propaganda. Doob includes in the term the involuntary effects obtained by the propagandist. He is the first to have stressed the possibility of this unintentional character of propaganda, contrary to all American thought on the subject, except for David Krech and Richard S. Crutchfield, who go even further in gauging the range of unintentional propaganda, which they even find in books on mathematics.

59. Mao's theory of the "mold."

60. This is one of the points common to all American works on micro-sociology.

61. At the conference on ideological problems held in Moscow at the end of December 1961, the need to "shape the Communist man" was reaffirmed, and the propagandists were blamed for the twenty-year delay in achieving this goal.

2

A Prolegomenon to the Future Study of Rhetoric and Propaganda

Critical Foundations

Beth S. Bennett and Sean Patrick O'Rourke

Introduction

Interest among rhetorical scholars in the nature of persuasion, as it is differentiated by the terms *rhetoric* and *propaganda,* is common and long-standing. In part, such interest persists due to the fact that as we introduce students to the role of rhetoric in civic life and in democratic decision making, we continue to have the need to discuss the relationship between rhetoric and propaganda. In the summer of 2001, though, a series of events seemed to warrant a fresh examination of that relationship.

In July 2001, the International Society for the History of Rhetoric (ISHR) held its biennial conference in Warsaw, Poland. This venue constituted the first time the organization had met in a former Eastern bloc country and had been chosen to encourage scholars throughout Eastern Europe to attend. The leadership of ISHR sought to infuse the conference with new ideas and perspectives from scholars who might otherwise be prohibited from attending due to travel costs. Among the differences of this conference was an unusually large number of papers dealing with issues of public participation in newly emerging democratic governments and of the threats posed by government-controlled media. The former was referred to as "rhetoric," the latter as "propaganda." The scholars who presented these papers, with their painful and often haunting firsthand accounts of the effects of propaganda, wanted to examine more specifically the functional differences between rhetoric and propaganda but seemed to lack a more critical framework for studying the way political persuasion acted in their societies.

In August 2001, in Greece, the International Association for Greek Philosophy held its 13th conference in Rhodes. The theme of the conference was the philosophy of communication. Among the various issues raised at that conference was a common concern over the role of mediated communication in effecting the concept of "globalization." While the economic progress promised Europeans with the acceptance of the Euro as common currency was perceived as "good globalization," the general influence of Western capitalism was feared as potentially "bad globalization." In particular, some argued, the economic clout of Western communication media, especially in the absence of effective competing media voices, threatened to erode individual cultures and national identities as well as silence opposing viewpoints.

Still later that summer came a third motivation. International events, occurring in the aftermath of the devastating September 11 attacks, spawned public interest in the general concept of propaganda. American media sources reported on the dissemination of "public relations" pamphlets, together with food relief packets, in Afghanistan as "positive propaganda," which sought to help correct America's image problems in the Middle East. Such measures were justified in the media as a necessary response to the "negative propaganda" being communicated in the Islamic world against the United States. The public discussion about propaganda in this context revealed at least two critical issues. First, although there were some media voices expressing concern at the American government's use of blatant propaganda, the consensus seemed to convey the idea that such propaganda was acceptable because it only targeted "other people" and it was for a "good cause," to benefit America in the "War on Terrorism." Certainly, the ethical questions raised by applying the rationale of "the end justifies the means" to excuse the methods used to disseminate popular institutional or educational policies seem to be prime material for classroom discussion. Furthermore, the rhetorical tradition provides much support for arguing against using expedience alone as justification.

But a second, corollary issue raised by this public discussion seemed more problematic. Surprisingly, public awareness of propaganda—of how it works and why it has been critiqued historically as a negative force in society—was largely confused or used synonymously with the terms *public relations, persuasion,* and of course, *rhetoric.* As society has been transformed into one that relies primarily on mediated communication for all types of public discourse, the common tendency to label all mass-mediated persuasion as propaganda tends to reinforce this conflation. Nonetheless, the loss of any functional or conceptual distinctions among suasory efforts seems at least uninformative, if not disturbing. Throughout the history of rhetoric, from Plato in his *Gorgias* to Donald C. Bryant in his 1953 essay, "Rhetoric: Its Functions and Its Scope," critics have deliberately drawn distinctions between rhetoric and propaganda. On the other hand, evidence of the conflation of rhetoric and propaganda, under the general notion of persuasion, has become increasingly obvious, especially in the classroom, where students seem incapable of differentiating among the suasory forms of communication pervasive now in our heavily mediated society. As Quintilian reminds us, "It is not surprising—we have taught them, they hear it from us" (*"Nec mirum: nos docuimus, ex nobis audiunt"*; *Institutio Oratoria* I. ii. 7–8). Apparently, not only is the term *rhetoric* itself misunderstood, but also the value of rhetorical education in terms of participating in democratic societies and functioning critically within the public domain seems to be largely ignored or unknown. Perhaps we need to revisit the historical distinction that has existed between rhetoric and propaganda, though, as Bryant remarked, "One can hardly hope to clarify here what may remain obscure in the work of . . . twenty centuries; but in proper humility, no doubt [we] can try" (p. 402).

Orientation and Goals

Herein, our aim is to establish some foundations for developing a functional, critical framework for differentiating between rhetoric and propaganda in today's society, whether for political, economic, or institutional purposes. Admittedly, we may raise more issues than we provide definitive answers, but what we believe is important is beginning such a discussion among rhetorical scholars. We begin with a discussion of the significance of distinguishing between rhetoric and propaganda, both on traditional, historical grounds and in terms of current intellectual and pedagogical concerns. Then, we offer a brief excursus on key issues in the history of rhetoric pertaining to the use and abuses of rhetorical efforts. Following that discussion is a review of significant work by contemporary scholars attempting to define propaganda.

In the final section of this essay, we offer a preliminary lexicon and sketch a theoretical outline for future studies of persuasive discourse. Working from within and drawing on the Western rhetorical tradition, we first note the importance of the question for studies of public discourse and locate rhetoric and propaganda on a "spectrum of influence." We then offer a typology of propaganda, including a basic distinction between political and commercial propaganda, and an examination of six dimensions of the rhetoric/propaganda relationship: *audience, choice, response, means, "truth,"* and *communicator*.

The Significance of the Problem

At least since the time of Plato, the misuse and abuse of persuasive discourse has been a central theme in the history of rhetoric. The traditional Greek distinction between *peitho* and *dolos,* Plato's attack on sophistical training in the *Gorgias* (as well as his insistence that rhetoric as a true art be held to higher standards), the moral underpinnings of the *orator perfectus* found in Cicero and Quintilian, and the dispute over the place of rhetoric in early Christian education all evidence the importance of this controversy in the Western rhetorical tradition. Drawing in part on this tradition, Pope Gregory XV stirred into the dispute a new term, *propaganda*—literally, "propagating or spreading widely the faith"—when he established the *Sacra Congregatio de Propaganda Fide* in 1622. The new term, associated with deliberate, strategic persuasion aimed at the masses, came to be used as a pejorative label for indicting opposing political discourse, particularly in the 20th century. For example, historians often use the term to dismiss the historical worth of the discourse of agitators, political activists use the term to denigrate the arguments of the opposition, and nation-states label as propaganda any discourse critical of their foreign policy.

In late 19th- and early 20th-century America, interest in propaganda studies was increasing at the same time rhetoric was losing its identity as an academic discipline to the extracurricular activity of public speaking and debate or, in English departments, to the study of composition. Early propaganda studies began as polemical analyses of socioeconomic problems but quickly developed into a scientific field of study focusing on institutional types of political propaganda. After the first few decades in the 20th century, rhetoric was largely ignored by communication scholars outside of the field of speech or public address. As a result, the 20th century witnessed an intellectual separation between scholarship on propaganda by communication scientists and scholarship on rhetoric from humanistic scholars in speech or in composition. Communication science tended to focus on effective, strategic persuasion in mass media, while speech or rhetorical studies concentrated on public address skills and the development of effective, responsible civic leadership.

The problems created by separating scholarly research on communication effects from scholarship dealing with the educational goals for civic participation and responsible leadership were already emerging in the post–World War II era. As Bryant (1953) warned then,

> If enlightened and responsible leaders with rhetorical knowledge and skill are not trained and nurtured, irresponsible demagogues will monopolize the power of rhetoric, will have things to themselves. If talk rather than take is to settle the course of our society, if ballots instead of bullets are to effect our choice of governors, if discourse rather than coercion is to prevail in the conduct of human affairs, it would seem like arrant folly to trust to chance that the right people shall be equipped offensively and defensively with a sound rationale of informative and suasory discourse. (pp. 419–420)

But, in the second half of the 20th century, rather than mending this academic split, scholars concerned with the nature of public persuasion soon found themselves divided further by new exigencies.

Rhetorical scholars, who viewed the traditional aim of their discipline as "to prepare students to contribute to the public good" (Couture, 2004, p. 2), had to confront what has been called "the post-modern critique of the autonomous agent" (Geisler, 2004, p. 10). Traditional, humanistic rhetoric has been blamed for promoting an ideology of agency that assumes equal access to society's mainstream public forums, thereby seeming to serve only the politically powerful or privileged. At the same time, communication scholars have had to reconsider their conceptualization of persuasion due to the rapid development of new communication technologies. As Timothy A. Borchers (2002) comments, "The nature of persuasion in contemporary culture is changing. Many theorists say that we are living in a time of chaos, instability, and upheaval. A confluence of forces—technological and cultural—influences how we communicate with others" (p. 4). David Kaufer (2004) argues that the technological means afforded by new media not only sever the traditional connection between institutional infrastructure and the ability to communicate to the masses but also remove communication barriers created by the absence of proximity, entitlement, or shared frames of reference. Nevertheless, although new technologies have opened access to mass communication and provided rhetorical agency more universally, perhaps, than ever before, they have failed to provide grounds for improving the quality of public communication (Kaufer, 2004, pp. 154–157).

As a result, in the midst of this explosion of means for public persuasion in today's society, the need to establish some critical foundations for differentiating among suasory efforts, between rhetoric and propaganda, seems especially important for at least three reasons. First, the general public response seems to be an increased sense of alienation from the political forces and culture at work in public persuasion. Societies that aim for democratic governance rely on the public engagement of their citizens in the process. Yet, in the United States, according to the National Commission on Civic Renewal, "We are in danger of becoming a nation of spectators. . . . Too many of us . . . lack confidence in our capacity to make basic moral and civic judgments, to join with our neighbors to do the work of community, to make a difference" (qtd. in Asen, 2004, p. 189).

Second, mass media today afford increased opportunities for the public expression of private identities or lives, but not necessarily for public rhetoric, that is, reciprocal exchange of different or conflicting views (Couture, 2004, p. 9). Typically, we find that audiences are no longer required to relate to others who are different from themselves; rather, they are entertained with guile and charm and told only what they want to hear. James E. Combs and Dan Nimmo (1993, pp. 45–47) have labeled this a new form of propaganda, *palaver*, which rewards audiences with happy endings and fertile grounds for indulging in their own interests and desires. The result, as Barbara Couture (2004) notes, is that "public responsibility for dealing with difference" is shifted to the private sphere where it can be ignored or denied (p. 11).

Finally, public persuasion does have an impact on the public good, regardless of how much we are aware of that influence. Being able to make critical distinctions between rhetoric and propaganda will enable us to analyze the persuasive processes more fully and to hold sources accountable for the influence they wield. The public tends to rely on sources they trust to tell them the truth, so the choices made from among communication goals and means used to achieve those goals reveal the ethical judgments of those sources. Borchers (2002) claims,

> As the persuasion industry becomes more sophisticated, the lines between persuasion, coercion, and violence are becoming increasingly blurred. . . . Persuasive communication that allows individuals to consciously choose their beliefs and behaviors is ethical whereas that which denies choice is unethical. (p. 54)

For the advancement of scholarship in both rhetoric and propaganda, our methods of historical or critical investigation need to be equally sophisticated.

Good Rhetoric and Bad: A Brief Excursus

When we seek to maintain, alter, or reinforce the views and behaviors of others; acquire their materials, assistance, or support; or gain general adherence to our own views, values, and policies, we seek, broadly speaking, to "influence." This is, of course, an unusually kind term for what has taken place across the centuries for, as history amply demonstrates, human creativity is rarely as abundant as when influence is the concern. In the history of rhetoric, different individuals have raised various questions about the need to harness the power of rhetoric to restrict the potential for its abuse.

Plato's Critique

In the *Gorgias,* Plato first identified many of the fears and concerns about the unconstrained use of rhetorical skill in a democratic society. In differentiating between "a true art" of rhetoric and that which he saw as problematic or dangerous, Plato provides vocabulary that became central to maintaining that distinction. In the *Phaedrus,* he discusses the importance of using the power of rhetoric to create a "dialogic" relationship with the hearer. Growing out of his critique of the abuse of rhetorical power in his own society came his advice about "the true art of rhetoric," as different from popular or manipulative rhetoric (see Table 2.1).

Popular rhetoric, as characterized by Plato in Phaedrus's performance of Lysias's speech, was not a threat to the hearer once he was able to judge for himself the difference between the discourse of Lysias and that of Socrates.

Table 2.1   Distinctions From Plato's Critique

True Rhetoric *Socrates's Second Speech*	Popular Rhetoric *Lysias/Phaedrus's Speech*	Manipulative Rhetoric *Socrates's First Speech*
Good technique Passion Sincerity (truth) Good intentions toward the hearers	Effective technique Commonly accepted ideas Popular (reasonable) Unacknowledged intentions	Highly skilled technique Excluding competing ideas Appearance of reason Real intentions hidden from hearers
Rhetoric Good because it puts what is the good of the hearer before self and makes clear to the hearer what intentions are motivating the matter	*Demagoguery* Problematic because it flatters the hearer and leads to wrong action, but it is rendered ineffective against competent hearers	*Propaganda* Evil because it is dishonest with the hearers and "short-circuits" their ability to reason or to judge for themselves

But manipulative rhetoric, Socrates's own initial effort, was dangerous precisely because it was designed to deceive—to hide the true intentions of the *rhetor* behind highly effective technique. In addition to these distinctions, Plato seems to suggest that persuasion targeting a large, public audience could hardly be "good" because of the need to flatter the unknowing masses. For Plato, the scope of "the true art of rhetoric" is limited to the few with the knowledge and wisdom to use it responsibly. Nonetheless, his critique focused on the importance of establishing an ethical relationship between the rhetor and the hearer and insisted that the rhetor aim for the betterment of the hearer.

The Aristotelian Audience-Centered Tradition

Crucial to Plato's view of rhetoric was the notion of a hearer competent enough to discern sincerity and truth. But it was Aristotle's *"Art" of Rhetoric* that assumed an audience-centered foundation to the decision-making process and placed *ethos* at the center of his system of argumentative proof. Accordingly, what developed as the distinction in the history of rhetoric, especially rhetoric in the classical sense of political rhetoric of speech making, emphasized rhetoric as the skill of "a deliberate proponent in a welter of competing social positions" (Sproule, 1997, p. 28). As such, the rhetor had to be able to "adapt remarks to lay audiences" and "to rely upon an assumed practical wisdom" that hearers would use to make judgments about the rhetor's position. This traditional focus on the audience in the process of persuasion has resulted in several ideological commitments:

1. Audience members and their views are understood as different from self.

2. Winning adherence entails convincing the audience to *choose* from among competing options.

3. Showing respect or validating the beliefs and values of the audience means being flexible, adaptive (both in ideas and in language use).

4. The democratic process should be approached as a marketplace of ideas, engaging in "consensus building."

Thus, technical skills in rhetoric have been viewed as necessary for "making real a plausible social knowledge for the purpose of building coalitions of belief that might lead to action" (Sproule, 1997, p. 28).

Nonetheless, prompting judgments that rely on the hearers and their beliefs, as well as on the rhetor's skills at adapting arguments to them, makes such suasion vulnerable to at least three types of abuse:

1. It may target uncritical common places or stereotypical thinking to build consensus or to win adherence.

2. It may normalize populist standards that are not necessarily beneficial and force out legitimate competition.

3. It may coerce the individual, in the process of building social cohesion/consensus, to subordinate the self to the group's ideas, fostering intolerance for difference.

If the hearers are not trained in critical thinking or committed to reasoned judgments, then the process can easily change to demagoguery or propaganda with an unscrupulous rhetor.

The Isocrates-Cicero-Quintilian Tradition of the Orator-Statesman

Beginning with the educational philosophy of Isocrates and further developed in the works of Cicero and Quintilian emerged the tradition of properly inculcating virtue into would-be oratorical civic leaders. These authors all stressed the necessity of an ethical base to rhetorical practice and located that base in the virtuous character of the speaker. They provided little in the way of a functional distinction between ethical and unethical rhetoric. But they recognized that the orality of rhetorical activity afforded hearers an enhanced opportunity to judge *ethos,* the truth and sincerity of the rhetor, for themselves. That is, public speakers risked judgment of themselves because their hearers knew them and could assess their credibility against the message they were attempting to convey.

The Fall of Rhetoric—The Rise of Propaganda

As written communication came to replace oral forms of official public discourse, the opportunity for independent public judgment did not exist. Yet, despite the increased reliance on written discourse, the oral tradition of rhetoric remained a central part of a liberal arts education well into the 19th century. But, within the academic climate of the late 1800s, the traditional study of rhetoric was at a disadvantage. According to Michael Sproule, in his 1997 study on *Propaganda and Democracy,* rhetoric was being forced to compete with science as a method for creating practical knowledge for the American public (p. 28). By the end of the 19th century, rhetoric was generally perceived as a method of communicating knowledge discovered by logic or science, and the emphasis was on technical competence in written composition. As Sproule describes the fall of rhetoric,

> Where rhetorical instruction once had organized itself around argumentation and persuasion, now its goal was to transmit information . . . [focusing on] appropriate words and producing efficient sentences. . . . [so,] the transition from sausive "rhetoric" to technologized "composition" marked a conscious shift away from concern with symbolic manipulation. (This semantic shift presaged the turn to objectivity in the 1940's signaled by the replacement of the term *propaganda* by *communication*.) (pp. 28–29)

As rhetoric was disappearing from the academic curriculum, interest in the study of propaganda was growing. As a result, those who wrote about propaganda in the first half of the 20th century did so largely unaware of the traditions of rhetoric and the problems addressed so skillfully by Plato and those who followed. The chief deficiency in these early studies, then, is that they tend to lump all persuasion into the category of propaganda.

The studies published in the 1930s and 1940s provide good examples of the problem. White (1939), examining the propaganda of fascist states, distinguishes only between propaganda, the object of which is "to induce great masses of people to think alike and in the way desired," and reason, which is "engaged in a serious and sober search for truth" (p. 23). Lee and Lee (1939/1979), drawing on their close affiliation with the Institute for Propaganda Analysis, offer little better. They define propaganda as "opinion expressed for the purpose of influencing actions of individuals or groups" (p. 15). Hummel and Huntress (1949) are similarly overinclusive when they claim that "propaganda means *any attempt to persuade anyone to a belief or to a form of action*" (p. 2). Doob (1948) argues that propaganda is "*the attempt to affect the personalities and to control the behavior of individuals towards ends considered unscientific or of doubtful value in a society at a particular time*" (p. 240), a definition that is more specific but still of little help to those seeking to differentiate between types of persuasion and the way they function.

The characteristic common to all of these studies is the conflation of rhetoric and propaganda, with little more than simplistic and often unexplored distinctions between reason and emotion or instruction and indoctrination. In a society where the system of government is based, at least in part, on the full, robust, give-and-take of persuasion in the context of debate, this conflation is deeply troubling. To the extent that all persuasive activity was lumped together with "propaganda" and given the "evil connotation" (Hummel & Huntress 1949, p. 1) the label carried, persuasive speech (i.e., rhetoric) would never hold the central place in education or democratic civic life it was designed to.

The Contemporary Problem of Defining Propaganda

At the time, of course, the prevailing conception of the American public was as competent participants in the traditional democratic process, and so the early study of propaganda focused on uncovering institutional deceptions and lies for the public's awareness. At the time, theories of public opinion and of public communication painted a picture of the rational, self-sufficient American not at all vulnerable to propagandized communication. Sproule (1997, pp. 92–94) traces a variety of social and political forces that worked to change that perception—from a public competent to decide when given sufficient information, to an incompetent public that needed proper training, to a public, confused by the complexity of public communication and media sources, that needed to be properly managed by the power elites for the good of the country. As the conception of the American public and its competency to make complex decisions in an increasingly complex, mediated society changed, Sproule argues, the study of propaganda was taken over by communication science, and it became the study of predicted effects—a "managed" approach to social influence.

Jacques Ellul (1962, English 1965)

Standing somewhat apart from this tradition (and complicating it) is the work of Jacques Ellul, who, in 1962, published his *Propaganda: The Formation of Men's Attitudes* (English translation 1965). This work, arguably the most sophisticated work on propaganda of its generation, takes a decidedly humanist perspective. Ellul analyzes the external and internal characteristics of propaganda, delineates different types (political and sociological, vertical and horizontal, rational and irrational, propaganda of agitation and propaganda of control), and discusses the conditions that give rise to propaganda, our social and individual need for it, and the effects it has on us. He closes with a discussion of propaganda and democracy.

Unfortunately, Ellul's (1962/1965) work is a perfect example of Sproule's (1997) claim that those studying propaganda did not address its relationship with rhetoric. France had formally banned rhetoric from the school curriculum in the late –19th century, and despite a classical education in the humanities and the law, Ellul evidences no knowledge of the tradition of rhetoric. He does provide an ethical perspective from which to assess propaganda. However, we are left *without* any explicit criteria to distinguish rhetoric from propaganda, and we are left *with* a haunting sense that "democracy's need of propaganda," as Ellul puts it, may well make such a distinction irrelevant or impotent. Indeed, Ellul and, following him in at least these regards, Philip Taylor (1995) argue,

> Propaganda is a social phenomenon and therefore operates in several directions, that it is not simply a message communicated from the powers to the public but also a reciprocal message, self reinforcing and flexible, which must contain the logic and elements of truth, which must explain and make sense of political reality to the point that the propaganda message will become significant of a whole political cosmology. (cited in Taithe & Thornton, 2000, p. 3)

From this perspective, rhetoric and propaganda are one, and any attempt to distinguish one from the other is in vain. Others have rejected this view, seeing the value in making distinctions between rhetoric and propaganda, and have attempted to address the problem.

Taithe and Thornton (2000)

In "Propaganda: A Misnomer of Rhetoric and Persuasion?" Taithe and Thornton (2000) argue that "Western culture and literature . . . entirely rests on the art of . . . rhetoric" (p. 2). They suggest that the postmodern rediscovery of the centrality of language, the now-famous "linguistic turn," allows us to see what earlier students of propaganda perhaps could not: that propaganda is "a secular branch of rhetoric." Concerned that the definitions of rhetoric and propaganda must be refined if they are to be of any use in historical analysis, Taithe and Thornton offer the Aristotelian definition of rhetoric as "the faculty of discovering in the particular case what are the available means of persuasion" (Taithe & Thornton, 2000, p. 2; cf. Aristotle, 333 b.c.e./1975) and seek to narrow the definition of propaganda to "the expression of a secular cosmology, a political grammar of the conscious and unconscious" (p. 3). This view takes notice of the close affinity between the two but also sees them as "not totally interchangeable" (p. 3).

Pratkanis and Aronson (2001)

Similarly, Pratkanis and Aronson (2001) seek to distinguish the two "arts." Although they do not use the term *rhetoric,* they do differentiate "mindless propaganda" from "thoughtful persuasion" (pp. 25–32). Using Petty and Cacioppo's (1986) work on "peripheral" and "central" persuasion, Pratkanis and Aronson urge that propaganda takes advantage of our natural inclination to conserve cognitive energy in our media-drenched environment. They distinguish propaganda from persuasion, then, on the basis of the audience response: Propaganda promotes and functions best on a "mindless" audience (i.e., one devoting little thought to the message), while persuasion promotes and functions best when addressed to a "thoughtful" audience (i.e., one devoting concentrated thought to the message).

Jowett and O'Donnell (1999)

Jowett and O'Donnell (1999) go considerably farther in their thinking about the problem. They define propaganda as "*the deliberate and systematic attempt to shape perceptions, manipulate cognitions, and direct behavior to achieve a response that furthers the desired intent of the propagandist*" (p. 6). As they note, the last element, the goal, is the key to the difference between propaganda and persuasion, for propaganda, unlike persuasion, seeks only the satisfaction of the propagandist. Persuasion, Jowett and O'Donnell claim, is a transactive process in which the desired outcome is mutual understanding or the mutual fulfillment of the needs of both persuader and persuadee. Persuasion seeks voluntary change from an active audience. Propaganda, they argue, often seeks to appear to be informative or persuasive communication. To appear so, the propagandist employs techniques of identity concealment, control of information flow, management of public opinion, and manipulation of behavior (pp. 23–35). As such, Jowett and O'Donnell's work provides one of the key bases for our own approach to the problem. The other important basis is the earlier work of Donald C. Bryant.

Bryant (1953)

> Propaganda, after all, is only a word for anything one says for or against anything. Either everything, therefore, is propaganda, or nothing is propaganda, so why worry? (Bryant, 1953, p. 401)

Donald C. Bryant (1953) reports this comment, allegedly by a radio commentator of the day, at the beginning of his essay on the functions and scope of rhetoric. While acknowledging that propaganda, as well as advertising, public relations, and what he calls "commercial, political, and national 'information' services," are all "great users of rhetoric," rather than of coercion or force, Bryant attempts to provide a full account of the province of rhetoric to make specific distinctions from those other uses of public persuasion (p. 411). Using Aristotle's system of rhetoric as his foundation, Bryant (1953) explains how rhetoric has traditionally been understood as "the art of prose whose end is giving effectiveness to truth" and that effectiveness here refers to "what happens to an audience, usually a popular or lay audience as distinguished from the specialized or technical audience of the scientific or dialectical demonstration" (p. 406). Although in our current age of specialization, we might want to argue otherwise, Bryant claims, "No matter what the audience, when the speaker evinces skill in getting into their minds, he evinces rhetorical skill" (p. 406). Bryant argues that the province for such skill should be defined more specifically, as Aristotle suggested, as a method for pursuing public questions about the contingent—questions of justice and injustice, expedience and inexpedience, the good and the bad, honor and dishonor. It is the way in which we "adjust ideas to people and people to ideas," and it is defined by these characteristics:

1. It functions as the rationale of both informative and suasory discourse.

2. It operates chiefly in the areas of contingent, rather certain knowledge.

3. Its aim is to attain maximum probability, as a basis for public decision making.

4. It serves to organize and animate all subject matters which have a relevant bearing on the decision. (p. 408)

From this perspective, then, Bryant (1953) labels propaganda *et alia* as partial or misused rhetoric, primarily because propagandists use techniques that are either "anti-reason" or "pseudo-reason" to effect action (p. 416). He says that advances in knowledge and in opportunity via the media have enabled both the propagandist and the advertiser to use techniques such as "suggestion, reiteration, imaginative substitution, verbal irrelevance and indirection, and emotional and pseudological bullying . . . beyond the fondest dreams of the sophists and the historic demagogues" (p. 416). He characterizes both as deriving "rhetorical solutions" to their problems, carefully gauging their efforts to the special or mass audience they have targeted. But neither prefers the use of reason to shorter, quicker ways to results. As he states, "They concentrate—forcibly where possible, rhetorically where necessary—on the exclusion of competing ideas, on the short-circuiting or by-passing of informed judgment" (p. 417). Their kinship to rhetoric, he warns, is "too strong to be ignored and too important to be denied" (p. 417). For Bryant, what distinguishes rhetoric is that it aims to combine morality, both in the character of its user and in the means employed, with reason and effectiveness. As he explains, "The moral disturbances which rhetoric and rhetorical activity seem to breed . . . arise when the speaker tries so to adjust ideas to people that the ideas are basically falsified, or when he attempts so to adjust people to ideas as to deform or anesthetize the people" (p. 413).

A Typology of Propaganda

In more than 50 years since Bryant (1953) made that observation, we have witnessed, along with a renewed interest in propaganda studies and a resurrection of rhetoric in the academy, an explosion in communication technologies that affords greater opportunities and challenges for those who study acts

Table 2.2   Propaganda in a "Spectrum of Influence"

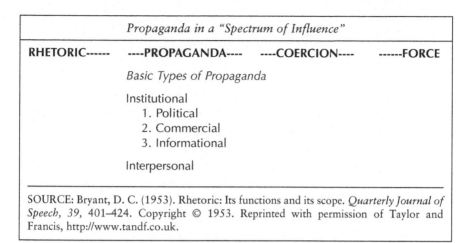

Propaganda in a *"Spectrum of Influence"*
RHETORIC------   ----**PROPAGANDA**----   ----**COERCION**----   ------**FORCE**
Basic Types of Propaganda
Institutional
1. Political
2. Commercial
3. Informational
Interpersonal

SOURCE: Bryant, D. C. (1953). Rhetoric: Its functions and its scope. *Quarterly Journal of Speech, 39*, 401–424. Copyright © 1953. Reprinted with permission of Taylor and Francis, http://www.tandf.co.uk.

of public persuasion. The pressing social, political, and economic exigencies facing us today, we believe, make now an appropriate time to reengage the conversation about the relationship between rhetoric and propaganda. Our attempt here is to provide a greater context for the discussion of rhetoric and propaganda. We begin by placing rhetoric on a "spectrum of influence," which includes moving from left to right (see Table 2.2).

Our main effort is focused on the first two terms on the left side of the spectrum, although, at some later point, we hope to at least sketch the implications of our thinking for the two terms on the right side of the spectrum as well.

Distinguishing Rhetoric and Propaganda

We begin by acknowledging that some of the traditional criteria or characteristics fail to make adequate distinctions because of the problematic nature of public discourse today. Consider the following:

1. Personal (or individual) discourse versus institutional (or group) effort-mediated communication confuses the actual source responsible for the message, resulting in virtually no risk of self for public judgment

2. Revealed intent versus hidden intent—informed choice versus manipulated choice

3. Interactive, dialogic relationship versus unilateral communication (media)

4. Technique used to render truth effective versus technique used effectively to hide the truth

5. The problem of ends/means rationality, where desirable ends justify the use of questionable or troubling means of persuasion

To address such issues critically, we sought a way to analyze the binary opposition that seems to exist between rhetoric and propaganda.

Because rhetoric and propaganda share certain techniques, audiences, intentions, and forms, we admit that distinctions between the two most often are drawn in shades and degrees. Few cases fit easily and neatly into one camp or the other, nor should we expect them to do so. After all, propaganda is only effective when it most resembles what it is not. Thus, to analyze acts of persuasion as either highly rhetorical or highly propagandistic, we needed to identify variables that describe the opposition.

In terms of difference, rhetoric and propaganda seem consistently distinguished at six key points. Several of these points resemble themes developed in the works of the scholars reviewed above and whose efforts have made this study possible. To paraphrase Bernard of Chartres, "If [and that's a big "if" here] we can one day see farther than those who came before, it is only because we are standing on the shoulders of giants" (Salisbury, 1962, p. 167). A second source is also our chief concern, developing our students' ability to function fully and capably in a mass-mediated democratic society. For that to be possible, the democratic process has to retain (or regain) certain key elements. A third source for our variables was our ongoing study of seemingly "successful" propaganda and its means of success.

We offer our preliminary distinctions in Table 2.3.

Within this table, rhetoric is on the left, propaganda is on the right, and the key variables for their opposition are centered between them. We discuss each of these variables briefly below.

Other (Audience)

We see important differences in the way rhetoric and propaganda approach the "other." This is the audience variable. In rhetoric, the other tends to be seen as a coparticipant in decision making and, therefore, as a person worthy of the presumption of equal respect. The audience in rhetoric, we assume, even in large groups, is still seen to be human—bundles of contradictions, no doubt, full of hopes and fears, reason, passion, and imagination, as well as bigoted, pigheaded, and stubborn, for that is what it means to be human. But as Miss Rose Gordon once said to Sean, "Honey, you just got to make your way in this ol' pig iron world." And that is what rhetoric does.

Table 2.3   Preliminary Distinctions Based on Democratic Process

Rhetoric	Issues Relevant to Democratic Process	Propaganda
Participant in decision making; person worthy of equal respect	1. **Other (Audience)**	Target or recipient; instrument of propagandist's will
Significant and informed	2. **Nature of Choice**	Limited because not fully informed
Thinking, reasoned	3. **Desired Response**	Reactionary; thinking response is short-circuited
Effective and ethical appeals Reason is primary, supported with both logic and imagination to appeal to emotions	4. **Appropriate Means** Use of reason Use of emotion Use of imagination	Most effective appeals Emotional appeals designed imaginatively to produce the quickest action
Socially constructed; constituted and reconstituted in open debate	5. **Determining Contingent "Truth"**	Determined by primary goal; determined by propagandist; often irrelevant or glossed
Coparticipant in decision making; seeks to engage others; post-Copernican; often less powerful	6. **Self (Communicator)**	More important than others; above, greater; pre-Copernican; often more powerful

In propaganda, on the other hand, the other tends to be seen as a target or recipient, as something to be struck or filled. The vocabulary of marketing, now so unfortunately adopted by many of our students, has them referring to themselves as "target audiences" of the latest political campaign ads or GAP jeans commercial pitches. It is, of course, cool and hip to use terms of art. But as targets, they are instruments of the propagandists' will and, as such, subject to manipulation, for they are means to the propagandists' ends, not human beings entitled to their own ends and empowered with the individual means of reason, judgment, and will to get there.

Nature of Choice

Because the propagandist tends to view the other in an instrumental way and usually seeks efficient use of that instrument to achieve the desired ends, he or she generally seeks to limit the field of choice open to the audience. This choice is limited by strict control of information flow, by appeals to the need to "act now," and by concealing or obscuring source information.

In rhetoric, on the other hand, the persuaders try to offer the audience a wider range of significant choice. This is not to say that the rhetor ever fully explains all points of view and all sides of an argument. Rather, in rhetoric, the speaker engages in the give-and-take of public *controversia* and seeks to promote an open investigation into the claims and counterclaims made.

Desired Response

Rhetoric, in this way, seeks to promote a thinking response. By thinking, we mean, following Hannah Arendt (1978), a reasoned, self-reflexive, deliberate engagement of a person's cognitive and affective functions. We do not mean to suggest here the old dichotomy between reason and emotion, logic and rhetoric. We mean that rhetoric seeks to engage the whole person— rational, emotional, moral.

Propaganda, of course, wants little of this. Propaganda usually seeks to short-circuit a thinking response. It prefers a reactionary, behavioral response where thought is minimized, reflection diminished, and investigation largely eliminated. It seeks to limit the aspects of response to the affective dimension and envisions nothing less desirable than a thinking target.

Means

Propaganda, therefore, chooses the most effective means to its ends. Most often, these come in the form of emotional appeals imaginatively constructed to produce immediate action. Such appeals are often designed to bypass reason and judgment and are unconstrained, but often cloaked in, by ethical concerns. In propaganda, the other is probed for weakness—needs, desires, unfulfilled dreams, identity issues, and the like—and those weaknesses are exploited. The propagandist uses the means most likely to pierce the emotional armor of the "target."

Rhetoric, of course, also seeks to use effective appeals. However, rhetoric aims to temper the desire for effective persuasion with a concomitant preference for ethical appeals. In such appeals, we believe, reason is primary, and the inventive challenge is to appeal, with reason, to the whole person, to engage that person in a thinking response that encourages investigation, questioning, and response.

Nature of Truth

Obviously, then, rhetoric and propaganda assume very different conceptions of truth. Rhetoric assumes that, in a democratic polity, the "true" and the "good" are socially discovered and/or constructed in the public sphere. Rhetoric celebrates open debate because this is the venue in which political and social "truth" is constituted and reconstituted in a participatory manner. And truth is arrived at with due consideration of factual claims, applicable values and beliefs, relevant burdens of proof, and appropriate standards of judgment.

Propaganda, on the other hand, tends to see "truth" as determined by the propagandist with reference to his or her primary goal. Often irrelevant or glossed, "truth" is otherwise open to a nearly limitless variety.

Self

As should be clear at this point, in rhetoric, the persuader views himself or herself as a coparticipant in decision making, one who seeks to engage others, one whose view of the universe is post-Copernican in that everything does not revolve around the self. The rhetor is often, but not always, of equal or lesser power than many others.

The propagandist, on the other hand, is always more important than others. He or she lives in a pre-Copernican universe where everything does, in fact, revolve around the self. Often, the propagandist is or works on behalf of those in some position of power and sees himself or herself as greater and more important than the rest of society.

Toward a Critical Appraisal of Rhetoric and Propaganda

Admittedly, we offer here but a preliminary sketch, something to be expanded as we continue to investigate the problem of distinguishing rhetoric and propaganda in today's heavily mediated, growingly globalized society. We have attempted to distinguish rhetoric and propaganda conceptually, recognizing that both public and private manifestations of rhetorical effort—that which is produced—may easily require different criteria for critical appraisal. For example, we see four modes in which the products of persuasion could be investigated and assessed:

1. The mode of *presentation* of the source—authentic, revealed, hidden, deceptive, or false.

2. The mode of *power* established with the audience—equal/explicit, ambiguous, superior/explicit, or superior/implicit.

3. The mode of intellectual or personal *engagement of the audience*—deliberative dialogue, rational dialogue, logical demonstration, or information dissemination.

4. The mode of *source intent*—promote thought, reflection, and deliberation or knee-jerk reaction, emotional short-circuiting, and end of propagandist.

Still, the schema as it stands now provides at least an initial framework, a set of *topoi,* for those who want to be able to differentiate among various types of public suasion, be they students or scholars, advertisers or consumers, political leaders or constituents. Our aim has been to initiate, not end, such a critical discussion.

References

Arendt, H. (1978). *The life of the mind* (2 vols.). London: Secker and Warburg.

Aristotle. (333 B.C.E./1975). *The "art" of rhetoric* (J. H. Freese, Trans.). Cambridge, MA: Harvard University Press.

Asen, R. (2004). A discourse theory of citizenship. *Quarterly Journal of Speech, 90,* 189–211.

Borchers, T. A. (2002). *Persuasion in the media age.* Boston: McGraw-Hill.

Bryant, D. C. (1953). Rhetoric: Its functions and its scope. *Quarterly Journal of Speech, 39,* 401–424.

Combs, J. E., & Nimmo, D. (1993). *The new propaganda: The dictatorship of palaver in contemporary politics.* White Plains, NY: Longman.

Couture, B. (2004). Reconciling private lives and public rhetoric: What's at stake? In B. Couture & T. Kent (Eds.), *The private, the public, and the published* (pp. 1–13). Logan: Utah State University Press.

Doob, L. W. (1948). *Public opinion and propaganda.* New York: Holt.

Ellul, J. (1965). *Propaganda: The formation of men's attitudes* (K. Kellen & J. Lerner, Trans.). New York: Alfred A. Knopf. (Original work published 1962)

Geisler, C. (2004). How ought we to understand the concept of rhetorical agency? Report from the ARS. *Rhetoric Society Quarterly, 34,* 9–17.

Hummel, W., & Huntress, K. (1949). *Analysis of propaganda.* New York: William Sloane.

Jowett, G. S., & O'Donnell, V. (1999). *Propaganda and persuasion* (3rd ed.). Thousand Oaks, CA: Sage.

Kaufer, D. S. (2004). The influence of expanded access to mass communication on public expression: The rise of representatives of the personal. In B. Couture & T. Kent (Eds.), *The private, the public, and the published* (pp. 153–166). Logan: Utah State University Press.

Lee, A. M., & Lee, E. B. (1979). *The fine art of propaganda.* San Francisco: International Society for General Semantics. (Original work published 1939)

Petty, R. E., & Cacioppo, J. T. (1986). *Communication and persuasion: Central and peripheral routes to attitude change.* New York: Springer-Verlag.

Pratkanis, A. R., & Aronson, E. (2001). *Age of propaganda* (2nd ed.). New York: W. H. Freeman.

Salisbury, John of. (1962). *The metalogicon: A twelfth-century defense of the verbal and logical arts of the trivium* (D. D. McGarry, Trans.). Berkeley: University of California Press. (Original work published in the 12th century)

Sproule, J. M. (1997). *Propaganda and democracy: The American experience of media and mass persuasion*. Cambridge, UK: Cambridge University Press.

Taithe, B., & Thornton, T. (2000). Propaganda: A misnomer of rhetoric and persuasion? In B. Taithe & T. Thornton (Eds.), *Propaganda: Political rhetoric and identity, 1300–2000* (pp. 1–24). Oxford, UK: Sutton.

Taylor, P. M. (1995). *Munitions of the mind: A history of propaganda from the ancient world to the present day*. Manchester, UK: Manchester University Press.

White, A. B. (1939). *The new propaganda*. London: Victor Gollancz.

3

War Propaganda and the American Revolution

The Pen and the Sword

Gladys Thum and Marcella Thum

Practically every American has heard of the Boston Massacre. If asked what happened that March night in 1770, most Americans would say, "A troop of British soldiers shot down in cold blood a group of unarmed American patriots." Is that what happened? Not exactly.

That night in Boston a lone British sentry was on duty at the Customs House on King Street. Small boys began pelting him with snowballs, taunting him, calling him "Lobster-back." The people of Boston resented the British soldiers, quartered in their city to quell colonial protests against royal taxes. Rowdies and ne'er-do-wells from the nearby wharf area quickly joined the boys, along with curious passersby, until a crowd of about sixty had gathered. The sentry, alarmed, called out the guard.

Ten British soldiers, armed with muskets, ran to the sentry's aid and ordered the crowd to disperse. The boys ran off. But many of the men stayed,

SOURCE: From Gladys Thum and Marcella Thum, "War Propaganda and the American Revolution: The Pen and the Sword," in *The Persuaders: Propaganda and Peace and War*. Copyright © 1974. Reprinted with permission from the Spectrum Literary Agency.

most of them still roisterous, eager for a fight. They picked up clubs, stones, bottles, and threw them at the soldiers. Several soldiers were hit. One was knocked down. Outnumbered, provoked and afraid, the soldiers lowered their muskets into firing position. A British captain, Thomas Preston, appeared on the scene and cried, "Don't fire! Don't fire!"

His cry came too late. A volley rang out in the cold night air. Men crumpled to the ground, their blood staining the white snow a bright crimson. Both soldiers and colonists stared down in dismay at the fallen men. The officer ordered retreat.

Shortly thereafter, the British soldiers involved were tried. Two of the soldiers were convicted by the Boston jury, not of murder but of manslaughter, and were branded on the hand and dismissed. The remainder of the soldiers and Captain Preston were acquitted. The jury? Not British officers but Boston citizens. The soldiers' attorney? John Adams, later to become second President of the United States.

Then why has this incident, which was quite simply a group of battered and outnumbered soldiers firing into a mob that was attacking them, come down in our history books as "the Boston Massacre"? The answer can be summed up in the name of one man: Samuel Adams. Samuel Adams, considered a failure and a black sheep by his family, called a "radical" and "agitator" by his contemporaries, was a man who despised tyranny and was dedicated to liberty. He believed the colonies could obtain their freedom and throw off the yoke of British rule only by arousing the emotions of the colonists, binding them together against a common enemy, the British.

The King Street tragedy he turned into an "atrocity" story, deliberately inflaming public opinion and stirring up hatred against the British government. Some historians have even speculated that Adams himself deliberately helped gather the crowd that eventually provoked the shooting. In either case, Samuel Adams set about propagandizing. He spoke at town meetings, taverns, hostels, wherever he could, denouncing the King Street soldiers (and thereby through Misleading Association, all British soldiers) as cold-blooded murderers and depicting the American victims as innocent, patriotic martyrs. He had broadsides and leaflets distributed throughout the American colonies, with accusations containing emotionally Loaded Words like "massacre" to show the Americans' innocence and "murder" to show the British guilt, and added such phrases as "wallowing in their gore" to show British callousness.

To these carefully selected words of Samuel Adams, calculated to arouse the anti-British anger of American readers, were added pamphlets and leaflets written by other equally ardent believers in freedom. Among those who followed Adams' lead was his friend, Paul Revere, who struck off and distributed an engraving of the "massacre." This famous engraving supposedly pictured the event as it happened but, if you look closely, you will see it is actually pictorial propaganda. Soon, Samuel Adams' distorted version of the tragedy became widely accepted as the truth throughout the colonies.

Although the Massachusetts Historical Society, more than a century later in 1887, aware of the truth, protested the raising of a monument to the victims of "the Boston Massacre," most Americans, because of Samuel Adams, still think of the King Street incident as a cold-blooded massacre and the Americans involved as innocent martyrs, enshrined among our first national heroes. For Samuel Adams, however, the propagandistic use of the Boston shooting was only the beginning of a long campaign to inflame the colonists to revolt against the British.

It was a revolt that did not come overnight. Adams' anti-British propaganda and agitation took several years to achieve its end. For the colonists were accustomed to British rule and considered themselves British subjects. And the colonies were thinly settled with people, too spread out to feel involved with each other. Also, revolution was a serious and dangerous step and, against a powerful country like England, must have seemed to many a hopeless cause. In addition, the colonists for the most part were content with things as they were. They were not so personally engaged with the British government in their daily lives as to feel concerned. In short, they were a "silent majority" who were not ready to do anything radical.

In order to shake the apathy and indifference of the people, Adams used an ancient propaganda device: Appeal to Fear. To do this, he helped to form and then received the aid of the Sons of Liberty, a group of men dedicated to agitating against the British—and against any colonists who sympathized with British rule. American colonists who showed loyalty to the king by buying imported British goods were denounced publicly through broadsheets distributed by the Sons of Liberty. The names of loyalist merchants were circulated on a blacklist and their shops boycotted.

But the Sons of Liberty did not rely alone on verbal Appeals to Fear, through threats and economic coercion. The Tory publisher John Mein was hanged in effigy and physically attacked, as were other loyalist printers. James Rivington in New York was burned in effigy and his printing press destroyed by the Sons of Liberty. Samuel Adams put to work early an important rule of propaganda: silence or eliminate opposition newspapers so that only stories and propaganda favorable to your cause will be read or reach the ears of the people.

Adams' master propaganda stroke, however, was an idea he proposed on November 2, 1772, at a Boston town meeting. It was a simple plan, but a shrewd and necessary one. Arousing temporary hatred of British tyranny was not enough. If rebellion were to come and to succeed, all of the people in all of the colonies from Massachusetts to Georgia had to be united. And to be united, each colony must be kept informed of what the other colonies were doing and saying. So at Adams' suggestion the Committees of Correspondence were formed.

These committees, established in every important town, linked their members through a continual exchange of letters. A web of correspondence was formed that tied all the thirteen colonies together. These letters unified and informed people. But they did more. The letters—regularly printed by colonial newspapers—made certain that anti-British charges reached all points of the colonies, influencing public opinion, shaping attitudes and arousing resistance against the crown. The Committees of Correspondence became in effect a propagandist arm of a national government—before there even was a national government.

When the Revolutionary War began, Adams was joined by another outstanding American propagandist and dedicated lover of freedom: Thomas Paine. Paine used emotion-stirring words, dramatic, yet simple language filled with ringing phrases that were easily remembered, as well as Name Calling and ridicule of King George in order to downgrade the monarch in the minds of the colonists. Although other men, such as James Otis and John Dickinson, also wrote pamphlets urging liberty, their writings were more sober, and were directed toward the educated men of property. Paine appealed directly to the common man. His famous pamphlet *Common Sense* is credited with doing more to inflame the emotions of the colonists against the British monarchy than any other document.

A century and a half later, the man in charge of American propaganda activities in World War I, George Creel, referred to Thomas Paine as "a master propagandist who played upon the hearts of the Colonists with a strong, sure touch. It is not too much to say that his pen was no less mighty than the sword of Washington."

George Washington must have thought so, too. During the bitter war year of 1776, Washington ordered read aloud in every one of his camps, words from another of Paine's pamphlets, entitled *The Crisis:*

"These are the times that try men's souls. The summer soldier and the sunshine patriot will, in this crisis, shrink from the service of their country; but he that stands it now, deserves the love and thanks of man and woman. Tyranny, like hell, is not easily conquered . . ."

George Washington himself did not depend entirely on the sword. He recognized the power of words to arouse the soldiers' will to stand and fight— or retreat and run. Not only did he support the publication of colonial patriot newspapers to help unite the colonists behind him, but he also encouraged the dissemination of rumors that spread fear and dissent among the enemy. And he became a propagandist himself.

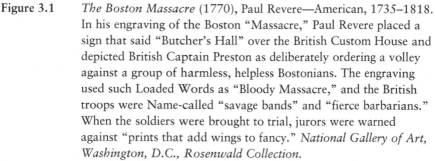

Figure 3.1   *The Boston Massacre* (1770), Paul Revere—American, 1735–1818. In his engraving of the Boston "Massacre," Paul Revere placed a sign that said "Butcher's Hall" over the British Custom House and depicted British Captain Preston as deliberately ordering a volley against a group of harmless, helpless Bostonians. The engraving used such Loaded Words as "Bloody Massacre," and the British troops were Name-called "savage bands" and "fierce barbarians." When the soldiers were brought to trial, jurors were warned against "prints that add wings to fancy." *National Gallery of Art, Washington, D.C., Rosenwald Collection.*

One of his propaganda efforts began when more than a thousand volunteer backwoodsmen, rugged men in buckskins, joined his army. Undisciplined, these frontiersmen made poor soldiers. In fact, Washington had to court-martial an entire platoon for "disobedient and mutinous behavior." But the frontiersmen had one great virtue: they could shoot much farther and more accurately with their long rifles than other soldiers could with their muskets.

PROSPECT HILL.	BUNKUR' HILL.
I. Seven Dollars a Month. — —	I. Three Pence a Day.
II. Fresh Provisions, and in Plenty. — . —	II. Rotten Salt Pork.
III. Health. — — — —	III. The Scurvy.
IV. Freedom, Ease, Affluence and a good Farm.	IV. Slavery, Beggary and Want.

Figure 3.2   The Bunker Hill leaflet—American propaganda tossed at British soldiers. The same appeals—food, money, medical care—are used in psychological warfare leaflets today.

Washington encouraged stories of the deadly accuracy of the frontiersmen to be placed in colonial newspapers. One such story in the *Pennsylvania Press* carried a Fear-Appeal warning to the British: "The worst of them [frontiersmen] will put a ball into a man's head at a distance of 150 or 200 yards, therefore advise your officers who shall hereafter come out to America to settle their affairs in England before their departure." It was reported, perhaps too optimistically, that when stories reached England of these "shirt-tail men, with their cursed twisted gun" recruitment in the British army dropped abruptly.

When the time was ripe, Washington gave a further twist to his propaganda. Taking advantage of the fears of the British soldiers (some of whom were already acquainted with the deadly aim of American frontiersmen from the French-Indian wars), Washington suggested that a number of his American troops who were *not* backwoodsmen should adopt the frontiersmen's distinctive fringed leather hunting shirt and long rifles, because such a uniform "carried no small terror to the enemy who thinks every such person a complete marksman." The rifles these men carried were, of course, simply weapons for military battle. They became weapons for propaganda as well when American propagandists publicized them, exaggerating their prowess, to instill fear in the enemy soldiers *before* battle.

Even more effective than this weapon propaganda, were the new efforts of the untiring Committees of Correspondence. At the instigation of Samuel Adams, they had helped to unite public opinion in the colonies against the British. Now the committees dealt with another propaganda need: to destroy the morale of the enemy soldier.

At the Battle of Bunker Hill, the American forces, poorly trained and low on ammunition, held Prospect Hill; the British forces, facing them, held Bunker Hill. The American soldiers were furnished with propaganda leaflets,

Massacre, and the bigots they ...
Hours to the Gates of this City many Thousands of our
brave Brethren in the Country, deeply affected with our
Distresses, and to whom we are greatly obliged on this
Occasion—No one knows where this would have ended,
and what important Consequences even to the whole
British Empire might have followed, which our Modera-
tion & Loyalty upon so trying anOccasion, and ourFaith
in the Commander'sAssurances have happily prevented.

Last Thursday, agreeable to a general Request of the
Inhabitants, and by the Consent of Parents and Friends,
were carried to their *Grave* in Succession, the Bodies
of *Samuel Gray, Samuel Maverick, James Caldwell,*
and *Crispus Attucks,* the unhappy Victims who fell in
the bloody Massacre of theMonday Evening preceeding!

On this Occasion most of the Shops in Town were
shut, all the Bells were ordered to toll a solemn Peal, as
were also those in the neighboring Towns of Charlestown
Roxbury, &c. The Procession began to move between
the Hours of 4 and 5 in the Afternoon ; two of the unfortunate Sufferers, viz. Mess. *JamesCaldwell* and *Crispus
Attucks,* who were Strangers, borne from Faneuil-Hall,

Figure 3.3   Coffin—Much of the propaganda iconography in the American
Revolution dealt with death. From the black border indicating
the "death" of the *Pennsylvania Journal* to the depiction of the
so-called "Boston Massacre," images of death played a prominent
part in conveying the seriousness of the struggle. This illustration
of the coffins of four men killed in the Boston Massacre is yet
another example of this phenomenon.

which they were told to wrap around bullets or rocks to make them "fly
well" and heave them into British entrenchments. Although the delivery
method left something to be desired, the propagandist appeals were clearly
stated: better pay, better food, better health, better treatment if the British
soldiers shifted to the other—the American—side. What was not stated was

what the leaflet was actually "selling"—desertion and the risk of death in front of a firing squad if caught.

Although the effect of the Bunker Hill propaganda leaflets was not recorded, the American colonial propagandists are known to have been highly successful in a later attempt. This time the Committees of Correspondence aimed their propaganda at the under-paid, poorly fed, badly treated Hessian soldiers that had been hired by the British army. The colonial assembly passed a law granting a German captain who deserted and brought with him forty men: "800 acres, four oxen, one bull, three cows and four hogs." Under the law, even a German private who deserted was offered 50 acres and livestock. The law was translated into German, by the Committees of Correspondence, printed, and distributed to Hessian troops. What this propaganda appeal actually was "selling" was desertion. It sold well. Statistics show that after the war, of the 30,000 Germans hired to fight, only slightly more than half returned to Germany. A few had died from wounds and disease, but thousands more had deserted; many had joined the American army and fought against their former comrades.

Stung by the success of the American propaganda leaflets, the British tried propaganda, too. In 1779, the British General Clinton issued a proclamation promising freedom and security to any Negro slave who came over to the British. Many did. South Carolina lost 25,000 slaves, and Georgia and Virginia many thousands more. The slaves who responded to the propaganda assumed they would receive the appeal—freedom—when they took the article being sold—desertion of their masters. Unfortunately, propaganda appeals need not be "real." After the war, many of these black people who had believed the propaganda were resold in the West Indies or forced to turn fugitive. Although some were trained by the British and put into military units, only a few hundred managed to leave the country with the British troops.

In view of the lack of faith behind this appeal, it is satisfactory to record that this particular propaganda backfired on the British. They thought that mass desertion of slaves would bring the colonial South to its knees, fearful of slave uprisings, ready to admit defeat. Instead, many powerful Southern slave owners, who otherwise might have remained loyal to the British, were outraged by Clinton's proclamation and became firm revolutionists.

The revolutionary propagandists had attempted to accomplish what was to become standard procedure for later, more modern psychological warfare campaigns:

1. Unite the people against a common foe.

2. Destroy the morale of enemy troops.

A third and equally essential task remained: Influence any and all foreign allies to your cause. If such countries as France, Spain or Holland could be persuaded to help, it would mean survival to the new republic. But established royal governments seldom wished to ally themselves with new revolutionary republics. Revolutionaries in the eighteenth century were regarded with even more suspicion and distrust than they are today. However, American propaganda efforts overseas were assisted by two factors.

First: France, Spain and Holland feared and were jealous of England's power. Second: the Continental Congress, with uncommonly good sense, sent Benjamin Franklin to serve as commissioner from America to France. Already admired in French scientific circles and surprisingly effective in winning the affection of the French people, Franklin, the diplomat, was well aware of what his job was. He had to publicize America's side of the war, erase suspicion of American revolutionaries and increase the European feeling of dislike toward England.

Franklin had had experience in the work. He had been in England at the time of the battle of Lexington. An American Salem clipper ship had managed to beat by eleven days the crossing of a British sloop bringing the news of the battle to England. Promptly, Franklin had spread the American version of the battle to English and European newspapers—naturally, with blame for the battle placed squarely on the British. When the British sloop and the British report had appeared with accusations of "treasonous minutemen" at Lexington, the British story had been anti-climatic and had already been discounted.

With this experience behind him, Franklin, arriving as American commissioner in France, immediately began placing pro-American stories in as many French newspapers as possible. And though England was also flooding Europe with news stories giving the British version of what was happening in the colonies, Franklin also managed, through friends, to place favorable American accounts of the war in Dutch, German and Irish newspapers.

So important did Franklin consider the steady flow of pro-American news and propaganda into European publications that he suggested to the Continental Congress that they use special light, fast sailing ships to send him regular news. With this news he could "refute the false news of our adversaries."

The Continental Congress, however, could not afford to supply fast new ships for Franklin. And, although the Committees of Correspondence tried to send American newspapers and letters to France, the British navy captured often the ships that carried them. So, unable to count on a regular supply of information from home, Franklin improvised.

As aware as Samuel Adams of the propaganda value of an atrocity story, Franklin arranged to have printed in European newspapers a letter supposedly sent by the Seneca Indians (allies of the English) to the British governor in Canada. In the letter the Senecas bragged about sending eight packages of American scalps—including those of women and children—to King George to show Indian "faithfulness."

The letter was what is often called "black propaganda"—propaganda that does not reveal its true source. Some historians believe Franklin wrote the letter. No one knows. As propaganda, it was brilliant. French and Dutch, even English, citizens read the letter and reacted with horror and revulsion toward the British for employing savages to fight their war. Franklin also publicized in Dutch newspapers stories of cruel treatment of American prisoners of war by the British. These stories, many of which were based on truth, also helped rouse sympathy for the American cause.

While Franklin was spreading his propaganda abroad, in the colonies another "atrocity" rumor began: that the British had deliberately caused a smallpox epidemic in Boston by sending newly inoculated soldiers among the people—just before the evacuation of British troops from the city. Many citizens of Boston believed this "atrocity" rumor. General Washington even warned his troops not to enter the city without permission "as the enemy with a malicious assiduity, have spread the infection of smallpox through all parts of the town." The rumor was spread by American sympathizers in Europe. It can be considered the first appearance in history of germ warfare propaganda, used later by Communists against Americans in the modern-day war in Korea.

Partly as a result of these efforts, by the end of the war, France, Holland and Spain were supporting the American cause. France, of course, actually sent vitally needed troops, troops that helped to bring about the British surrender at Yorktown.

Compared to the elaborate and costly propaganda campaigns conducted by modern governments in wartime, the American revolutionists' efforts must be regarded as primitive. Yet, the techniques used by Samuel Adams, Thomas Paine and Benjamin Franklin have been studied and copied by many past and present-day governments.

4

We Become Propagandists

Thomas C. Sorenson

"The public be damned!" exclaimed William H. Vanderbilt nearly a century ago, but the public would not be damned. Today its voice is heard and heeded around the world. In America, public opinion is king: the man in the White House nervously awaits its next reading by Gallup or Harris, and so do a great many other people.

There are those who scorn public opinion, who agree with Thoreau that it is "a weak tyrant compared with our own private opinion." They may be right, but public opinion nonetheless must be reckoned with—and not only in our own country. It can elevate men and ideas to great power, and break them overnight. It can sometimes start wars, and sometimes stop them. A nation sensitive about its relations with other nations had better also be sensitive about the attitudes and enthusiasms of other peoples.

Before World War I most Americans were curious but not overly concerned about foreign opinion. Protected by two oceans, weary of the internecine quarrels of the Old World and absorbed in the task of building a new civilization, this country went its own way. When others criticized them, Americans were either angry or unconcerned. Theirs was "God's country"; what did it matter what others thought?

SOURCE: "We Become Propagandists," pp. 1–30 from *The Word War: The Story of American Propaganda* by Thomas C. Sorenson, copyright © 1968 by Thomas C. Sorenson. Reprinted with permission of HarperCollins Publishers.

In time of war the situation was a little different. God and right were on America's side, of course, but it was fervently hoped that others also recognized it. At the very beginning of the nation, the merits of the colonialists' cause were proclaimed abroad by a talented collection of indefatigable propagandists headed by wily old Benjamin Franklin. At the battlefront, crude leaflets promised amnesty and free land to Hessian mercenaries and British soldiers if they would desert, and five thousand Hessians—one-sixth of the total force—did defect.

During the Civil War the Union sought support from antislavery elements in Europe. In 1863 a group of laborers in Manchester sent President Lincoln a resolution supporting his Emancipation Proclamation, expressing a view contrary to much influential opinion in England. Lincoln replied in an open letter that created some excitement, for in disregard of diplomatic precedent he spoke directly to the people of another country:

> I have understood well that the duty of self-preservation rests solely with the American people, but I have at the same time been aware that the favor or disfavor of foreign nations might have a material influence in enlarging or prolonging the struggle.

"The favor of nations." The United States has needed it in every crisis and conflict, but it has never come easy. For it is based, after all, on the much-discussed "image" of America abroad, and that image is a highly elusive picture: part fact and part mirage, part expectation and part disillusionment. It is a picture magnified by the modern mass media, blurred by the fantasies of Hollywood, distorted by the falsifications of our adversaries, and complicated by the sheer size of America's population, wealth, power, and problems.

The image is actually many and often contradictory images: great wealth and grinding poverty, unparalleled freedom and racial discrimination, awesome power and frustrating impotence, responsible leadership and irresponsible policies, sophisticated technology and unsophisticated politicians. Some of the flickering foreign images of America are true, some half true, and others simply false.

"It is fashionable in certain circles," Walter Lippmann has written in the Washington *Post,*

> to dismiss scornfully a serious concern about what foreign nations think of us. This is a reaction to the naïve and often silly American wish to be loved by everybody. But the reaction has gone much too far. For it is not true that in the real world of affairs a great power, even the strongest, can afford to ignore the opinions of others. It cannot overawe them all. It must have friends who trust it and believe in it and have confidence that its power will be used wisely.[1]

If this nation is to have such friends, especially when it needs them most, then it must actively seek the friendship of others. Our example alone is not sufficient, so we must persuade others of its validity. We call this our "information program"; others call it propaganda.

That label, in this century, has become widely distasteful. Most Americans identify it with Hitler's "big lie," Soviet speeches in the United Nations, and—for an older generation—"perfidious Albion" enticing this country into World War I. To propagandize means in many minds to lie, to exaggerate, to manipulate, to subvert. So the U.S. Government employs a euphemism, but in this book we will not.

The word *propaganda* first appeared in the seventeenth century, when Popes Gregory XV and Urban VIII established a College of Propaganda to educate priests for missionary work; the Catholic Church still maintains a committee of cardinals, the *Congregatio de Propaganda Fide,* to supervise its worldwide missions. In modern times the word has become associated with the efforts of secular organizations or nations to influence the thinking and actions of others.

There are several categories of propaganda used by nations to influence one another. Each involves different but overlapping methods: battlefield psychological warfare, to undermine the enemy's will to fight; tactical political propaganda, seeking to win support on immediate issues of the day; the long-range influencing of motivations and attitudes in support of long-term national objectives; and indirect propaganda through the influencing of the educational processes of other nations.

The American Government today is engaged in all these types of propaganda. Yet, despite a firm American belief in the importance of public opinion, no one prior to the mid-1940s ever seriously considered an organized, government-sponsored effort to influence foreign peoples in peacetime. It seemed to many an unclean and improper function of a democratic government, particularly after international persuasion was debased by the false propaganda of the Nazis, Fascists, and Communists. It took Cold War with the Soviet Union to make foreign propaganda a permanent feature of American Government.

There would, perhaps, be fewer qualms about American propaganda if it were better understood that there is not necessarily a conflict between veracity and advocacy, that it is possible to be both truthful and persuasive. American propaganda has not always been persuasive, but it has always tried to be truthful.

In this day of rapid and multiple communications, few lies will stand undetected for long. Everyone is watching everyone else, and the spotlight is brightest on the most powerful and the most righteous. Once a politician or a nation is caught in a lie, an increasingly sophisticated public will view subsequent utterances with skepticism if not outright disbelief. And the greater the number of lies, the greater the skepticism.

When he was head of America's propaganda program, Edward R. Murrow put it this way: "To be persuasive we must be believable; to be believable we must be credible; to be credible we must be truthful. It is as simple as that."[2]

Of course, closed societies, Communist or otherwise, do have a certain advantage, especially over the short run. They can suppress or lie about what goes on in their own countries, while preventing others from checking the facts. But the truth will out, even in tyrannies (as the truth about Stalin did in the Soviet Union, once his successors started admitting it), and in any case dictators cannot prevent outsiders from telling the truth once it becomes known.

American propagandists do have a problem, however, for which the truth is no solution: the double standard applied to the conduct of nations. More is expected and demanded of the United States than of other nations. The ink-throwers and window-breakers went after U.S. libraries and embassies when the United States supported the Bay of Pigs invasion of Cuba in 1961, but they were silent when the Soviet Union nearly precipitated World War III by smuggling missiles into Cuba in 1962. The pickets and paint-splashers harassed President Johnson and Vice President Humphrey about Vietnam during their travels abroad in 1966 and 1967, but they made no complaint when Hanoi and the Vietcong launched their campaign of terror and subversion in South Vietnam.

For U.S. propagandists this double standard is often frustrating and always exasperating, but perhaps in the long run it works to America's advantage. For it exists in part because many foreigners know and cherish the principles of Jefferson, Lincoln, Wilson, and Franklin Roosevelt, and they expect Americans to live up to them—even if the rest of the world does not.

The truth, then, is no cure-all. Nevertheless, Murrow was basically correct: credibility, in the long run, cannot be achieved without truthfulness. "There was never a country in the world that aired its dirty laundry the way the U.S.A. does," commented an influential Cologne publisher to an American friend, but he spoke with great admiration and sympathy, not disapproval.

While good propaganda is truthful, the truth—out of context and unexplained—is not always good propaganda. It is not good propaganda to tell the world of racial disturbances without, at the same time, reciting the steady if unspectacular progress toward an integrated society. It is not good propaganda to tell the world of an increased commitment of American military power in some far corner of the world without making it clear why that power is there.

Moreover, the sheer volume of events forces any medium, government or private, to be selective, not inclusive, and to pay attention to one development at the expense of another. No disseminator of information can tell all the truth all the time, even if it does not tell any falsehoods. It must select bits and pieces of the truth, although to remain credible it must not omit any of major significance.

Effective U.S. Government propaganda is the selective but credible dissemination of truthful ideas and information for the purpose of persuading other people to think and act in ways that will further American purposes. It is a definition that has stood the tests of time and trial.

The Creel Committee

The first major test came in 1917, when the American Government for the first time since the Revolution launched a serious campaign of foreign propaganda. A week after Congress declared war, President Wilson by Executive Order created a Committee on Public Information composed of the Secretaries of State, War, and Navy, and headed by a journalist friend, George Creel. Creel did not call his operation propaganda, "for that word, in German hands, had come to be associated with deceit and corruption,"[3] but propaganda was what it was, nonetheless.

The committee's representatives, working with the Military Intelligence Bureau, arranged for leaflets to be sent by gun, balloon, and airplane over the German lines. Enemy soldiers were encouraged to surrender by promises of food and fair treatment. Stories were fed to newspapers in neutral countries, and then often unwittingly transmitted to German papers by neutral and even German correspondents. Books, exhibits, pamphlets, and movies were produced for foreign consumption. Copies of Wilson's speeches and his photograph were distributed in great numbers.

Creel and his associates sought to educate their colleagues in the government, and in Allied governments, on the significance of public opinion to the war effort. Publicist Edward L. Bernays, a youthful member of the committee's Foreign Press Bureau in New York, talked Tomáss Masaryk into proclaiming Czechoslovakia's independence on a Sunday rather than a Friday, in order to assure better press coverage. ("That, sir, is making history in the cables," Masaryk protested at first. "Sir, cables make history," Bernays replied. Masaryk went along.)

The fledgling propagandists had to learn while doing, and they made many mistakes. "When we started out," Creel recalled later, "it was as if the Babylonians were asked to invent the threshing machine." But they learned fast. Though often flamboyant and amateurish, the Creel Committee played a major part in making Wilson and U.S. war aims widely known and appreciated throughout the world. And it did so in the face of severe handicaps. In neutral nations its representatives frequently found themselves undercut by chauvinistic British and French propagandists, as well as by Germans. In this country Creel and his associates, like their successors of later years, were viewed with suspicion by the Secretary of State, most U.S. diplomats, and important elements of the press, public, and Congress.

Annoyed by Congressional sniping, Creel nearly sank the whole effort with an imprudent remark to reporters in May, 1918. Asked if he thought all Congressmen were loyal, Creel shot back: "I do not like slumming, so I won't explore into the hearts of Congress for you." He later apologized publicly, but Congress never forgave him, even though Wilson told a group of angry Senators, "Gentlemen, when I think of the manner in which Mr. Creel has been maligned and persecuted I think it a very human thing for him to have said."[4]

Creel had been an early supporter of Wilson; during the 1916 campaign he had written a partisan book, *Wilson and the Issues,* and his actress wife was a long-time friend of Wilson's daughter Margaret. Consequently, there were some, especially Republicans, who saw Creel more as a propagandist for the Wilson Administration than for the American nation. Although the House Appropriations Committee gave his operation a clean bill of health after a thorough investigation at the height of the war (even as Congress cut his budget request in half), the lawmakers interrupted an orderly termination of the Creel Committee by abolishing it in mid-1919, leaving it without "power to rent a building, employ a clerk, transfer a bank balance, or to collect a dollar."

Creel's difficulties may have made him overly sensitive to criticism. According to Bernays, Creel's failure to work closely with the press at the Paris Peace Conference "helped to lose the peace for us."[5] After the Armistice, eleven employees of Creel's New York office were assigned to attend the Peace Conference, although Creel had earlier announced that propaganda operations were being terminated with the end of hostilities. On November 21, 1918, the press quoted Bernays as saying that the purpose of the "press mission" was "to interpret the work of the Peace Conference by keeping up a worldwide propaganda to disseminate American accomplishments and ideals."

Congressional Republicans immediately accused Creel of planning to control American press coverage of the conference. He promptly denied it: "The one proper effort of the Committee . . . will be to open every means of communication to the press of America without dictation, without supervision, and with no other desire than to facilitate in every manner the fullest and freest flow of news."[6] Then he cabled his Paris office: "Contrary to the press, the people I sent abroad . . . will have nothing to do but purely mechanical work in connection with distribution."[7]

Creel followed this with another public statement: "The representatives of the Committee [do] not in any manner constitute an official Peace Conference press mission. . . . Their sole duties will be the completion of the Committee's foreign work and settlement of contracts and business details." He told Wilson he would insist upon "the government's immediate and complete surrender of every supervisory function as far as news was concerned."[8] But freedom of the press was not the issue; everyone favored that. The need was to make America's position at Paris clear to the world and rally support for it. This was not realized, and not done.

Creel himself did little in Paris, and prevented the New York group from working with the press. Wilson put Ray Stannard Baker in charge of press relations, but Baker was inexperienced and inept. Had Wilson been able to deal with the press himself, with the flair of a Roosevelt or a Kennedy, little damage would have been done. But he was not, and the government failed to make its case effectively with the news media. Bernays believes that if Creel "had insisted on following the original plan, [Wilson's] communication with the media in the U.S." would have been assured and "the course of history possibly altered."[9]

But Creel did not insist, Wilson was defeated on the treaty issue, and America again turned its back on the world. The "normalcy" of Warren G. Harding succeeded Wilson's "New Freedom," and there was no place for foreign propaganda in the frenzied twenties or the depression years that followed.

Then Adolf Hitler came to power in Germany. Relying heavily on the propaganda of fear, he occupied the Rhineland in 1936, seized Austria in early 1938, blackmailed Britain and France at Munich into letting him take the Czech Sudetenland that autumn, and swallowed the rest of that hapless democracy the next spring. The Bolsheviks, after their takeover in Russia, also made propaganda an important instrument of foreign policy. So did the short-lived Communist regime in Hungary. Holland began international broadcasting in 1927, France in 1931, and Britain in 1932 with the British Broadcasting Corporation (BBC) Empire Service. Fascist Italy had a Ministry of Propaganda, similar to Hitler's.

The Propaganda of War

The most active early practitioners of modern political propaganda were the European dictators, and they gave it the bad name which has lasted to this day. As Hitler's mouthpiece, Dr. Josef Goebbels, saw it, "Propaganda has only one object—to conquer the masses." The Nazis believed in total propaganda: total control over the minds of the German people and as much control as could be obtained over the minds of others. Vast sums were spent. Propagandists were assigned to German embassies abroad, and "front" groups established. Hitler and the Third Reich were exalted, and every weakness— real or invented—of the democracies was proclaimed and reiterated.

Too little and too late, in propaganda as in military prowess, the United States sought in the late 1930s to develop a capability of its own. The initial concern was with Nazi and Fascist propaganda in Latin America. President Roosevelt in 1938 established an Inter-departmental Committee for Scientific and Cultural Cooperation and, within the State Department, a Division of Cultural Cooperation. In August, 1940, after the fall of France, Roosevelt appointed young Nelson Rockefeller to be Coordinator of Commercial and Cultural Affairs between the American Republics (later retitled Coordinator of Inter-American Affairs). Rockefeller launched an exchange-of-persons program with Latin-American countries, and opened offices in them to cultivate opinion leaders and sponsor libraries and jointly operated binational cultural centers.

In 1941 the war drew nearer. Britain was given desperately needed Lend-Lease assistance and U.S. war production greatly increased, but the country was sharply divided between "interventionists" who favored all-out help to the Allies and "isolationists" who believed the war was none of our business or too far gone to win. In this climate Roosevelt created a government bureau to provide Americans with information on the defense effort. Delighting in alliteration and chary of anything smacking of the propaganda machines of the enemy, he named the new organization the Office of Facts and Figures, and appointed not a huckster or a journalist but a poet—Archibald MacLeish—to head it.

Also in 1941 Roosevelt established yet another agency, this one for foreign intelligence and clandestine political action and sabotage. Heading it was a lawyer and former military officer, William J. (Wild Bill) Donovan, who was given the deliberately innocuous and misleading title of Coordinator of Information. Playwright Robert E. Sherwood, a Roosevelt speech writer during the 1940 campaign, persuaded Donovan to set up what in effect was a division of the new agency called the Foreign Information Service. Sherwood recruited a few friends to help him and began beaming broadcasts and news material abroad. Congress and the public knew little about this foreign propaganda effort, and it was probably just as well, for its legal basis was questionable.

On December 7 the Japanese attack on Pearl Harbor put America in the war all the way. It now was both necessary and politically possible to step up propaganda abroad. In February, 1942, bringing together the facilities of eleven private shortwave stations, Sherwood launched a government-sponsored shortwave broadcasting station and named it the Voice of America.

Four months later, on June 13, Roosevelt consolidated the bits and pieces of the foreign and domestic propaganda effort into an Office of War Information (OWI). He instructed OWI to supervise or coordinate all government information activities except Rockefeller's Latin-American operation. Elmer Davis, a renowned and scholarly Indiana-born journalist who had gone from the *New York Times* to become a celebrated radio news reporter, was installed as OWI's Director. Sherwood remained head of what then became the Overseas Branch of OWI. Offices abroad were named the United States Information Service (USIS).

From its birth the Office of War Information was embroiled in controversy. Davis had few peers as a thinker, writer, and broadcaster, but he was never comfortable in the bureaucratic jungle of war-time Washington. A part of Congress and the public considered propaganda to be unclean and un-American, and—as in Creel's time a generation earlier—some suspected that OWI was chiefly interested in propagandizing on behalf of the Democratic Administration.*

OWI's staff was also a problem. Davis and his colleagues naturally recruited personnel from two sources: the communications media and the foreign-born community, especially those of the latter who had a good grasp of the language, culture, and mentality of the Old World. OWI's employees were well educated and unusually articulate. But some were more concerned with the politics of their native lands than with American policy; a high percentage were political liberals or even farther to the left, and most had been exempted from military service. All this aroused doubts about OWI among those elements of Congress and the public that viewed intellectuals, the political left, and "foreigners" with suspicion.

With some justification, it was the domestic activities of OWI that at first were most criticized, just as Creel's home-front operations had been during World War I. A domestic "ministry of propaganda" was anathema to most Americans who gave the matter much thought. As a result, the domestic operation never really got under way; pleased, the critics then turned their fire on OWI's overseas effort. Davis himself was the target of repeated personal attacks, and his impatience with critics and criticism only further antagonized his opponents.

---

*Creel wanted an important position in OWI, but was turned down by the Roosevelt Administration.

Moreover, OWI was plagued with internal problems. Davis' hastily recruited staff had a high proportion of prima donnas, all competing with one another. Sherwood's Overseas Branch in New York, which had been in action before OWI was formed, resented and sometimes ignored Davis and his senior staff in Washington. After Roosevelt finally gave Davis his full support, three of Sherwood's principal assistants quit in a huff in early 1944. Later in the year, Sherwood himself resigned to work in the Roosevelt re-election campaign and was succeeded by Edward W. Barrett, a former associate editor of *Newsweek*. Under his skillful direction, harmony was restored.

Not all the trouble was internal. Other elements of the government, from the White House on down, were neither as understanding nor as helpful as they should have been. The State Department, the War and Navy departments, and especially the Office of Strategic Services (OSS)**—the new subversion-espionage-intelligence agency—were jealous of their prerogatives and not fully cognizant of the uses of propaganda and psychological warfare. Consequently, they often sought to keep OWI—at worst—impotent and—at best—out of their hair.

OWI was told too little and too late about what was going on. The State Department and the military were given the responsibility of providing it with policy guidance, but the guidance was often neither prompt nor specific. OWI did not participate in policy-making, and Davis was not a member of Roosevelt's "war cabinet." In fact, Davis rarely saw the President and almost never alone, in sharp contrast to Creel's close relationship with Wilson. Roosevelt, the consummate politician who should have had a good understanding of the potential of propaganda, seemed to view OWI as a censorship agency, which, unlike the Creel Committee, it was not.

Many military officers thought of war exclusively in terms of men and weapons, not of words, although General Eisenhower in Africa and Europe, General MacArthur in the Pacific, and General Stilwell in Burma did encourage psychological warfare operations in their theaters. One sarcastic Allied

---

**This forerunner of the present-day Central Intelligence Agency was headed by the same Colonel Donovan who had briefly served as Coordinator of Information and in that capacity supervised Sherwood's pre-OWI Foreign Information Service. It took nine months after OWI's creation to define and divide foreign propaganda responsibilities between OWI and OSS, and during that period they spent almost as much time fighting each other as fighting the enemy. Donovan's organization wanted as much control as possible over American propaganda, and believed the emphasis should be put on unattributable "black" propaganda. OWI, on the other hand, felt that truthful information disseminated under the American label would be the most effective propaganda in wartime. In the end OWI prevailed, the feud was brought to a halt, and good working relations developed.

officer wrote to Eisenhower's psychological warfare chief: "The army insists on the killing of our enemies, not persuading or arguing them out of the war. . . . Paper will not kill Germans."[10] No one, of course, claimed that it would. Davis understood "that the war is going to be won primarily by fighting, but we can point to plenty of proof in history . . . that victory of the fighting forces can be made easier" by psychological warfare and propaganda.

Davis won some converts, but not enough. Psychological factors were not adequately considered in making and enunciating policy, and OWI had only partial success as an advocate and clarifier of American war aims. Wallace Carroll, an OWI senior official, wrote later that "while Americans attained considerable skill in the use of propaganda as an instrument of war, they failed completely to develop the arts of persuasion as an instrument of foreign policy."[11] And the Army General Board, in its final report on the war, concluded that propaganda had been "a neglected and ineptly used political and diplomatic weapon."

Two Big Problems: Vichy and "Unconditional Surrender"

OWI had little success in dealing with the two biggest propaganda problems of the war. Both were prime examples of the neglect and ineptness of which the Army General Board spoke.

The first grew out of the Allied invasion of French North Africa in November, 1942. At the beginning, all was rosy. Eisenhower told OWI's Deputy Director: "I don't know much about psychological warfare but I want to give it every chance."[12] Percy Winner, a former foreign correspondent, went on Eisenhower's staff as his propaganda adviser. He obtained the cooperation of the British counterpart to OWI and organized an Anglo-American team that planned broadcasts, drafted statements for issuance by Allied leaders, and produced thirty million leaflets for distribution in Africa and metropolitan France. "From that time on," Sherwood recalled later, "there was no major Allied landing from Normandy to the Philippines that did not have a Psychological Warfare Division as part of the force."[13]

But unforeseen political difficulties limited the impact of OWI's propaganda. The main objective, of course, was to minimize or eliminate French military resistance in North Africa. A secondary goal was to keep alive French hopes for liberation. Achievement of the first objective required gaining the support of—or at least neutralizing—Marshal Pétain's Vichy-based government of unoccupied France which still exercised sovereignty over North

Africa. This meant excluding General Charles de Gaulle and his Fighting French movement, whom Vichy viewed as traitors.

The hoped-for soft response from Vichy was not forthcoming, however. The embittered Pétain cried, "We shall defend ourselves," and there was scattered opposition by French forces. Vichy's top military man, Admiral Jean Darlan, happened to be in Algiers when the invasion took place. After brief resistance, he surrendered French forces there. But fighting continued in Oran and Morocco, whereupon Darlan—with the approval of Pétain—offered to cooperate, at a price.

Eisenhower had the choice of dealing with the Fascist-minded Darlan or continuing to fight. Ike chose the former, and French resistance was ended by Darlan in the name of Pétain. The Darlan accord prompted a wave of surprise and anger in America and Britain. The conquered peoples of Western Europe wondered if a precedent had been set for dealing with Hitler's stooges after liberation. Enemy propagandists were quick to exploit the situation.

Partly at the prompting of OWI, President Roosevelt sought a week later to reassure the world. Describing the Darlan deal as "only a temporary expedient justified solely by the stress of battle," he agreed that "no permanent arrangement should be made with Admiral Darlan. . . . We are opposed to Frenchmen who support Hitler and the Axis. The future French government will be established . . . by the French people themselves after they have been set free." He said he had "asked for the abrogation of all laws and decrees inspired by Nazi governments or Nazi ideologies."

Despite Roosevelt's words, the deeds OWI needed to reassure world opinion were not quickly forthcoming. Under the Eisenhower-Darlan agreement, the communications media of North Africa remained largely in the hands of Vichyites. And, to avoid offending them and anti-Zionist Arab leaders, Eisenhower's headquarters imposed a ban on OWI references in North Africa to the reforms Roosevelt had promised.

Anxiously trying to appraise the situation, Elmer Davis sent one of his deputies—Milton Eisenhower, the General's brother—to North Africa for a firsthand report. Eisenhower concluded that reforms were going forward but could not be publicized without unnecessarily antagonizing local French and Arab authorities, that the military advantages of the deal outweighed its political liabilities, and that OWI should therefore suffer in silence.

Understandably, De Gaulle was enraged by the American recognition of Darlan, which undermined his whole position. His radio in Brazzaville and his representatives in the United States and Britain attacked the Darlan accord and pressed De Gaulle's claim to be the exclusive legitimate spokesman of France. In one of the more curious if temporary alliances of the war, the Russians—and Communists everywhere—joined in the attacks, and Dr. Goebbels exploited the controversy to suit Nazi ends.

Time and the Casablanca Conference of Roosevelt and Churchill eventually reduced the controversy to controllable proportions. Darlan was assassinated, Gaullists were included in the North African administration, and the worst of the Vichy laws repealed. German and Italian resistance in North Africa ended in the spring of 1943. A French Committee of National Liberation, dominated by De Gaulle, was established, and in August won full U.S. and British diplomatic recognition.

Eisenhower probably made the right decision in quickly ending French resistance by dealing with the Vichyites. Lives were saved, and the campaign was brought to a successful conclusion sooner than if the French had fought us. But politically it was a defeat: it cast doubt on the Roosevelt-Churchill proclamation of the Atlantic Charter, aroused suspicions of American motives among the captive peoples of Europe, handed both the Nazis and the Communists a useful club with which to beat us, and generated animosities in the heart of Charles de Gaulle which still trouble Britain and America.

Although the Casablanca Conference helped smooth over one major psychological problem, it also added another: "unconditional surrender." The official communiqué of the January, 1943, conference made no mention of the doctrine. However Roosevelt, at a press conference, had remarked that the Allies would settle for no less than "unconditional surrender" by the Axis Powers. Churchill apparently had opposed the concept when FDR first mentioned it to him, but he told the House of Commons three weeks later that Roosevelt, "with my full concurrence . . . decided that the note of the Casablanca Conference should be the unconditional surrender of our foes."

Both men had been concerned about persistent rumors of a negotiated peace. They also wanted to avoid a repetition of what happened after World War I: the rise of the myth in Germany that German armies had not been beaten but were betrayed on the home front. Roosevelt wanted to make it clear that this war would end only when the Axis Powers were unquestionably defeated, and acknowledged and accepted that defeat unconditionally. He explained that unconditional surrender did not mean oppression of the defeated populations but punishment of their leaders and elimination of their ideology.

Dr. Goebbels' propagandists, however, told the German people that unconditional surrender would mean total destruction of their nation. The Nazi line was unwittingly given a boost in September, 1944, by public disclosure of the Morgenthau Plan to turn industrial Germany into an agricultural nation. OWI played down this draconian scheme, but it caused an international uproar, nonetheless.***

Even Stalin at his 1943 Teheran meeting with Roosevelt and Churchill warned that the demand for unconditional surrender would only stiffen German resistance. OWI joined Secretary of State Hull, General Eisenhower, and others in recommending that the Allies soften the phrase or at least define more precisely what it meant. But Roosevelt refused to water down or back away from the words. "Germany understands only one kind of language," he wrote Hull. And he pointed to Lee's capitulation to Grant at Appomattox as both unconditional and generous—a comparison questionable on both counts.

After the war, Allen W. Dulles—who had dealt with the German underground for OSS and later became head of CIA—argued that Goebbels twisted the formula of unconditional surrender "into the formula 'total slavery' and very largely succeeded in making the German people believe that was what unconditional surrender meant."[14] Eisenhower, in 1964, agreed. Nonetheless, it appears today that the quarrel over the doctrine was largely meaningless. There is little proof that the outcome of the war, or postwar developments, were substantially affected one way or another. Polls taken after the war showed a majority of Germans had been prepared to accept unconditional surrender, if not the Morgenthau Plan. And the doctrine did enhance the confidence of the conquered peoples of Europe in our ultimate war aims and quiet fears raised by the Darlan deal.

OWI's Contributions to Victory

OWI made its mark not so much in the Darlan and "unconditional surrender" controversies as in day-to-day, mostly unsung efforts to maintain Allied morale, undermine the morale of the enemy, and weaken his will to resist. OWI started from scratch, learned while doing—and often failed while learning. Its propagandists were inexperienced and untrained, and what was remembered of the Creel Committee offered few helpful precedents. But OWI did learn, and its successes were not inconsiderable.

***The plan was named after its principal author, Secretary of the Treasury Henry Morgenthau, Jr., who was one of the few officials doing much thinking about postwar Germany. Roosevelt, like many Americans haunted by visions of another aggression-bent Germany rising from the ashes, approved Morgenthau's scheme and obtained Churchill's endorsement. The plan was, of course, never carried out.

Then as now, some of the most effective propaganda projects were the simplest. One was the brain child of author Leo Rosten, who was serving a stint with OWI in Washington. He was asked to come up with a propaganda scheme for January 30, 1943, which was both the tenth anniversary of Hitler's accession to power and Roosevelt's birthday. The war was still running in Germany's favor, and Hitler and Goebbels were certain to make the most of the anniversary.

When it appeared likely that Hitler would broadcast to the world at 11 A.M., the hour he became Chancellor, Rosten proposed that the RAF bomb Berlin at that precise moment and knock the Nazi radio off the air while the world listened. The project went off without a hitch. With perfect timing, RAF Mosquito bombers hit Berlin a few seconds after 11 o'clock. Hitler had a sore throat, but Hermann Goering spoke in his place. A few seconds after the fat *Reichsmarschall* began speaking, explosions were heard in the background. Shouts and sounds of confusion followed, then Radio Berlin went off the air. Germany was not invincible, after all.[15]

The first daylight raid on Berlin did not win the war; it probably did not even shorten it by one day. But it gave new hope and courage to the conquered peoples of Europe in a striking example of successful propaganda of the deed. And it was probably the only time the enemy's radio broadcast our own propaganda message!

Allied radios had their effect, too. Despite Nazi jamming, nearly two-thirds of the German population listened to broadcasts from the West. While the BBC had a head start, and its programs were superior to those of the Voice of America, VOA had its share of the audience, and that share grew as the war progressed.

In 1942 OWI began producing a four-page tabloid newspaper, *L'Amérique en Guerre*, for distribution in France. At first, only a few copies were circulated in unoccupied France through our embassy at Vichy. Then the British Royal Air Force, and later the U.S. Army Air Corps, began dropping the little newspaper over the cities of occupied France. Circulation rose to seven million per week before D-day in 1944, compared to the grand total of three million American leaflets distributed throughout all of World War I. *L'Amérique* was factual, nonargumentative, and attractive in design. It emphasized Allied victories and held out hope of liberation. Similar newspapers were produced for conquered Norway and neutral Spain and Ireland.

Various other specialized publications, designed for specific audiences or specific purposes, were distributed. In North Africa leaflets were scattered over enemy lines by artillery and air drops, encouraging "honorable" surrender in the face of "overwhelming odds." Labeled safe-conduct passes, the leaflets were so successfully that they were used with increasing effectiveness throughout the war (and later in Korea and Vietnam). OWI produced posters for pasting on walls in the wake of advancing Allied armies.

In mid-1943 the U.S. Eighth Air Force began dropping OWI leaflets in its daylight bombing raids over Germany. The first leaflet, a million of which were scattered over two cities, had an American flag on one side and on the other the simple but ominous statement, "Adolf Hitler declared war on the United States on December 11, 1941." Later, a little weekly newspaper, *Sternebanner* (*Star-Spangled Banner*) was produced and dropped in great numbers. The newspaper was good propaganda: straightforward, low-key, and factual—so factual that it occasionally carried news unfavorable to the Allies. There were some objections to inclusion of this kind of material, but the purpose was to make *Sternebanner* believable to its German readers, and credibility could not be achieved without objectivity.* * * *

Partly as a result of a massive propaganda campaign, more than a million Italian troops still behind Axis lines when Marshal Badoglio surrendered refused to stick with Mussolini and had to be interned by the Germans. The Italian Navy, after being urged by U.S. radio broadcasts every quarter-hour to deliver itself to the Allies, did just that—prompting a British admiral to comment that American propagandists had "accomplished in one day" what he had not been able to do in three years.

The admiral's remarks were timely if exaggerated because OWI had gotten into trouble at the time of Mussolini's overthrow by Badoglio. The Duce was ousted without warning on a Sunday night, and in the absence of guidance OWI had to devise its own line for VOA broadcasts. It decided to say that the Allies should not celebrate prematurely because the King and Badoglio were Fascists who were continuing the war. The BBC took a more optimistic note, which turned out to be the official line. Newspapers scolded OWI for working at cross-purposes with Allied policy, and President Roosevelt publicly reprimanded it. As a result, a binational committee to coordinate propaganda in Europe and avoid contradictory lines was established.

Except for fast-breaking or unexpected developments, OWI had a reasonably efficient system for providing policy guidance to its staff. Each week a Central Directive was drafted, approved by an Overseas Planning Board (which included representatives of OWI, the Office of Inter-American Affairs, the State Department, OSS, the Joint Chiefs of Staff, and Britain's Political Warfare Executive), and flashed to all OWI offices.

---

* * * *Some military men had their doubts about the leaflets. One of Bill Mauldin's famous "Up Front" cartoons showed "Joe" loading and firing a cannon while "Willie" instructed the telephone operator: "Tell them leaflet people the Krauts ain't got time fer readin' today."

Most major projects were jointly planned by overseas posts and Washington headquarters. Among these were psychological pressures on the Germans to make Rome an "open city," clever baiting of Goering's *Luftwaffe* in 1944 to get German planes up in the air where they could be destroyed, efforts to make it appear the Germans were committed to holding the Atlantic Wall against the Allied invasion so that our successful landings would look all the more impressive, and (after D-day) pressing the theme of "overwhelming force" to give German soldiers an honorable rationale for surrendering.

With the end of the European war, OWI turned its full attention to telling the Japanese that their cause was hopeless. In July, 1945, the Japanese Government advised Washington through neutral diplomats that it was prepared to discuss surrender. But the Japanese armies and people were not told, and they fought on—until OWI told them through radio and a massive leaflet drop. The surrender would have come in any event, but Japanese officials later admitted that, once their people knew peace was in the offing, they had no choice but to surrender on our terms. Foreign affairs expert Paul Linebarger subsequently wrote that this "one operation alone probably repaid the entire cost of OWI through the war."[16] *****

Assessing the effectiveness of propaganda is difficult in war or peace, because it is only one factor leading to a given result. And propaganda's failures are more visible than its success. During World War II Allied propaganda could not break the morale of the German home front, but neither could strategic bombing, which cost thousands of lives and billions of dollars. It was crushing military defeat—not propaganda—that finally undermined the faith of the German people in Hitler, and the atomic bomb—not propaganda—that finally ended Japan's will to resist. Yet U.S. propaganda did have considerable impact.

After the war Secretary of War Stimson and General Eisenhower paid tribute to OWI. Stimson said that "the political and social stresses created within Germany and Japan [by propaganda] were cogent forces which undermined the enemies' strength and sapped their resolution." Agreeing, Eisenhower wrote that "the spoken and written word was an important contributing factor in undermining the enemy's will to resist. . . . Psychological warfare has proved its right to a place of dignity in our military arsenal." And one of the sharpest Congressional critics of OWI, Representative Everett Dirksen of Illinois, reversed his position after a tour abroad and went out of his way to praise the agency.

*****From start to finish, OWI's Overseas Branch spent $110,800,000, a tiny fraction of the hundreds of billions spent on the war and only 60 percent of one year's budget of the peacetime U.S. Information Agency in the late 1960s.

James P. Warburg, Deputy Director of OWI, concluded after the war that, in the year following the North African invasion, "Allied strategic propaganda contributed greatly toward driving Italy out of the war; Allied front-line propaganda brought about the surrender of large numbers of German and Italian troops, prevented the French fleet from falling into the hands of the Germans, and delivered the Italian fleet into Allied hands"—a much too generous appraisal. After the Italian surrender in 1943, however, says Warburg, "strategic propaganda accomplished but little due to the absence of a clear pro-democratic foreign policy," although "front-line propaganda continued to be effective."[17]

Wallace Carroll, who held important OWI positions in London and Washington, believes World War II "Showed that propaganda is a weapon of definite but limited utility. Used wisely against suitable targets and *in conjunction with military or political action,* it can achieve notable results. Used unwisely *without regard for its limitations,* it can prove as futile as a badly calculated air or artillery bombardment."[18]

The italics are mine, and this rule applies equally in war or peace. Propaganda unrelated to policy is almost certain to be ineffective and can be harmful. Used as one of several instruments in a coordinated campaign with specific and realistic objectives, it can do much. That, perhaps, is the most important lesson of propaganda taught by World War II; it is a lesson repeatedly retaught in the peacetime propaganda operations that followed.

It would be comforting to think the lesson was so obvious and so well learned that we could take it for granted, but the record of the two decades since the war indicates otherwise. U.S. propagandists now as then must continually fight for a place at the policy-makers' table. Sometimes they succeed and sometimes they do not. In OWI's time and today, American propaganda is vastly more pertinent and more effective when they do.

The Propaganda of Peace

The experience gained in the early 1940s provided the framework and the trained cadres for peacetime propaganda. But the transition was not easy. Americans were tired of war agencies, war controls, and war spending. Even before the Japanese had signed the surrender documents, President Truman by Executive Order transferred OWI and the propaganda functions of the Office of Inter-American Affairs to a newly created bureau in the State Department, the Interim International Information Service. He asked Secretary of State James Byrnes to make recommendations on the future of American propaganda.

Truman did recognize that "the nature of present day foreign relations makes it essential for the United States to maintain information activities abroad as an integral part of the conduct of our foreign affairs."[19] But most of the old hands in the State Department, traditionalists in the conduct of diplomacy, took a contrary view, and they set out to put propaganda in its place—as they saw it. They had support from many members of Congress who had disapproved of OWI and saw little need for a similar program in peacetime. And their boss Secretary Byrnes, himself a former Senator, shared many of their views.

Elmer Davis and hundreds of his wartime OWI colleagues, among them many of his most talented people, returned to private life. William Benton, who had made money and a name for himself in advertising (Benton & Bowles), education (University of Chicago), and publishing (*Encyclopaedia Britannica*), was appointed to the newly created position of Assistant Secretary of State for Public Affairs and given the task of reducing and reorganizing the propaganda machine.

Benton set out to cut the staff (thirteen thousand at war's end) and programs to acceptable size. He consolidated broadcasting operations in New York City, eliminated all OWI magazines except the Russian-language *Amerika*, reduced the news service by four-fifths, and dropped OWI's radio-photo transmission system. In the wake of large-scale resignations, he cut the staff back even further.

Where Benton used a scalpel, however, the Bureau of the Budget used a cleaver and Congress an ax. Despite the fact that the United States was already having trouble with Russia and diplomats were warning of more to come, despite the fact that much of the war-weary world was confused and hostile, Benton had to fight the Bureau of the Budget, and then Congress, for every penny needed to maintain even a skeleton propaganda service.

Although he assiduously wooed Congress, Benton's abrasive personality did not always help. The Voice of America was cut back from 3,200 live pro-grams in some forty languages to slightly more than half that. Many other operations were eliminated entirely. Benton finally got an appropriation of $19 million and acceptance of a "permanent" Office of International Information and Cultural Affairs in the State Department, comprised of what was left of OWI and State's limited cultural program.

Yet, despite the drastic budget cuts and the hostility within the State Department and in Congress, the program remained alive. Benton made dozens of speeches across the country to promote his cause. He persuaded the skeptical American Society of Newspaper Editors to appoint a committee to study the program and tour overseas posts; it concluded that a real need existed and that Benton's people were doing a good job.

One man, however, more than any other, contributed to the growing sentiment in America that a strong, permanent information program was a necessity. That man was Josef Stalin. In conference after conference, Soviet intransigence blocked efforts to settle the issues of the postwar world. Allies in battle became adversaries in peace, and the newly created United Nations was more disunited than anything else. In Churchill's memorable words, Stalin had rung down an "iron curtain" from "Stettin in the Baltic to Trieste in the Adriatic." Communist governments, backed by the occupying Red Army, were installed in the capitals of Eastern Europe. Although the Soviets did reluctantly withdraw from the Iranian province of Azerbaijan, Communist guerrillas threatened to take over Greece and Moscow applied increasing pressure on Turkey.

Americans grudgingly faced up to a world that was unpleasantly different from their wartime anticipations. In a striking analogy with 1918, the people in 1946 repudiated the Administration that had led them to victory and elected a Republican Congress. But there the analogy ended; where the mood after World War I had been strictly isolationist, this time it was internationalist, at least among the leadership. Henry Cabot Lodge, Sr. had been a bitter foe of Wilson's blueprint for peace, but the chairman of the Senate Foreign Relations Committee in the Eightieth Congress—Arthur Vandenberg of Michigan—was a stout collaborator in constructing a bipartisan foreign policy. In the spring of 1947 Congress approved the Truman Doctrine for unprecedented U.S. assistance to Greece and Turkey. Two months later, Secretary of State George C. Marshall proposed, and Congress subsequently approved, a program of massive economic aid to the shattered nations of Europe.

For the foreign information program, the change in Congressional sentiment came none too soon. The second time Benton went to the Hill for an appropriation, he was cut back $5 million, and it would have been more had not Truman and Marshall intervened. The information program all but disappeared in another State Department reorganization. But Stalin's ambitions, Benton's educational campaign, and the new bipartisanship in Congress resulted in the passage in early 1948 of Public Law 402, the Smith-Mundt Act.

Senator H. Alexander Smith of New Jersey and Representative (later Senator) Karl Mundt of North Dakota, both Republicans, became convinced that the country needed an effective foreign information program. They believed such a program required specific authorization by Congress so that it would not—in the words of one observer—continue to be viewed in the State Department as an "illegitimate child at a family reunion."[20] A few Senators were opposed, and there was even more resistance in the House, but Smith and Mundt, greatly aided by Vandenberg, stuck to their guns.

As finally passed, the legislation was neither very sophisticated nor very explicit. But it did provide a statutory basis for a permanent foreign information program, the basic legislation which to this day underlies the operations of the U.S. Information Agency. (USIA was not created by P.L. 402, however; that came more than five years later.)

The objectives of the Smith-Mundt Act were "to promote a better understanding of the United States in other countries, and to increase mutual understanding" between Americans and foreigners. The Act provided for "an information service to disseminate abroad information about the United States, its people and policies," and "an educational exchange service to cooperate with other nations in (a) the interchange of persons, knowledge, and skills; (b) the rendering of technical and other services; (c) the interchange of developments in . . . education, the arts and sciences."

Carrying out the new law, the State Department created two new offices, the Office of International Information (OII) and the Office of Educational Exchange (OEX), under the Assistant Secretary of State for Public Affairs. A year later, following a recommendation by the Hoover Commission on Government Reorganization that the Assistant Secretary be relieved of daily operational burdens, a general manager was appointed under the Assistant Secretary to direct the International Information and Educational Exchange Program (USIE), which included both OII and OEX.

The Smith-Mundt Act provided the authority for the foreign information program, but of course it did not provide the appropriations. Members of the Appropriations Committees were less international-minded than their brethren who specialized in foreign affairs. Radio scripts, art exhibits, nearly everything that was produced, were carefully scrutinized on Capitol Hill, and there was hardly a product that was not found wanting by some legislators. One Congressman even proposed that all VOA scripts be edited by a committee of the Daughters of the American Revolution.

In early 1948, his welcome with Congress well worn, Benton returned to his encyclopedic interests and was succeeded by a career Foreign Service Officer, George V. Allen. Only forty-four, the North Carolina–born Allen had risen rapidly in government service to become Ambassador to Iran two years earlier. A former newspaperman, he had some appreciation of the communications media. More importantly, he could impress his skeptical fellow Foreign Service Officers on the importance of the program. More effective than Benton with Congress, Allen talked the Hill into appropriating $11,320,000 for foreign relay stations to make the Voice of America more audible in many corners of the world, including the Soviet Union.

There was much for the Information Service and its Voice to say. A "full and fair picture" concept resulted in too many stories about the wealth of

America, with its countless automobiles and refrigerators, and such stories alienated as many foreigners as they attracted. But stories of greater urgency were also communicated. Although the Marshall Plan program had its own information service in Europe, State Department propagandists elsewhere told the exciting story of European recovery under freedom, contrasting it with the declining living standards in Soviet-held Eastern Europe. When the Communists blockaded Berlin, USIS posts went all out in publicizing the Western airlift which kept the former German capital supplied—and free— in the winter of 1948–49. Similar treatment was given President Truman's "Point Four" proposal, in his 1949 Inaugural Address, for extending technical assistance to underdeveloped countries.

The "Campaign of Truth"

But it was Stalin who again gave the information program a big boost. In late 1949 the Soviet Union exploded its first atomic bomb, and the shock waves were felt more in Washington than anywhere else. The National Security Council, in a detailed study of Soviet capabilities and intentions, came to the conclusion that a major propaganda effort should be undertaken in addition to massive U.S. rearmament. Edward W. Barrett, summoned back from *Newsweek* to be Assistant Secretary of State, agreed after making his own quick study.

Barrett was a good choice to succeed Allen, who had been named Ambassador to Yugoslavia. Among the ablest of the wartime propagandists, Barrett also was well regarded by his fellow American journalists. Secretary of State Acheson summoned him to Washington shortly after Christmas, 1949, to urge him to take the job, then took him to see the President. Barrett was deeply impressed by Truman, but in a different way than he had been when he met Roosevelt during the war. Truman had "the simplicity and friendliness of, say, the corner merchant," he wrote later. "Yet here was a man who clearly understood the problem of international information work far better than Roosevelt ever had."[21]

Once in office, however, Barrett had no more access to Truman than Allen. But he was helped by the presence in the White House of George Elsey, a young aide who became interested in propaganda, passed Barrett's suggestions to Truman, and served as a friend at court.

Influenced by recommendations from all sides, Truman decided to propose a major propaganda offensive in a Washington speech to the American Society of Newspaper Editors in April, 1950. Barrett suggested that he call his proposal a "campaign of truth" to avoid the "propaganda" label, and Truman agreed. The President's words were widely publicized:

We must make ourselves heard round the world in a great campaign of truth.
This task is not separate and distinct from other elements of our foreign policy.
It is a necessary part of all we are doing . . . as important as armed strength or
economic aid.

Barrett set four goals for the new campaign: (1) Creating a "healthy international community" with confidence in American leadership; (2) presenting
America fairly and countering misrepresentations and misconceptions about
it; (3) discouraging aggression by showing that America wants peace but is
prepared for war; (4) reducing Soviet influence by weakening the will of its
officials at home while encouraging non-Communist forces elsewhere.

In retrospect the Barrett program appears overambitious if not naïve. But
our propagandists did not know what they could accomplish until they tried—
and once again skepticism in Congress was a major obstacle. Like his prede-
cessors and successors, Barrett spent a disproportionate amount of time cajoling
on Capitol Hill, with only partial success. Senator Pat McCarran of Nevada
almost succeeded in getting the program abolished in early 1950. Then Stalin,
once again, came to the rescue. On June 25, 1950, the Soviet-backed government of North Korea invaded South Korea, American forces rushed to the
rescue, and Moscow began a propaganda offensive to persuade the world it was
the United States that was at fault. That year, at least, Congress was generous
in its appropriation, nearly tripling the program's funds.******

In the wake of the Korean outbreak, the worldwide propaganda operation
grew rapidly. It was not without growing pains: some decisions were made
hastily and carelessly; not all of the thousands of persons hurriedly employed
were of top caliber; and some USIS posts were assigned more people than they
needed. But the program had its effect, as the Soviets demonstrated indirectly
through their increased attacks upon it. Although jamming limited the audi-
bility of the Voice of America in Soviet cities, *Pravda* and Tass revealed the
Kremlin's sensitivity by replying to VOA "lies." One by one USIS offices were
forced to close in the satellite countries of Eastern Europe. The Soviets made
distribution of the USIS magazine *Amerika* so difficult that it was discontinued in 1952 (though resurrected four years later).

On this side of the Iron Curtain, staffs and budgets were enlarged, and
the beginnings of a genuine professionalism began to appear. Washington
permitted more decisions to be made in the field on what to say and how to

---

******A year later, though, tired of the Korean War, Congress was its old stubborn
self. In 1950 the chairman of the Senate Appropriations Committee, Kenneth
McKellar of Tennessee, had lavishly praised the Alabama-born Barrett as a true
Southern gentleman. In 1951, however, he opened a hearing by asking him, "Are you
a Communist?" McKellar's colleagues were equally difficult if more rational.

say it. A management consultant firm, called in to make an independent study, concluded in 1951 that "the program today is in a sounder position, conceptually and management-wise, than at any time since the Department of State took over" in 1945.

By mid-1951 Barrett could boast of a number of accomplishments, although on examination they proved to be more accomplishments of growth than of persuasion. He told members of his staff, whose morale was slipping under a mounting barrage of Congressional criticism, that they could "look with pride" on having: improved and expanded VOA broadcasts to make them the "most effective single weapon the free world has behind the Iron Curtain"; recruited "two of the nation's ablest advertising men, a dozen well-known newspaper correspondents, [and] an outstanding radio executive"; opened six and laid plans for another twenty-nine new USIS posts abroad, for a total of 133; issued two million copies of 277 American books and documents in foreign languages; tripled the audience for USIS films "to a rate of 400,000,000 persons a year"; and won participation "in top policy-making."

It was a record of impressive growth under difficult circumstances. "However unfair the current sniping may seem," Barrett told his staff, "keep up the good work—well aware that your efforts, added to those of loyal public servants in other fields, may well mean the difference between peace and war."[22]

Reorganization Again

Shaken by the mixed foreign reaction to events in Korea, the Pentagon pressed for a still stronger information service, one in which it would have a hand. The State Department objected to too much military control of the program, and President Truman compromised by creating an interdepartmental strategy committee with representatives of the Secretary of Defense and the Joint Chiefs of Staff. Barrett served as chairman. Later in 1951 the President established a higher-level group called the Psychological Strategy Board (PSB), comprised of the Under Secretary of State, the Deputy Secretary of Defense, and the Director of Central Intelligence. The original group then became the Psychological Operations Coordinating Committee.

The two bodies had little impact, however. Both were long on ideas but short on power to carry them out. Though members of PSB were high-ranking, they were not the heads of their departments, and the departments resisted what they considered encroachments on their preserves. Philosophical abstractions and recommendations on operational tactics were handed down; both were largely ignored.

Barrett, meanwhile, was never fully satisfied with the administration of the program within the State Department. Rigid departmental regulations, written more for negotiators and diplomatic observers than for propagandists, limited the program's flexibility. The Assistant Secretary for Public Affairs, one of several Assistant Secretaries, had to compete with his colleagues for the Secretary's attention—and he had almost no contact with the President. Immersed in daily operations (despite the help of a general manager), he had little time to work with the department's top officers on basic policies.

Barrett and others recommended consolidation of USIE's two offices into an International Information Administration (IIA), still within the State Department but semiautonomous in administration. Its administrator would receive policy guidance from the Assistant Secretary but would report directly to the Secretary, and would have a relatively free hand in operations. The reorganization plan was accepted and Barrett resigned in early 1952. At Secretary Acheson's recommendation, President Truman appointed Howland Sargeant, who had been Deputy Assistant Secretary from 1947 to 1951, to succeed him.******* Dr. Wilson Compton, president of Washington State University, was appointed the first administrator of IIA.

Sargeant's appointment was logical; he had considerable experience in the field, and it probably would have been difficult to find anyone as competent outside the government in the last year of the long Roosevelt-Truman Administration. But Compton, sixty-one, was an unlikely choice, best known as the least famous of the famous Compton brothers. A former college teacher (of economics) and administrator, he had little government experience and none in communications. But he was a Republican and knew Congress from his twenty-six years as a lobbyist for the National Lumber Manufacturers Association, and those apparently were the qualifications that Acheson, under heavy fire from Republicans on Capitol Hill, prized most highly.

Compton never had a chance. Congressional criticism increased instead of slackening, and the experienced bureaucratic infighters in the State Department ran rings around him. After a few months in office, Compton complained to Acheson that the promised "semi-autonomy" in personnel and budget had not been forthcoming. "To achieve such semi-autonomy implies a high degree of consolidation of authorities and responsibilities which

---

*******Barrett later became dean of the Columbia University School of Journalism in New York; Sargeant now heads Radio Liberty, which broadcasts to the Soviet Union.

heretofore have been widely dispersed. There is within the Department a reluctance to accept these changes, and if not a resistance at least a formidable inertia."

Some of that "formidable inertia" stemmed from the Secretary of State himself. Acheson believed the information program had only marginal value because, as he wrote later, "world opinion simply does not exist on matters that concern us." And he complained of the tendency of the American "to stare like Narcissus at his image in the pool of what he believes to be world opinion."[23]

Inertia and indifference in Washington handicapped overworked field officers, but many nonetheless improved their operations and came up with imaginative projects. One of the most imaginative—and most successful—flowered in the Middle East. Annually, many thousands of Muslims travel long distances to make the required pilgrimage or *haj* to Mecca. In the hot summer of 1952, several thousand pilgrims were stranded in Beirut when airlines oversold their space. At the suggestion of the American Legation and USIS in Beirut, U.S. Air Force transports carried 3,318 *hajis* to Saudi Arabia. Although the United States was not in good favor in the area because of its support for Israel, Muslims of every nationality praised the gesture. Local newspapers published thousands of USIS-supplied pictures and words on the airlift, and pamphlets, radio programs, and posters were produced to keep the story alive for months.

At home, however, there were only setbacks for the propaganda program during 1952. It was an election year, and partisanship intensified the bitterness of the attacks on the State Department, on Secretary Acheson, and on the Information Administration. General Eisenhower, the Republican candidate for President, made the information program a campaign issue. Senator Joseph R. McCarthy of Wisconsin, riding the crest of an irresponsible campaign against "Communists" in the State Department, let his charges far outrun the facts, and fear and uncertainty lay heavily on the land.

The real danger to America continued to be foreign, totalitarian, Communist. But many Americans, seeking scapegoats for their frustrations, looked for devils at home, not abroad. In the year ahead, the greatest opposition to an effective U.S. foreign information program would come not from Stalin or Mao Tse-tung but from the junior Senator from Wisconsin.

Notes

1. Walter Lippmann, "As Others See Us," syndicated column in the Washington *Post*, June 10, 1965.

2. Statement by Edward R. Murrow, Director of the U.S. Information Agency, before the Subcommittee on International Organizations and Movements of the Committee on Foreign Affairs, House of Representatives, Washington, D.C., March 28, 1963.

3. George Creel, *How We Advertised America* (New York: Harper & Brothers, 1920).

4. James R. Mock and Cedric Larson, *Words That Won the War* (Princeton: Princeton University Press, 1939), p. 61.

5. Edward L. Bernays, *Biography of an Idea: Memoirs of Public Relations Counsel Edward L. Bernays* (New York: Simon and Schuster, 1965), p. 177.

6. Creel, *op. cit.,* p. 402.

7. Mock and Larson, *op. cit.,* p. 332.

8. Creel, *op. cit.,* p. 408 and p. 402.

9. Bernays, *op. cit.,* p. 177.

10. Robert A. McClure, Foreword to Daniel Lerner's *Sykewar* (New York: Macmillan, 1949), p. 133.

11. Wallace Carroll, *Persuade or Perish* (Boston: Houghton Mifflin, 1948), p. 370.

12. *Ibid.,* p. 12

13. Robert E. Sherwood, *Roosevelt and Hopkins* (New York: Harper & Brothers, 1948), p. 630.

14. Allen W. Dulles, *Germany's Underground* (New York: Macmillan, 1946), p. 133.

15. Leo Rosten, "The World of Leo Rosten: The Day I Bombed Berlin," *Look.*

16. Edward W. Barrett, *Truth Is Our Weapon* (New York: Funk & Wagnalls, 1950), pp. 13–14.

17. James P. Warburg, *Unwritten Treaty* (New York: Harcourt Brace, 1946).

18. Carroll, *op. cit.,* pp. 362–363.

19. Executive Order 9608, issued by President Truman, August 31, 1945.

20. Barrett, *op. cit.,* p. 54.

21. *Ibid.,* p. 75.

22. *Ibid.,* pp. 89–91.

23. Dean Acheson, "The American Image Will Take Care of Itself," *New York Times Magazine,* February 28, 1965.

5

The Bolshevik Revolution and the War of Ideologies (1917-39)

Philip Taylor

T he 'war to end all wars' did not live up to its name. Neither did the peace treaties that concluded it herald a return of world peace. As the Chief of the Imperial General Staff noted in 1919 after counting 44 wars in progress, 'this peace treaty has resulted in wars everywhere.' The year 1918 may have seen the end of the Great War but international conflict none the less remained. Most notably, there was an intensification of a struggle that had begun with the Bolshevik seizure of power in Russia in 1917 and which has raged intermittently ever since, sometimes as open war, sometimes postponed, and mostly, since 1945, as Cold War. It is essentially a struggle between two diametrically opposed ideologies in which propaganda has always played a central role. The Bolshevik Revolution may well have taken Russia out of the First World War, but it also led to a new and significant development in the conduct of international affairs. After 1917, propaganda became a fact of everyday life. For Lenin and his successors, who owed so much to the successful employment of propaganda in securing power at the expense of the tsars, propaganda also became an essential ingredient in the ideological war against capitalism and the struggle for world revolution. But

SOURCE: From *Munitions of the Mind* by Philip Taylor, 1990, Manchester University Press, Manchester, UK. Reprinted with permission.

it also had to be used to spread the word internally to the vast majority of peasants initially untouched by the actual events of the revolution in St Petersburg but whose lives were to be changed radically by them, particularly during the crucial days of the Civil War (1918–21).

The crusading element in Marxist ideology, to bring the essential 'truth' to the peasants and working classes of both Russia and the wider world, combined with the experience of underground struggle and covert resistance, led to great emphasis being placed by Lenin and his supporters on the role of propaganda in helping to secure power and to maintain it. The Russian revolutionaries were, of course, great publicists. Working from underground presses, frequently from abroad, they began to distribute their ideas long before the revolution itself through such publications as *Iskra* ('The Spark') and *Pravda* ('Truth'). Yet despite the reputation of *Iskra* for lighting the spark that fuelled the revolution, its importance as a propaganda newspaper was never matched by its popularity. It was printed in Munich, edited by Plekhanov, and smuggled into Russia via Switzerland under the supervision of Lenin's wife Krupskaya, but its somewhat doctrinaire and intellectual style made it rather heavy reading and its circulation never reached more than 40,000. Following the 1904 split between the Bolsheviks and the Mensheviks, *Iskra* passed into the latter's hands, whereupon the Bolsheviks founded other papers. Trotsky was responsible for founding *Pravda* in 1912 and its circulation rose steadily thanks to its simpler and more readable style. During its first two years, the paper was closed down nine times by the authorities.

The Great War gave impetus to the Bolshevik cause, particularly when, following the abdication of the tsar in February 1917, Russia continued its involvement. The Germans even helped the Bolsheviks produce a version of *Pravda* for the trenches that helped to foster pacifist agitation and the paper reopened in Petrograd. *Izvestia* ('News') was founded. Also at home, the Bolsheviks were able to play upon growing war-weariness with their ideological messages through the use of such masterly slogans as 'Peace, Land and Bread' and 'All Power to the Soviets.' And, of course, there was the oratorical skill of Lenin himself. From his position in exile before 1917 he also had every opportunity to study the propaganda battles being waged on the various military and civilian fronts; he returned to Russia as an expert in the role which indoctrination and mass persuasion could play both at home and abroad. Perhaps this, ironically, was the greatest German propaganda achievement of the First World War.

A major obstacle to Lenin was the illiteracy of the mass of the Russian people and thus the relatively limited role which newspapers could play. *Izvestia* had the largest circulation with 400,000 copies at its highest point; *Pravda*'s was barely a third of that—tiny figures given the size of the Russian population. Yet the masses *were* historically and culturally receptive to icons, which had formed a central role in their daily and spiritual life for centuries. If that tradition could be adapted to transmit political images through modern means of communication, then the Bolsheviks stood a good chance of getting their message across. This meant using posters, and before long the Bolsheviks were producing posters of such design and imagination that they have often been regarded as works of art. Indeed posters of the Civil War period are regarded as being among the most impressive contributions to pictorial art ever made by the Soviet Union. The poster, like the icon, could present symbols in a simple and easily identifiable way, even to barely literate peasants. A style of visual story-board poster—not unlike the modern cartoon strip—emerged that is still popular today. Experimentation in this new form led men with no formal artistic training, such as D. S. Orlov and V. Deni, to emerge as the principal exponents of poster art. But it was Mikhail Cheremnykh who originated the most distinctive posters of the Civil War period—the 'Satire Window' format, sometimes known as the ROSTA windows. ROSTA were the initials of the Bolsheviks' Telegraph Agency, set up in September 1918, and this organization published its own newspapers. Because of severe paper shortages, however, Cheremnykh devised the idea of wall newspapers to be pasted in busy parts of Moscow and in shop windows. Posters soon followed and the idea quickly spread to other cities. By the end of the Civil War, ROSTA had nearly fifty agencies around the country using these methods, the window posters of the poet Mayakovsky being especially successful. But their success was limited to the Civil War period. They often attracted more artistic than political attention, and the avant-garde movement which pioneered them accordingly went into decline after 1921.

The Allied invasion of Russia in support of the White counter-revolutionaries began before the First World War ended. While Britain, France, and Germany slugged it out on the Western Front, the fighting being intensified by the release of German troops from the east following the Russo-German treaty of Brest-Litovsk in March 1918, Allied troops (principally Japanese) landed at Vladivostok on the Pacific coast of Russia in the following month. But the western powers at this stage were not motivated by ideological considerations. Alarmed at Russia's departure from the war, the move was designed to keep Germany distracted in the east. Hence the British occupation of Murmansk in March 1918 and of Archangel on 1 August. Even so, from Siberia, the Civil War spread to the Cossack territories and the Caucasus, but it was only after the defeat of Germany that the European Powers could afford to intervene more intensively. This gave time for Trotsky to build up the new Red Army and for the *Cheka,* the secret police, to establish its grip on the domestic population.

Following the Armistice with Germany, Allied intervention increased dramatically. The French landed at Odessa in the south in December, while the British and Japanese reinforced their detachments in northern Russia and in the Far East, the latter being joined by American forces. But, after four years of bloody war, public support for Allied intervention declined, particularly after the failure of the White generals Kolchak and Denekin to make substantial progress in their offensives of 1919. Poland took up the cause and attacked Russia in 1920 but, despite the help of the Ukrainians, suffered a series of defeats at the hands of the Red Army. The Treaty of Riga was signed in March 1921. By that time, most Allied troops had been withdrawn, with the Japanese finally evacuating completely in 1925. The White cause had collapsed. The Bolsheviks had survived.

The role of propaganda in all this chaos and confusion is difficult to evaluate. The Whites, to be sure, were less skilled in this as in most other areas, particularly in their failure to capture the support of the peasants. Their ideology also lacked the cohesion of their opponents. The presence of foreign troops on Russian soil in support of the Whites helped the Reds to play on nationalistic desires to drive the invaders out of Mother Russia but, as will be seen, this was not without its irony given the international aspirations of the Bolsheviks. But Russia was far from being a unified country; separatist elements exploited by the Whites in various republics made disintegration a very real possibility. The Bolsheviks for their part seized upon the disunity of their opponents while themselves unifying the towns and countryside behind their own party organization. This was done through a combination of agitation, terror, and propaganda. Lenin's land decree—his first act in power—was itself a masterstroke of propaganda and served to provide the basis by which the peasants could be won over. Activists went out into the countryside to take the news to the peasants that they now owned the land, to organize them, and to agitate.

However, as the Civil War dragged on, food shortages in the cities led to requisitioning, and this merely alienated the peasantry. The Bolsheviks responded with increased 'education' (i.e., propaganda) and the Commissariat of Enlightenment was formed to supervise public readings for the illiterate peasants, workers, and soldiers. The young—always a primary target for any aspiring propaganda state—were organized and indoctrinated through the Komsomol. Agit-ships went down rivers and agit-trains went into the countryside to take the message to the people. Agitational outposts, *agitpunkty,* were set up at railway stations complete with libraries and lecture halls for the purpose of establishing links 'between the localities and the centre, to agitate, to carry out propaganda, to bring information, and to supply literature.' Even the names of the agit-trains and agit-ships had a propaganda purpose:

V.I. Lenin, The October Revolution, and *Red Star.* Each of these were highly decorated mobile propaganda units, covered in posters, flags, and slogans. They carried about a hundred people (including Cheka officers and representatives of all the leading Bolshevik committees) to organize selected local officials, a complaints section (always busy), its own press, a wireless transmitter, and, most important of all, a film projector.

Lenin's often quoted view that 'for us the most important of all arts is the cinema' reflected an appreciation of the role which the new mass media could play in the revolutionary context. Although the situation varied from city to city and from town to countryside, on average only two out of five adults were literate in the Russia of 1920. The most effective means of reaching the majority of uneducated Russians was by using film. For Lenin, the cinema was primarily an educational device—for political education, that is. For the audiences, it was primarily a medium of entertainment (Charlie Chaplin being particularly popular). For many peasants, who had never seen a film until the agit-trains brought one to them, it was a miracle. The fact that films at this time were silent helped to overcome the problem of communicating to the numerous different nationalities with their different languages. Foreign films, often portraying ideas that were incompatible with Bolshevik ideology, were popular and had to be countered by a domestic film industry that was not yet capable of meeting the needs of the revolution. Indeed, the Civil War momentarily destroyed the Russian film industry. It was not until 1927, after a period of reconstruction, that Soviet films earned more at the box-office than imported products. Lenin had nationalized the Russian film industry in August 1919 but, starved of film stock and equipment from abroad, not to mention the shortages of electricity and of those many technicians, actors, and directors who had fled the revolution, it was unlikely that film propaganda itself played a significant role in determining the final outcome of the revolution. What the available films did in the countryside was to attract a curious audience, whereupon the officials from the agit-trains would disembark to deliver their message using classic techniques of crowd manipulation.

From this disastrous beginning, however, the Soviet film industry soon began to produce one of the most acclaimed bodies of work in the history of world cinema. A national production company, Sovkino, was established in 1925 and new studios were set up in Moscow, Leningrad, Kiev, and Odessa; thirteen were functioning across the nation by 1928 producing 123 films in that year, each reaching an average audience of 2½ million people. Virtually all the films were made to serve the State. *Battleship Potemkin* (1926), made by Sergei Eisenstein, portrayed the 1905 mutiny at Odessa but its message had more to do with propaganda than with history. Eisenstein's next film, *October* (1927), made to commemorate the tenth anniversary of the revolution, fell into a similar category. They had the feel of documentaries but concentrated on events rather than individuals. As a result, they are often mistaken even today as being film 'records' of what actually happened in the 1905 and 1917 revolutions rather than re-enactments designed to serve the interests of the Soviet state in the 1920s. Pudovkin's *End of St Petersburg* (1927), another anniversary classic, paid more attention to the human elements of the revolutionary struggle, but here again its message was symbolic and propagandistic rather than historical. Such films legitimized the revolution and thereby the regime that inherited it. They appear, however, to have created a greater impression abroad than they did at home.

Although the Soviets pioneered new methods of domestic propaganda that were watched with great interest by other countries, it was their foreign propaganda that caused most concern abroad. The Bolshevik leadership was certainly quick to appreciate the role propaganda could play in undermining the position of the 'capitalist-imperialist' powers and spreading its ideas about world revolution. In October 1917, for example, the Bolsheviks published various secret treaties that had been negotiated by the tsarist regime with the Allies, notably the 1915 Treaty of London. The embarrassment this caused the Allies—at a time when President Wilson was calling for national self-determination—was to contribute towards Italian disillusionment with the Paris Peace Settlement. Moreover, influenced by Trotsky's theories of world revolution, the role of propaganda in spreading an international class-based ideology that recognized no national frontiers was a serious threat to established regimes suffering from the intense socio-economic and political chaos caused by the First World War. Great hopes that the theories were about to become a reality with the revolution in Germany, followed by the establishment of a short-lived communist regime in Hungary, were reflected in the foundation of the Third International, or Comintern, in March 1919. Comintern agents were included in the staff of Soviet diplomatic missions; indeed, in the years immediately following the revolution, Soviet foreign policy and Soviet propaganda became virtually indistinguishable.

For Russia's former allies, the replacement of 'Prussian militarism' by Bolshevism as the principal perceived threat to civilization as they knew it was clearly a matter requiring urgent counter-measures. The British Empire, in particular, was a primary target for the Comintern and was identified as the main bastion of the world 'capitalist-imperialist' order. Troubles in Ireland, India, and Palestine provided ideal opportunities to stir up revolutionary activity. But Britain had also largely dismantled its efficient wartime propaganda machinery and had to rely on military intervention in the Civil War as its best means of stopping Comintern activities. Following the Red victory, the Communist International continued its activities, but the chance for world revolution seemed to have passed. Aid was given to the Chinese communists until Russian advisers were expelled in 1928. And the chance seemingly provided by the General Strike in Britain in 1926 also seemed to have faded. Following the death of Lenin in 1924 and the internal struggle for power which followed, resulting in Trotsky's expulsion and Stalin's accession, the economic chaos that the Civil War had created in Russia required urgent attention. With the adoption of the first Five Year Plan and of the policy of Socialism in One Country by the end of the 1920s, the Comintern went into decline.

Fear of Bolshevism in the western democracies, however, remained. The formation of 'Little Moscows' in 1919 throughout Europe and America had rocked the established order. The Red Flag had even been hoisted over Glasgow Town Hall! Calls for the workers of the world to unite were made with the aid of the new medium of radio. For Lenin, radio was 'a newspaper without paper . . . and without boundaries.' When Radio Moscow began transmissions in 1922, it was the most powerful transmitter in the world. In 1925, it added the world's first short-wave transmitter. In the following year, when the General Strike in Britain conjured up memories of 'Red Clyde' and the widespread strikes of 1919, Radio Moscow tried to fuel the agitation until the British government jammed its broadcasts. Despite the Russian promise in the 1921 Anglo-Soviet Trade Agreement not to attack Britain by propaganda, violations continued throughout the next ten years, although by the end of the decade, with a more introspective Stalin in charge, the threat was felt to have subsided. Democracy in Britain, France, and America had survived its immediate post-war crises. Counter-measures (such as the banning of *The Battleship Potemkin* and other Soviet classics) seemed to have prevented the spreading of the Bolshevik word, and the powers looked forward to the restoration of peace amidst hopes for world disarmament.

The new spirit of optimism in the late 1920s saw important developments in the communications revolution: 1927 in fact was almost as momentous a year as 1896. That was the year of Charles Lindbergh's historic solo trans-Atlantic flight, which heralded the beginning of the end of North America's geographic isolation from Europe. With the rapid development of international civil aviation routes, the world was becoming more like a global village. The telephone also contributed to the feeling of a shrinking world, and in 1927 communication was established across the Atlantic by radio-telephone. In the same year, the British Broadcasting Company became the British Broadcasting Corporation with the motto 'Nation shall speak peace unto Nation' and, within five years, the BBC had initiated its Empire Service designed to enable the far-flung peoples of the British Empire to remain in constant touch with the mother country. Australian broadcasts were heard in

Britain for the first time in 1927. That year also witnessed the arrival of the first commercially successful talking picture, *The Jazz Singer*. Radio and the cinema, both in their infancy during the First World War, were the first true mass media and their implications for politics, propaganda, and warfare were to be far-reaching. In Glasgow, Baird demonstrated the transmission of colour television pictures in 1927 (the Russians had demonstrated the technology of television before even the First World War), although this particular medium was not to receive its real significance as a propaganda medium until the late 1940s.

The World Economic Depression that resulted from the collapse of the American stock market in 1929 quickly dashed the short-lived optimism of the late 1920s. In Germany, Hitler began his rapid rise to power and was appointed Chancellor in 1933. He then began to dismantle the Weimar democracy and establish the Nazi totalitarian state using many of the propaganda methods pioneered by the British and the Soviets. Meanwhile, the Japanese, also badly hit by the Depression, decided to abandon any notion of international collective security and attacked Manchuria in late 1931. World opinion was shocked by the first newsreel footage of military operations against civilians with the Japanese bombing of Chinese towns. The League of Nations, established in 1919 to safeguard a lasting peace, did nothing to punish the aggressor or protect the small power involved. Hitler walked out of both the World Disarmament Conference and the League of Nations and began rearming Germany. Mussolini attacked Abyssinia in 1935. Again the League was unable to prevent aggression. The Americans, never a League member, passed Neutrality Acts and tried to isolate themselves from mounting European aggression. France was in the middle of a political and economic crisis and was rocked by a series of scandals and riots. Britain, the only true world power with interests stretching from Europe through the Mediterranean to the Far East, found herself confronted by three potential enemies but totally unprepared to meet force with force. Russia, which could have helped by virtue of both her European and Far Eastern interests, decided to abandon her isolation and entered the League in 1934. A pact with France followed the next year. Whatever unfinished business Stalin had at home, the advent of a regime in Germany dedicated to the overthrow of communism was a threat he could not ignore. By the mid-1930s Europe was once again becoming increasingly polarized into two opposing camps and the ideological conflict between the forces of the left and the right was to become even more acute when the Spanish Civil War broke out in July 1936.

Coming as it did so rapidly after the crises in Europe, the Far East, and Africa, many observers felt that the Spanish Civil War could quite easily develop into a second world war. As in the case of the Russian Civil War, the

European powers became involved in affairs that might at first appear to have had little to do with them. But although the Second World War broke out in 1939, Poland, not Spain, was the immediate cause. This was to some extent due to the fact that Britain and France, at least, tried desperately to limit the effects of the Spanish Civil War and prevent it from spreading into a wider conflict by a non-intervention agreement. Russia, Germany, and Italy, however, honoured the agreement more in the breach. They exploited the conflict for their own purposes and it became a major battleground in the international propaganda war of the 1930s—a dress rehearsal for things to come. By the late 1930s, in other words, propaganda had become an established fact of everyday life. International broadcasting, State-controlled cinemas and newspapers, public opinion polls, mass rallies: all these were new features of an age characterized by an ideological struggle with worldwide dimensions thanks to the technology of the communications revolution. As such, truth was a major casualty long before the actual fighting began.

6

Restructuring the Means of Communication in Nazi Germany

David A. Welch

The Ministry for Popular Enlightenment and Propaganda

It was during the early part of 1933 that Goebbels was making the final plans for a Ministry of Propaganda. However, because Goebbels was so involved in the forthcoming elections on 5 March, it was decided to delay announcing the creation of the new ministry until after the Nazis' electoral success was guaranteed. From Goebbels' own account of his rise to power it is quite clear that the decision to create such a ministry had been agreed for some time:

> We are thinking of a Ministry of Public Education within which film, radio, art, culture and propaganda would be combined. Such a revolutionary organisation will be under central control and firmly embody the idea of the Reich. This is a really big project, as big as the world has seen. I am to start at once working out the structure for this Ministry.[1]

Goebbels is said to have been initially unhappy with the open use of 'Propaganda' in the title on the grounds that it was psychologically

SOURCE: D. Welch, *Third Reich: Politics and Propaganda*, pp. 23–49, copyright © 1993, reprinted by permission of Taylor & Francis Books, Ltd.

counter-productive. Given his voluminous writings on the subject and that he felt confident enough to form the Nazi Party Reich Propaganda Directorate in 1930, this claim, which is based on little substantive evidence, seems out of character to say the least. The Ministry for Popular Enlightenment and Propaganda (Reichsministerium für Volksaufklärung and Propaganda—RMVP), was established by a presidential decree, signed on 12 March 1933 and promulgated on the following day, which defined the task of the new ministry as the dissemination of 'enlightenment and propaganda within the population concerning the policy of the Reich Government and the national reconstruction of the German Fatherland.' In June Hitler was to define the scope of the RMVP in even more general terms, making Goebbels responsible for the 'spiritual direction of the nation.' Not only did this vague directive provide Goebbels with room to out-manoeuvre his critics within the Party; it also put the seal of legitimacy on what was soon to be ministry's wholesale control of the mass-media. Nevertheless, Goebbels was constantly involved in quarrels with ministerial colleagues who resented the encroachment of this new ministry on their old domain.

Analysing the political function of propaganda in the Third Reich is further complicated by the fact that it was simultaneously channelled through three different institutions: the RMVP, the Central Propaganda Office of the Party, and the Reich Chamber of Culture. Moreover, the political structure of the Third Reich was based on the twin pillars of the Party and the State. According to Hitler, it was the task of the State to continue the 'historical development of the national administration within the framework of the law,' while it was the function of the Party to 'build its internal organisation and establish and develop a stable and self-perpetuating centre of the National Socialist doctrine in order to transfer the indoctrinated to the State so that they may become its leaders as well as its disciples.'[2] The creation of the RMVP in March 1933 was a significant step towards the merging of the Party and the State. Goebbels continued to be head of Party Propaganda, but he greatly strengthened both his own position within the Party and the scope of propaganda by setting up this new ministry—the first of its kind in Germany.

Two days after his appointment as Minister for Propaganda Goebbels outlined his view of the role of the new ministry in a revealing speech to representatives of the German press:

> We have established a Ministry for Popular Enlightenment and Propaganda. These two titles do not convey the same thing. Popular enlightenment is essentially something passive; propaganda, on the other hand, is something active. We cannot be satisfied with just telling the people what we want and

enlightening them as to how we are doing it. We must replace this enlightenment with an active government propaganda that aims at winning people over. It is not enough to reconcile people more or less to our regime, to move them towards a position of neutrality towards us, we would rather work on people until they are addicted to us.[3]

With the creation of the RMVP, propaganda became primarily the responsibility of the State, although its departments were to be supported and reinforced by the Party's Central Propaganda Office (Reichspropagandaamt), which remained less conspicuous to the general public. Indeed, the two institutions would often merge into one apparatus: not only would their respective organisations and responsibilities correspond closely, but many of the leading positions in the Ministry and the Reichspropagandaleitung were held by the same officials. Originally Goebbels had planned only five departments for the new ministry, to embrace radio, press, active propaganda, film, and theatre and popular education, but by April 1933 it had acquired its basic structure and was divided into seven departments. During the war even Goebbels' staunch anti-bureaucratic stance could not prevent the RMVP escaping the process of expansion and bureaucratisation, and the number of departments actually increased to fourteen. However, in the context of this study I have confined my discussion to the more important departments. Accordingly, the division of labour within the ministry can be broken down along the following lines. The wide variety of responsibilities of the departments points to a remarkably comprehensive organisational structure:

Department I: Legislation and Legal Problems; Budget Finance, and Accounting.

Department II: Co-ordination of Popular Enlightenment and Propaganda ('active propaganda'); Regional Agencies of the Ministry; German Academy of Politics; Official Ceremonies and Demonstrations; National Emblems; Racial Questions; Treaty of Versailles; Opposing Ideologies; Youth Organisations; Public Health and Sport; Eastern and Border Questions; National Travel Committee.

Department III: Radio; National Broadcasting Company (Reichsfunkgesellschaft).

Department IV: National and Foreign Press; Journalism; Press Archives; News Service; National Association of German Press.

Department V: Film; Film Picture Industry; Film Censorship, Newsreels.

Department VI: Theatre.

Department VII: Music, Fine Arts; People's Culture.

The RMVP began with only 350 administrative and executive officials. Goebbels retained a notoriously low opinion of civil servants and once confided in his diary that 'just as you cannot expect a cow to lay eggs, so you cannot expect a bureaucrat to look after the interests of the State properly.'[4] As a new creation, the RMVP was from the beginning staffed by fanatical young Nazis, generally with better educational qualifications than the average Nazi activist. Goebbels had declared that his staff should never exceed 1,000, and he also agreed to meet the costs of the RMVP from radio licenses. Fortunately for the new minister, the purchase of radios increased dramatically during the Third Reich, and it has been estimated that over 80 per cent of the ministry's current expenditure was recovered from this source.[5] Goebbels saw the RMVP as the main policy- and decision-making body, providing directions and delegating responsibilities to the numerous subordinate agencies that lay under its control. The most important of these was the Reich Chamber of Culture (Reichskulturkammer).

The Reich Chamber of Culture

Kulturpolitik (cultural policy) was an important element in German life, but the Nazis were the first party systematically to organise the entire cultural life of a nation. As the RMVP ominously proclaimed when it announced the Theatre Law of 15 May 1934: 'The arts are for the National Socialist State a public exercise; they are not only aesthetic but also moral in nature and the public interest demands not only police supervision but also guidance.' The Reich Chamber of Culture was set up by a law promulgated on 22 September 1933. It represented a triumph for Goebbels in his bitter struggle with the Nazi 'ideologist' Alfred Rosenberg, who before 1933 had claimed responsibility for cultural matters through the establishment of his 'Combat League for German Culture.' The Reich Chamber of Culture allowed the Minister of Propaganda to organise the various branches of the arts and cultural professions as public corporations. Seven individual areas were organised as separate chambers: literature, theatre, music, radio, film, fine arts, and the press. Goebbels was designated president of the Reichskulturkammer (RKK), with power to appoint the presidents of the subordinate chambers. The creation of the RKK is an excellent example of the process of *Gleichschaltung*. This was the term employed by the Nazis when they came to power, and referred to the obligatory assimilation within the State of all political, economic and cultural activities. The RKK acted as an agent of this 'coordination' in that it allowed the RMVP to exert its control over almost all aspects of German cultural life. As Minister for Propaganda, Goebbels acted as president of the seven chambers, and through him their jurisdiction spread down to both the nation's regional administration (*Länder*) and the Party's own specifically political areas (*Gaue*). This not only facilitated the RMVP's control over individual chambers but, equally importantly, allowed the ministry to co-ordinate its propaganda campaigns.

The chief function of each chamber was to regulate conditions of work in its particular field. This involved the keeping of a register and the issuing of work permits. Nobody refused such a permit could be employed in his or her profession. To be refused membership of the chamber, therefore, spelt professional ruin. To those sympathetic to the regime, on the other hand, enforced membership of such an immense organisation represented financial security and public recognition. The law which established the RKK conferred on Goebbels the power to exclude all those who were considered racially or artistically objectionable.

As the Nazi revolution was to bring about a new consciousness, which would transcend the political structure, it followed that artists too had a revolutionary role to play. In one of his first speeches as Minister for Propaganda Goebbels outlined the future role of German art:

> Modern German art's task is not to dramatise the Party programme, but to give poetic and artistic shape to the huge spiritual impulses within us. . . . The political renaissance must definitely have spiritual and cultural foundations. Therefore it is important to create a new basis for the life of German art.[6]

Under the Nazis, art was seen as an expression of race and would underpin the political renaissance that was taking place. Whereas Modernism was associated with 'decadent' Jewish-Liberal culture, art under National Socialism would be rooted in the people as true expression of the spirit of the People's Community (*Volksgemeinschaft*). At the height of his power, Hitler gave a succinct summary of his concept of culture and the role of artists in a speech delivered on 18 July 1937 at the opening of the House of German Art in Munich, which was intended to house officially approved art:

> During the long years in which I planned the formation of a new Reich I gave much thought to the tasks which would await us in the cultural cleansing of the people's life; there was to be a cultural renaissance as well as a political and economic reform. . . . As in politics, so in German art-life, we are determined to make a clean sweep of empty phrases. . . . The artist does not create for the artist. He creates for the people, and we will see to it that the people in future be called to judge his art. No one must say that the people have no understanding for a really valuable enrichment of its cultural life. . . . The people in passing through these galleries will recognise in me its spokesman and counsellor.

It will draw a sigh of relief and gladly express its agreement with this purification of art. . . . The artist cannot stand aloof from his people.[7]

This speech defined what was and what was not artistically desirable in
the Third Reich. Moreover, it was believed that, by establishing the seven
chambers under the umbrella of the RKK, such a control mechanism would
allow the regime largely to dispense with a formal system of censorship,
since artists had either been purged or, if they remained, would exercise self-
censorship for fear of losing their livelihood. In practice the regime became
increasingly sensitive to artistic criticism of any kind, and Goebbels was
eventually persuaded that once a work of art had been officialy approved
it was not the function of critics to criticise it. On 13 May 1936 Goebbels
issued a proclamation which banned the writing of critical reviews on the
same evening as the performance (*Nachtkritik*). Justifying his position, the
Minister for Propaganda declared: 'Artistic criticism no longer exists for its
own sake. In future one ought not to degrade or criticise a well-meaning or
quite respectable artistic achievement for the sake of a witty turn of phrase.'[8]
Such measures were clearly intended as a warning to critics not to question,
by means of hostile reviews, officially approved artistic works (which would
range from a piece of sculpture to a feature film). However, on 27 November
1936 Goebbels decided to ban all art criticism by confining critics to writing
merely 'descriptive' reviews (*Kunstbetrachtungen*). In future all critics would
need a special license from the RKK, and these licenses would only be given
to critics over the age of thirty. The day following Goebbels' famous order,
his press chief at the RMVP, Alfred Ingemar Berndt, informed the Reich
Chamber of Culture:

Judgement of art work in the National Socialist State can be made only on the
basis of the National Socialist viewpoint of culture. Only the Party and the State
are in a position to determine artistic values. . . . If a license has been issued by
those who are appointed to pass judgement on art, the reporter, may of course,
employ the values thereby established. This situation will arise only rarely,
however.[9]

It can be seen that art criticism was never an aesthetic but always a political question. In practice art criticism came more and more to resemble publicity material distributed by the State to promote a particular venture or
activity. Although the ban met with some hostility (especially abroad), the
first manifestation of such a mentality occurred as early as 10 May 1933, a
few months before the RKK was established, in Berlin's Franz Joseph Platz,
with the barbarous ceremony of the 'Burning of the Books.' The works of

'undesirable and pernicious' writers were thrown on a ceremonial bonfire, and Goebbels made a speech, broadcast on German radio, in which he referred to such writers as 'the evil spirit of the past,' and declared:

> the age of extreme intellectualism is over . . . the past is lying in flames . . . the future will rise from the flames within our hearts . . . Brightened by these flames our vow shall be: the Reich and the Nation and our Führer Adolf Hitler: Heil! Heil! Heil!.[10]

From now on the State would determine what was 'good' and what was 'bad' literature. However, since its establishment Goebbels and the RMVP had become embroiled in a struggle for power with Alfred Rosenberg, who had set up a Party agency, the 'Reich Office for the Encouragement of German Literature' and vied with Goebbels for ultimate control of censorship. In November 1933, Goebbels had requested all State governments to consult with the Reich Chamber of Literature before banning books. The matter was finally resolved by a decree of 25 April 1935 which established the supreme authority of the Reich Chamber of Literature, who were now empowered to draw up an 'index' of all 'damaging and undesirable literature,' which threatened 'the National Socialist cultural aspirations.' If the police now wished to ban or confiscate a work of literature, they were obliged to request its inclusion in this 'confidential' index.

Kulturpolitik in the Third Reich had a 'revolutionary' role in an attempt to create a 'people's culture' which would express the new art forms of the National Socialist revolution. Government statistics regularly purported to show the increasing number of 'people's theatres,' 'people's films,' 'people's sculpture,' 'people's radios,' etc., all of which were intended to reflect the manner in which art was being brought to the people and expressing the 'national community.' Objectivity and opinion, however, were eliminated, and replaced by a definition of truth as defined by the Nazi regime. Conformity of opinion and action were also secured within the *Kunstwelt* itself. Addressing the opening of the 'Week of German Books' (an annual event) in Weimar in October 1936, Goebbels argued that writers, for example, should no longer follow their own whims but feel obliged to work for the nation: 'Now the pen has been compelled to serve the nation like the sword and the plough,' he declared.[11]

In order that art should reflect the ideological precepts of National Socialism, it was imperative that artists themselves should be sympathetic towards the aims and ideals of the new regime. Accordingly a 'cleansing' process of *Entjudung* eliminated Jews and other political undesirables from working in German cultural life. The result of these measures was inevitably an overwhelming cultural mediocrity that produced 'safe,' conventional art, rather than the vibrant 'people's culture' that the regime purported to encourage. In 1941 Goebbels was forced to admit at a press conference: 'The National Socialist State has given up the ambition of trying to produce art itself. It has wisely contented itself with encouraging art and gearing it spiritually and intellectually to its educative function for the people.'[12] Before taking up these issues and analysing the themes disseminated by the regime, I should first like to discuss the major channels of communication and the manner in which they were 'coordinated' into the Ministry for Propaganda, the RKK, and the Central Propaganda Office of the Party.

Radio

When Goebbels became Minister for Propaganda, the newspaper and film industries were still privately owned; the broadcasting system, however, had been State-regulated since 1925 by means of the Reich Radio Company (Reichsrundfunkgesellschaft—RRG). Under this system, 51 per cent of the capital was owned by the Ministry of Posts, which also appointed a Radio Commissioner (Reichsfunkkommissar). However, the RRG had little say over programme content, which was the responsibility of nine regional broadcasting companies, who owned the remaining 49 per cent of the capital.[13]

Although the Nazis had failed to gain access to this medium while in opposition, once in power the 'coordination' of German radio proved comparatively easy, despite a few initial setbacks. From the moment he assumed power, Goebbels recognised its propaganda potential and he was determined to make the most of this relatively new medium. In his address to representatives of the press on 15 March 1933, Goebbels had revealed that the radio would have the responsibility of bringing the people closer to the National Socialist State. He hinted that the Nazis had already gone some way to achieving this, because

> our radio propaganda is not produced in a vacuum, in radio stations, but in the atmosphere-laden halls of mass gatherings. In this way every listener has become a direct participant in these events. I have a vision of a new and topical radio, a radio that really takes account of the spirit of our time . . . a radio that is aware of its great national responsibility.

Goebbels clearly saw in radio an instrument not only to create uniformity but also to guide public opinion towards the Nazi concept of 'national community' as the ideological obverse to the class conflict that has been such a feature of Weimar politics. The theme of *Volksgemeinschaft* also figured prominently in his first address to managerial staff of German radio in the Haus des Rundfunks on 25 March 1933. Goebbels began by flattering his audience ('I hold radio to be the most modern and the most important instrument of mass influence that exists anywhere'), and he continued: 'I am also of the opinion—and one shouldn't say this out loud—that in the long term radio will replace newspapers.' The Minister for Propaganda concluded his speech by declaring:

> I am placing a major responsibility in your hands, for you have in your hands the most modern instrument in existence for influencing the masses. By means of this instrument you are the creators of public opinion. If you perform this well, we shall win over the people. . . . As the piano is to the pianist, so the transmitter is to you, the instrument that you play on as sovereign masters of public opinion.[14]

In his efforts to consolidate his control over radio, Goebbels' immediate problem was to break down the federal structure, over which the Reich possessed limited economic and political control. He also had to contend with resistance from Hermann Göring, who, as Prussian Minister of the Interior, supported the independence of the regional authorities for radio. Thus before Goebbels could assert his new ministry's control over radio, indeed over all rival agencies, he was obliged to persuade Hitler to issue a supplementary decree on 30 June 1933 which laid out in detail those responsibilities which were to be transferred to RMVP from other ministries and rival agencies. The regulations stated:

> The Reich Minister for Popular Enlightenment and Propaganda is responsible for all influences on the intellectual life of the nation; public relations for the State, culture, and the economy, for instructing the domestic and foreign public about them and for the administration of all the institutions serving these purposes.[15]

Although this decree stated unequivocally that responsibility for radio now rested with the RMVP, to clear this matter up still required a personal letter from Hitler (dated 15 July) to the Reichsstatthalter (Governors), who had assumed control of *Länder* governments on behalf of the Reich. In fact it would take several months more before the whole broadcasting system was unified under a drastically purged 'Reich Radio Company,' which would in theory be subordinate to Department III of the RMVP. The nine regional stations now became merely branches (renamed 'Reich Radio Stations') with general managers centrally controlled by the Ministry for Propaganda. Once this organisational structure had been established, the RMVP could then implement what it termed *Rundfunkeinheit,* complete unity in all radio matters. This entailed a 'pooling-together' of all broadcasting resources, very much on the model of fascist Italy. The first important step towards integrating the technical, commercial and listening side of radio came with the formation on 8 July 1933 of the RRG under the new Director of Broadcasting, Eugen Hadamovsky, a former motor mechanic, who had originally formed a 'voluntary' organisation called the 'National Socialist Radio Chamber' on 3 July. Six months later this would become the official Reich Chamber of Radio. Hadamovsky was also given the additional title of Reich Transmitter Leader (Reichssendeleiter) and in his capacity as overlord for broadcasting he quickly established a direct link to Goebbels and was largely responsible for approving all important broadcasts. Membership of the RRG now became compulsory for everyone connected with broadcasting, whether radio engineers or salesmen of wireless sets. Within a year, however, control of the manufacturing side of the industry would be removed from the Reich Chamber of Radio and transferred to the Reich Ministry of Economics. The Chamber would also be frustrated in its attempts to implement legislation (*Reichsrundfunkrecht*) that would secure complete control of broadcasting for the RMVP. Although a working compromise would eventually be reached between the RMVP and the radio industry in the form of a voluntary liaison committee, the original concept of an integrated 'radio unity' can be seen to have been hopelessly illusory.[16]

Despite these setbacks, the new masters of German broadcasting never lost their faith in the medium. It was a faith confirmed as early as 1934 by the results of the radio campaign to reincorporate the Saarland into Germany. During the Weimar Republic, radio had been used by successive governments as a means of contacting German-speaking minorities (*Volksdeutsche*) living abroad. Under the Treaty of Versailles, the future of the Saar was to be settled by a League of Nations plebiscite in 1935. In January 1934, however, Goebbels had pre-empted this by setting up a specific office to coordinate propaganda broadcasts into the Saar area with the innocuous title of the Westdeutsche Gemeinschaftsdients. He also distributed cheap radio sets and encouraged National Socialist listeners' associations to organise community listening to important Nazi events. The content of these broadcasts was based on highly charged emotional appeals to past German grievances. In January 1935, 91 per cent of those who voted in the plebiscite opted for the return of their province to a National Socialist Germany.

Although the Nazis were unlikely to lose in the plebiscite, there can be little doubt that Goebbels' broadcasts played a decisive part in achieving such a clear majority. It should be noted that in conjunction with these broadcasts the Nazis instigated a ruthless campaign of 'whispered propaganda' (*Flüsterpropaganda*).

This was a typical Nazi psychological device, intended to convince the voter that the Party knew how individuals voted and therefore, by implication, that they would be punished or rewarded accordingly. Needless to say, the success of the Saarland campaign convinced Nazi agitators that the planned use of radio propaganda could achieve almost any political goal.

The technical mobilisation of German radio as the 'voice of the nation' is a history of remarkable accomplishment. To increase the number of listeners, the Nazis persuaded manufacturers to produce one of the cheapest wireless sets in Europe, the VE 3031 or *Volksempfänger* ('people's receiver'). The 'people's radio' was heavily subsidised so that it would be affordable to all workers. In fact two versions of radio receivers were quickly produced: one for 75RM, and the *Volksempfänger* for 35RM payable in instalments. A poster issued by the RMVP advertising the *Volksempfänger* showed one of these uniform radio sets surrounded by thousands of people, with the caption: 'All Germany listens to the Führer with the People's Radio.' One-and-a-half million sets were produced during 1933, and in 1934 the figure for radio sets passed the 6 million mark, indicating an increase of more than 1 million in a single year. The long-term aim was to install a set in every home in Germany. Indeed, by the beginning of the war over 70 per cent of all households owned a wireless set—the highest percentage anywhere in the world. The 'people's receivers' were designed with a limited range, which meant that Germans who purchased them were unable to receive foreign broadcasts. Great emphasis was placed on the encouragement of community listening, changing listeners' thinking from what Hadamovsky referred to as 'the anarchic intellectualism of the individual to the organically developed spirituality of the community.'[17] Moreover, in order to ensure the widest possible listening audience, local Party branches were encouraged to organise community listening. On these occasions an army of National Socialist radio functionaries (*Funkwarte*) took charge of the event and staged what came to be referred to as 'National Moments' (*Stunden der Nation*). When a speech by a Nazi leader or an important announcement was to be made, this network of radio wardens established loudspeakers in public squares, factories, offices, schools, even restaurants. Sirens would howl and professional life throughout the nation would stop for the duration of the 'community reception' in an effort to persuade the individual citizen to identify with the nation. The radio warden was also responsible for popularising the radio and encouraging people to share their sets with friends and neighbours. In addition, these wardens, who were invariably Party members, forwarded criticism of and requests for specific programmes. The radio warden became notorious during the war, when he reported those Germans listening to foreign broadcasts.

The radio soon came to be regarded as the Nazi regime's principal propaganda medium for the dissemination of National Socialist ideas and in the creation of a single public opinion. In order to achieve these objectives, special emphasis was placed on political broadcasts. Listeners soon learned to associate signature tunes with various Party leaders who would make regular speeches over the radio. Hitler's speeches were preceded by his favourite march, the *Badenweiler*; Goebbels' annual eulogy on Hitler's birthday was accompanied by Wagner's 'Meistersinger' overture, and the Führer's speech on Heroes' Day by Beethoven's 'Eroica' symphony. It has been estimated that in 1933 alone, fifty speeches by Hitler were transmitted. By 1935, Hitler's speeches reached an audience of over 56,000,000. The radio was, not surprisingly, described as 'the towering herald of National Socialism,' the means of expression of a united State. In his desire to create 'one single public opinion' Goebbels maintained that it was imperative that this 'spiritual weapon of the totalitarian State' should enjoy the confidence of the people. With the radio, he declared, 'we have destroyed the spirit of rebellion.'

Although the radio continued to play an important part in the Nazis' propaganda arsenal, it was not without its shortcomings. The first disappointment was the discovery that Hitler, if confined in the studio without an audience, was uncomfortable, and ineffective as a speaker. Accordingly from October 1933, when he announced Germany's departure from the League of Nations, until the end of the war Hitler did not speak in a studio again. Instead his speeches would be transmitted from public meetings (often specially assembled for the purpose), where he gained direct contact with an audience and was thus provided with the essential stimulus for his speaking.

The second disappointment was that in the middle of the war the intense concentration on political broadcasting was proving to be counter-productive with the average listener. Radio wardens were reporting that listeners were so bored that they were switching off. Therefore in 1942 Goebbels decided that almost 70 per cent of transmissions should be devoted to light music in order to guarantee a large audience for the important political bulletins. Thus there were limits to radio's ability to create uniformity of opinion and action. But Goebbels learned to mix the content of transmissions accordingly, and this corresponded to his wider belief as Minister for Propaganda in mixing entertainment with propaganda. Despite these drawbacks, there can be little doubt that the most impressive achievement of Nazi broadcasting lay in the creation of such a mass listening public. Neither fascist Italy nor the Soviet Union used the radio to such a degree on its less literate population.

Press

The *Gleichschaltung* of the press proved infinitely more complicated for the Nazis than the radio, which had, for some time, experienced a degree of State involvement. The press, on the other hand, was associated with a whole plethora of political parties, pressure groups, religious bodies and private companies. In 1933 Germany could boast more daily newspapers than the combined total of Britain, France and Italy.

According to O. J. Hale,[18] the Third Reich adopted a three-pronged approach to the control of the press: first, all those involved in the press industry were rigorously controlled; second, the Party's publishing-house, the Eher Verlag, gradually acquired the ownership—directly on indirectly—of the vast majority of the German press; and finally, the RMVP controlled the content of the press by means of the State-controlled press agency (Deutsches Nachrichtenbüro) and daily press briefings and directives. The response of the publishers and journalists to the Nazi take-over is most revealing. The publishers' association (Verein deutscher Zeitungsverleger), effectively 'coordinated' themselves. They immediately sought a *modus vivendi* with the new regime by first of all replacing politically 'unacceptable' members and then appointing Max Amann, the head of Eher Verlag, as chairman of their organisation, under the revised title of the 'Association of German Newspaper Publishers' (Reichsverband deutscher Zeitungsverleger). On 15 November 1933, Amann was appointed president of the Reich Press Chamber to which the publishers were affiliated. The Reich Association of the German Press (Reichsverband der deutschen Presse) likewise felt compelled to appoint the Nazi press chief, Otto Dietrich, as their chairman. On 30 April 1933, the Association announced that membership would be compulsory and that all members of the Association would be screened for their 'racial and political reliability.'

In his speech to the press of 15 March 1933, Goebbels referred to the press as a piano on which the Government could plan to influence the public in whatever direction it desired. However, although the Nazis looked upon the press as an instrument of mass influence, they were aware that their success had been due more to the spoken than to the printed word. In order to reassure his audience, Goebbels presented himself to the press as a fellow-journalist who had experienced the frustrations of working in opposition to the Government of the day: 'If opposition papers claim today that their issues have been forbidden, they can talk to me as a fellow-sufferer. There is, I think, no representative of any newspaper banned fifteen times, as mine was!' According to Goebbels, the press must not 'merely inform; it must also instruct.' He argued that there was 'no absolute objectivity,' and the press should expect to receive not simply information from the Government but also instructions: 'We want to have a press which cooperates with the Government just as the Government wants to cooperate with the press. . . . We do not want a state of daily warfare.' He also urged the press to change its style of reporting in order to reflect the 'crusading' spirit of the time: 'The reader should get the impression that the writer is in reality a speaker standing behind him.' Newspapers in the Third Reich were to capture the atmosphere of the emotion-laden mass meetings. In this respect, the Party newspaper, the *Völkischer Beobachter,* would give the lead.

One of the most important tasks confronting the RMVP when it came to power was the elimination of alternative sources of information. However, the fact that the German press was not centralised like its British counterpart proved a major obstacle. The lack of a 'national' press, together with long-standing regional loyalties, persuaded Goebbels to undertake the *Gleichschaltung* of the German press in gradual stages. This would have the dual advantage of allowing Nazi journalists to be trained for their future role and more importantly, not suddenly breaking readers' habits.

The emergency decree issued immediately following the Reichstag fire on 28 February 1933 allowed the regime to suspend publication and include the spreading of rumours and false news as treasonable offences. The Reichstag fire served as the pretext for the suppression of the Communist and Social Democratic press, which was either destroyed or taken over by Nazi newspapers. Catholic and other middle-class democratic dailies soon followed, as Nazi-controlled advertising agencies switched their contracts to the Nazi press. However, some liberal papers, notably the *Frankfurter Zeitung* and the *Berliner Tageblatt,* were still permitted to publish. So too, for a while, was the flourishing *Generalanzeiger* press, which showed little interest in politics; but its confessional character posed a moral threat and its popularity a competitive one. The Nazis disapproved of both and eventually undertook measures to prohibit them.[19] At the beginning of 1933, the Nazis owned fifty-nine daily newspapers with a combined circulation of only 782,121, which represented only 2.5 per cent of the population. By the end of the year, they had acquired a further twenty-seven dailies and increased their circulation by 2.4 million copies per day. In 1934, they would acquire the large Jewish publishing firm of Ullstein. By 1939 the Eher Verlag, largely as a result of Amann's ordinances, controlled, either directly or indirectly, two-thirds of the German press. Many of these papers retained their old names so that their readers would be unaware of the change of ownership. The elimination of many non-Party newspapers was followed by the fusion of Germany's two principal news agencies, Wolff's Telegraphisches Büro and Hugenberg's Telegraphen-Union, into a new official agency, the Deutsches Nachrichtenbüro (DNB). It was soon providing over half the material which appeared in the German press, and newspapers were often confined to simply publishing verbatim a story put out by the news agency.

The other important instrument of political control over the newspaper industry was the Reich Press Chamber, and particularly the professional institutions under its tutelage. The Reich Association of the German Press became a corporate member of the Press Chamber, which not only acted as a kind of labour exchange for the profession by keeping registers of 'racially pure' editors and journalists, but also regarded the 'regulation of competition' within the industry as a perfectly legitimate function. The Press Chamber was determined to imbue all members with a strong National Socialist bias and to educate a new generation of journalists along strict Party lines so that they would, in Goebbels' words, 'take a stand for the new Reich and its Führer, not because they have to, but because they wish to do so.'

Having regulated both entry into the profession and the flow of news from its source, Goebbels then tackled the problem of editorial policy and content. From 1933 the press department of the RMVP took over the daily press conferences which had been a regular feature of journalistic life during the Weimar Republic. The content of the newspapers was rigidly controlled through the very detailed directives issued by the RMVP, which even covered the length of articles on particular topics and where they should be placed in the paper. Admission to these conferences was now severely controlled along Party and racial lines. As one senior journalist for the *Frankfurter Zeitung* observed:

> The press conference *with* the Reich Government established in 1917 was changed by the National Socialists on their seizure of power in Germany in 1933 into a 'press conference of the Reich Government.' So it was now an insti-tution of the Government. There it gave directives, laid down language varia-tions, and brought the 'press into line.' . . . Before 1933, these press conferences were run by journalists and the Government was their guest; after they were run by the Government.[20]

Such restrictions were soon to be reinforced by the so-called 'Editors' Law' (*Schriftleitergesetz*) of 4 October 1933. From now on editors of newspapers and political periodicals would be made responsible for any infringement of Government directives. In effect, the law reversed the roles of the publisher and the editor, reducing the publisher to the position of a business manager.[21] The obligatory character of all directives and decrees was stressed repeatedly, ruling out editorial independence. Clause 14 of the regulations obliged editors to keep out of the newspapers everything 'which is calculated to weaken the strength of the Reich abroad or at home, the resolution of the community, German defence, culture or the economy, or to injure the religious sensibili-ties of others, as well as everything offensive to the honour or dignity of a German.' By turning the individual editor into the regime's censor, this piece of legislation went a considerable way towards achieving uniformity of the press by transforming journalism into a public corporation. Editors and journalists could now only work if they were officially accredited, and Goebbels, as Minister for Propaganda was appointed president of the Press Association with the power to veto any journalist entering the profession. A system of professional courts was set up to enforce the law with the power to reprimand, fine or expel offenders.[22]

Once some degree of uniformity had been achieved, Goebbels believed it important that the content of the press should not become lifeless. This proved difficult given the fact that newspapers were restricted to publishing Government directives. Therefore the themes commonly associated with Nazi propaganda—charismatic leadership, appeals to national unity, anti-Semitism, etc.—were supplemented by special appeals and special campaigns aimed at securing repeated gestures of conformity from the people. Such appeals and campaigns were ideally suited to the medium of the press. They would take the form of a positive discussion of the deeds of the Führer, or of some aspect of the Volk community life, such as the 'Strength through Joy' programme. A particular favourite of Goebbels was the campaign to obtain more public money for the 'Winter Help' schemes. This invariably manifested itself in the slogan 'A Sacrifice for the Community,' by which housewives and workers were urged to restrict their eating consumption to the *Eintopfgericht* ('one-pot meal') in order to conserve food, especially meat ('the meal of sacrifice for the Reich'). Alternatively, there was the annual 'National Day of Solidarity,' which developed out of 'Winter Help' and which was a sort of plebiscite for the regime. Here the press was urged to stress not only the amount of money that was collected for the community, but also the uniqueness of the event and the voluntary character of the donations.

The press was also instrumental in the Nazis' virulent anti-Semitic campaigns. Sections of the press, particularly *Der Stürmer* and the *Völkischer Beobachter,* continued to depict the Jew as barbaric and 'subhuman' and denounced alleged Jewish 'criminality' and the 'conspiracy' of foreign Jews against Germany. Campaigns waged in these papers might be used to prepare the public for some forthcoming anti-Jewish legislation. The press was also directed to answer foreign criticism of their racial policy by means of counter-attacks which were also intended to heighten people's awareness of their Aryan origins and characteristics. Anti-Semitic propaganda became so omnipresent that in terms of everyday journalism few news items or articles could be published without such a slant.

Quantitatively as well as qualitatively, the national press declined during the Third Reich. When the Nazis came to power there were approximately 4,700 daily newspapers, reflecting a variety of political persuasions. The NSDAP controlled less than 3 per cent of all German dailies and periodicals; in 1944, 82 per cent of the remaining 977 newspapers were firmly under the

Party's control. Between 1933 and 1938 a total of 10,000 periodicals and learned journals had been reduced to 5,000, a decline symbolising the basic anti-intellectualism of National Socialism in general.

The overriding feature of the press until the outbreak of war at least was the deliberate sacrifice of speedy reportage of news in favour of staggeringly comprehensive, but unwieldy, press directives. In many respects Nazi propagandists favoured broadcasting at the expense of the press. Hitler, who was a voracious newspaper reader, is said to have been hostile to the press and to journalists. Not only did he believe that pictures and spoken words had greater impact than printed words, but he also resented the press for its vehement criticism of him during the years when the Nazis were in opposition. Although he rarely received journalists, he would occasionally praise the press for their performance. The most celebrated occasion was on 10 November 1938, when he addressed 400 representatives of the German press in Munich. Complimenting them for their work preceding the Munich Conference, Hitler went on to describe the role of press propaganda both abroad and at home as 'decisive' in the acquisition of the Sudetenland by Germany: 'Gentlemen, this time we have actually obtained 10 million men with over 100,000 square kilometres of territory through propaganda in the service of an idea. This is something momentous.'[23] Goebbels, on the other hand, who recognised good journalism, was never entirely happy about the drab uniformity of the German press which was the outcome of his policy. He nevertheless defended the press laws by arguing that the free expression of opinion could seriously threaten the National Socialist State, and continued to reject suggestions that problems should be frankly discussed in the press. His directives became so minutely detailed that the papers were virtually written for the editors by the Ministry for Propaganda. The Government strait-jacket so destroyed journalistic initiative that Goebbels was prompted to remark in his diary: 'No decent journalist with any feeling of honour in his bones can stand the way he is handled by the press department of the Reich Government . . . Any man who still has a residue of honour will be very careful not to become a journalist.'

Film

Hitler and Goebbels shared an interest in film. Shortly after his appointment as Minister for Popular Enlightenment and Propaganda, Goebbels declared that the German cinema had been given the mission of conquering the world as the vanguard of the Nazi troops. Film propaganda was Goebbels' special interest, for he believed in the power of the cinema to influence people's thoughts and beliefs, if not their actions.

As early as the 1920s the National Socialists had infiltrated their members into many spheres of public life.[24] The entire organisation of the Party, the division into administrative sectors and the structure of leadership were built up as a state within a state. The Nazis were therefore well placed to take control of a film industry which had to a large extent prepared itself to be controlled. The *Gleichschaltung* of the German cinema was affected behind the scenes by a process of which the ordinary citizen was largely unaware. To achieve this end, a plethora of complex laws and decrees and an intricate state machinery were instigated to prevent non-conformity. Pursuing a policy that was to become traditional in the Third Reich, the Party organisation was kept separate from State administration at both national and regional levels, while at the same time remaining closely linked with it.

During 1932 the industry was still recoiling from the continuing effects of the recession in world trade and the advent of talking films, which involved considerable expenditure at a time when total receipts were falling, companies were going bankrupt and cinemas were changing hands at an alarming rate.[25] The German film industry responded with the so-called 'SPIO-Plan' of 1932; SPIO (Spitzenorganisation der deutschen Filmindustrie e.V.) was the industry's main professional representative body, and its principal concern was to strike a satisfactory relationship between the production, distribution and exhibition sectors, while at the same time retaining the traditional structure of the industry. Significantly, SPIO was dominated by the large combines (particularly Ufa), and it was no surprise that they should produce a plan that discriminated so blatantly against the German Cinema Owners' Association (Reichsverband Deutscher Lichtspieltheater e.V.), whom they accused of flooding the market with too many cinemas, price-cutting and retaining a disproportionate share of total receipts. The Cinema Owners' Association retorted by complaining, quite justifiably, that they were expected to exhibit films they were given regardless of their suitability in terms of box-office appeal.

In the months following Hitler's appointment as Chancellor in January 1933 the divisions within the Party which had flared up in 1932 became an issue again. Certain organisations—such as the Nazi 'trade union,' the Nationalsozialistische Betriebszellen Organisation (NSBO), and the Fighting League for German Culture (Kampfbund für deutsche Kultur—KfdK)—put forward radical solutions to the film industry's problems, demanding centralisation and the banning of all films which offended *the völkische Weltanschauung*. Goebbels, on the other hand, was more realistic and appreciated that the *Filmwelt* did not welcome these forces of Nazi extremism. He was unwilling to undertake an immediate nationalisation of the industry, not only on ideological grounds but for the pragmatic reasons that Alfred Hugenberg, who owned the largest film company, Ufa, was a member of the new cabinet as Minister of Economics and that the Party in general depended on big business for its finances.

However, on 9 February 1933, at the Cinema Owners' annual conference, the Nazi elements demanded that their leader, Engl, should be elected to the Association's board. Their argument that the small owners faced bankruptcy in the face of unfair competition from the large combines seemed to be confirmed when the SPIO-Plan was published nine days later. On 18 March the entire board of the Cinema Owners' Association resigned, thus giving Engl and the NSDAP complete control. They responded by demanding that all cinema owners express unconditional loyalty to Engl's leadership within two weeks.[26]

Cinema owners were not the only sector of the industry to be effectively 'coordinated' in this manner; throughout March and April the NSBO had been active in all spheres of film production—from cameramen to film actors and composers. When the Nazis banned all trade unions in early May, the industry's 'official' trade union DACHO (Dach-Organisation der Filmschaffenden Deutschlands e.V.) was dissolved and absorbed into the NSBO, which was itself transferred automatically to the German Labour Front (Deutsche Arbeitsfront), the only permissible trade union; DACHO therefore had little chance of preventing is own dissolution, though there is no evidence of any united stand being organised.

The film industry presented a number of structural, economic and artistic problems for the builders of the new German society. Significant of the high estimation of the cinema in the Third Reich is the fact that the Reich Film Chamber (Reichsfilmkammer) was founded by Goebbels some months before the Reich Chamber of Culture, of which it became a part. The creation of the Reichsfilmkammer (RFK) on 14 July 1933 is an excellent example of the process of coordination in that it allowed the RMVP to exert its control over both film-makers and the film industry as a whole. The structure of the RFK was scarcely changed after it had been incorporated into the Reich Chamber of Culture (RKK). Its head and all-responsible president was subordinate only to the president of the RKK, that is, the Minister for Propaganda. The first president of the RFK was Dr Fritz Scheuermann, a financial expert who had been involved in secret plans to implement the recommendations of the SPIO-Plan, which had been merged with the RFK in July. Scheuermann was assisted by a vice-president, Arnold Räther, who was also head of the Film Office of the NSDAP Propaganda Office. There was an Advisory Council (*Präsidialrat*) consisting of financial experts from the RMVP and the banks; and specialist advisory councils taken from the individual *Fachgruppen*, as the former SPIO elements were now called. The various sections of the industry were grouped together into ten departments. These ten departments controlled all film activities in Germany. The centralisation, however, did not lead to what the Minister of Propaganda claimed—the harmonisation of all branches of the industry—but it did harm the substance of the German film by limiting personal and economic initiative and artistic freedom.

It must also be remembered that the *Filmwelt* greeted the Nazis with some misgivings. The industry was not entirely convinced that it could expect much constructive assistance from the new regime. To offset these fears and also to gain control over film finance, a Filmkreditbank (FKB) was established. It was announced on 1 June 1933 as a provider of credit for the crisis-ridden film economy, which had been badly hit by the costs of installing equipment for the new 'talking movies' and the effects of the slump on film audiences.

The idea of the Filmkreditbank had originally been proposed in the SPIO-Plan with the aim of encouraging independent production by lending money to approved film-makers at highly competitive rates. In practice the FKB was to create the beginnings of the National Socialists' disastrous film policy and to result in the dependence of private film producers on the Nazi State. However, at the time of its inauguration the FKB was greeted with great enthusiasm from all sides of the film industry. By 1936, the FKB was financing over 73 per cent of all German feature films. The result was that the smaller companies' share of the market continued to decline as the process of concentration was relentlessly increased. This proved a further step towards creating dependence and establishing a State monopoly in order to destroy independent initiative.

The Filmkreditbank functioned to all intents and purposes as a normal commercial undertaking, except that it was not expected to make large profits. It took the form of a private limited-liability company formed out of the Reichskreditgesellschaft, SPIO (acting as a cover for the Reichsfilmkammer), and a number of the main banks. However, within a year the banks transferred their shares to the RFK and on Goebbels' personal initiative the president of the latter became the Filmkreditbank's chairman. The procedure for securing finance from the bank was that a producer had to show that he could raise 30 per cent of the production costs as well as convincing the FKB that the film stood a good chance of making a profit. The film then became the property of the bank until the loan was repaid. Thus private finance was excluded from all freedom of credit and opportunities for profit. Within a short time this financial body would also become an important means of securing both economic and political conformity. The FKB acting on behalf of the Government, could refuse all credit at the pre-production stage until a film reflected the wishes of the regime. Significantly, there is no evidence to suggest that the film industry was unwilling to accept this form of self-censorship.

Apart from regulating the financing of films, one of the main purposes of establishing the Reichsfilmkammer was the removal of Jews and other *entartete Künstler* (degenerate artists) from German cultural life, since only racially 'pure' Germans could become members. Whoever wished to participate in any aspect of film production was forced to become a member of the RFK. By 1936, the Party had begun publishing a new illustrated film magazine, *Der deutsche Film,* with the intention of disseminating party policy relating to the film industry through consciously anti-Semitic propaganda. Statistics were published in film magazines and books, which purported to expose an overwhelmingly Jewish influence in film production. Although the industry had been heavily dependent on Jewish artists and executives, these figures were a gross exaggeration. However, because Nazi propaganda identified Jewish influence with the downfall of German culture, it was only to be expected that the Party would use the struggle in the film industry to stir up racial hatred. Not surprisingly, these policies resulted in the emigration of all those who either could not or would not submit to such conditions. The loss of talent was severe, but the Nazis were able to retain a reservoir of talented actors, technicians and artistic staff.

On 28 March 1933, Goebbels introduced himself to the *Filmwelt* at a SPIO-DACHO function at the Kaiserhof. Goebbels presented himself as an inveterate film addict (which he was), and showed considerable ingenuity in mitigating many of the industry's fears caused by the already extensive exodus. Films, he said, were to have an important place in the culture of the new Germany. But he warned that film-makers must, in future, learn to regard their profession as a service, and not merely as a source of profit. Goebbels went on to mention four films that had made a lasting impression on him. They were *Battleship Potemkin, Anna Karenina, Die Nibelungen,* and *Der Rebell.* According to Goebbels, the German cinema was in a state of spiritual crisis which 'will continue until we are courageous enough radically to reform German films.' National Socialist film-makers, he argued, 'should capture the spirit of the time.' What was not required in these films was 'parade-ground marching and the blowing of trumpets.' In calling for the industry's cooperation in this new venture Goebbels concluded by declaring that with this new conviction 'a new moral ethos will arise,' allowing it 'to be said of German films, as in other fields, "Germany leads the world!"'

To consolidate his position, Goebbels still desired more power than he had hitherto secured through the Reichskulturkammer legislation. He also needed some form of legal confirmation to be able to supervise films in the early stages of production. Goebbels settled both these issues by creating a revised version of the Reich Cinema Law (*Reichslichtspielgesetz*), which became law on 16 February 1934. This legislation attempted to create a new 'positive' censorship by which the State encouraged 'good' National Socialist films instead of merely discouraging 'bad' ones.

The new Cinema Law anticipated three different channels through which this positive censorship could be achieved: a compulsory script censorship, an increase in the number of criteria according to which the Censorship Office (*Filmprüfstelle*) might ban a film, and an enlarged system of distinction marks (*Prädikate*) awarded by the regime to worthy films.

The most significant innovation of the Cinema Law was the institution of a pre-censor (*Vorzensor*), a role undertaken by an RMVP official called the Reich Film Director (*Reichsfilmdramaturg*). If a producer wished to make a film, he had first to submit a 'treatment' to the *Dramaturg*, who was appointed directly by Goebbels. If this was passed, the full scenario could be written, and this would have to be approved before shooting could begin. In most cases the *Dramaturg* could supervise every stage of production. The orders issued and the changes suggested by him were binding. As the representative of the RMVP, he could even interfere with the censorship exercised by the Censorship Office in Berlin.

The new film legislation greatly extended the powers of censorship, which it prescribed in some detail. It replaced the original law of 12 May 1920, which had regulated films during the Weimar Republic. Although the Weimar censorship was initially a democratic one—'films may not be withheld on account of political, social, religious, ethical, or ideological tendencies'—the intervention of the censor was permitted when 'a film endangers public order or safety . . . or endangers the German image or the country's relationship with foreign states.' The examination of films was delegated to two censorship offices (*Prüfstellen*), in Berlin and in Munich. Each office had two chairmen, who examined films with the aid of four assessors drawn from the teaching and legal professions and the film industry itself. However, the 1934 law joined the two *Prüfstellen* together and incorporated them as a subsidiary office of the RMVP. The procedure by which the Censorship Office reached its decision was also revised. Under the 1920 law, decisions were arrived at by means of a majority vote and if a film was banned its producer could appeal to the Supreme Censorship Office (*Oberprüfstelle*). After 1934 the power to decide whether or not a film should be exhibited rested entirely with the chairman.

According to Paragraph 4 of the 1934 Cinema Law, all kinds of films were to be submitted to the censor. Public and private screenings were made equal in law. Even film advertising in the cinemas was censored. For each print of a film a censorship card had to be issued which contained the official report on the film together with an embossed stamp of the German Eagle. In all matters concerning censorship, the Minister for Propaganda had the right of intervention. He could either appeal to the *Oberprüfstelle* or, by circumventing the *Prüfstelle,* he could forbid the release of various films directly. In the Second Amendment to the Cinema Law, of 28 June 1935, Goebbels was given extra powers to ban any film without reference to the *Prüfstelle* if he felt it was in the public's interest. Not only was the entire censorship apparatus centralised in Berlin, but the previous rights of local governments to request re-examination of films was now the exclusive prerogative of the RMVP.

In addition to direct censorship, the film industry depended on a system of distinction marks (*Prädikate*), which was really a form of negative taxation. During the Weimar Republic these distinction marks were considered an honour and an opportunity to gain tax reductions. Under the Nazis, however, a film had to obtain a *Prädikate* not only to benefit from tax deductions but to be allowed to be exhibited at all. Films without these distinction marks needed special permission to be shown. A further incentive was that producers with a *Prädikate* now received an extra share of the film's profits. By 1939, there were eleven distinctions, ranging from 'politically and artistically especially valuable' to 'culturally valuable.' 'Film of the Nation' (*Film der Nation*) and 'valuable for youth' (*Jugendwert*) differed from the others in that they carried no tax relief. However, these were special awards which greatly enhanced a film's status. Furthermore, they were decisive for selection in schools and Nazi youth organisations. After 1938 no cinema owner was allowed to refuse to exhibit a film with a political distinction mark if a distributor offered one.

The *Prädikate* system not only produced certain financial advantages but also helped to establish the appropriate expectations and responses on the part of cinema audiences. These distinction marks were naturally a key to the political and propaganda content in the description of films. 'Politically valuable' clearly reflected a political message that was completely acceptable to the Party, whereas 'artistically valuable' was understood in the sense of cultural propaganda and was given only to the prestige films and those reserved for export.

Secure in the knowledge that film censorship had been reorganised according to the principles of the NSDAP, Goebbels now embarked on his next project, the nationalisation of the film industry. In fact this would be carried out in two stages, largely through a process of which the ordinary citizen was totally unaware. When the Nazis came to power there were four major film companies operating in Germany. To have nationalized them immediately would have damaged their contacts with foreign distributors, which in turn would have reduced the not-inconsiderable revenue and foreign currency earned from Germany's film exports. It seemed advisable, therefore, to proceed warily with the nationalisation of the cinema industry and not alarm the outside world unnecessarily. However, as German film exports continued to decline under the Nazis and production costs continued to increase, the RMVP decided secretly to buy out the major shares in the film companies and to refer to them as *staatsmittelbar* (indirectly State-controlled), rather than State-owned. Germany's military victories 1939/40 had created a German-dominated film monopoly in Europe which the RMVP believed it could only exploit if the film industry produced 100 films per year. Towards the end of 1941 it became increasingly clear that this target was not being reached. The only solution, it was decided, lay in a complete take-over by the State. To this end the nationalisation of the film industry was completed in 1942. On 10 January 1942 a giant holding company, Ufa-Film GmbH (call Ufi to distinguish it from its precedessors) assumed control of the entire German film industry and its foreign subsidiaries. Every aspect of film-making was now the immediate responsibility of Ufi. The Reichsfilmkammer had become merely a bureaucratic adminstrative machine and Ufi, thanks to its vertical organisation was a mere receiver of orders from the RMVP. This represented an enormous concentration of a mass medium in the hands of the National Socialist State and, more specifically, of the Minister for Popular Enlightenment and Propaganda. With his task completed Goebbels could sit back and reflect on the wisdom of his actions:

> Film production is flourishing almost unbelievably, despite the war. What a good idea of mine it was to take possession of the films on behalf of the Reich several years ago! It would be terrible if the high profits now being earned by the motion-picture industry were to flow into private hands.[27]

An analysis of the different types of film produced during the Third Reich reveals a good deal about Goebbels' *Filmpolitik*. Of the 1,097 feature films produced between 1933 and 1945, only about one-sixth were overtly propagandist with a direct political content. The majority of these films were 'State-commissioned films' (*Staatsauftragsfilme*) including politically the most important films, which were given disproportionate funding and publicity.

Such films were invariably classified at the time as *Tendenzfilme*. This was a term employed during the Third Reich to describe a certain type of film that exhibited 'strong National Socialist tendencies.' In other words, without necessarily mentioning National Socialism, these films advocated various principles and themes identifiable with Nazism which the Ministry for Propaganda wished to disseminate at intermittent periods. Of the entire production of feature films, virtually half were either love stories or comedies, and a quarter dramatic films like crime thrillers or musicals. Yet all went through the pre-censorship process and all were associated with the National Socialist ideology in that they were produced and performed in accordance with the propagandist aims of the period. In a highly politicised society like the Third Reich, even the apolitical becomes significant in that so-called 'entertainment films' tend to promote the official world-view of things and to reinforce the existing social and economic order. Propaganda is as important in reinforcing existing beliefs as it is in changing them, and even the most escapist entertainment can, as Goebbels noted, be of value to the national struggle, 'providing it with the edification, diversion and relaxation needed to see it through the drama of everyday life.'[28] The comparatively small number of overt political films was supplemented by documentary films and newsreels, which became increasingly important during the war.

Thus the themes that recur in the Nazi cinema are central to their *Weltanschauung,* and these ideas were repeated at carefully chosen intervals. Goebbels therefore chose to keep prestigious film propaganda at its maximum effectiveness by spacing out the films concerned—except, that is, for the newsreels (*Deutsche Wochenschau*), which depended on their ability to capture the immediacy of events. The full-length documentaries were all the more effective for their comparative rarity. Perhaps the two best-known documentaries of the Nazi period are Leni Riefenstahl's *Triumph des Willens* (*Triumph of the Will,* 1935) about the 1934 Party rally in Nuremberg, and *Olympiade* (*Olympia,* 1938), a four-hour record of the 1938 Olympic Games held in Berlin, which proved an ideal vehicle for Nazi propaganda to foreign countries.

Surprisingly enough, there was very little sign of an overall pattern or strategy of film propaganda. It is true that a trilogy of films eulogised the *Kampfzeit* (time of struggle), and glorified the Nazi Movement and its martyrs in 1933 (*SA-Mann Brand, Hitlerjunge Quex, Hans Westmar*). Similarly, in 1940, three films were produced which were intended to prepare the German people for the final solution of the 'Jewish problem' (*Die Rothschilds, Jud Süss, Der ewige Jude*). Equally, 1941 marked the highest concentration of *Staatsauftragsfilme* commissioned by the RMVP. But Goebbels' main concern was to keep the important themes of Nazi ideology constantly before the public by releasing an optimum number of State-commissioned films. In accordance with Hitler's dictum of orientating the masses towards specific topics, a number of these propaganda films attempted, together with carefully coordinated campaigns in the press and radio, to dramatise aspects of the National Socialist programme that were deemed important. Such films would include *Das alte Recht* (*The Old Right,* 1934), the justification of the State Hereditary Farm Law; *Ich für Dich—Du für mich* (*Me for You—You for Me,* 1934), emphasising the importance of *Blut und Boden* (blood and soil) and defining the source of strength of the 'master race' in terms of peasant virtues and the sacredness of German soil; *Ewige Wald* (*Eternal Forest*, 1936), an attempt to create national solidarity and the need for 'living space' (*Lebensraum*); *Der Herrscher* (*The Ruler*, 1937), providing analogies with Hitler's teachings and calling for strong leadership; *Sensationsprozess Casilla* (*The Sensational Trial of Casilla*, 1939), anti-American propaganda designed to ridicule the American way of life; *Heimkehr* (*Homecoming*, 1941), about the sad fate of German nationals living abroad; *Ich klage an* (*I Accuse*, 1941), an exposition of the Nazis' euthanasia campaign.

This strategy illustrates Goebbels' desire to mix entertainment with propaganda. For, unlike Hitler, Goebbels believed that propaganda was most effective when it was insidious, when its message was concealed within the framework of popular entertainment. Goebbels therefore encouraged the production of feature films which reflected the ambience of National Socialism rather than those that loudly proclaimed its ideology. The result of Goebbels' *Filmpolitik* was a monopolistic system of control and organisation which maintained profits and managed to quadruple the annual number of cinema-goers between 1933 and 1942. Film was only one factor in reaching an uncritical audience; but it had an important function, in the sense that when people read newspapers or listened to the radio they were more conscious of the propaganda content. The cinema, on the other hand, was associated with relaxation and entertainment and was therefore all the more dangerous, particularly as the *Gleichschaltung* of the German cinema had been carried out behind the scenes. It is clear that when the Nazis assumed power they thought highly of film as a propaganda weapon. The need for conformity in a police state meant that the film industry had to be reorganised according to the ideals of the NSDAP. Like all forms of mass communication, film had to correspond to the political *Weltanschauung* and the propaganda principles of the Party. The communications media—the press, radio and film—had a circular interrelationship in that they supplied each other with themes in the manner prescribed by the State, and supported each other in their effect by a simultaneous and graduated release of information, which was circulated, controlled, and modulated by the State. This control remained of paramount importance to Goebbels and Hitler, both of whom continued to recognise its importance as a source of their 'popularist' appeal. In his diary entry for 20 June 1941, Goebbels recorded: 'The Führer praises the superiority of our system compared with liberal-democratic ones. We educate our people according to a common world-view (*Weltanschauung*), with the aid of films, radio and the press, which the Führer sees as the most important tools of popular leadership. The State must never let them out of her hands.'[29]

Notes

1. J. Goebbels, *Von Kaiserhof zur Reichkskanzlei* (Munich, 1935), entry of 23 January 1932.

2. Hitler made these points in his final address to the Nuremberg Party Congress of September 1935. The full speech is reproduced in N. H. Baynes (ed.), *The Speeches of Adolf Hitler,* 2 vols. (Oxford, 1942), vol. 1, pp. 438–69.

3. Speech to representatives of the press, 15 March 1933; taken from Wolffe Telegraphisches Buro (WTB) press agency report of 16 March 1933, deposited Bundesarchiv, Koblenz.

4. L. P. Lochner (ed.), *The Goebbels Diaries* (London, 1948), entry of 26 April 1942, p. 137.

5. Quoted in M. Balfour, *Propaganda in War* (London, 1979), p. 15.

6. Quoted in O. Kalbus, *Von Werden deutscher Filmkund,* Teil 2: *Der Trefilm* (Altona and Bahrenfeld, 1935), p. 101.

7. Baynes (ed.), *The Speeches of Adolf Hitler,* vol. 1, pp. 584–92.

8. *Film-Kurier,* 13 May 1936.

9. Völkischer Beobachter, 29 November 1936. Also quoted in D. S. Hull, *Film in the Third Reich* (Berkeley and Los Angeles, 1969), p. 96. Hull uses the *New York Times* as his source.

10. Quoted in Lochner (ed.), *Goebbels Diaries,* p. xxvii. Lochner, who witnessed the scene, added that 'the few foreign correspondents who had taken the trouble to view this "symbolic act" were stunned. What had happened to the "Land of Thinkers and Poets"? they wondered.'

11. Cf. Bramsted, *Goebbels and National Socialist Propaganda,* p. 68.

12. E. Frolich, 'Die Kulturpolitische Presskonferenz des Reichspropaganda Ministeriums,' *Vierteljakrskeft für Zeitgeschictr,* 22 April 1974, pp. 358–9; quoted in J. Noakes and G. Pridham (eds.), *Nazism 1919–1945,* Vol. 2 *State, Economy and Society* (Exeter, 194), p. 409.

13. For detailed accounts of broadcasting in the Third Reich, see A. Diller, *Rundfunkpolitik im Dritten Reick* (Gutersloh, 1964); H. Pohle, *Der Rundfunk als Instrument der Politik* (Hamburg, 1955); J. Hale, *Radio Power, Propaganda and International Broadcasting* (London, 1975) especially ch. 1, "The Nazi Model," pp. 1–16.

14. H. Heiber (ed.), *Goebbels Reden,* 2 vols. (Düsseldorf, 1971), vol. 1, pp. 82–107 for the full speech.

15. Quoted in Diller, *Rundfunkpolitik,* p. 89.

16. The Radio Chamber, which seems to have lost its way, was in fact dissolved in October 1939, when the outbreak of war provided a convenient excuse to disband it. Its duties were taken over by the Reichs-Rundfunk-Gesellschaft.

17. Quoted in Pohle, *Der Rundfunk,* p. 327, and Balfour, *Propaganda in War,* p. 20.

18. O. J. Hale, *The Captive Press in the Third Reich* (Princeton, NJ, 1964).

19. On 24 April 1935 the 'Anordnung zur Beseitigung der Skandalpresse' prohibited newspapers 'who maintain their character and sale by reporting events in an unsuitable way, so as to create sensation and to reflect on the press in general.'

20. The journalist was Fritz Sanger; quoted in J. Wulf (ed.), *Presse and Funk im Dritten Reich* (Gutersloh, 1964), p. 79.

21. In 1936 attempts were made to restore to the publisher some of the powers taken away from them by the *Schriftleitergesetz,* but it was quickly removed from the cabinet agenda when the extent of the opposition became clear.

22. It has been estimated that between mid-1934 and mid-1943 there were some 1,290 reported cases of newspapers and periodicals being reprimanded for carrying 'unwanted' topics. See K. Koszyk and M. Lindermann, *Geschichte der deulschen Press, 1914–1945* (Berlin, 1966–72).

23. For the full text of Hitler's speech, which was off the record, see 'Rede Hitlers vor der deutschen Presse,' *Vierteljakrsshefte für Zeitgeschickte,* vol. 6, no. 2, April 1958, pp. 175–91. For a first-hand account of Hitler's views on the press, see O. Dietrich, *12Jahre mit Hitler* (Munich, 1955); English edition *The Hitler I Knew* (London, 1971).

24. The process is described in D. Orlow, *The History of the Nazi Party 1919–33* (London, 1971).

25. The number of cinemas had fallen from just over 5,000 in 1929 to 2,196 in 1932.

26. For further details of the organization of the Nazi cinema, see D. Welch, *Propaganda and the German Cinema, 1933–1945* (Oxford, 1983), pp. 6–38.

27. Lochner (ed.), *The Goebbels Diaries,* entry for 22 January 1942, p. 5.

28. Goebbels' speech to the Reichsfilmkammer, 15 February 1941; quoted in Welch, *Propaganda and the German Cinema,* p. 45. For detailed analysis of Nazi films see ibid.: G. Albrecht, *Film im Dritten Reich* (Stuttgart, 1982); F. Courtagde and P. Cadera, *Histoire du cinema nazi* (Paris, 1972); E. Leiser, *Nazi Cinema* (London, 1974); R. Taylor, *Film Propaganda: Soviet Russia and Nazi Germany* (London, 1979); B. Drewniak, *Der deutsche Film 1938–1945, Ein Germany* (Düsseldorf, 1987); J. Wulf (ed.), *Theater und Film im Dritten Reich Eime Dokumentation* (Gutersloh, 1964).

29. F. Taylor, (ed.), *The Goebbels Diaries, 1939–1941* (London, 1982), p. 419.

7

The Rhetoric of Hitler's "Battle"

Kenneth Burke

The appearance of *Mein Kampf* in unexpurgated translation has called forth far too many vandalistic comments. There are other ways of burning books than on the pyre—and the favorite method of the hasty reviewer is to deprive himself and his readers by inattention. I maintain that it is thoroughly vandalistic for the reviewer to content himself with the mere inflicting of a few symbolic wounds upon this book and its author, of an intensity varying with the resources of the reviewer and the time at his disposal. Hitler's "Battle" is exasperating, even nauseating; yet the fact remains: If the reviewer but knocks off a few adverse attitudinizings and calls it a day, with a guaranty in advance that his article will have a favorable reception among the decent members of our population, he is contributing more to our gratification than to our enlightenment.

Here is the testament of a man who swung a great people into his wake. Let us watch it carefully; and let us watch it, not merely to discover some grounds for prophesying what political move is to follow Munich, and what move to follow that move, etc.; let us try also to discover what kind of "medicine" this medicine-man has concocted, that we may know, with greater accuracy, exactly what to guard against, if we are to forestall the concocting of similar medicine in America.

SOURCE: From *The Philosophy of Literary Form* by Kenneth Burke, 3rd ed., 1973 (original 1941), University of California Press, Berkeley, CA. Reprinted with permission.

Already, in many quarters of our country, we are "beyond" the stage where we are being saved from Nazism by our *virtues*. And fascist integration is being staved off, rather, by the *conflicts among our vices*. Our vices cannot get together in a grand united front of prejudices; and the result of this frustration, if or until they succeed in surmounting it, speaks, as the Bible might say, "in the name of" democracy. Hitler found a panacea, a "cure for what ails you," a "snakeoil," that made such sinister unifying possible within his own nation. And he was helpful enough to put his cards face up on the table, that we might examine his hands. Let us, then, for God's sake, examine them. This book is the well of Nazi magic; crude magic, but effective. A people trained in pragmatism should want to inspect this magic.

1

Every movement that would recruit its followers from among many discordant and divergent bands, must have some spot towards which all roads lead. Each man may get there in his own way, but it must be the one unifying center of reference for all. Hitler considered this matter carefully, and decided that this center must be not merely a centralizing hub of *ideas*, but a mecca geographically located, towards which all eyes could turn at the appointed hours of prayer (or, in this case, the appointed hours of prayer-in-reverse, the hours of vituperation). So he selected Munich, as the *materialization* of his unifying panacea. As he puts it:

> The geo-political importance of a center of a movement cannot be overrated. Only the presence of such a center and of a place, bathed in the magic of a Mecca or a Rome, can at length give a movement that force which is rooted in the inner unity and in the recognition of a hand that represents this unity.

If a movement must have its Rome, it must also have its devil. For as Russell pointed out years ago, an important ingredient of unity in the Middle Ages (an ingredient that long did its unifying work despite the many factors driving towards disunity) was the symbol of a *common enemy*, the Prince of Evil himself. Men who can unite on nothing else can unite on the basis of a foe shared by all. Hitler himself states the case very succinctly:

> As a whole, and at all times, the efficiency of the truly national leader consists primarily in preventing the division of the attention of a people, and always in concentrating it on a single enemy. The more uniformly the fighting will of a people is put into action, the greater will be the magnetic force of the movement and the more powerful the impetus of the blow. It is part of the genius of a great

leader to make adversaries of different fields appear as always belonging to one category only, because to weak and unstable characters the knowledge that there are various enemies will lead only too easily to incipient doubts as to their own cause.

As soon as the wavering masses find themselves confronted with too many enemies, objectivity at once steps in, and the question is raised whether actually all the others are wrong and their own nation or their own movement alone is right.

Also with this comes the first paralysis of their own strength. Therefore, a number of essentially different enemies must always be regarded as one in such a way that in the opinion of the mass of one's own adherents the war is being waged against one enemy alone. This strengthens the belief in one's own cause and increases one's bitterness against the attacker.

As everyone knows, this policy was exemplified in his selection of an "international" devil, the "international Jew" (the Prince was international, universal, "catholic"). This *materialization* of a religious pattern is, I think, one terrifically effective weapon of propaganda in a period where religion has been progressively weakened by many centuries of capitalist materialism. You need but go back to the sermonizing of centuries to be reminded that religion had a powerful enemy long before organized atheism came upon the scene. Religion is based upon the "prosperity of poverty," upon the use of ways for converting our sufferings and handicaps into a good—but capitalism is based upon the prosperity of acquisitions, the only scheme of value, in fact, by which its proliferating store of gadgets could be sold, assuming for the moment that capitalism had not got so drastically in its own way that it can't sell its gadgets even after it has trained people to feel that human dignity, the "higher standard of living," could be attained only by their vast private accumulation.

So, we have, as unifying step No. 1, the international devil materialized, in the visible, point-to-able form of people with a certain kind of "blood," a burlesque of contemporary neo-positivism's ideal of meaning, which insists upon a *material* reference.

Once Hitler has thus essentialized his enemy, all "proof" henceforth is automatic. If you point out the enormous amount of evidence to show that the Jewish worker is at odds with the "international Jew stock exchange capitalist," Hitler replies with one hundred per cent regularity: That is one more indication of the cunning with which the "Jewish plot" is being engineered. Or would you point to "Aryans" who do the same as his conspiratorial Jews? Very well; that is proof that the "Aryan" has been "seduced" by the Jew.

The sexual symbolism that runs through Hitler's book, lying in wait to draw upon the responses of contemporary sexual values, is easily characterized:

Germany in dispersion is the "dehorned Siegfried." The masses are "feminine." As such, they desire to be led by a dominating male. This male, as orator, woos them—and, when he has won them, he commands them. The rival male, the villainous Jew, would on the contrary "seduce" them. If he succeeds, he poisons their blood by intermingling with them. Whereupon, by purely associative connections of ideas, we are moved into attacks upon syphilis, prostitution, incest, and other similar misfortunes, which are introduced as a kind of "musical" argument when he is on the subject of "blood-poisoning" by intermarriage or, in its "spiritual" equivalent, by the infection of "Jewish" ideas, such as democracy.[1]

The "medicinal" appeal of the Jew as scapegoat operates from another angle. The middle class contains, within the mind of each member, a duality: its members simultaneously have a cult of money and a detestation of this cult. When capitalism is going well, this conflict is left more or less in abeyance. But when capitalism is balked, it comes to the fore. Hence, there is "medicine" for the "Aryan" members of the middle class in the projective device of the scapegoat, whereby the "bad" features can be allocated to the "devil," and one can "respect himself" by a distinction between "good" capitalism and "bad" capitalism, with those of a different lodge being the vessels of the "bad" capitalism. It is doubtless the "relief" of this solution that spared Hitler the necessity of explaining just how the "Jewish plot" was to work out. Nowhere does this book, which is so full of war plans, make the slightest attempt to explain the steps whereby the triumph of "Jewish Bolshevism," which destroys *all* finance, will be the triumph of *"Jewish"* finance. Hitler well knows the point at which his "elucidations" should rely upon the lurid alone.

The question arises, in those trying to gauge Hitler: Was his selection of the Jew, as his unifying devil-function, a purely calculating act? Despite the quotation I have already given, I believe that it was *not*. The vigor with which he utilized it, I think, derives from a much more complex state of affairs. It seems that, when Hitler went to Vienna, in a state close to total poverty, he genuinely suffered. He lived among the impoverished; and he describes his misery at the spectacle. He was *sensitive* to it; and his way of manifesting this sensitiveness impresses me that he is, at this point, wholly genuine, as with his wincing at the broken family relationships caused by alcoholism, which he in turn relates to impoverishment. During this time he began his attempts at political theorizing; and his disturbance was considerably increased by the skill with which Marxists tied him into knots. One passage in particular gives you reason, reading between the lines, to believe that the dialecticians of the class struggle, in their skill at blasting his muddled speculations, put him into a state of uncertainty that was finally "solved" by rage:

The more I argued with them, the more I got to know their dialectics. First they counted on the ignorance of their adversary; then, when there was no way out, they themselves pretended stupidity. If all this was of no avail, they refused to understand or they changed the subject when driven into a corner; they brought up truisms, but they immediately transferred their acceptance to quite different subjects, and, if attacked again, they gave way and pretended to know nothing exactly. Wherever one attacked one of these prophets, one's hands seized slimy jelly; it slipped through one's fingers only to collect again in the next moment. If one smote one of them so thoroughly that, with the bystanders watching, he could but agree, and if one thus thought he had advanced at least one step, one was greatly astonished the following day. The Jew did not in the least remember the day before, he continued to talk in the same old strain as if nothing had happened, and if indignantly confronted, he pretended to be astonished and could not remember anything except that his assertions had already been proved true the day before.

Often I was stunned.

One did not know what to admire more: their glibness of tongue or their skill in lying.

I gradually began to hate them.

At this point, I think, he is tracing the *spontaneous* rise of his anti-Semitism. He tells how, once he had discovered the "cause" of the misery about him, he could *confront it*. Where he had had to avert his eyes, he could now *positively welcome* the scene. Here his drastic structure of *acceptance* was being formed. He tells of the "internal happiness" that descended upon him.

This was the time in which the greatest change I was ever to experience took place in me.

From a feeble cosmopolite I turned into a fanatical anti-Semite.

and thence we move, by one of those associational tricks which he brings forth at all strategic moments, into a vision of the end of the world—out of which in turn he emerges with his slogan: "I am acting in the sense of the Almighty Creator: *By warding off Jews I am fighting for the Lord's work*" (italics his).

He talks of this transition as a period of "double life," a struggle of "reason" and "reality" against his "heart."[2] It was as "bitter" as it was "blissful." And finally, it was "reason" that won! Which prompts us to note that those who attack Hitlerism as a cult of the irrational should emend their statements to this extent: irrational it is, but it is carried on under the *slogan* of "Reason." Similarly, his cult of war is developed "in the name of" humility, love, and peace. Judged on a quantitative basis, Hitler's book certainly falls under the classification of hate. Its venom is everywhere, its charity is sparse.

But the rationalized family tree for this hate situates it in "Aryan love." Some deep-probing German poets, whose work adumbrated the Nazi movement, did gravitate towards thinking *in the name of* war, irrationality, and hate. But Hitler was not among them. After all, when it is so easy to draw a doctrine of war out of a doctrine of peace, why should the astute politician do otherwise, particularly when Hitler has slung together his doctrines, without the slightest effort at logical symmetry? Furthermore, Church thinking always got to its wars in Hitler's "sounder" manner; and the patterns of Hitler's thought are a bastardized or caricatured version of religious thought.

I spoke of Hitler's fury at the dialectics of those who opposed him when his structure was in the stage of scaffolding. From this we may move to another tremendously important aspect of his theory: his attack upon the *parliamentary*. For it is again, I submit, an important aspect of his medicine, in its function as medicine for him personally and as medicine for those who were later to identify themselves with him.

There is a "problem" in the parliament—and nowhere was this problem more acutely in evidence than in the pre-war Vienna that was to serve as Hitler's political schooling. For the parliament, at its best, is a "babel" of voices. There is the wrangle of men representing interests lying awkwardly on the bias across one another, sometimes opposing, sometimes vaguely divergent. Morton Prince's psychiatric study of "Miss Beauchamp," the case of a woman split into several sub-personalities at odds with one another, variously combining under hypnosis, and frequently in turmoil, is the allegory of a democracy fallen upon evil days. The parliament of the Habsburg Empire just prior to its collapse was an especially drastic instance of such disruption, such vocal diaspora, with movements that would reduce one to a disintegrated mass of fragments if he attempted to encompass the totality of its discordancies. So Hitler, suffering under the alienation of poverty and confusion, yearning for some integrative core, came to take this parliament as the basic symbol of all that he would move away from. He damned the tottering Habsburg Empire as a "State of Nationalities." The many conflicting voices of the spokesmen of the many political blocs arose from the fact that various separationist movements of a nationalistic sort had arisen within a Catholic imperial structure formed prior to the nationalistic emphasis and slowly breaking apart under its development. So, you had this Babel of voices; and, by the method of associative mergers, *using ideas as imagery,* it became tied up, in the Hitler rhetoric, with "Babylon," Vienna as the city of poverty, prostitution, immorality, coalitions, half-measures, incest, democracy (i.e., majority rule leading to "lack of personal responsibility"), death, internationalism, seduction, and anything else of thumbs-down sort the associative enterprise cared to add on this side of the balance.

Hitler's way of treating the parliamentary babel, I am sorry to say, was at one important point not much different from that of the customary editorial in our own newspapers. Every conflict among the parliamentary spokesmen represents a corresponding conflict among the material interests of the groups for whom they are speaking. But Hitler did not discuss the babel from this angle. He discussed it on a purely *symptomatic* basis. The strategy of our orthodox press, in thus ridiculing the cacophonous verbal output of Congress, is obvious: by thus centering attack upon the *symptoms* of business conflict, as they reveal themselves on the dial of political wrangling, and leaving the underlying cause, the business conflicts themselves, out of the case, they can gratify the very public they would otherwise alienate: namely, the businessmen who are the activating members of their reading public. Hitler, however, went them one better. For not only did he stress the purely *symptomatic* attack here. He proceeded to search for the "cause." And this "cause," of course, he derived from his medicine, his racial theory by which he could give a noneconomic interpretation of a phenomenon economically engendered.

Here again is where Hitler's corrupt use of religious patterns comes to the fore. Church thought, being primarily concerned with matters of the "personality," with problems of moral betterment, naturally, and I think rightly, stresses as a necessary feature, the act of will upon the part of the individual. Hence its resistance to a purely "environmental" account of human ills. Hence its emphasis upon the "person." Hence its proneness to seek a noneconomic explanation of economic phenomena. Hitler's proposal of a noneconomic "cause" for the disturbances thus had much to recommend it from this angle. And, as a matter of fact, it was Lueger's Christian-Social Party in Vienna that taught Hitler the tactics of tying up a program of social betterment with an anti-Semitic "unifier." The two parties that he carefully studied at that time were this Catholic faction and Schoenerer's Pan-German group. And his analysis of their attainments and shortcomings, from the standpoint of demagogic efficacy, is an extremely astute piece of work, revealing how carefully this man used the current situation in Vienna as an experimental laboratory for the maturing of his plans.

His unification device, we may summarize, had the following important features:

(1) Inborn dignity. In both religious and humanistic patterns of thought, a "natural born" dignity of man is stressed. And this categorical dignity is considered to be an attribute of *all* men, if they will but avail themselves of it, by right thinking and right living. But Hitler gives this ennobling attitude an ominous twist by his theories of race and nation, whereby the "Aryan" is elevated above all others by the innate endowment of his blood, while other "races,"

in particular Jews and Negroes, are innately inferior. This sinister secularized revision of Christian theology thus puts the sense of dignity upon a fighting basis, requiring the conquest of "inferior races." After the defeat of Germany in the World War, there were especially strong emotional needs that this compensatory doctrine of an *inborn* superiority could gratify.

(2) Projection device. The "curative" process that comes with the ability to hand over one's ills to a scapegoat, thereby getting purification by dissociation. This was especially medicinal, since the sense of frustration leads to a self-questioning. Hence if one can hand over his infirmities to a vessel, or "cause," outside the self, one can battle an external enemy instead of battling an enemy within. And the greater one's internal inadequacies, the greater the amount of evils one can load upon the back of "the enemy." This device is furthermore given a semblance of reason because the individual properly realizes that he is not alone responsible for his condition. There *are* inimical factors in the scene itself. And he wants to have them "placed," preferably in a way that would require a minimum change in the ways of thinking to which he had been accustomed. This was especially appealing to the middle class, who were encouraged to feel that they could conduct their businesses without any basic change whatever, once the businessmen of a different "race" were eliminated.

(3) Symbolic rebirth. Another aspect of the two features already noted. The projective device of the scapegoat, coupled with the Hitlerite doctrine of inborn racial superiority, provides its followers with a "positive" view of life. They can again get the feel of *moving forward,* towards a *goal* (a promissory feature of which Hitler makes much). In Hitler, as the group's prophet, such rebirth involved a symbolic change of lineage. Here, above all, we see Hitler giving a malign twist to a benign aspect of Christian thought. For whereas the Pope, in the familistic pattern of thought basic to the Church, stated that the Hebrew prophets were the *spiritual ancestors* of Christianity, Hitler uses this same mode of thinking in reverse. He renounces this "ancestry" in a "materialistic" way by voting himself and the members of his lodge a different "blood stream" from that of the Jews.

(4) Commercial use. Hitler obviously here had something to sell—and it was but a question of time until he sold it (i.e., got financial backers for his movement). For it provided a *noneconomic interpretation of economic ills.* As such, it served with maximum efficiency in deflecting the attention from the economic factors involved in modern conflict; hence by attacking "Jew finance" instead of *finance,* it could stimulate an enthusiastic movement that left "Aryan" finance in control.

Never once, throughout his book, does Hitler deviate from the above formula. Invariably, he ends his diatribes against contemporary economic ills by a shift into an insistence that we must get to the "true" cause, which is centered in "race." The "Aryan" is "constructive"; the Jew is "destructive"; and the "Aryan," to continue his *construction,* must *destroy* the Jewish *destruction.* The Aryan, as the vessel of *love,* must *hate* the Jewish *hate.*

Perhaps the most enterprising use of his method is in his chapter, "The Causes of the Collapse," where he refuses to consider Germany's plight as in any basic way connected with the consequences of war. Economic factors, he insists, are "only of second or even third importance," but "political, ethical-moral, as well as factors of blood and race, are of the first importance." His rhetorical steps are especially interesting here, in that he begins by seeming to flout the national susceptibilities: "The military defeat of the German people is not an undeserved catastrophe, but rather a deserved punishment by eternal retribution." He then proceeds to present the military collapse as but a "consequence of moral poisoning, visible to all, the consequence of decrease in the instinct of self-preservation . . . which had already begun to undermine the foundations of the people and the Reich many years before." This moral decay derived from "a sin against the blood and the degradation of the race," so its innerness was an outerness after all: the Jew, who thereupon gets saddled with a vast amalgamation of evils, among them being capitalism, democracy, pacifism, journalism, poor housing, modernism, big cities, loss of religion, half measures, ill health, and weakness of the monarch.

2

Hitler had here another important psychological ingredient to play upon. If a State is in economic collapse (and his theories, tentatively taking shape in the pre-war Vienna, were but developed with greater efficiency in post-war Munich), you cannot possibly derive dignity from economic stability. Dignity must come first—and if you possess it, and implement it, from it may follow its economic counterpart. There is much justice to this line of reasoning, so far as it goes. A people in collapse, suffering under economic frustration and the defeat of nationalistic aspirations, with the very midrib of their integrative efforts (the army) in a state of dispersion, have little other than some "spiritual" basis to which they could refer their nationalistic dignity. Hence, the categorical dignity of superior race was a perfect recipe for the situation. It was "spiritual" in so far it was "above" crude economic "interests," but it was "materialized" at the psychologically "right" spot in that "the enemy" was something you could *see.*

Furthermore, you had the desire for unity, such as a discussion of class conflict, on the basis of conflicting interests, could not satisfy. The yearning for unity is so great that people are always willing to meet you halfway if you will give it to them by fiat, by flat statement, regardless of the facts. Hence, Hitler consistently refused to consider internal political conflict on the basis of conflicting interests. Here again, he could draw upon a religious pattern, by insisting upon a *personal* statement of the relation between classes, the relation between leaders and followers, each group in its way fulfilling the same commonalty of interests, as the soldiers and captains of an army share a common interest in victory. People so dislike the idea of internal division that, where there is a real internal division, their dislike can easily be turned against the man or group who would so much as *name* it, let alone proposing to act upon it. Their natural and justified resentment against internal division itself, is turned against the diagnostician who states it as a *fact*. This diagnostician, it is felt, is the *cause* of the disunity he named.

Cutting in from another angle, therefore, we note how two sets of equations were built up, with Hitler combining or coalescing *ideas* the way a poet combines or coalesces *images*. On the one side, were the ideas, or images, of disunity, centering in the parliamentary wrangle of the Habsburg "State of Nationalities." This was offered as the antithesis of German nationality, which was presented in the curative imagery of unity, focused upon the glories of the Prussian Reich, with its mecca now moved to "folkish" Vienna. For though Hitler at first attacked the many "folkish" movements, with their hankerings after a kind of Wagnerian mythology of Germanic origins, he subsequently took "folkish" as a basic word by which to conjure. It was, after all, another noneconomic basis of reference. At first we find him objecting to "those who drift about with the word 'folkish' on their caps," and asserting that "such a Babel of opinions cannot serve as the basis of a political fighting movement." But later he seems to have realized, as he well should, that its vagueness was a major point in its favor. So it was incorporated in the grand coalition of his ideational imagery, or imagistic ideation; and Chapter XI ends with the vision of "a State which represents not a mechanism of economic considerations and interests, alien to the people, but a folkish organism."

So, as against the disunity equations, already listed briefly in our discussion of his attacks upon the parliamentary, we get a contrary purifying set; the wrangle of the parliamentary is to be stilled by the giving of *one* voice to the whole people, this to be the "inner voice" of Hitler, made uniform throughout the German boundaries, as leader and people were completely identified with each other. In sum: Hitler's inner voice, equals leader-people identification, equals unity, equals Reich, equals the mecca of Munich, equals plow, equals sword, equals work, equals war, equals army as midrib, equals responsibility (the personal responsibility to the absolute ruler), equals sacrifice, equals the theory of "German democracy" (the free popular choice of the leader, who then accepts the responsibility, and demands absolute obedience in exchange for his sacrifice), equals love (with the masses of feminine), equals idealism, equals obedience to nature, equals race, nation.[3]

And, of course, the two keystones of these opposite equations were Aryan "heroism" and "sacrifice" vs. Jewish "cunning" and "arrogance." Here again we get an astounding caricature of religious thought. For Hitler presents the concept of "Aryan" superiority, of all ways, in terms of "Aryan humility." This "humility" is extracted by a very delicate process that requires, I am afraid, considerable "good will" on the part of the reader who would follow it:

The Church, we may recall, had proclaimed an integral relationship between Divine Law and Natural Law. Natural Law was the expression of the Will of God. Thus, in the middle ages, it was a result of natural law, working through tradition, that some people were serfs and other people nobles. And every good member of the Church was "obedient" to this law. Everybody resigned himself to it. Hence, the serf resigned himself to his poverty, and the noble resigned himself to his riches. The monarch resigned himself to his position as representative of the people. And at times the Churchmen resigned themselves to the need of trying to represent the people instead. And the pattern was made symmetrical by the consideration that each traditional "right" had its corresponding "obligations." Similarly, the Aryan doctrine is a doctrine of resignation, hence of humility. It is in accordance with the laws of nature that the "Aryan blood" is superior to all other bloods. Also, the "law of the survival of the fittest" is God's law, working through natural law. Hence, if the Aryan blood has been vested with the awful responsibility of its inborn superiority, the bearers of this "culture-creating" blood must resign themselves to struggle in behalf of its triumph. Otherwise, the laws of God have been disobeyed, with human decadence as a result. We must fight, he says, in order to "deserve to be alive." The Aryan "obeys" nature. It is only "Jewish arrogance" that thinks of "conquering" nature by democratic ideals of equality.

This picture has some nice distinctions worth following. The major virtue of the Aryan race was its instinct for self-preservation (in obedience to natural law). But the major vice of the Jew was his instinct for self-preservation; for, if he did not have this instinct to a maximum degree, he would not be the "perfect" enemy—that is, he wouldn't be strong enough to account for the ubiquitousness and omnipotence of his conspiracy in destroying the world to become its master.

How, then, are we to distinguish between the benign instinct of self-preservation at the roots of Aryanism, and the malign instinct of self-preservation at the roots of Semitism? We shall distinguish thus: The Aryan self-preservation is based upon *sacrifice,* the sacrifice of the individual to the group, hence, militarism, army discipline, and one big company union. But Jewish self-preservation is based upon individualism, which attains its cunning ends by the exploitation of peace. How, then, can such arrant individualists concoct the world-wide plot? By the help of their "herd instinct." By their sheer "herd instinct" individualists can band together for a common end. They have no real solidarity, but unite opportunistically to seduce the Aryan. Still, that brings up another technical problem. For we have been hearing much about the importance of the *person.* We have been told how, by the "law of the survival of the fittest," there is a sifting of people on the basis of their individual capacities. We even have a special chapter of pure Aryanism: "The Strong Man is Mightiest Alone." Hence, another distinction is necessary: The Jew represents individualism; the Aryan represents "super-individualism."

I had thought, when coming upon the "Strong Man is Mightiest Alone" chapter, that I was going to find Hitler at his weakest. Instead, I found him at his strongest. (I am not referring to *quality,* but to *demagogic effectiveness.*) For the chapter is not at all, as you might infer from the title, done in a "rise of Adolph Hitler" manner. Instead, it deals with the Nazis' gradual absorption of the many disrelated "folkish" groups. And it is managed throughout by means of a spontaneous identification between leader and people. Hence, the Strong Man's "aloneness" is presented as a *public* attribute, in terms of tactics for the struggle against the *Party's* dismemberment under the pressure of rival saviors. There is no explicit talk of Hitler at all. And it is simply *taken for granted* that *his* leadership is the norm, and all other leaderships the abnorm. There is no "philosophy of the superman," in Nietzschean cast. Instead, Hitler's blandishments so integrate leader and people, commingling them so inextricably, that the politician does not even present himself as candidate. Somehow, the battle is over already, the decision has been made. "German democracy" has chosen. And the deployments of politics are, you might say, the chartings of Hitler's private mind translated into the vocabulary of nationalistic events. He says *what he thought* in terms of *what parties did.*

Here, I think, we see the distinguishing quality of Hitler's method as an instrument of persuasion, with reference to the question whether Hitler is sincere or deliberate, whether his vision of the omnipotent conspirator has the drastic honesty of paranoia or the sheer shrewdness of a demagogue trained in *Realpolitik* of the Machiavellian sort.[4] Must we choose? Or may we not, rather, replace the "either—or" with a "both—and"? Have we not by now offered grounds enough for our contention that Hitler's sinister powers of persuasion derive from the fact that he spontaneously evolved his "cure-all" in response to inner necessities?

It was Machiavelli's hope that, for this roundabout project, he would be warded with a well-paying office in the prince's administrative bureaucracy.

3

So much, then, was "spontaneous." It was further channelized into the anti-Semitic pattern by the incentives he derived from the Catholic Christian-Social Party in Vienna itself. Add, now, the step into *criticism*. Not criticism in the "parliamentary" sense of doubt, of hearkening to the opposition and attempting to mature a policy in the light of counter-policies; but the "unified" kind of criticism that simply seeks for conscious ways of making one's position more "efficient," more thoroughly itself. This is the kind of criticism at which Hitler was adept. As a result, he could *spontaneously* turn to a scapegoat mechanism, and he could by conscious planning, perfect the symmetry of the solution towards which he had spontaneously turned.

This is the meaning of Hitler's diatribes against "objectivity." "Objectivity" is interference-criticism. What Hitler wanted was the kind of criticism that would be a pure and simple coefficient of power, enabling him to go most effectively in the direction he had chosen. And the "inner voice" of which he speaks would henceforth dictate to him the greatest amount of realism, as regards the tactics of efficiency. For instance, having decided that the masses required certainty, and simple certainty, quite as he did himself, he later worked out a 25-point program as the platform of his National Socialist German Workers Party. And he resolutely refused to change one single item in this program, even for purposes of "improvement." He felt that the *fixity* of the platform was more important for propagandistic purposes than any revision of his slogans could be, even though the revisions in themselves had much to be said in their favor. The astounding thing is that, although such an attitude gave good cause to doubt the Hitlerite promises, he could explicitly explain his tactics in his book and still employ them without loss of effectiveness.[5]

Hitler also tells of his technique in speaking, once the Nazi party had become effectively organized, and had its army of guards, or bouncers, to maltreat hecklers and throw them from the hall. He would, he recounts, fill his speech with *provocative* remarks, whereat his bouncers would promptly swoop down in flying formation, with swinging fists, upon anyone whom these provocative remarks provoked to answer. The efficiency of Hitlerism is the efficiency of the one voice, implemented throughout a total organization. The trinity of government which he finally offers is: *popularity* of the leader, *force* to back the popularity, and popularity and force maintained together long enough to become backed by a *tradition*. Is such thinking spontaneous or deliberate—or is it not rather both?[6]

Freud has given us a succinct paragraph that bears upon the spontaneous aspect of Hitler's persecution mania. (A persecution mania, I should add, different from the pure product in that it was constructed of *public* materials; all the ingredients Hitler stirred into his brew were already rife, with spokesmen and bands of followers, before Hitler "took them over." Both the pre-war and post-war periods were dotted with saviors, of nationalistic and "folkish" cast. This proliferation was analogous to the swarm of barter schemes and currency-tinkering that burst loose upon the United States after the crash of 1929. Also, the commercial availability of Hitler's politics was, in a low sense of the term, a *public* qualification, removing it from the realm of "pure" paranoia, where the sufferer develops a wholly *private* structure of interpretations.)

I cite from *Totem and Taboo:*

> Another trait in the attitude of primitive races towards their rulers recalls a mechanism which is universally present in mental disturbances, and is openly revealed in the so-called delusions of persecution. Here the importance of a particular person is extraordinarily heightened and his omnipotence is raised to the improbable in order to make it easier to attribute to him responsibility for everything painful which happens to the patient. Savages really do not act differently towards their rulers when they ascribe to them power over rain and shine, wind and weather, and then dethrone them or kill them because nature has disappointed their expectation of a good hunt or a ripe harvest. The prototype which the paranoiac reconstructs in his persecution mania is found in the relation of the child to its father. Such omnipotence is regularly attributed to the father in the imagination of the son, and distrust of the father has been shown to be intimately connected with the heightened esteem for him. When a paranoiac names a person of his acquaintance as his "persecutor," he thereby elevates him to the paternal succession and brings him under conditions which enable him to make him responsible for all the misfortune which he experiences.

I have already proposed my modifications of this account when discussing the symbolic change of lineage connected with Hitler's project of a "new way of life." Hitler is symbolically changing from the "spiritual ancestry" of the Hebrew prophets to the "superior" ancestry of "Aryanism," and has given his story a kind of bastardized modernization, along the lines of naturalistic, materialistic "science," by his fiction of the special "blood-stream." He is voting himself a new identity (something contrary to the wrangles of the Habsburg Babylon, a soothing national unity); whereupon the vessels of the old identity become a "bad" father, i.e., the persecutor. It is not hard to see how, as his enmity becomes implemented by the backing of an organization, the rôle of "persecutor" is transformed into the rôle of persecuted, as he sets out with his like-minded band to "destroy the destroyer."

Were Hitler simply a poet, he might have written a work with an anti-Semitic turn, and let it go at that. But Hitler, who began as a student of paint-ing, and later shifted to architecture, himself treats his political activities as an extension of his artistic ambitions. He remained, in his own eyes, an "archi-tect," building a "folkish" State that was to match, in political materials, the "folkish" architecture of Munich.

We might consider the matter this way (still trying, that is, to make precise the relationship between the drastically sincere and the deliberately schem-ing): Do we not know of many authors who seem, as they turn from the rôle of citizen to the rôle of spokesman, to leave one room and enter another? Or who has not, on occasion, talked with a man in private conversation, and then been almost startled at the transformation this man undergoes when addressing a public audience? And I know persons today, who shift between the writing of items in the class of academic, philosophic speculation to items of political pamphleteering, and whose entire style and method changes with this change of rôle. In their academic manner, they are cautious, painstaking, eager to present all significant aspects of the case they are considering; but when they turn to political pamphleteering, they hammer forth with vituper-ation, they systematically misrepresent the position of their opponent, they go into a kind of political trance, in which, during its throes, they throb like a locomotive; and behold, a moment later, the mediumistic state is aban-doned, and they are the most moderate of men.

Now, one will find few pages in Hitler that one could call "moderate." But there are many pages in which he gauges resistances and opportunities with the "rationality" of a skilled advertising man planning a new sales campaign. Politics, he says, must be sold like soap—and soap is not sold in a trance. But he did have the experience of his trance, in the "exaltation" of his anti-Semitism. And later, as he became a successful orator (he insists that revolu-tions are made solely by the power of the spoken word), he had this "poetic" rôle to draw upon, plus the great relief it provided as a way of slipping from the burden of logical analysis into the pure "spirituality" of vituperative prophecy. What more natural, therefore, than that a man so insistent upon unification would integrate this mood with less ecstatic moments, particularly when he had found the followers and the backers that put a price, both spir-itual and material, upon such unification?

Once this happy "unity" is under way, one has a "logic" for the develop-ment of a method. One knows when to "spiritualize" a material issue, and when to "materialize" a spiritual one. Thus, when it is a matter of materialis-tic interests that cause a conflict between employer and employee, Hitler here disdainfully shifts to a high moral plane. He is "above" such low concerns. Everything becomes a matter of "sacrifices" and "personality." It becomes crass to treat employers and employees as different *classes* with a corresponding difference in the classification of their interests. Instead, relations between employer and employee must be on the "personal" basis of leader and follower, and "whatever may have a divisive effect in national life should be given a unifying effect through the army." When talking of national rivalries, however, he makes a very shrewd materialistic gauging of Britain and France with relation to Germany. France, he says, desires the "Balkanization of Germany" (i.e., its breakup into separationist movements—the "disunity" theme again) in order to maintain commercial hegemony on the continent. But Britain desires the "Balkanization of *Europe,*" hence would favor a fairly strong and unified Germany, to use as a counter-weight against French hegemony. *German* nationality, however, is unified by the *spiritual* quality of Aryanism (that would produce the national organization via the Party) while this in turn is *materialized* in the myth of the blood-stream.

What are we to learn from Hitler's book? For one thing, I believe that he has shown, to a very disturbing degree, the power of endless repetition. Every circular advertising a Nazi meeting had, at the bottom, two slogans: "Jews not admitted" and "War victims free." And the substance of Nazi propaganda was built about these two "complementary" themes. He describes the power of spectacle; insists that mass meetings are the fundamental way of giving the individual the sense of being protectively surrounded by a movement, the sense of "community." He also drops one wise hint that I wish the American authorities would take in treating Nazi gatherings. He says that the presence of a special Nazi guard, in Nazi uniforms, was of great importance in building up, among the followers, a tendency to place the center of authority in the Nazi party. I believe that we should take him at his word here, but use the advice in reverse, by insisting that, where Nazi meetings are to be permitted, they be policed by the authorities alone, and that uniformed Nazi guards to enforce the law be prohibited.

And is it possible that an equally important feature of appeal was not so much in the repetitiousness per se, but in the fact that, by means of it, Hitler provided a "world view" for people who had previously seen the world but piecemeal? Did not much of his lure derive, once more, from the *bad* filling of a *good* need? Are not those who insist upon a purely *planless* working of the market asking people to accept far too slovenly a scheme of human purpose, a slovenly scheme that can be accepted so long as it operates with a fair degree of satisfaction, but becomes abhorrent to the victims of its disarray? Are they not then psychologically ready for a rationale, *any* rationale, if it but offer them some specious "universal" explanation? Hence, I doubt whether the appeal was in the sloganizing element alone (particularly as even slogans can only be hammered home, in speech after speech, and two or three hours at a stretch, by endless variations on the themes). And Hitler himself somewhat justifies my interpretation by laying so much stress upon the *half-measures* of the middle-class politicians, and the contrasting *certainty* of his own methods. He was not offering people a *rival* world view; rather, he was offering a world view to people who had no other to pit against it.

As for the basic Nazi trick: the "curative" unification by a fictitious devil-function, gradually made convincing by the sloganizing repetitiousness of standard advertising technique—the opposition must be as unwearying in the attack upon it. It may well be that people, in their human frailty, require an enemy as well as a goal. Very well: Hitlerism itself has provided us with such an enemy—and the clear example of its operation is guaranty that we have, in him and all he stands for, no purely fictitious "devil-function" made to look like a world menace by rhetorical blandishments, but a reality whose ominousness is clarified by the record of its conduct to date. In selecting his brand of doctrine as our "scapegoat," and in tracking down its equivalents in America, we shall be at the very center of accuracy. The Nazis themselves have made the task of clarification easier. Add to them Japan and Italy, and you have *case histories* of fascism for those who might find it more difficult to approach an understanding of its imperialistic drives by a vigorously economic explanation.

But above all, I believe, we must make it apparent that Hitler appeals by relying upon a bastardization of fundamentally religious patterns of thought. In this, if properly presented, there is no slight to religion. There is nothing in religion proper that requires a fascist state. There is much in religion, when misused, that does lead to a fascist state. There is a Latin proverb, *Corruptio optimi pessima,* "the corruption of the best is the worst." And it is the corruptors of religion who are a major menace to the world today, in giving the profound patterns of religious thought a crude and sinister distortion.

Our job, then, our anti-Hitler Battle, is to find all available ways of making the Hitlerite distortions of religion apparent, in order that politicians of his kind in America be unable to perform a similar swindle. The desire for unity is genuine and admirable. The desire for national unity, in the present state of the world, is genuine and admirable. But this unity, if attained on a deceptive basis, by emotional trickeries that shift our criticism from the accurate locus of our trouble, is no unity at all. For, even if we are among those who happen to be "Aryans," we solve no problems even for ourselves by such solutions, since the factors pressing towards calamity remain. Thus, in Germany, after all the upheaval, we see nothing beyond a drive for ever more and more upheaval, precisely because the "new way of life" was no new way, but the dismally oldest way of sheer deception—hence, after all the "change," the factors driving towards unrest are left intact, and even strengthened. True, the Germans had the resentment of a lost war to increase their susceptibility to Hitler's rhetoric. But in a wider sense, it has repeatedly been observed, the whole world lost the War—and the accumulating ills of the capitalist order were but accelerated in their movements towards confusion. Hence, here too there are the resentments that go with frustration of men's ability to work and earn. At that point a certain kind of industrial or financial monopolist may, annoyed by the contrary voices of our parliament, wish for the momentary peace of one voice, amplified by social organizations, with all the others not merely quieted, but given the quietus. So he might, under Nazi promptings, be tempted to back a group of gangsters who, on becoming the political rulers of the state, would protect him against the necessary demands of the workers. His gangsters, then, would be his insurance against his workers. But who would be his insurance against his gangsters?

Notes

1. Hitler also strongly insists upon the total identification between leader and people. Thus, in wooing the people, he would in a roundabout way be wooing himself. The thought might suggest how the Führer, dominating the feminine masses by his diction, would have an incentive to remain unmarried.

2. Other aspects of the career symbolism: Hitler's book begins: "Today I consider it my good fortune that Fate designated Braunau on the Inn as the place of my birth. For this small town is situated on the border between those two German States, the reunion of which seems, at least to us of the younger generation, a task to be furthered with every means our lives long," an indication of his "transitional" mind, what Wordsworth might have called the "borderer." He neglects to give the date of his birth, 1889, which is supplied by the editors. Again there is a certain "correctness" here, as Hitler was not "born" until many years later—but he does give the exact date of his war wounds, which were indeed formative. During his early years in Vienna and Munich, he foregoes protest, on the grounds that he is "nameless." And when his party is finally organized and effective, he stresses the fact that his "nameless" period is over (i.e., he has shaped himself an identity). When reading in an earlier passage of his book some generalizations to the effect that one should not crystallize his political views until he is thirty, I made a note: "See what Hitler does at thirty." I felt sure that, though such generalizations may be dubious as applied to people as a whole, they must, given the Hitler type of mind (with his complete identification between himself and his followers), be valid statements about himself. One *should* do what he *did*. The hunch was verified: about the age of thirty Hitler, in a group of seven, began working with the party that was to conquer Germany. I trace these steps particularly because I believe that the orator

who has a strong sense of his own "rebirth" has this to draw upon when persuading his audiences that his is offering them the way to a "new life." However, I see no categorical objection to this attitude; its menace derives solely from the values in which it is exemplified. They may be wholesome or unwholesome. If they are unwholesome, but backed by conviction, the basic sincerity of the conviction acts as a sound virtue to reinforce a vice—and this combination is the most disastrous one that a people can encounter in a demagogue.

3. One could carry out the equations further, on both the disunity and unity side. In the aesthetic field, for instance, we have expressionism on the thumbs-down side, as against aesthetic hygiene on the thumbs-up side. This again is a particularly ironic moment in Hitler's strategy. For the expressionist movement was unquestionably a symptom of unhealthiness. It reflected the increasing alienation that went with the movement towards world war and the disorganization after the world war. It was "lost," vague in identity, a drastically accurate reflection of the response to material confusion, a pathetic attempt by sincere artists to make their wretchedness bearable at least to the extent that comes of giving it expression. And it attained its height during the period of wild inflation, when the capitalist world, which bases its morality of work and savings upon the soundness of its money structure, had this last prop of stability removed. The anguish, in short, reflected precisely the kind of disruption that made people *ripe* for a Hitler. It was the antecedent in a phrase of which Hitlerism was the consequent. But by thundering against this *symptom* he could gain persuasiveness, though attacking the very *foreshadowings of himself.*

4. I should not want to use the word "Machiavellian," however, without offering a kind of apology to Machiavelli. It seems to me that Machiavelli's *Prince* has more to be said in extenuation than is usually said of it. Machiavelli's strategy, as I see it, was something like this: He accepted the values of the Renaissance rule a *fact.* That is: whether you like these values or not, they were there and operating, and it was useless to try persuading the ambitious ruler to adopt other values such as those of the Church. These men believed in the cult of material power and they had the power to implement their beliefs. With so much as "the given" could anything in the way of benefits for the people be salvaged? Machiavelli evolved a typical "Machiavellian" argument in favor of popular benefits, on the basis of the prince's own scheme of values. That is: the ruler, to attain the maximum strength, requires the backing of the populace. That this backing be effective as possible, the populace should be made as strong as possible. And that the populace be as strong as possible, they should be well treated. Their gratitude would further repay itself in the form of increased loyalty.

5. On this point Hitler reasons as follows: "Here, too, one can learn from the Catholic Church. Although its structure of doctrines in many instances collides, quite unnecessarily, with exact science and research, yet it is unwilling to sacrifice even one little syllable of its dogmas. It has rightly recognized that its resistibility does not lie in a more or less great adjustment to the scientific results of the moment, which in reality are always changing, but rather in a strict adherence to dogmas, once laid down, which alone give the entire structure the character of creed. Today,

therefore, the Catholic Church stands firmer than ever. One can prophesy that in the same measure in which the appearances flee, the Church itself, as the resting pole in the flight of appearances, will gain more and more blind adherence."

6. Hitler also paid great attention to the conditions under which political oratory is most effective. He sums up thus:

"All these cases involve encroachments upon man's freedom of will. This applies, of course, most of all to meetings to which people with a contrary orientation of will are coming, and who now have to be won for new intentions. It seems that in the morning and even during the day men's will power revolts with highest energy against an attempt at being forced under another's will and another's opinion. In the evening, however, they succumb more easily to the dominating force of a stronger will. For truly every such meeting presents a wrestling match between two opposed forces. The superior oratorical talent of a domineering apostolic nature will now succeed more easily in winning for the new will people who themselves have in turn experienced a weakening of their force of resistance in the most natural way, than people who still have full command of the energies of their minds and their will power.

"The same purpose serves also the artificially created and yet mysterious dusk of the Catholic churches, the burning candles, incense, censers, etc."

8

'Why We Fight'

Social Engineering for a Democratic Society at War

David Culbert

The past decade has seen an important shift in emphasis by historians interested in World War II, from battles and strategy to transportation of supplies, secret codes and morale—what might be termed the 'soft' side of military history.[1] We look to the war's indirect effects on the home front for which industrial productivity and military manpower requirements are responsible. Geoffrey Perrett is correct in describing a social revolution which occurred within the United States between 1941 and 1945, the actuality which New Deal slogans had been unable to bring about.[2] The key to that revolution is economic prosperity combined with technological innovation, in a society whose distinctive contribution is often a triumph of scale. Within the American Army, acceptance of social science research techniques and heavy reliance on media technology suggests that generals can sometimes be True Believers. Total war proved the right time to give innovation a massive degree of support.[3]

SOURCE: From David Culbert, "'Why We Fight': Social Engineering for a Democratic Society at War," in Ken Short (Ed.), *Film and Radio Propaganda in World War II*. The University of Tennessee Press, 1983, pp. 173–191. Reprinted with permission.

Military enthusiasm for social science research and media technology relates to the concept of Social Engineering, an outgrowth of behavioural psychology arguing that human behaviour can be manipulated towards socially desirable goals.[4] Critics of industrial societies had long complained that as technology spread its benefits, it also eroded traditional values. Optimistic social scientists believed that a 'humane' or 'liberal' use of film could reaffirm the values of a democratic society. In practice the relation between film and social science proved to be symbiotic: each used the other to gain popular acceptance.

There is another way of defining social engineering: the need to offer a *reason* why to an educated citizenry. 'Give me the man who knows that for which he fights,' Oliver Cromwell declared, 'and loves that which he knows.' Mass education made it harder to avoid factual explanations; if the Light Brigade really charged into battle without knowing 'the reason why'; few citizens could be found in Depression America so willing to follow authority blindly. In 1916, 1.7 million Americans were in high school; in 1940, 7.1 million. In 1916, 400,000 attended college; in 1940, 1.4 million.[5] Franklin Roosevelt's 'fireside chats' assumed educated Americans who wanted explanations for citizen obligations. Acceptance of state policy, everyone seemed to agree, demanded some reason why. Not necessarily the whole truth, mind you, but at least plausible justification.

As a result the Army found new responsibilities in the area of morale, long a matter of interest to field commanders, but now allied with the 'science' of public relations and behavioural psychology. Within the Army the Morale Branch, or the Information and Education Division or I&E as it was finally called, became the centre for dramatic experimentation, an entire division which might have been called the Center for Social Engineering. Dedicated to offering reasons why, its seven orientation films, the *Why We Fight* series, must be considered one of its greatest achievements. The title suggests a fascination with reason, and the propagandist's understanding of combining patriotism with selected facts. The medium showed a sturdy faith in technology's ability to wed the educated citizen to his soldier's calling.

Brigadier General Frederick H. Osborn headed I&E.[6] A wealthy New Yorker without prior military service, Osborn had impeccable family connections and a genius for administration. His father was one of Secretary of War Henry Stimson's close friends; an uncle, Henry Fairfield Osborn, had been largely responsible for the rise to international prominence of New York's Museum of Natural History. Osborn, also a board member of the Social Science Research Council, with a scholarly study of eugenics to his credit, came to the Army persuaded that morale could be determined by scientific means, and that traditional morale boosters—sports, camp songfests, 'decks of cards and dice and tonettes'—belonged to a bygone era.

Osborn also had a physical presence of immense value when selling new ideas to possibly resistant career types; he was, as Alfred Kazin remembers him, 'spectacularly tall.' When Osborn needed to, he could also be a tough fighter amidst the empire-builders who saw wartime as just the right moment for any number of elaborate ideas.

The most important reason for Osborn's success was not his ability to keep immensely-gifted people working in some sort of harmony, but the backing of Secretary of War Stimson, and, in particular, General George C. Marshall, Army Chief of Staff. Osborn's greatest interest lay in social science research and the group headed by Samuel Stouffer which introduced *What the Soldier Thinks*. For General Marshall, a more important I&E priority was film. As a Civilian Conservation Corps Commander in the Pacific northwest during the 1930s, he had seen how effective feature films shown off the back of trucks could be for morale.[7] Since President Roosevelt never put much stock in a civilian propaganda agency, really elaborate film programmes required the backing of the military and the protection 'wartime defence' afforded.

What really turned Marshall into a zealous proponent of educational film was his intense dissatisfaction with existing methods of troop indoctrination— mandatory orientation talks. Few human beings are inspiring public speakers; the Army's canned lectures made it less likely that individual delivery could be effectively related to the subject—especially in 'recreation halls' where the talks were given. The Bureau of Public Relations prepared 15 lectures in the autumn of 1941 to explain foreign affairs, 1919–39, to all new troops. The results were disastrous; most commanders considered orientation a waste of time or a mandatory rest hour. Few could see how the past could be made vivid and interesting enough to make some uninformed eighteen-year-old see why he was being inducted.[8]

Although these talks failed completely, the idea of using film for orientation was not Marshall's alone; it was an idea whose time had come. A single film, Leni Riefenstahl's *Triumph of the Will* (1935) did more to make all of World War II's belligerents rely on film for morale purposes than anything else. *Triumph of the Will* showed military leaders and filmmakers the world over how compelling a device film could be for the propagandist. Also effective distribution of the film to remote parts of Germany suggested that film could unify an entire population.

There are extraordinary similarities between the concept and practice of information, orientation, and propaganda but the *Why We Fight* series is propaganda, no doubt about it. Facts were selected with an eye to offering emotional reasons for supporting one's own war effort, the cause of one's allies, and for fearing and hating one's enemies. The specific content of the seven completed films (the final film was originally in two parts) cannot be discussed here, but the series justified American participation as unavoidable. *Prelude to War* conveniently simplified things by dividing the world into free and slave; *The Nazis Strike* showed the *blitzkrieg* in the Low Countries and Poland, and made the enemy appear suitably threatening; *Divide and Conquer* attributed the collapse of France to fifth columnists—it seemed at times to lecture more about internal subversion than the reality of France's collapse. *The Battle of Britain* pulled out all the stops to make the heroism of the British admirable enough to paper over memories of Chamberlain; *The Battle of Russia* used Soviet and German footage to depict Soviet heroism, especially at Stalingrad. Not only was the film effective, but its official origin made it one of the most persuasive attempts at quieting persistent anti-Soviet sentiment inside the United States. *The Battle of China* was a fairy tale, or flatfooted propaganda which relied on too much Hollywood feature footage. The film was formally withdrawn from circulation but later reissued. *War Comes to America* went over the same ground as *Prelude to War,* but was more concerned with visualising the American people and tracing the growth of pro-war sentiment than in defining the universal threat of Fascism. Especially interesting was the use of Gallup poll data to document graphically changes in public opinion.[9]

To term the *Why We Fight* films propaganda is not to dismiss them as a tissue of lies. They were truthful in the way Emily Dickinson sensed all effective propaganda must be:

> Tell all the truth, but tell it slant—
>
> Success in circuit lies.
>
> . . .
>
> The truth must dazzle gradually,
>
> Or every man be blind.

A technological society depends on propaganda to persuade its citizens that its actions are legitimate. It becomes an enterprise, Jacques Ellul argues, 'for perverting the significance of events and of insinuating false intentions.' Michael Balfour distinguishes between the method of science and art of propaganda, 'inducing people to leap to conclusions without adequate examination of the evidence.'[10] Ellul struggles to relieve propaganda of its negative or pejorative connotations, for he feels that propaganda is necessary to modern decision-making, that in practice it cannot be separated from information, education, or public relations, and that with more education we become even more susceptible to the allure of propaganda. The reason, Ellul believes, is obvious:

Modern man worships 'facts'—that is, he accepts 'facts' as the ultimate reality
. . . Facts in themselves provide evidence and proof, and he willingly subordi-
nates values to them; he obeys what he believes to be necessity, which he somehow connects with the idea of progress.

In spite of Ellul, the cynical definition of propaganda offered by F. M.
Cornford finds continued acceptance: 'that branch of the art of lying which
consists in very nearly deceiving your friends without quite deceiving your
enemies.'[11]

The more thought one gives to the struggle between ends and means the
more slippery the concept of objective truth becomes; the less easy to say with
certainty what the contextual significance of any fact is. Education assumes the
rational man as an attainable ideal; given sufficient facts or sufficient perception of objective reality, so one is taught to believe, it is possible to know the
truth about public issues of the day. But propaganda lies behind every opinion
we hold on public issues. No moral or religious code arms the citizen sufficiently in the quest for separating what is true from what is not. 'Arguments
can easily cancel one another out,' Balfour concludes, 'and the upshot of discussion may be that all possible courses of action seem open to objection, so
that Mr Valiant-for-Truth ends up as Mr Facing-both-Ways.'

Such concerns have the greatest importance to an understanding of the *Why
We Fight* films, whose technical expertise is extraordinary, but whose overall
purpose is a mixture of twisted fact, deceit, simplification and emotion of what,
in World War II, was proclaimed the 'strategy of truth,' or the 'propaganda of
fact.'[12] A *New Yorker* cartoon which appeared a few years ago makes the same
point. We see a room of filing cabinets variously labelled 'our facts,' 'their facts,'
'semi-facts,' 'good facts,' and 'bad facts.' The original purpose of the films was
to define war aims in an exciting but truthful fashion; in the end truth took a
back seat to emotional patriotism. Or, as Peter Kenez argues, one really distinguishes issue-propaganda from a nation's *Weltanschauung*-propaganda. The
former allows for cynical decisions about gradations of truth; the latter may not
be apparent except to those outside the culture.[13]

The series became mandatory viewing for all military personnel in 1942;
eventually three found commercial distribution in movie theatres within
the United States. Worldwide distribution followed the addition of foreign-
language soundtracks in French, Spanish, Russian and Chinese. In England
Churchill wanted to see the series widely distributed but the Ministry of
Information's Film Division generally disliked the series and did what it could
to restrict circulation.[14]

The Army proved a hotbed of intrigue, for career men deeply resented I&E
civilians given high rank just after Pearl Harbor. Osborn spent much of his

time protecting I&E activities from diehard opposition of officers in the field, and rivals in the Signal Corps and Office of War Information, whose activities were termed 'an amazing cloud of double talk, recrimination . . . and no small amount of chicanery.'[15] Osborn wanted morale film but sensed that the proposal of the Signal Corps, for 'John Doughboy, an inspirational poem set to music and picturized,' was not what the doctor ordered.[16]

Even among those of good will, problems of distribution and proper utilisation proved further hindrances. One base might have 50 prints of the same film (49 unneeded) while another had none. The 16mm projector was too fragile for the demands placed upon it in the field. Murphy's Law was also in evidence when it came to spare parts—the various projectors all used different parts and many turned to cannibalisation.

Some commanders thought that film taught as if by magic, or knowingly sabotaged orders that troops see particular films. They would march their troops for six hours, feed them a big meal, place them in an over-heated room and proceed to screen several hours of detailed instructional material. In such a regimen technological innovation was reduced to the subliminal. I&E found that enthusiasts for the potential of audiovisual instruction needed all of their charisma in selling techniques to career officers certain that push-ups were the key to discipline and close-order drill the zenith of creative soldiering.

Hollywood's Frank Capra received the assignment to make the *Why We Fight* films. A Sicilian-born immigrant who studied chemical engineering at the Californian Institute of Technology, Capra had enjoyed a string of commercial hits including *It Happened One Night* (1934), *Mr. Deeds Goes to Town* (1936) and *Mr. Smith Goes to Washington* (1939). Under five feet tall, and up from the bottom, Capra identified with the little guy; to him the American Dream was real and wonderful.[17] A sense of the comic tempered the faith of the zealot. Capra had worked as an editor ('cutter') for comedies in the 1920s; he understood that straight preaching could empty any commercial theatre in the land. The *Why We Fight* films represent Capra's personal values and beliefs. There is humour and plenty of patriotic emotion; the world divides neatly into places where the little guy ('John Q. Public') has a chance against the regimented world of Fascism. The people, we are told in all seven films in the series, will surely triumph over the tyranny of Fascism.

In 1940 Capra accepted a reserve commission in the Army Signal Corps which meant he had made himself available well before Pearl Harbor. Many in Hollywood did the same (someone said they were 'acting like a bunch of kids') though few were directors of Capra's stature.[18] In November 1942 Capra testified under oath about how he got the *Why We Fight* assignment. Because of the distortions in Capra's *Autobiography*, his earlier testimony is worth quoting in full:

Q: What were the circumstances?

A: Of my commissioning? [11 February 1942]

Q: Yes.

A: About a year or two prior to that . . . Colonel Schlossberg of the
      Signal Corps and Colonel Wright had come out in connection with the
      training film program. At that time I expressed to Colonel Schlossberg
      my desire to be of any use that I could in the war program, and that if
      I could be of any use to call upon me. On December 8 . . . 1941, I was
      called upon by Colonel Schlossberg and Captain Si Walters, both of
      the Signal Corps, who were visiting at Warner Brothers where I was
      shooting a picture on the set. They came to me and asked me if I was
      still willing to join the service and I said I was. So I signed an applica-
      tion which they brought out to me then. Subsequently to that, before
      being commissioned they asked me to come to Washington on an
      interview with General Osborn who was then head of the Morale
      Branch. I did, and I met General Osborn and we talked and he told me
      of his program and what he was trying to do, for which I had great
      sympathy, and I agreed to help him in any way that I could. He asked
      that I come into the Army just as soon as I could . . . The first job
      I was assigned to was the putting into film of a series of 15 lectures
      that were to be delivered to the armed forces by the Bureau of Public
      Relations.[19]

   Work began with a group of Hollywood scriptwriters all temporarily
located at the Library of Congress in Washington. In March an optimistic
press release announced that the films would be issued 'twice a month,'
though the final film in the series was not actually released until June 1945.[20]
Capra set to work lining up talent and scrounging film from newsreel companies. The importance of his project, and his knowledge of men in the industry enabled him to get many of the best cutters, screenwriters and directors in
Hollywood.[21]
   Capra was supposed to make documentary films but, he claims, had never
seen one. Records from the Central Files of the Museum of Modern Art Film
Library (MOMA) tell a good deal Capra fails to mention in his unreliable
autobiography. MOMA Curator Iris Barry secured a print of *Triumph of the
Will* on a visit to Germany in 1936.[22] She sent this and other film material to
Washington since editing equipment was located in the cooling tower of the
Department of the Interior (where Capra's friend Edgar Peterson had made a
couple of educational films). Capra and his staff first saw Riefenstahl's film

in the splendid new fifth-floor auditorium of National Archives in March 1942.[23]

Nazi footage had already been translated and analysed at MOMA under a grant arranged by Nelson Rockefeller; Siegfried Kracauer is the best known of those who worked on the project.[24] MOMA learned of additional German footage seized by the Treasury Department and arranged to have it transferred to New York, first telling Capra about this new source. Capra took the footage himself, then refused to let MOMA analysts come to the cooling tower except late at night. In the meantime Richard Griffith, a MOMA employee, formally joined the Capra unit as an expert on compilation footage.[25] MOMA's crucial role (the provision of *Triumph of the Will* alone entitles the Film Library to such recognition) has never been documented since those who planned to tell the story never got around to publishing what they knew.

Editing techniques in *March of Time* obviously influenced Capra. The extensive narration and the recreation of historic events within what purported to be a factual presentation encouraged Capra to find his own style of filmmaking in which many of the distinctions between documentary and fiction film were blurred. Especially influential was *The Ramparts We Watch,* which traced shifts in American attitudes from isolationism to interventionism (the very theme of *War Comes to America* and, less fully, *Prelude to War*). The use of footage from *Feldzug in Polen* not only suggested exactly how to cut enemy footage into one's own propaganda film, but the exact source. Only someone with a poor memory, or the instincts of a showman would, as Capra has, neglect to note the obvious connections with the *Why We Fight* series.[26]

In April Eric Knight joined the Capra unit. Now there was someone well informed about British documentary films who could influence Capra's thinking. Born in England, Knight had been film critic for the Philadelphia *Public Ledger,* and contributor to journals seen by British documentary filmmakers. Knight captured the interest of Paul Rotha, who lectured at MOMA in 1937. Rotha and Knight exchanged thousands of pages of single-spaced letters, only a few of which have appeared in print. Knight saw all of the important British documentaries, either in New York, or on his own trips back to Britain, the last of which took place in autumn 1941. Rotha of course was greatly influenced by John Grierson, chief spokesman for the British documentary movement, who in turn as a young man studied at the University of Chicago where he was specifically introduced to the concept of Social Engineering by political scientist Charles Merriam.[27]

Eric Knight was an extraordinary catalyst in the planning of the *Why We Fight* scripts during the spring and summer of 1942. In May he prepared a detailed analysis of the philosophical bases of propaganda which helped outline basic possibilities just as I&E was setting up shop. Knight argued that 'positive assertion of your beliefs and aims' was more effective than 'refutation of enemy assertions'; he claimed that film is possibly the best means of propaganda for the home front. Film, he added, 'is peculiarly adept at expressing most glibly one of the subtlest tricks of the propagandists: to state a well-known truth, and bracket it with a new truth or a half-truth or a patent lie.'[28] The *Why We Fight* series, from the outset, was created by people immensely intrigued by the way combination of image and narration can be used to make viewers conclude something based as much on emotion as documented fact. Knight knew about filmmaking and scriptwriting, in fact it was he who wrote the scripts for the first four films in the series and not, as Capra remembers, Anthony Veiller. Knight's almost daily letters to his wife during the summer of 1942 provide a fascinating glimpse of how the films were conceived. Knight wrote the *Army Pocket Guide to Britain* in the summer of 1942; the exact wording from the Guide is found in *Battle of Britain*. And Knight had spent time at Fort Sill, Oklahoma, in 1934, seeing how the Army made official training films. Thus Knight could understand, for example, the need for careful explanation of military tactics which might otherwise seem inexplicable to a modern viewer of *Divide and Conquer*. Finally, Knight had long been interested in animation. He was assigned to work at the Disney studio in July 1942 to work out the extraordinary animated inserts for the first four films.[29] The Disney staff considered what they did all in a day's work, but the *Why We Fight* series has the most brilliant animated maps ever to appear in official films; the poor inserts in such war documentary classics as *Desert Victory* (1943) or *San Pietro* (1945) suggest why Disney was indeed the best in the business.

The achievement of the series owes much to others besides Knight and Capra. Anatole Litvak, who directed the *Battle of Russia*, and Veiller were important to the success of each film. Walter Huston and Veiller did the narration (Veiller was the voice of the little guy, or the sceptic). Dimitri Tiomkin, uncharitably termed the 'world's loudest composer,' did the scoring. William Hornbeck, one of Hollywood's most experienced cutters, did the editing. And Capra had a hand in the contents of each film, here insisting on an emotional touch; there, a bit of humour; here, faster pacing; there, music up. Above all, Capra was Mr Film to the Army; he guarded his troops from educational filmmakers in other branches of the service.[30]

A chronology of the making of the series is as follows. In the autumn of 1941 the Army's Bureau of Public Relations prepared 15 orientation lectures on foreign affairs. Right after Pearl Harbor a group of screenwriters met at the Library of Congress to begin putting these lectures into film form. Capra saw some of the available compilation footage in March. In May Knight began revising draft scripts in light of what he knew about documentary films and the compilation footage at hand. During the summer of 1942 Capra, Knight, Litvak and Veiller argued round-the-clock in Hollywood about the wording of the scripts. The conception of the series was fixed by September 1942, some of the scripts in pretty complete form, much of the compilation footage chosen thanks to the work of Richard Griffith. After the spring of 1943, an administrative shakeup put Capra's independent 834th Signal Service Photographic Detachment under the Army Pictorial Service, the latter soon headed by Lyman Munson, Jr, Capra's West Point supervisor at I&E. Now Capra had a hand in every sort of film project that sounded important, and was often out of the country, which meant that the final two *Why We Fight* films were subject to all sorts of delays.[31]

The technical perfection of each film, the time necessary for completion and the expensive production shots were not originally intended. Like Topsy, the series just grew and grew. Knight found what was happening, the arguments and the resulting delays, terribly frustrating, but Capra and Litvak were perfectionists, insisting that their orientation films be the very best possible.[32] In selling the concept of film as a medium for orientation, there is much to recommend Capra's insistence on perfection, but as a result the first in the series, *Prelude to War,* was released only in November 1942. This meant that millions went through basic training without seeing any of the series, though most later saw them at military theatres. It is important to remember that the impact of the series was much greater in quality 35mm prints shown in post theatres, instead of the ancient 16mm copies which are generally available today. As a general proposition, for American soldiers, audiovisual instruction existed mostly on paper until the autumn of 1943. Not only were films not ready, but distribution and effective utilisation remained acute problem areas until that time.

Prelude to War was a big hit. Capra says it was his favourite in the series since after that his favoured position as military filmmaker was assured. Henry Stimson noted in his diary that it was a 'most powerful picture . . . when we came out we felt very somber.' Marshall, Stimson, and the other most significant military leaders in Washington felt that now they had a weapon to win the hearts and minds of their troops. They had no qualms about special pleading; in total war, here was total success. They knew what they were getting because the factual content of the script was subject to endless official supervision. In July 1942 Colonel Herman Beukema, who had supervised the 15 orientation lectures, was sent to the Capra unit to work out details on battle tactics in the scripts.[33] In the Pentagon and other Washington civilian agencies as many as 50 offices checked the contents of each script.

Rough cuts were screened in the Pentagon theatre by Stimson, Marshall, and other high-ranking officers.

Such minute attention from those directing the war is particularly significant.[34] Such concern suggests the need to place film in a prominent place in any overall appraisal of war aims. Such official concern enables us to accept one of Capra's most extreme claims: the *Why We Fight* series really does define American official war aims. Not Capra but official Washington deserves the credit (or blame) for factual omissions, for a varnishing of the truth, for what is conveniently passed over. The films represent a classic example of the strategy of truth so much talked of at the time. Only *The Battle of China* strained everyone's credulity too far. The recall of General Joseph Stillwell made it public knowledge that something was seriously wrong with a film that ignored the existence of the Chinese Communists and pretended that a united China was throwing out the Japanese invader. The film, released in the fall of 1944, was withdrawn briefly, then used anyway. At least 3.75 million people had seen it by 1 July 1945.[35]

Ironically, the research techniques of social science undermined the value of the Capra series. No scientific sample could show that a will to win had been instilled solely through these films.[36] How could one be sure that soldiers had not learned about the nature of the enemy from a thousand other sources of information? All one could prove was a marginal improvement, in those tested, in specific factual details. Was such a little mouse all that emerged from the vast mountain of expenditure? Nobody could say for sure. Nevertheless, 'Why Korea?' and 'Why Vietnam?' films were made, with lower budgets and little evidence of success.[37]

There are two ways of responding to a question about proof that the series increased the patriotic zeal of the viewer (a variant of the immensely-complex problem of relating mass media to political decision-making). One is the brilliant appendix of Ellul's *Propaganda,* where he demolishes the methodology of the scientific sample, asserting that film's effects are much more widespread than any questionnaire can discover and that film's impact relates to group participation in a way that defies sampling.[38]

Some never saw the films; some slept through them; some film enthusiasts worried about theatrical touches; others, perhaps looking for an emotional reason to support official war aims, found the films remarkable. Alfred Kazin, son of Russian immigrants, recalls, some 35 years later, the impact of *The Battle of Russia* on him:

Everything came to a head one glowering winter day [1944] at a great army camp and hospital in southern Illinois. . . . Sitting in the dark post theater, we were all of us at ease; we were at the movies. On the screen, the dear exciting movie screen, best friend many an American ever had, jagged arrow leaped across the map to show the Nazis poised against France in 1940, against England, finally against Russia on June 22, 1941. Loud thunderclaps of music burst against my brain as I sat with hundreds of soldiers in the theater. In the excitement and terror of seeing the large swastika map move across England, I felt together with these men, knew that with the trustworthy old American movie magic working on us like a liberating storm, our political souls were being cleansed and invigorated. We would come out of the theater knowing what was agreed on all sides—that it was our privilege to erase the evil in the world that was Hitler.

Now *The Battle of Russia* comes on, and there it is, the real thing. This is not the visual Walt Disney diagrams. . . . On the sound track, abysmal mourning, low Slavic chords, muttering thunder. On the screen, a dead muddy winter scene as old men and women from a village in the Ukraine stoop over the muddy blood-soaked ravines where their people have been left after being shot by the Nazis. The Russian sky behind them is dark and soggy, rain is coming on, and the villagers bend in agony over their dead. Now they are playing broken chords from the *Pathétique*. Nothing I was to see after the war in Russia and East Berlin, with its vast sarcophagi of Russian soldiers, was to bring out the torment of the Russians in the Hitler war as did those scattered shots from captured Nazi news-reels and Soviet sources which I saw on a snow-soaked day at a camp in Illinois. Sitting in the post theater, embracing Russia as my parents had not been allowed to embrace it, I see coming together the divided forces of the Red Army encir-cling the Germans at Stalingrad. Two long lines of Russian soldiers are running to each other in the snow, hugging each other, bussing each other man to man in the hearty Russian fashion. Stalingrad! Long lines of anti-aircraft guns are lined up in this 'beautiful' ballet of war, the katusha rockets whiz brilliantly through the air, soldiers are slithering through the snow toward a ruined apart-ment house. Doughty, cheeky, round Red Army men, all bundled up in their winter greatcoats, are striding toward victory. The movie makes it easy to sit in southern Illinois and to accept that lovely Russian sacrifice in my behalf. I lose all separateness, feel absolutely at one with the soldiers in that dark theater.

It was a physical shock, walking out of the theater in the gray dripping twilight, watching the men plodding back to their barracks in the last slant of light, to realize how drained I was, how much I had been worked over, appealed to. In the end, as so often happened to us after a terrific American movie, we were stupefied. There was no magic bridge between a snowed-on American sol-dier and the movie he was forced to see about the sufferings of the Old World.[39]

How, as well, can we hope to know the precise impact of this film on Russian audiences—Stalin approved the distribution of this film to commer-cial theatres throughout the Soviet Union in 1944?

There is a second way of responding to the effectiveness of these films, a way social scientists did not choose to explore. We must, as historians, be satisfied with certain kinds of data, none by itself conclusive, relating to distribution, and focus our attention primarily on conception and filmic realisation, for here proper documentation survives, and here we can see the significance of the entire series. The *Why We Fight* series represented a pioneering attempt at standardising orientation; they did a better job of instilling morale than canned lectures—which is not to say that they were superior to an individual commander able to speak brilliantly to his troops. The problem is the inability of any army to find enough such commanders to handle millions of men. In such a situation standardised instruction involving audiovisual techniques is literally the only alternative. And since the series soon was intended to explain war aims to a world audience, it took on obligations far beyond the confines of basic training. Those who have argued that America lacked an emotional involvement in World War II as compared with World War I have surely overlooked the ardent emotionalism of those who sponsored and those who made the *Why We Fight* series.

The worldwide impact of the Capra series suggests how varied the lessons of the past become when one looks from outside one's own culture. Karsten Fledelius says that the Capra series influenced an entire generation of Danish documentary film-makers, and to this day in Denmark is considered a model for effective films of *persuasion*. In 1947, the Soviet director Pudovkin predicted that *Why We Fight*-style films would become a permanent feature of international communications. Montage, based on actuality footage, would break down international barriers. 'I am convinced,' he wrote,

> that this form of the documentary feature film will gain ever-increasing significance in the post-war period, first, because we need no longer doubt that it can be understood by all the peoples of the world, and second, because, thanks to this advantage, it can be widely used for fully and profoundly acquainting peoples with one another and can serve to a very considerable degree in expressing universal ideas in a graphic and striking way.[40]

Such an optimistic prediction, though incorrect, suggests two reasons why tough-minded American scholars who find the emotional patriotism of the series too much to take, are guilty of varying degrees of ethnocentrism. First, the person outside American society sees the *Why We Fight* films as important collective statements of an American mythology to the rest of the world. The films are seen as documents of New Deal ideology, with their exaggerated notions of populist democratic concepts. Secondly, the series suggests a technical means for amplifying leadership; it seems a successful Roosevelt-era device for using technology to lead a mass society. The British documentary film movement favoured cadre propaganda—the vanguard as target, not the masses. Roosevelt and Capra hoped to communicate with the masses of the world, and succeeded.[41]

World War II destroyed Capra as an effective filmmaker. In a recent interview, he offered a convincing explanation for what happened:

> The war was a terrible shock to me. I hated the unnecessary brutality. Women and children being killed, terrified, huddling in fear. Going around dropping bombs on women and children. *What the hell is wrong with us?* I thought that perhaps I had put too much faith in the human race—you know, in the pictures I made. Maybe they were too much as things should be.[42]

The *Why We Fight* series also says something important about technological innovation and the military. We can perceive a central goal of leaders in twentieth-century society—the necessity of providing an educated citizenry a reason why—from these seven films. Film was the chosen tool of enthusiasts for Social Engineering. The Army way, veterans say, is to send ten times as much of everything in hopes that one-tenth will arrive where it can do some good. Those who consider the series tendentious ignore the reality of the need to give citizens an emotional feeling of patriotic community in total war. In Britain, *In Which We Serve* had a demonstrably greater impact than *A Diary for Timothy,* in spite of the latter's subtle artistry.

Each nation in World War II had the major problem of spelling out war aims so as to instil sufficient civilian zeal for sacrifice. Churchill may have been correct in his insistence that nobody ever won a war with his mouth, but World War II was a moment when everyone looked to film in hopes that propaganda might have the desired effect.[43] The *Why We Fight* films defined American war objectives to military and civilian audiences throughout the world in a way Roosevelt's Four Freedoms never could. It is the medium of film which provides the most comprehensive statement of war aims produced in America between 1941 and 1945.

Notes

1. See, for example, James MacGregor Burns, *Roosevelt: The Soldier of Freedom* (New York, 1970); Richard R. Lingeman, *Don't You Know There's a War On? The American Home Front, 1941–1945* (New York, 1970); Richard Polenberg, *War and Society: The United States, 1941–1945* (New York, 1972); John Morton Blum, *V Was for Victory: Politics and American Culture During World War II* (New York, 1976); and Allan M. Winkler, *The Politics of Propaganda: The Office of War Information, 1942–1945* (New Haven, 1977).

2. Geoffrey Perrett, *Days of Sadness, Years of Triumph: The American People 1939–1945* (Baltimore, 1974), pp. 9–12.

3. For the relation between social science and film see Thomas Cripps and David Culbert, 'The Negro Soldier (1944): Film Propaganda in Black and White,' *American Quarterly*, vol. XXXI (Winter, 1979), pp. 616–40; Thomas Cripps, 'Movies, Race, and World War II: *Tennessee Johnson* as an Anticipation of the Strategies of the Civil Rights Movement,' *Prologue*, vol. XIV (Summer, 1982), pp. 49–67; and David Culbert, 'Walt Disney's Private Snafu: The Use of Humor in World War II Army Film,' *Prospects*, vol. I (December, 1975), pp. 80–96.

4. For a good analysis of social engineering see Chapter XVI, 'Science and Democratic Social Structure,' in Robert K. Merton, *Social Theory and Social Structure* (rev. edn, Glencoe, IL., 1957); see also Alvin M. Weinberg, 'Can Technology Replace Social Engineering,' in Albert H. Teich (ed.), *Technology and Man's Future* (New York, 1972), pp. 27–35. For the origin of the term see H. S. Person, 'Engineering,' in Edwin R. A. Seligman *et al.* (eds.), *Encyclopaedia of the Social Sciences*, vols. V–VI (New York, 1931), p. 542.

5. Samuel A. Stouffer *et al.*, *Studies in Social Psychology in World War II: Vol. I The American Soldier: Adjustment During Army Life; Vol. II Combat and Its Aftermath; Vol. III Experiments in Mass Communication; Vol. IV Measurement and Prediction* (Princeton, N.J., 1949–50), vol. I, pp. 65, 57 [hereafter SSP].

6. There is a vast literature about morale and its importance. See Wesley Frank Craven and James Lea Cate (eds.), *Services Around the World*, vol. VII of *The Army Air Forces in World War II* (Washington, DC, 1958), pp. 431–76, for a good introduction to the problem. The scientific study of morale was an outgrowth of World War I. See Edward L. Munson, *The Management of Men: A Handbook on the Systematic Development of Morale and the Control of Human Behavior* (New York, 1921); Munson's son was in I&E and had much to do with the film programme; he too wrote a widely-used guide to morale: Colonel Edward Lyman Munson, Jr, *Leadership for American Army Leaders, The Fighting Forces Series* (rev. edn, Washington, DC, 1944). Alfred Kazin, *New York Jew* (New York, 1979), p. 115.

7. After 1945, Marshall was attacked for being a New Deal liberal because of his involvement with CCC camps. See Senator Joe McCarthy, *The Story of General George Marshall* (n.p., n.d. [Milwaukee, 1952]), pp. 10–11.

8. Report, Osborn to Marshall, 6 August 1945, 9, 319.1 cos, Box 371, Records of the Chief of Staff, Troop Information & Education, RG 319, Modern Military Records, National Archives, Washington, DC; Osborn and A. D. Surles to Chief Signal Officer, 10 December 1941, 062.2 ocsigo, Box 750, A43-B-28, Washington National Records Center, Suitland, Maryland [hereafter *MMR-NA; WNRC*]. On Marshall's intense commitment to the welfare of the average soldier see Forest C. Pogue, *George C. Marshall: Organizer of Victory, 1943–1945* (New York, 1973), in particular pp. 80–114. For a practical guide to government records relating to film production, see David Culbert, 'Note on Government Paper

Records,' pp. 235–43, in Bonnie G. Rowan (ed.), *Scholars' Guide to Washington, D.C. Film and Video Collections* (Washington, DC, 1980).

9. For information about the series see William Murphy, 'The Method of *Why We Fight*,' *Journal of Popular Film*, vol. I (1972), pp. 185–96; also helpful is Karsten Fledelius, *et al.*, '*Why We Fight*: An Example of Wartime Orientation' (Copenhagen, 1974); and Thomas William Bohn, *An Historical and Descriptive Analysis of the Why We Fight Series* (New York, 1977); Richard W. Steele, 'The Greatest Gangster Movie Ever Filmed: *Prelude to War, Prologue*, vol. XI (Winter, 1979), pp. 221–36.

10. Jacques Ellul, *Propaganda: The Formation of Men's Attitudes* (New York, 1973), p. 58. For the relation between film and propaganda see David Culbert (ed.), *Mission to Moscow* (Madison, 1980). Michael Choukas, *Propaganda Comes of Age* (Washington, DC, 1965), p. 37, provides a reasonable definition of propaganda: 'the controlled dissemination of deliberately distorted notions in an effort to induce action favorable to predetermined ends of special interest groups.' Michael Balfour, *Propaganda in War 1939–1945: Organisations, Policies and Publics in Britain and Germany* (London, 1979), p. 421.

11. Ellul, *Propaganda*, pp. xv, 137; Cornford, *Microsmographia Academica: Being a Guide for the Young Academic Politician* (London, 1966), p. 5.

12. Balfour, *Propaganda in War*, p. 422. For a good discussion of the problem see Paul F. Lazarsfeld and Robert K. Merton, 'The Psychological Analysis of Propaganda,' in Writers' Congress, *The Proceedings of the Conference Held in October 1943 Under the Sponsorship of the Hollywood Writers' Mobilization and the University of California* (Berkeley, California, 1944), pp. 362–80.

13. Peter Kenez argued with me about propaganda every waking hour during the Bellagio Conference, to my vast intellectual profit.

14. Mandatory viewing announced in War Department Circular 368, 1942. The War Activities Committee agreed to commercial release of *Prelude to War* on 27 May 1943; *Battle of Russia*, 11 November 1943; *War Comes to America*, 14 June 1945; War Activities Committee, *Movies at War 1945* (New York, 1945). For overseas theatrical distribution of the first five in the series in 'Australia, New Zealand, Tasmania, Egypt and the Middle East, Africa (south of the Equator) and India' see Overseas Motion Picture Bureau Report, 16 November–15 December, 1943, Box 19, entry 6, Records of the Office of War Information, RG 208, *WNRC*; Frances Thorpe and Nicholas Pronay, *British Official Films in the Second World War: A Descriptive Catalogue* (Oxford, 1980), p. 237. Pronay told me at the Bellagio Conference that *War Comes to America* was withheld from British cinemas because of its pronouncements regarding isolationism and the United Nations.

15. Munson to Capra, 17 December 1943, 062.2 ocsigo, Box 49, A45–196; concerning OWI opposition see Nelson Poynter to Lowell Mellett, 10 November 1942, Box 1438, entry 264, RG 208, both in *WNRC*; and Secret Minutes, Meeting of General Council, 10 May 1943, 8, 334 ocs, Box 30, Records of the Office of Chief of Staff, RG 165, *MMR-MA*.

16. Osborn and A. D. Surles to Chief Signal Officer, 10 December 1941, 062.2 ocsigo, Box 750, A43-B28, *WNRC*.

17. Frank Capra, *The Name Above the Title: An Autobiography* (New York, 1971), pp. xi–xii, 3–16; *Movie-Made America: A Cultural History of American Movies* (New York, 1976), pp. 205–14. The newly-opened Frank Capra Archive, Wesleyan University, Middletown, CT, should offer important information about Capra's wartime work. The war years files may be opened to scholars in 1983; Jeanine Basinger, Curator, to author, 22 August 1982.

18. Sol Levinson to Richard Schlossberg, 8 December 1941, 333.9 ig, Box 1161, Records of the Inspector General, RG 159, *WNRC*.

19. Capra verbatim transcript, 25 November 1942, 318, 333.9 ig, Box 1165, RG 159, *WNRC*. Osborn's call on 8 December is corroborated in Army Pictorial Service, *Summary Report on Photographic Activities of the Signal Corps Since August 4, 1941 in the Fields of Motion Pictures and Visual Aids* (typescript, Washington, DC, 26 February 1943, 412, copy in US Army Center for Military History Library, Washington, DC [hereafter *APS Summary Report*]).

20. Press Release, 2 March 1942, 'BPR-War Dept' folder, Box 3, Lowell Mellett Papers, Franklin D. Roosevelt Library, Hyde Park, NY. In Osborn to Chief Signal Officer, 2 March 1942, 062.2 ocsigo, Box 750, A43-B28, *WNRC*, he speaks of 'six 30-minute pictures to emphasize, to supplement, or to substitute for the present fifteen one-hour lectures.' On 1 March Marshall, Capra, and Osborn talked for an hour about the projected films, *APS Summary Report*, 434. The group at the Library of Congress consisted of Jerome Chodorov, John Sanford, Julius and Philip Epstein, Ted Paramore, S. K. Lauren, Leonard Spigelgass, and Capra. Munson to Robert Cutler, 18 August 1945, 062.2 ocsigo, Box 49, A45–196, *WNRC*.

21. Those who wrote drafts of the scripts included John Gunther, William Shirer, Leonard Spigelgass, Anthony Veiller, and Eric Knight. Editors and directors included Merrill White, William Hornbeck, Anatole Litvak and, of course, Capra himself.

22. Details, including the legal contract, are found in 'German folder-UFA,' Central Files, Museum of Modern Art Film Library, New York, NY [hereafter *CF-MOMA*]. I am grateful to Eileen Bowser for opening these records to me.

23. For instance, March 1942: 'Projected 30 reels of German propaganda films from our archive for Capra . . . sent him English transcripts of the commentary and visuals.' April 1942: 'Duped our print of *Triumph des Willens* and provided Major Capra with a print, at cost.' [Iris Barry], 'Special Activities for Government Offices from Jan 42 to Jan 43,' 'OSS' folder, *CF-MOMA*.

24. On 9 March 1942, Richard Griffith sent Capra rough transcriptions of visuals and commentary for *Triumph des Willens, Feldzug in Polen,* and *Flieger, Funker, Kanoniere.* 'They're rather curiously phrased,' he added, 'because Dr. Kracauer wrote them when he was just beginning to learn English.' On 15 March Griffith sent Capra a list of all the stock footage and foreign films he could locate which would be appropriate to each of the 15 orientation lectures. Both in 'War Dept' folder, *CF-MOMA*.

25. [Barry], 'Brief Report of Work by MOMA on Contract OEMcr-112 as of 4 January 1943,' in 'CIAA' folder, *CF-MOMA*.

26. Raymond Fielding, *The March of Time, 1935–1951* (New York, 1978), in particular pp. 243–72.

27. P. Rotha, *Documentary Diary: An Informal History of the British Documentary Film, 1928–1939* (London, 1973), pp. 19–21, 171–212; Rotha (ed.), *Portrait of a Flying Yorkshireman: Letters from Eric Knight in the United States to Paul Rotha in England* (London, 1952); Rachael Low, *Films of Comment and Persuasion of the 1930s* (London, 1979), p. 178. Erik Barnouw helped me gain access to Eric Knight's widow, who has an important collection of Eric Knight Papers in her possession. Bary Karl, *Charles E. Merriam and the Study of Politics* (Chicago, 1975).

28. Munson to Col. Watrous, 26 May 1942, Box 2, Lyman Munson Papers, Manuscript Division, University of Wyoming, Laramie, WY.

29. David Culbert, '"A Quick, Delightful Gink": Eric Knight at the Walt Disney Studio,' *Funnyworld* (No. 19, Fall, 1978), pp. 13–17.

30. The fervour with which Capra viewed his assignment is suggested in a memorandum he sent his unit on 22 August 1942, ending: 'THE GREATEST GLORY THAT CAN COME TO ANY MAN IS TO JOIN THE SERVICE WHEN HIS COUNTRY IS IN DANGER.' 062.2 ocsigo, Box 3, A46–484, *WNRC*; telephone interview with Capra, 18 January 1977. It was only in August 1942 that the series was named *Why We Fight*.

31. 'General Surles . . . "borrowed" Colonel Capra and some of his best men to organize and direct the making of pictures of American troops in combat.' Osborn to Marshall, 12 February 1944, 062.2 ocs, Box 133, RG 165, *MMR-NA*.

32. Knight to Eric Knight, 24 August 1942, Eric Knight Papers, Quakertown, PA [hereafter Knight MSS].

33. Stimson Diary, Yale University, 23 October 1942; telephone interview with Capra, 18 January 1977; Knight to Jere Knight, 21 July 1942, Knight MSS; Munson to Robert Cutler, 18 August 1945.

34. Telephone interviews with General Osborn, 4 November, 5 November 1976; Pogue, *Marshall, Organizer of Victory*, pp. 91–2; Capra, *Name Above the Title*, pp. 325–67.

35. Figures from F. H. Osborn, *Information and Education Division* (privately printed, October 1945), p. 7, copy kindly sent me by General Osborn; telephone interview with Osborn, 10 November 1976; Surles (with concurrence of Osborn) to Munson, 4 January 1945, 062.2 ocsigo, Box 749, A43-B28, *WNRC*.

36. *SSP*, III; interview with Irving Janis (who worked for I&E's Research Branch and helped write *SSP*), New Haven, Connecticut, 7 February 1978.

37. Many films on such subjects are briefly described in DA PAM 108–1, *Index of Army Motion Pictures and Related Auto-Visual Aids* (Washington, DC, January 1977), in particular pp. 154–6, 184–91.

38. Ellul, *Propaganda*, Appendix I, pp. 259–302.

39. Kazin, *New York Jew*, pp. 129–31.

40. Comment at Bellagio Conference session devoted to American film propaganda; Vsevold Pudovkin, 'The Global Film,' *Hollywood Quarterly*, vol. II (July, 1947), p. 330, quoted in William J. Blakefield, 'A History and Analysis of "Know Your Enemy-Japan,"' Master's thesis, University of Maryland, 1981.

41. Comments by Fledelius, Pronay at Bellagio Conference.

42. Quoted (without Karp's interpolations) in Walter Karp, 'The Patriotism of Frank Capra,' *Esquire,* vol. XCV (February 1981), p. 35.

43. Balfour, *Propaganda in War,* p. 437.

9

The Function of
Psychological Warfare

Paul M. A. Linebarger

P sychological warfare, in the broad sense, consists of the application of parts of the science called psychology to the conduct of war; in the narrow sense, psychological warfare comprises the use of propaganda against an enemy, together with such military operational measures as may supplement the propaganda. Propaganda may be described, in turn, as organized persuasion by non-violent means. War itself may be considered to be, among other things, a violent form of persuasion. Thus if an American fire-raid burns up a Japanese city, the burning is calculated to dissuade the Japanese from further warfare by denying the Japanese further physical means of war and by simultaneously hurting them enough to cause surrender. If, after the fire-raid, we drop leaflets telling them to surrender, the propaganda can be considered an extension of persuasion—less violent this time, and usually less effective, but nevertheless an integral part of the single process of making the enemy stop fighting.

Neither warfare nor psychology is a new subject. Each is as old as man. Warfare, being the more practical and plain subject, has a far older written

SOURCE: From Paul M. A. Linebarger, "The Function of Psychological Warfare," in *Psychological Warfare*. New York: Duell, Sloan and Pearce, 1954, pp. 168–174. Published by permission of The Estate of Paul M. A. Linebarger c/o Ralph M. Vicinanza, Ltd.

history. This is especially the case since much of what is now called psychology was formerly studied under the heading of religion, ethics, literature, politics, or medicine. Modern psychological warfare has become self-conscious in using modern scientific psychology as a tool.

In World War II the enemies of the United States were more fanatical than the people and leaders of the United States. The consequence was that the Americans could use and apply any expedient psychological weapon which either science or our version of common sense provided. We did not have to square it with Emperor myths, the Führer principle, or some other rigid, fanatical philosophy. The enemy enjoyed the positive advantage of having an indoctrinated army and people; we enjoyed the countervailing advantage of having skeptical people, with no inward theology that hampered our propaganda operations. It is no negligible matter to be able to use the latest findings of psychological science in a swift, bold manner. The scientific character of our psychology puts us ahead of opponents wrapped up in dogmatism who must check their propaganda against such articles of faith as Aryan racialism or the Hegelian philosophy of history.

Psychological Warfare as a Branch of Psychology. Good propaganda can be conducted by persons with no knowledge of formal psychology. The human touch, the inventive mind, the forceful appeal—things such as these appear in the writings of gifted persons. Thomas Paine never read a word of Freud or Pavlov, yet Paine's arguments during the Revolutionary War played subtly on every appeal which a modern psychologist could catalogue. But war cannot, in modern times, assume a statistical expectation of talent. Psychology makes it possible for the able but ordinary statesman or officer to calculate his persuasion systematically and to obtain by planning those results which greater men might hit upon by genius.

What can psychology do for warfare?

In the first place, the psychologist can bring to the attention of the soldier those elements of the human mind which are usually kept out of sight. He can show how to convert lust into resentment, individual resourcefulness into mass cowardice, friction into distrust, prejudice into fury. He does so by going down to the *unconscious* mind for his source materials. (During World War II, the fact that Chinese babies remain unimpeded while they commit a nuisance, while Japanese babies are either intercepted or punished if they make a mess in the wrong place, was found to be of significant importance in planning psychological warfare.)

In the second place the psychologist can set up techniques for finding out how the enemy really does feel. Some of the worst blunders of history have arisen from miscalculation of the enemy state of mind. By using the familiar statistical and questionnaire procedures, the psychologist can quiz a small cross section of enemy prisoners and from the results estimate the mentality of an entire enemy theater of war at a given period. If he does not have the prisoners handy, he can accomplish much the same end by an analysis of the news and propaganda which the enemy authorities transmit to their own troops and people. By establishing enemy opinion and morale factors he can hazard a reasoned forecast as to how the enemy troops will behave under specific conditions.

In the third place, the psychologist can help the military psychological warfare operator by helping him maintain his sense of mission and of proportion. The deadliest danger of propaganda consists of its being issued by the propagandist for his own edification. This sterile and ineffectual amusement can disguise the complete failure of the propaganda *as* propaganda. There is a genuine pleasure in talking-back, particularly to an enemy. The propagandist, especially in wartime, is apt to tell the enemy what he thinks of him, or to deride enemy weaknesses. But to have told the Nazis, for example, "You Germans are a pack of murderous baboons and your Hitler is a demented oaf. Your women are slobs, your children are halfwits, your literature is gibberish and your cooking is garbage," and so on, would have stiffened the German will to fight. The propagandist must tell the enemy those things which the enemy will heed; he must keep his private emotionalism out of the operation. The psychologist can teach the propaganda operator how to be objective, systematic, cold. For combat operations, it does not matter how much a division commander may dislike the enemy; for psychological warfare purposes, he must consider how to persuade them, even though he may privately thirst for their destruction. The indulgence of hatred is not a working part of the soldier's mission; to some it may be helpful; to others, not. The useful mission consists solely of making the enemy stop fighting, by combat or other means. But when the soldier turns to propaganda, he may need the advice of a psychologist in keeping his own feelings out of it.

Finally, the psychologist can prescribe media—radio, leaflets, loud-speakers, whispering agents, returned enemy soldiers, and so forth. He can indicate when and when not to use any given medium. He can, in conjunction with operations and intelligence officers, plan the full use of all available psychological resources. He can coordinate the timing of propaganda with military, economic or political situations.

The psychologist does not have to be present in person to give this advice. He does not have to be a man with an M.D. or Ph.D. and years of postgraduate training. He can be present in the manuals he writes, in the indoctrination courses for psychological warfare officers he sets up, in the current propaganda line he dictates by radio. It is useful to have him in the field, particularly at the higher command headquarters, but he is not indispensable. The psychologist in person can be dispensed with; the methods of scientific psychology cannot. (Further on, throughout this book, reference will be made to current psychological literature. The general history of psychology is described in readable terms in Gregory Zilboorg and George W. Henry, *A History of Medical Psychology,* New York, 1947, and in Lowell S. Selling, *Men Against Madness,* New York, 1940, cheap edition, 1942.)

Propaganda can be conducted by rule of thumb. But only a genius can make it work well by playing his hunches. It can become true psychological warfare, scientific in spirit and developed as a teachable skill, only by having its premises clearly stated, its mission defined, its instruments put in systematic readiness, and its operations subject to at least partial check, only by the use of techniques borrowed from science. Of all the sciences, psychology is the nearest, though anthropology, sociology, political science, economics, area studies and other specialties all have something to contribute; but it is psychology which indicates the need of the others.

Psychological Warfare as a Part of War. An infantry officer does not need to study the whole nature of war, in order to find his own job. Tradition, military skill, discipline, sound doctrine—these have done the job for him. Sun Tzu, Vegetius, Frederick, Clausewitz and a host of lesser writers on war have established the place of combat in war, and have appraised its general character.

How much the traditional doctrines may be altered in the terrible light of atomic explosion, no one knows; but though the weapons are novel, the wielders of the weapons will still be men. The motives and weaknesses within war remain ancient and human, however novel and dreadful the mechanical expedients adopted to express them.

Warfare as a whole is traditionally well defined, and psychological warfare can be understood only in relation to the whole process. It is no mere tool, to be used on special occasion. It has become a pervasive element in the military and security situation of every power on earth.

Psychological warfare is a part of war. The simplest, plainest thing which can be said of war—any sort of war, anywhere, anytime—is that it is *an official fight between men.* Combat, killing, and even large-scale group struggle are known elsewhere in the animal kingdom, but war is not. All sorts of creatures fight; but only men declare, wage, and terminate war; and they do so only against other men.

Formally, war may be defined as the "reciprocal application of violence by public, armed bodies."

If it is not *reciprocal,* it is not war, the killing of persons who do not defend themselves is not war, but slaughter, massacre, or punishment.

If the bodies involved are not *public,* their violence is not war. Even our enemies in World War II were relatively careful about this distinction, because they did not know how soon or easily a violation of the rules might be scored against them. To be public, the combatants need not be legal—that is, constitutionally set up; it suffices, according to international usage, for the fighters to have a reasonable minimum of numbers, some kind of identification, and a purpose which is political. If you shoot your neighbor, you will be committing mere murder; but if you gather twenty or thirty friends, together, tie a red handkerchief around the left arm of each man, announce that you are out to overthrow the government of the United States, and *then* shoot your neighbor as a counterrevolutionary impediment to the new order of things, you can have the satisfaction of having waged war. (In practical terms, this means that you will be put to death for treason and rebellion, not merely for murder.)

Finally, war must be *violent.* According to the law of modern states, all the way from Iceland to the Yemen, economic, political, or moral pressure is not war; war is the legalization, in behalf of the state, of things which no individual may lawfully do in time of peace. As a matter of fact, even in time of war you cannot kill the enemy unless you do so on behalf of the state; if you had shot a Japanese creditor of yours privately, or even shot a Japanese soldier when you yourself were out of uniform, you might properly and lawfully have been put to death for murder—either by our courts or by the enemies'. (This is among the charges which recur in the war trials. The Germans and Japanese killed persons whom even war did not entitle them to kill.)

The governments of the modern world are jealous of their own monopoly of violence. War is the highest exercise of that violence, and modern war is no simple reversion to savagery. The General Staffs would not be needed if war were only an uncomplicated orgy of homicide—a mere getting-mad and throat-cutting season in the life of man. Quite to the contrary, modern war—as a function of modern society—reflects the institutional, political complexity from which it comes. A modern battle is a formal, ceremonialized and technically intricate operation. You must kill just the right people, in just the right way, with the right timing, in the proper place, for avowed purposes. Otherwise you make a mess of the whole show, and—what is worse—you lose.

Why must you fight just so and so, there and not here, now and not then? The answer is simple: you are fighting against *men.* Your purpose in fighting is to make them change their minds. It is figuratively true to say that the war we have just won was a peculiar kind of advertising campaign, designed to make the Germans and Japanese like us and our way of doing things. They did not like us much, but we gave them alternatives far worse than liking us, so that they became peaceful.

Sometimes individuals will be unpersuadable. Then they must be killed or neutralized by other purely physical means—such as isolation or imprisonment. (Some Nazis, perhaps including the Führer himself, found our world repellent or incomprehensible and died because they could not make themselves surrender. In the Pacific many Japanese had to be killed before they became acceptable to us.) But such is man, that most individuals will stop fighting at some point short of extinction; that point is reached when one of two things happens:

Either, the defeated people may lose their sense of organization, fail to decide on leaders and methods, and give up because they can no longer fight as a group. This happened to the American Southerners in April, 1865. The President and Cabinet of the Confederate States of America got on the train at Richmond; the men who got off farther down the line were "refugees." Something happened to them and to the people about them, so that Mr. Davis no longer thought of himself as President Davis, and other people no longer accepted his commands. This almost happened in Germany in 1945 except for Admiral Doenitz.

Or, the defeated people can retain their sense of organization, and can use their political organization for the purpose of getting in touch with the enemy, arranging the end of the war, and preparing, through organized means, to comply with the wishes of the conquerors. That happened when Britain acknowledged American independence; when the Boers recognized British sovereignty; when Finland signed what Russia had dictated; and when Japan gave up.

Sometimes these things are mixed. The people might wish to make peace, but may find that their government is not recognized by the enemy. Or the victors may think that they have smashed the enemy government, when the new organization is simply the old one under a slightly different name, but with the old leaders and the old ideas still prevailing.

It is plain that whatever happens wars are fought to effect a psychological change in the antagonist. They are then fought for a psychological end unless they are wars of extermination. These are rare. The United States could not find a people on the face of the earth whose ideas and language were unknown to all Americans. Where there is a chance of communication, there is always the probability that one of the antagonistic organizations (governments)—which have already cooperated to the extent of meeting one another's wishes to fight—will subsequently cooperate on terms of primary advantage to the victors. Since the organizations comprise human beings with human ways of doing things, the change must take place in the minds of those specific individuals who operate the existing government, or in the minds of enough other people for that government to be overthrown.

The fact that war is waged against the minds, not the bodies, of the enemy is attested by the comments of military writers of all periods. The dictum of Carl von Clausewitz that "war is politics continued by other means" is simply the modern expression of a truth recognized since antiquity. War is a kind of persuasion—uneconomical, dangerous, and unpleasant, but effective when all else fails.

Ideology. An ideology is a system of deep-rooted beliefs about fundamental questions in human life and affairs.[1] Ideology also plays a part in psychological warfare. A difference in beliefs which does not touch fundamentals is commonly termed a difference of *opinion*. You may believe in high tariffs; and I, in no tariff. You may believe in One World; I may not. You may support Republicans; I, Democrats. Despite these differences both of us can still believe in dollars as a method of paying income, in marriage as a system of setting up the family, in private property for most goods industrial or personal, in the Government of the United States, in majority rule, in democratic elections, in free speech, and so on.

If our difference of opinion is so inclusive that we can agree on nothing political, our differences have gone from mere opinion into the depths of *ideology*. Here the institutional framework is affected. You and I would not want to live in the same city; we could not feel safe in one another's presence; each would be afraid of the effect which the other might have on the morals of the community. If I were a Nazi, and you a democrat, you would not like the idea of my children living next door to yours. If I believed that you were a good enough creature—poor deluded devil—but that you were not fit to vote, scarcely to be trusted with property, not to be trusted as an army officer, and generally subversive and dangerous, you would find it hard to get along with me.

It was not metaphysical theories that made Protestants and Catholics burn one another's adherents as heretics in early wars. In the seventeenth century, the Protestants knew perfectly well what would happen if the Catholics got the upper hand, and the Catholics knew what would happen if the Protestants came to power. In each case the new rulers, fearful that they might be overthrown, would have suppressed the former rulers, and would have used the rack, the stake, and the dungeon as preventives of counterrevolution. Freedom cannot be accorded to persons outside the ideological pale. If an antagonist is not going to respect your freedom of speech, your property, and your personal safety, then you are not obliged to respect his. The absolute minimum of any ideology is the assumption that each person living in an ideologically uniform area (what the Nazi General Haushofer, following Rudolf Kjellen, would call a *geo-psychic* zone) will respect the personal safety, etc., of other individuals in the same area.

In our own time, we have seen Spaniards get more and more mistrustful of one another, until years of ferocious civil war were necessary before one of the two factions could feel safe. Spain went from republican unity to dictatorial unity in four years; in neither case was the unity perfect, but it was enough to give one government and one educational system control of most of the country. The other countries of the world vary in the degree of their ideological cohesion. Scandinavia seemed serene until the German invasion brought to the surface cleavages, latent and unseen, which made Quisling a quisling. Russia, Italy, Germany and various other states have made a fetish of their ideologies and have tried to define orthodoxy and heresy in such a way as to be sure of the mentality of all their people. But most of the countries of the world suffer from a considerable degree of ideological confusion—of instability of basic beliefs—without having any immediate remedy at hand, or even seeking one.

Education. Education is a process usually institutional by which the people of a given area transmit to their successors, their own children, the purely practical information needed in modern life, together with a lot of other teachings designed to make good men and women, good citizens, good Christians or other believers, of them. In the democratic states this process is ideological only in some parts of the curriculum; elsewhere in the field of opinions, the government seeks to control ideology only negatively—through laws concerning obscenity, blasphemy, subversion, and so on.

In the states which are ideologically self-conscious and anxious to promote a fixed mentality, the process of education is combined with agitation and regulation, so that the entire population lives under conditions approximating the psychological side of war. Heretics are put to death or are otherwise silenced. Historical materialism and the Marxian "objectivity," or the *Volk*, or *Fascismo*, or *Yamato-damashii*, or "new democracy" is set up as the touchstone of all good and evil, even in unrelated fields of activity. Education and propaganda merge into everlasting indoctrination. And when such states go to war against states which do not have propaganda machinery, the more liberal states are at a disadvantage for sheer lack of practice in the administrative and mechanical aspects of propaganda. Education is to psychological warfare what a glacier is to an avalanche. The mind is to be in both cases captured, but the speed and techniques differ.

Salesmanship. Salesmanship is related to psychological warfare. Propaganda is often compared to another art of our time—industrialized salesmanship through mass printing and telecommunications. This bad parallel was responsible for much of the inept American propaganda overseas in the early part of the war; some of our propagandists had a fundamental misconception of the nature of wartime propaganda.

Allegiance in war is a matter of ideology, not of opinion. A man cannot want his own side to lose while remaining a good citizen in all other respects. The desire for defeat—even the acceptance of defeat—is of tragic importance to any responsible, sane person. A German who wanted the Reich to be overthrown was a traitor to Germany, just as any American who wished us to pull out of the war and exterminate American Jews would have been a traitor to his own country. These decisions cannot be compared with the choice of a toothpaste, a deodorant, or a cigarette.

Advertising succeeds in peacetime precisely because it does not matter; the choice which the consumer makes is of slight importance to himself, even though it is of importance to the seller of the product. A Dromedary cigarette and an Old Coin cigarette are both cigarettes; the man is going to smoke one anyhow. It does not matter so much to him. If Dromedaries are associated in his mind with mere tobacco, while Old Coins call up unaccountable but persistent memories of actresses' legs, he may buy Old Coins. The physical implements of propaganda were at hand in 1941–1942, but we Americans had become so accustomed to their use for trivial purposes that much of our wartime propaganda was conducted in terms of salesmanship.

In a sense, however, salesmanship does serve the military purpose of accustoming the audience to appeals both visual and auditory. The consequence is that competing, outside propaganda can reach the domestic American audience only in competition with the local advertising. It is difficult for foreign competition to hold attention amid an almost limitless number of professionally competent commercial appeals. A Communist or Fascist party cannot get public attention in the United States by the simple expedient of a "mass meeting" of three hundred persons, or by the use of a few dozen posters in a metropolitan area. Before the political propagandist can get the public attention, he must edge his media past the soap operas, the soft drink advertisements, the bathing beauties advertising Pennsylvania crude or bright-leaf tobacco. The consequence is that outside propaganda either fails to get much public attention, or else camouflages itself to resemble and to exploit existing media. Clamorous salesmanship deadens the American citizen to his own government's propaganda, and may to a certain extent lower his civic alertness; but at the same time, salesmanship has built up a psychological Great Wall which excludes foreign or queer appeals and which renders the United States almost impervious to sudden ideological penetration from overseas.

Psychological Warfare and Public Relations. Psychological warfare and public relations are different in the direction in which they apply. Psychological warfare is designed to reach the enemy. Public relations is designed primarily to reach the home audience. Both reach neutrals, sometimes confusingly much. In some nations, the two functions were combined in a single instrumentality, as in the Japanese *Joho Kyoku*. The American army and navy traditions of public relations are based on the ideas that the news should be as complete as military security may permit, that it should be delivered speedily and interestingly, that it should enhance the confidence of the people in their armed services, and that its tenor (no less than its contents) should not aid the enemy morale. These ideas are justified in terms of sound newspaper practice, but they can lead to a weak psychological warfare position when we must deal with an inventive and enterprising enemy.

It is not possible to separate public relations from psychological warfare when they use the same media. During World War II, the Office of War Information prepared elaborate water-tight plans for processing war news to different audiences; at their most unfortunate, such plans seemed to assume that the enemy would listen only to the OWI stations, and that the American public releases issued from the Army and Navy would go forth to the world without being noted by the enemy. If a radio in New York or San Francisco presented a psychological warfare presentation of a stated battle or engagement, while the theater or fleet public relations officer presented a very different view, the enemy press and radio were free to choose the weaker of the two, or to quote the two American sources against each other.

Psychological Warfare and Morale Services. All modern armies, in addition to public relations, also employ morale services facilities—officers or employees whose function it is to supply troops with entertainment, educational materials, political indoctrination, and other attention-getting materials. Morale services are the prime overt defense against enemy psychological warfare, and by a program of keeping the attention of the troops, can prevent the enemy from establishing effective communication. During World War II, the Armed Forces Radio Service of the United States established global radio service for Americans, and incidentally turned out material of top importance to United States propaganda. Naturally, enemy and allied peoples would pay more serious heed to communications from Americans *to* Americans than they would to materials which they knew had been concocted for themselves. The American morale services in the last war indignantly rejected the notion that they were a major propaganda facility, rightfully insisting that their audience counted on getting plain information, plain news, and plain education without ulterior propaganda content. The fact that in a theater of war *all communication has propaganda effect* was not always taken into account, and only on one or two critical occasions was there coordination of stress and timing.

It must be said, however, that propaganda by any other name is just as sweet, and that the conviction of the propagandist that he is not a propagandist can be a real asset. Morale services provided the American forces with news, entertainment, and educational facilities. Most of the time these morale facilities had huge parasitical audiences—the global kibitzers who listened to our broadcasts, read our magazines, bought our paper-bound books on the black markets. (It was a happy day for Lienta University at Kunming, Yünnan, when the American Information and Education set-up began shipping in current literature. The long-isolated Chinese college students found themselves deluged with good American books.)

The morale services lost the opportunity to ram home to their G.I.-plus-foreign audience some of the more effective points of American psychological warfare, but they gained *as propagandists* by not admitting, even to themselves, that they *were* propagandists. Since the United States has no serious inward psychological cleavages, the general morale services function coordinated automatically with the psychological warfare function simply because both were produced by disciplined, patriotic Americans.

In the experience of the German and Soviet armies, morale services were parts of a coordinated propaganda machine which included psychological warfare, public relations, general news, and public education. In the Japanese armies, morale services were directed most particularly to physical and sentimental comforts (edible treats, picture postcards, good luck items) which bore little immediate relation to news, and less to formal propaganda.

Related Civilian Activities. In a free nation, the big media of communication will remain uncoordinated even in time of war. The press, the stage, motion-pictures, part of the radio, book publishing and so on will continue. Psychological warfare has in such private facilities a constantly refreshed source of new material for news or for features. By a sparing but well considered liaison with censorship, psychological warfare can effect negative control of non-governmental materials, and can prevent the most overt forms of enemy propaganda from circulating on the home front.

News becomes propaganda when the person issuing it has some purpose in doing so. Even if the reporters, editors, writers involved do not have propaganda aims, the original source of the news (the person giving the interview; the friends of the correspondents, etc.) may give the news to the press with definite purposes in mind. It is not unknown for government officials to shift their rivalries from the conference room to the press, and to provide on-the-record or off-the-record materials which are in effect *ad hoc* propaganda campaigns. A psychological warfare campaign must be planned on the assumption that these civilian facilities will remain in being, and that they will be uncoordinated; the plan must allow in advance for interference, sometimes of a very damaging kind, which comes from private operations in the same field. The combat officers can get civilian cars off the road when moving armored forces into battle but the psychological warfare officer has the difficult task of threading his way through civilian radio and other communication traffic over which he has no control.

Psychological warfare is also closely related to diplomacy. It is an indispensable ingredient of strategic deception. In the medical field, psychological warfare can profit by the experiences of the medical corps. Whenever a given condition arises among troops on one side, comparable troops on the other are apt to be facing the same condition; if the Americans are bitten by insects, the same insects will bite the enemy, and enemy soldiers can be told how much better the American facilities are for insect repulsion. Finally, psychological warfare is intimately connected with the processing of prisoners of war and with the protection of one's own captured personnel.

Psychological warfare is a field to itself, although it touches on many sciences and overlaps with all the other functions of war. It is generally divisible into three topics: the general scheme of psychological warfare, the detection and analysis of foreign psychological warfare operations, and the tactical or immediate conduct of psychological warfare. It must be remembered, however, that psychological warfare is not a closed operation which can be conducted in private, but that—to be effective—psychological warfare output must be a part of the everyday living and fighting of the audiences to which it is directed.

Note

1. In his *The Political Doctrines of Sun Yat-sen*, Baltimore, 1937, page 17 and following, this author attempted to present some of the relationships of ideology to other methods of social control and, in connection with that enterprise, was furnished by the philosopher, A. O. Lovejoy, with a definition of "ideology" more systematic and more elaborate than the one used here.

10

Brainwashing: The Korean POW Controversy and the Origins of a Myth

Garth S. Jowett

Origins of the Term

The concept of "brainwashing" has been a lingering problem in the field of propaganda studies since the 1950s, when it was first introduced. While there are many definitions of *brainwashing,* depending on the ideological perspective of the user of the term, in general it pertains to the use of coercive psychological techniques to forcibly alter a person's beliefs and behavior, usually to achieve some political objective. The term initially came into wide use in the 1950s to describe the techniques used by the Chinese communists to bring about major alterations in the ideological attitudes and behavior of its vast population following the success of the communist revolution in 1949. Later, its use was extended to describe the psychological "torture" of foreigners imprisoned in communist China after the revolution and finally it found its greatest impact in the United States as an explanation for the disturbing behavior of many American POWs taken captive in the Korean War.

In the 1960s, the term *brainwashing* was used to describe a wide range of coercive persuasion techniques that new religious movements used to attract and convert inductees. The unexpected success of these groups, often called "cults," and the widespread publicity and concern about their growth and their apparent appeal for large numbers of young people demanded an answer. Brainwashing, or "mind control" as it was often called, was offered as a possible explanation when no other psychological explanations were able to adequately explain the process of conversion and submergence into religious movements. Gradually, as a result of serious scientific research and much discussion in the fields of psychology and psychiatry, the term fell out of favor as a serious scientific concept and is seldom used by reputable scientists today (Bromley & Richardson, 1980). The term has always been rather vague, and undoubtedly its association with the concept of propaganda has further tainted it beyond scientific redemption. Nevertheless, throughout the Cold War, the concept of brainwashing was a popular and common theme and provided a sinister undertone to how the West viewed the methodologies and strategies associated with communist propaganda activities.

There is almost universal agreement that the term is attributed to Edward Hunter (1902–1978), who, on September 19, 1950, published an article in the *Miami Daily News* titled "Brainwashing Tactics Forced Chinese Into Ranks of Communist Party." This article contained the first known printed utilization of this ambiguous but provocative term. Hunter, a rather enigmatic figure, was a CIA propaganda operator who worked undercover as a journalist and who had spent several years in China and Japan. For further examples of his work in this field, see Hunter (1951) and Hunter (1956). In an appearance before the Committee on Un-American Activities in 1958, Hunter described how he had developed the term *brainwashing*. He was interviewing individuals who had escaped from communist China in 1950 when one young man used the phrase *hsi nao* or "washed brain." Hunter noted,

> I immediately stopped him, asking what he meant. He laughed and said no that's nothing; it's only something we say when close relatives or friends get together. When somebody said something the paper or someone in government wouldn't like, a relative or friend was libel to say to him to watch out you'll get your brains washed. That was the first time I heard the word brainwashing. I was the first to use the word in writing in any language, and the first to use it in a speech in any language except for that small group of Chinese. That word and its connotation, against this background that I had been weaving ever since I started in journalism, especially during the years since the Civil War in China became acute, was like a streak of lightning, clarifying the pattern of which I had already discerned its shadows. Brainwashing was the new procedure, built up out of all earlier processes of persuasion, using the Pavlovian approach to make people react in a way determined by a central authority, exactly as bees in the hive. (*Communist Psychological Warfare*, 1958, p. 14)

The Korean War POW Controversy

The Korean War began on June 25, 1950, when the North Korean army marched across the border into South Korea on a false pretense that it had been attacked first. The United Nations, after a heated debate, was able to assemble an international force to go to the aid of the South Koreans in what was initially deemed to be only a "police action." The United States contributed more than 80% of the men and military equipment for this United Nations force. During the 3-year conflict, 1.8 million American servicemen and women were involved in this theater of war. The conflict was an unexpectedly bitter one waging up and down the Korean peninsula, the first real military confrontation between the forces of communism and capitalism. After an initial series of unexpected defeats, the American forces pushed the North Koreans back up the peninsula almost to the Yalu River near the Chinese border. This aggressive move precipitated an unexpected reaction when a force of well over 1 million Chinese soldiers poured over the border from China to join the battle. The war continued until June 1953, when the United Nations command and communist forces signed an armistice ending 3 years of fierce fighting in what were often very harsh geographical and climatic conditions. (There has never been an official ending to the war, and the armistice is still in force today.)

One of the unexpected aspects to emerge from the war was the controversial treatment of POWs on both sides. For the communists, the issue centered on the controversial policy approved by President Harry Truman known as "voluntary repatriation." Although this was contrary to the 1947 Geneva Convention on the treatment of enemy prisoners of war, which mandated the wholesale exchange of all POWs at the conclusion of a conflict, Truman's policy proved to be highly successful. In the end, nearly 50,000 North Korean and Chinese POWs dealt a severe propaganda defeat to their communist governments by choosing not to return to their homelands. Most of the Chinese defectors elected to go to the island of Fomosa, now known as Taiwan. The Chinese and North Koreans naturally objected very strongly to this, but it was carried out, and the discussion of the POW exchanges proved to be a sticking point at the lengthy armistice negotiations.

For the Americans, two related issues ultimately resulted in enormous hand-wringing and acrimony on the home front. In September 19, 1953, at the time that the POWs were being exchanged and repatriated on both sides, 23 American POWs refused repatriation, thus sparking an extensive debate among journalists, military officials, politicians, psychiatrists, and the soldiers themselves. The American military was surprised at this turn of events and held the men for a 90-day cooling-off period in the neutral military zone in

Panmunjom. For the next 3 months, the men were subjected to visits from military officials and politicians, as well as letters from their families begging them to reconsider. At the end of this period, only 2 of the men changed their minds, and the remaining 21 journeyed with their captors to China. The defection of these 21 men was immediately attributed to the effectiveness of the brainwashing techniques of their Chinese captors, and only later were more serious in-depth examinations made of the reasons for this unprecedented event.

On a much larger scale, this specter of brainwashing hung over the assessment of the behavior of all American POWs in the conflict. There were 7,190 American prisoners of war, and approximately 2,730 had died in captivity. This was a higher death rate than in any previous war. What was equally disturbing was a continued series of reports that the great majority of the American prisoners had in some way collaborated with their captors. As these revelations were made public, the mood in the press shifted away from sympathy for the POWs to one of suspicion and condemnation. This shift in journalistic perspectives, and ultimately the public's attitude, was precipitated to a large extent by a change in military policy away from lenient treatment of the collaborators toward a harsher program of pressing charges against those suspected of collaboration with the enemy. In the end, 13% of returning U.S. POWs were subjected to investigation on charges of collaboration; however, of the 565 cases, only 57 men were found guilty. Nonetheless, this did not stop the growing belief that collaboration had been widespread and that this was the result of something fundamentally unsound in the American psyche and culture.

There is little doubt that most American POWs were subjected to a great deal of both physical and psychological coercion while being held captive. In the early part of the war, the North Koreans treated their prisoners extremely harshly, killing a significant percentage of them either through deliberate murder or by physical neglect. Once the Chinese entered into the conflict and took over most of the prison camps, the conditions for the prisoners improved to some degree. The Chinese seldom resorted to killing their prisoners, but they did resort to a variety of coercive techniques to obtain information, destroy cohesiveness among the prisoners, sow seeds of ideological doubt about both the war and capitalism itself, and ultimately undermine the will to fight. The latter objective was so successful that no American prisoner of war successfully escaped from a Chinese prison camp, and there were few organized protests within these camps. (This is in marked contrast to the North Korean and Chinese POWs, who maintained rigid discipline in their camps and were constantly harassing their American guards.)

The Chinese techniques of coercive persuasion or brainwashing were well conceived, no doubt as a result of the extensive experience the Chinese had from using such techniques in their own country in the previous 2 years. Peter Watson (1978, p. 291), in his excellent book *War on the Mind,* summarized these procedures:

> The Chinese chose as directors of the brainwashing programs persons who had been educated in the United States during the previous 10 to 15 years and so understood the American mind and way of life. To begin with squads of captured American personnel would be placed in a general camp. The first efforts were directed at destroying the unity of the squad; leaders would be discouraged from acting as leaders and if they persisted would be moved to a special camp for "reactionaries." (It has to be remembered that all the time the prisoners were uncertain as to their fate: the dread of being killed no doubt made a personal situation much worse than it must appear to the reader.) Another tactic was the development of the informer system. The Communist understood enough group dynamics to know that in any group someone would turn informer from his own personal needs—to gain satisfaction, to feel superior and so forth. But they also ensured that, in the early stages at least, no one suffered as a result of informing. All they would do was have a chat with the man who had been informed upon and say that they realize he was really a "victim" of society and sympathize to an extent. This ensured two things: first, that the informant was not picked upon by his fellow group members and thus information kept coming in; second, longer term prisoners cease to trust anyone. This helped to break up the group, added to the soldiers' insecurity and anxiety, and made thought reform that much easier. (p. 291)

It was at this point that the indoctrination sessions were introduced. These consisted of both formal lessons and informal talks sessions and were designed to undermine the belief system of the prisoners. Initially, all the prisoners, after expecting death or torture, were informed that they were not to blame for the war personally, as they were merely pawns of the "imperialist Wall Street warmongers." While this may not seem terribly convincing, to those who had just been spared from death, it could have had a much more significant meaning. From all of the analysis done after the war on the nature of the "lessons" offered to the prisoners, it appears as if the emphasis was not so much on instilling ideological communism as it was in undermining the credibility of the United States. What was surprising is that very little communist literature was used, despite what we might see in movie depictions of Chinese POWs camps; instead, articles from the American press and American literature were used—*Time,* the *Wall Street Journal, Fortune,* and similar publications. The intention here was clear—to show the inherent contradictions in American life, emphasizing the difference in class structure, and attempting to sow doubt as to why they were imprisoned while others were making money back home. (Black prisoners, now part of the newly integrated

Figure 10.1   The Korean War POWs were subjected to lengthy and tiring lectures that were designed not so much to create change but to instill doubt about the capitalist system. Attendance at these daily (and sometimes twice-daily) lectures was mandatory. There was almost no evidence that these lectures had any large-scale effect, except as a means of controlling the POWs through the lethargy that comes with boredom.

U.S. Army, were subjected to lengthy lectures about the history of slavery and racism, conditions with which there were only too familiar, and therefore these revelations had very little impact on them.)

The psychological pressures applied to the prisoners consisted of not only long hours of communist indoctrination and study sessions but also intensive interrogations at all hours, which resulted in sleep deprivation. The men were also forced to write confessions of their complicity in the war and "self-criticisms" of their actions. Captured Air Force pilots were under intense pressure to sign confessions indicating their complicity in spreading germ warfare by dropping such weapons on North Korea. Unfortunately, under such duress, several pilots did sign such statements and appeared before international newsreel cameras to verify their confessions. After repatriation, all of these men recanted their confessions, claiming that they thought they would be sent home earlier or that this was one way to let their families know that they were alive; some even claimed that they knew that such charges would never be believed. Unfortunately, these germ warfare confessions only added to what had become a raging international controversy about the practice of

Figure 10.2   At the conclusion of lectures, the POWs were formed into discussion groups to further their understanding of the ideological arguments being put forth. Here too, there was little evidence that these discussions were seriously intended to bring about a massive shift in opinion; rather, they served to occupy the POW's time in nonproductive ways.

germ warfare on the part of the United States. Fifty years later, this issue remains unresolved and still has many people believing that the United States did drop biological weapons during the Korean War.

One issue that became a central focus of the analysis of American POWs' actions was the amount of physical torture used to bring about the collaboration and complacency that had been exhibited. There is little doubt that the North Koreans, when they had control of the POWs at the beginning of the war, were brutal and engaged in deliberate extermination. This has been attributed not only to a lack of facilities to hold the prisoners but also to a breakdown in the command system and the callousness of Oriental peasant soldiers (Hinkle & Wolff, 1957, p. 168). Once the Chinese took control of the prisoners, there was little evidence of such systematic brutality, and the emphasis shifted to more subtle physical torture, such as forcing individuals to stand at attention for long periods.

An enormous amount of time was spent attempting to indoctrinate the POWs, leading to the following question: What did this brainwashing achieve? It surely was not the intent of the Chinese to convert the majority of prisoners to communism. There is some evidence that the Chinese were able to obtain quite a bit of useful military information from prisoners who cooperated in providing detailed histories of themselves, but this obviously did not have a major impact on the outcome of the conflict. However, what is reasonably clear from the postwar studies of POW behavior is that they were quite successful in creating enough confusion and doubt in the minds of prisoners to reduce the potential for large-scale conflict and escape attempts in the prison camps, thus reducing the need for a large number of Chinese guards, who could be much more useful on the battlefront.

What was interesting to social scientists and psychiatrists regarding the effectiveness of the brainwashing was that it was culture specific to the American prisoners of war. There were prisoners taken from the other countries participating in the United Nations forces who were not as severely affected by this psychological coercion. The most famous of these groups were the several hundred Turkish soldiers imprisoned under very similar conditions and who survived almost to a man. The Turks maintained military and self-discipline, as well as a strong sense of cultural coherence. Perhaps it was because they did not relate to the communism versus capitalism argument or to the concept that rich Turks were behind the war that caused them to be immune to the brainwashing strategies of the Chinese. Eventually, the Chinese simply gave up on any indoctrination activities for the Turkish soldiers. Even the British soldiers, who one would imagine had similar values to the Americans, were not as deeply affected, with only one British soldier refusing to be repatriated at the conclusion of the conflict.

In a study undertaken by Major William Mayer, a U.S. Army psychiatrist who served in Korea and who researched almost 1,000 cases of POWs forcibly indoctrinated in North Korea, he was able to discern that the American soldiers had defects in three basic areas:

> In character development and self discipline; in general education, particularly about the operation of a democracy and the multi-cultural role of the world; and in military preparedness—while good on weapons and tactics and so on, they were weak on the psychological and moral side of war. These points have implications for the training of resistance to interrogation and brainwashing. (Watson, 1978, p. 294)

In fact, the majority of the American POWs who "collaborated" did so out of self-protection to gain extra food, clothing, or medication.

Once the extent of the collaboration had been made public, it was only a matter of time before the internal critique of what went wrong became a central topic of conversation in America. The journalist Eugene Kincaid published a book entitled *In Every War but One* (1959), in which he analyzed why the 21 GIs had defected and what was wrong with American society that caused so many men to act in what he considered to be a morally reprehensible and cowardly fashion. Kincaid noted that

> the roots of the explanation go deep into diverse aspects of our culture—home training of children, education, physical fitness, religious adherents, and the privilege of existing under the higher standard of living in the world. In the light of what happened in Korea, all these facets of American life might profitably be reexamined by our leaders in government, education, and religion. (p. 17)

Kincaid (1959) claimed that the POWs' treatment "rarely involved outright cruelty, but instead a highly novel blend of leniency and pressure" (p. 17).

The result of all of this soul-searching about the "softness" in American society and culture that could allow such morally reprehensible behavior on the part of its young soldiers reached into the highest circles of government and the military. In the government's sphere, there would be debates about the nature of education, physical fitness, and the very nature of patriotism itself. Of course, the ultimate responsibility lay at the feet of the communists, who now became even more suspect and demonized because of what appeared to be highly effective, although iniquitous, propaganda techniques. The U.S. military also undertook a series of studies as to what had happened in the Korean prisoner of war camps, and one of the most interesting results of their analysis of these events was the promulgation on August 17, 1955, by President Eisenhower of the new *Code of Conduct for Members of the Armed Forces of the United States*. The *Code of Conduct* was a document unprecedented in previous American military history, and never before had a president felt it necessary to specifically clarify and prescribe the principles of conduct for all the branches of the military. As Kincaid (1959) noted, "The fact that it was necessary to spell out what had always been taken for granted by Americans as constituting the unquestioned duties and obligations of our fighting men showed how greatly the Korean War differed from the seven previous major wars that this nation had fought" (p. 20). The code makes its points in six clearly stated articles:

I. I am an American fighting man. I serve in the forces which got my country and our way of life. I am prepared to give my life in their defense.

II. I will never surrender of my own free will. If in command I will never surrender my men while they have the means to resist.

III. If I am captive I will continue to resist by all means available. I'll make every effort to escape and aid others to escape. I will accept neither parole nor special favors from the enemy.

IV. If I become a prisoner of war I will keep faith of my fellow prisoners. I will give no information or take part in any action which might be harmful to my comrades. If I'm senior, I will take command. If not, I will obey the lawful orders of those appointed over me and will back them up in every way.

V. When questioned, should I become a prisoner of war, I am bound to give only name, rank, serve this number, and date of birth. I will evade answering further questions to the utmost of my ability. I will make no oral or written statements disloyal to my country and its allies or harmful to their course.

VI. I will never forget that I am an American fighting man, responsible for my actions, and dedicated to the principles which made my country free. I will trust in my God and in the United States of America.

Kincaid (1959) claimed that "the promulgation of the set of principles means that the Government of the United States, because of what happened in the prison camps of the Korean War, is prepared to try to mold a new set of fundamental attitudes in its citizens in the armed forces, with a view to helping them, and the nation itself, survive any future war" (p. 21).

The basic conclusion of most of the army studies regarding the behavior of the prisoners of war was that brainwashing was not very effective, and what little effect it had very quickly dissipated once the individual had been returned to his normal environment, where he would receive support from those familiar to him. However, the concept of brainwashing was intriguing enough for the CIA to embark upon an extensive series of experiments to gauge the potential of "thought control" as a potent weapon in the ongoing Cold War. The story of these experiments constitutes one of the saddest chapters in the history of the CIA, involving the use of dangerous drugs and other forms of psychological coercion that claimed several lives. Eventually, under a cloud of suspicion and faced with ongoing negative public scrutiny, the CIA withdrew from all such activities (Marks, 1979).

By the end of the decade, the issue of the Korean War prisoners of war faded from public memory as attention shifted to the more serious threats posed by the nuclear arms race between the Soviet Union and the United States. However, the concept of brainwashing had firmly established itself in American culture and became part of the common lexicon. While there is no clear scientific proof that brainwashing as such is possible, it remains a common mythology that we are all being subjected to largely unseen forces that manipulate our behavior in a matter that is fundamentally contradictory to our basic wills. In our popular culture, starting with the motion picture *The Manchurian Candidate* (1962) and novels such as *The Ipcress File* (1962), we have been constantly bombarded with images of such manipulation taking place. While much of this activity takes place in the realm of mad scientists and flashing lights, there is an underlying fear about the unknown. Despite the assurances of psychologists, psychiatrists, and those others who study the human brain, the notion of "brainwashing" as a distinct possibility remains as firmly entrenched as ever.

References

Bromley, D. G., & Richardson, J. T. (1980). *The brainwashing/deprogramming controversy: Sociological, psychological, legal and historical perspectives.* New York: Edwin Mellen.

Communist psychological warfare (brainwashing), Committee on Un-American Activities, House of Representatives, 85th Cong., 2nd session (1958) (testimony of E. Hunter).

Hinkle, L., & Wolff, H. (1957). Communist interrogation and indoctrination of "enemies of the states." *American Medical Association, Archives of Neurology and Psychiatry, 76,* 116–174.

Hunter, E. (1951). *Brainwashing in Red China: The calculated destruction of men's minds.* New York: Vanguard.

Hunter, E. (1956). *Brainwashing: The story of men who defied it.* New York: Farrar, Strauss and Cudahy.

Kincaid, E. (1959). *In every war but one.* New York: Norton.

Marks, J. (1979). *The search for the "Manchurian candidate": The CIA and mind control.* New York: Times Books.

Watson, P. (1978). *War on the mind: The military uses and abuses of psychology.* London: Hutchison.

Additional Sources

Carruthers, S. L. (1999). "Not just washed but dry-cleaned": Korea and the "brainwashing" scare of the 1950s. In G. D. Rawnsley (Ed.), *Cold War propaganda in the 1950s.* New York: St. Martin's.

Hyde, M. O. (1976). *Brainwashing & other forms of mind control.* New York: McGraw-Hill.

Lifton, R. J. (1961). *Thought reform and the psychology of totalism: A study of "brainwashing" in China.* New York: Norton.

Meerloo, J. A. M. (1956). *The rape of the mind: The psychology of thought control, menticide, and brainwashing.* Cleveland, OH: World Publishing.

Sargent, W. (1957). *Battle for the mind: A physiology of conversion and brainwashing.* London: Heineman.

Schein, E. (1961). *Coercive persuasion: A socio-psychological analysis of the "brainwashing" of American civilian prisoners by the Chinese communists.* New York: Norton.

White, W. L. (1957). *The captives of Korea: An unofficial white paper.* New York: Scribner.

11

The Influence of
the Built Environment

Victoria O'Donnell

P eople usually think of their lives as being separate from the built
environment because they move in and out of different places during the
course of daily life. Yet, behavior is the product of the complex functioning
of variables related to the individual on the one hand and variables related
to buildings, spaces, decor, color, furniture, and landscaping on the other.
How people are influenced by the built environment in the workplace,
restaurants, shopping malls, public housing, and political settings is the focus
of various kinds of researchers who are identified as environmental psychologists, behavioral ecologists, environmental engineers, and behavioral geographers. They conceptually and empirically study the link between the built
environment and behavior. An important journal in the field is *Environment & Behavior,* first published in 1969. Interdisciplinary in nature, it
includes research by psychologists, architects, urban planners, geographers,
and communication scholars who report experimental and theoretical
work that focuses on the influence of the physical environment on human
behavior.

SOURCE: An earlier version of this essay appeared in *Persuasion: An Interactive
Dependency Approach,* by Victoria O'Donnell and June Kable (1982). New York:
Random House.

The study of the influence of the physical environment on human behavior is also the study of persuasion and propaganda that grows out of a process in which the people who use the built environment play a central role. As Robert Sommer (1969), pioneer and leader in the field, said, "All people are builders, creators, molders, and shapers of the environment" (p. 7). The study of the environment includes human influence and behavior change; therefore, it can be studied as an important dimension of persuasion and propaganda. The physical environment has different effects on different people. Attitudes that a person has toward a particular environment and experiences within it and similar environments help determine whether or not that environment is perceived as familiar, comfortable, strange, or threatening.

The environment consists of a combination of physical and psychological components that continually influence one another in a dynamic and interactive way. David Seamon (1979) defined environmental experience as "the sum total of a person's first-hand involvements with the geographical world in which he or she typically lives" (p. 16). People react emotionally to their surroundings, responding to how aroused, pleasurable, and dominant they feel.

In order to understand the relationship between people's behavior and the environment, it is important to recognize that people and their environments are interactive. The environment-behavior interface produces behavior in various settings that is both learned by people as well as determined by the environment they occupy. For example, behavior during a church service or at a baseball game is the result of learning, observation of others, social exchange, and perception. People learn that certain behavior is required or discouraged because of the setting and constraints therein. Amos Rapoport, emeritus professor of architecture and planning, explored meaning in the environment in his book, *The Meaning of the Built Environment* (1982). He said that the environment can be seen as a series of relationships between things and things, things and people, and people and people. These relationships, which have patterns and structures, order people's lives and the settings for their lives. He viewed relationships as primarily spatial because objects and people are related through various degrees of separation and by space. His major thesis was that the environment communicates meaning. The environment reflects, channels, facilitates, and shapes who communicates with whom, under what conditions, how, when, where, and in what context. It connects and separates people to and from one another and things. Furthermore, the materials, forms, sizes, passageways, colors, and maintenance provide the users of the environment with meaning. Rapoport said that our homes and surroundings with their fences, porches, outer doors, walls, and inner doors control communication and indicate how far one can penetrate into them. Living rooms are usually in the front of homes to facilitate interaction with guests; whereas bedrooms tend to be in the back of homes or on a different level, indicating that these are private places.

Environmental psychologists, architects, city planners, and landscape architects study the appeal of areas in and around large city structures. Recognizing that there is meaning in the built environment, they preserve and create what they call a sense of place in malls, plazas, walkways, waterfronts, and other urban public spaces. As a result, there have been dramatic changes in urban areas all over the world, and these changes affect people's behavior in those places as well. Behavior depends upon the people's perception, for the perceived environment may not be the real environment.

Perception is the process of extracting information from situational components as well as from one's experiences. People attribute characteristics to an environmental situation through a perceptual filter made up of their own values, attitudes, beliefs, needs, and past experiences. Environmental perception is, as Ittelson, Proshansky, Rivlin, and Winkel (1976) maintained, "the source of our phenomenal experience of the world" (p. 123). What people know about the external world is apprehended through their senses. The phenomena they perceive have the characteristics they attribute to them because they interpret them, assign meaning to them, and give some sense of structure to them. The human brain orders and interprets the stimuli that are fed into it. Yi-Fu Tuan, a geographer, said in his book, *Topophilia* (1990), that people use their senses of vision, touch, hearing, and smell to recall emotionally charged memories of childhood scenes and places. These sensory perceptions are affected by individual differences in auditory and color sensitivity, temperament, and verbal and spatial skills. A person with a highly developed spatial sense, for example, will tend to see a place in its entirety rather than as a collection of elements.

Tuan also said that visitors and natives perceive places differently. A visitor brings fresh perspective to a novel scene. A native has an emotional and personal attachment to a place. Most Americans and Europeans, for example, would regard the Latin American rain forest, with its muggy humidity, screeching birdcalls, and exotic wildlife, as an uncomfortable and perhaps threatening environment. Yet to a native of the rain forest, it is a warm and friendly place. Imagine the same native who had never before left the rain forest in an American bar where loud hip-hop music is playing. Here the native would probably feel discomfort because it is a strange and unfamiliar environment with different sounds and frightening people. Many Americans would probably feel at ease in such a place.

When people perceive the environment in a specific situation, they take in valuable information on which to base their behavior. People can observe how much space they have, what demands it places on them, and consequently consider what might result from given behaviors under consideration. Physical environment affects behavior only when it is perceived, that is, only when it is transformed into social meaning. Intimate relationships between place and personal identity was a theme of Donald Appleyard (1979), an environmental designer and researcher, who believed that places could either bolster or suppress a sense of identity, which he considered to be a joint creation of individual and society. He said that places are rich sources of psychological memories, many of which played an important role in identity formation. Rapoport cited a startling example of Hertzberger's senior citizen's home in Amsterdam that was designed with white frame and black infil elements for aesthetic beauty but was perceived by the residents as looking like crosses and coffins representing death.

Thus, it is apparent that environmental meaning and any subsequent behavior are related to individual perception. Yet, there are those who believe that sometimes environment may have a direct effect on behavior. The Hawthorne studies of Elton Mayo and his associates in the 1930s were experiments designed to measure the impact of variations in the physical setting (lighting changes) on workers' performances (relay assembly and testing of telephone equipment). However, the researchers told the subjects that they were to be subjects of an experiment, then moved them to a special room where they were no longer under the watchful eyes of their supervisor. The different behavior, increased group interaction, could not be attributed to lighting changes alone because not only did the spatial differences allow easy contact among the subjects, but also there was evidence that they felt they had special status because they had been singled out for special treatment by their relocation. This made direct influence of lighting changes untenable (Steele, 1973).

Many employees believe that their work is affected by their surroundings. In 1978, Steelcase, Inc., a manufacturer of office furniture commissioned the opinion research firm of Louis Harris and Associates to conduct a study of the attitudes of office workers, corporate office planners, and professional office designers toward the offices of today and tomorrow. Their research was conducted among a national cross-section of 1,047 office workers, 209 executives with office planning responsibilities in *Fortune* 1300 lists of major corporations, and 225 office design professionals. A nearly unanimous 92% of the office workers perceived a connection between their personal satisfaction with their office surroundings and their job performances. Yet, 54% of the executives and 51% of the designers agreed that it would be desirable to adopt open-plan office designs that would allow more contact among the employees. Only 29% of the office workers agreed. The open-plan office is based on modular workstations, often referred to as "bull pens," with few or no floor-to-ceiling walls. The executives and designers supported the open-plan office because it would give them the ability to change office layouts with a minimum of cost, but the office workers perceived the open-plan designs to result in a lack of privacy, too much noise, and less individual space. Harris concluded that "a collision course" is indicated for the future unless executives and designers communicate about these issues. He recommended more employee participation in the office planning process to alleviate the intensity of the collision (Harris, 1980, pp. v–vii).

Open-plan offices were designed in the 1950s, with many companies converting to these types of design by the 1970s. The main incentive was cost-savings in construction and maintenance. Since the Harris study, many other studies have been conducted that revealed that office workers were most likely to complain about limited space in the open-plan system. Brennan, Chugh, and Kline (2002) conducted a study in a large Canadian firm where workers were relocated from traditional private offices with doors that closed to open-plan offices shared with two to four other workers. Ample time to get used to the new offices was built into the study, but the results showed major dissatisfaction even after the adjustment period.

Moving people away from their normal work environment is an important factor for employee training. Steele (1973) related the experience of a training director who tried holding seminars in the regular meeting room of a company but found that it failed because people had previous experiences in the room with upper management. In the meeting room, the trainees felt that their behavior had to be appropriate, and they were unwilling to take risks. They perceived the room as determining how they were to behave. The trainer subsequently rented space off-site. Many companies hold training sessions in resort-like locales. Alcoa of Pittsburgh holds some of its training sessions in historic Williamsburg, Virginia, and the Morgan Bank of New York City holds them in a resort hotel on Long Island. Their directors of training told me that off-site locales tended to reduce the hierarchical distance among employees and eliminate distractions that were normally in the workplace (interviews conducted in 1985).

Because most professionals and support staff spend their days in front of computer terminals, there have been massive modifications in workplace design. Workspaces have been designed with an aura of warmth to offset the high-tech equipment, but cool colors are used to direct attention inward in order to achieve visual and mental tasks. The cafeterias, on the other hand, offer a change of scenery and tend to be more upbeat with red, orange, and yellow walls and chairs and tables (Birren, 1982, p. 57).

Environmental features have different effects according to the individual differences and perceptions of the people who relate to them. The variations may be cultural and societal, or they may be consequences of position, age, income, technology, and/or social organization. K. A. Franck (1984), in an article about physical determinism, said, "The environmental feature and the type of society, or the environmental feature and the type of user, interact in their effects on the outcome variable and each may affect the outcome variable in its own right" (p. 418).

A study done in Padova, Italy, tested the hypothesis that courthouse architecture may affect the feelings of users as well as their estimates of likelihood of conviction of a wrongly accused friend. Subjects were exposed to a trial in the old courthouse built in a medieval style, originally built in 1345 and reconstructed in 1929, and in a new courthouse built in a modern style in 1991. The old courthouse has a residential look, warm colors, large windows, and a large wooden entry door. The new courthouse is a massive, gray, semicircular building with narrow windows and an entrance enclosed between two huge walls. It was seen by the subjects in the study as oppressive, threatening, and hostile. The modern courthouse elicited greater discomfort in participants who were already familiar with the building. Yet, regardless of familiarity, participants estimated a greater likelihood that the friend would be convicted when the trial took place in the newer building. Both courthouses were judged equally attractive, but the new one was judged more intimidating (Maass et al., 2000).

The role of the environment in the healing process has been extensively studied. Poor design of hospitals has been linked to negative patient consequences such as anxiety, elevated blood pressure, and an increased intake of drugs. Patients who had windows with a view of nature in their hospital rooms had shorter postoperative stays, took fewer moderate and strong analgesic doses, and had fewer postsurgical complications than those who had windows facing a brick wall (Devlin & Arneill, 2003).

Physical environment also means a sense of security, not only from the elements but also from people who might do harm. Throughout history, certain cities were defensible against attack due to their locations. Similarly, fortresses were built to protect cities. A close analogy to the fort in today's society is the secure living area for citizens who are fearful of crime. Gated communities have sprung up all over America. Apartment towers often have a single entrance with an armed guard at the door. Senior citizen complexes in many cities have single entrances and elevator keys.

People experience themselves and their activities according to their environment and the spatial setting. Architects and designers know that people's experience of space is related to action. When plans were made to rebuild the House of Commons in London after World War II, Sir Winston Churchill fought against new plans that departed from the traditional intimate space pattern that caused opponents to face one another across a narrow aisle. He felt that if the environment of the House of Commons was changed, then the British government would change as well. Churchill believed that people shape buildings and that buildings, in turn, shape people (Hall, 1959, p. 97).

How a person approaches, moves through, and departs from a room or a building creates a reaction to the image of its occupants. Every major monumental complex, such as the Acropolis of classical Greece or the Forbidden City of Imperial China, has created a sense of power. The Acropolis stood at the highest point of Athens with individual buildings forming a processional path to it. The Forbidden City in Peking creates a cumulative effect as it symmetrically aligns many buildings, gateways, plazas, and terraces that lead visitors to the center, creating awe and respect. Adolf Hitler had Albert Speer design the opulent Chancellery Wing in Berlin with an "approach to power":

> Arriving by car in the court of honor, distinguished guests ascended a short flight of stairs and proceeded through a succession of halls and salons, down the long marble gallery, to a reception hall, then presumably through the cabinet room, along another (redundant) hallway and finally arrived at the Fuhrer's workroom. So pleased was Hitler with the impact of this dramatic 'approach' to the seat of power that he had Speer double the length for his second new chancellery on the Konigsplatz, to something over a quarter of a mile. (Helmer, 1985, p. 39)

Executive offices in corporations are usually on the top floors where ceilings and doors are higher and made with custom details, walls are made of wood paneling or marble, desks are very large, and carpets are thick and plush. Expensive art is likely to hang on the walls. To gain entry to the upper floors, visitors have to pass through obstacles—acquire permission in the lobby, go through security, take special elevators, talk to a floor receptionist, and talk to the executive secretary. The shape and size of office furniture conveys subtle messages about the image of the occupants as well. Large desks, multiple work surfaces, and high-back chairs are seen as indicators of high status. Panoramic views extend the office out into the city skyline. June Collier, president of National Industries, a company that manufactures wiring assemblies for cars and aerospace appliances, decorated her office suite with African tribal masks and stuffed heads of wild animals that she killed on safari. Outside her door stands the lion that she shot in Kenya. Her intended message is "If I didn't get rattled when this lion turned up, I'm certainly not going to be worried by you" ("Personal Space," 1984, p. 35). She also has a glass display case that holds 21 nuggets of pure gold, some weighing more than a pound, and her desk ornaments, the ruler, tape dispenser, and stapler, are made of gold. She wants to make sure that her customers and visitors know that she equates monetary value with power and control.

The physical environment represents a nation's culture, its shared history, accumulated knowledge, values, and social customs. The physical artifacts of a culture reflect its values, and the behavior of its citizens reflects its customs and norms. The American culture values free enterprise, capitalism, and material goods. This is reflected in the prominence of shopping malls in communities of all sizes. Malls are centers for buying and selling goods as well as gathering places for entertainment, eating, and exercise. In the past, churches and cathedrals were the most important buildings in cities and communities. They had elaborate entry patterns with grand plazas, entry halls, and elaborate doors. Often they were the tallest buildings in the area. Today, commercial buildings attract the most effort, expense, and tradition. Al Qaeda terrorists flew the airplanes into the World Trade Center on September 11, 2001, presumably because those towers represented American success, progress, and competition.

Shopping malls have become mega-malls, such as the Mall of America in Minneapolis, where hundreds of stores are built around and above theme restaurants and amusement park rides. Ritzer (2004) refers to the mega-malls, theme parks, and casinos as "landscapes of consumption." Shopping malls use design, materials, lighting, and elevation to symbolize quality. Analysis of three large shopping malls in Dallas, Texas, by students in my persuasion class at the University of North Texas revealed that not only are the prestigious and expensive shops clustered together in subdued, lighted areas with natural plants and natural wood facades compared to the less expensive shops in harshly lighted areas with concrete facades and artificial plants, but also the mall floors actually begin to slope downward in the approaches to the less expensive shops and ascend upward in the approaches to the more expensive ones. Trends in the latter 1980s turned individual stores into a theater-like atmosphere to increase the stimulation of shopping. Stores like Laura Ashley are decorated to transport customers into exciting and romantic environments. The Ralph Lauren store on Chicago's Miracle Mile gives the impression of a stately home with paneled walls, a carved, spiral staircase, and elegant paintings on the walls. *Time* (Betts, 2004) has cited examples of two New York City stores, Ruehl No. 925 and Tory, that were designed to "create an environment in which shoppers feel as if they are browsing through someone's very stylish living room, maybe even their own" (p. 89). The Tory store, which sells clothing, was designed to look like designer Tory Burch's own living room. The psychological comfort of shopping in such environments is derived from a sense of fantasy and change from everyday life.

Architecture can be a symbol of a nation's ideology as well as a persuasive force that perpetuates an ideology. Architecture both reflects and influences people's beliefs, values, attitudes, and behavior. When visiting other nations, people can let the architecture help them better understand the societies that created these structures. When visiting Washington, D.C., it is impossible to view the memorials to Lincoln, Washington, and Jefferson without being influenced to believe that the history of the United States is based on the efforts of great individuals and that the greatness of the country is bigger than individuals and as impressive and indestructable as the monuments that represent its past. The war memorials to World War II, the Korean War, and the Vietnam War evoke a sense of honor, sadness, and closure rather than a celebration of victory; thus they express the nation's reluctance to go to war unless necessary. The new Museum of the American Indian's natural facade is surrounded by native plants and a wetland, while inside windows help track the sun's natural light as it falls on the displays. The role of nature in the lives of Native Americans is a central theme to the architecture.

A striking example of architecture as a persuasive and propagandistic force was in Nazi Germany. Hitler told Speer to design buildings and arenas that would be a visual dimension of Nazi ideology. Hitler wanted his buildings to act as permanent statements of the beliefs of the Third Reich and as symbols of Hitler as a great unifier and leader (Stuart, 1973). As a result of the monuments erected during his regime, Speer acquired the label "Master Builder." The massive size of Speer's buildings symbolized force, superiority, and power. The Lutzpold arena is an example of how a structure magnified Hitler and his rhetoric. The huge slab platforms symbolized the "new" Germany, and when Hitler spoke there, his stature and his message were viewed as massive, as strong, and as indestructible as the arena itself (Stuart, 1973). Speer's designs for Berlin included the Great Hall, public squares, and boulevards to provide a place for assembling vast crowds for speeches and parades (Helmer, 1985, p. 38). Napoleon III of France had his architect Baron Hausman deliberately widen the boulevards of Paris to prevent insurgent crowds from forming barricades across narrow city streets (Pinkney, 1958).

In many cities, low-income housing is hidden from the rest of the city. The poor, like prisons, garbage dumps, and industry, are kept at the back of the city. The suburbs, also away from the mainstream of a town or city, are not hidden but secluded to invoke a sense of privacy with fences and walls symbolizing territorial rights. The lengthy facades of Versailles in France and the Winter Palace in Leningrad caused people to feel a sense of awe and respect for their occupants. Long driveways and houses set on hills have the same effect.

People are often unaware of the persuasive and propagandistic effects that the environment has on them. Because of habitual behavior, much of people's responses to environmental forces is subconscious or, at least nonconscious, in nature. Franck (1984) said, "It is more likely that the physical environment affects behavior even when people are unaware of it; and such effects deserve the attention of researchers" (p. 422). Kuo and Sullivan (2001) found higher rates of violence and aggression among urban public housing residents living in buildings with common areas that were paved with little or no natural vegetation compared to their counterparts, who lived in architecturally similar buildings with common areas that had grass and trees.

A study by Maslow and Mintz (1956) found that subjects rated pictures of faces according to whether they were in an ugly or a beautiful room. The beautiful room was large and furnished with comfortable furniture, drapes, paintings, and a Navajo rug. The ugly room was a janitor's closet with gray walls, an overhead bulb with a torn lamp shade, and strewn with tin cans, pails, brooms, and cardboard boxes. The faces in the ugly room were rated negatively, while the faces in the beautiful room were rated positively. More interesting, however, were the reactions of the people who ran the experiment and who had to spend time in both rooms. They changed their behavior although they were unaware of it at the time. The researchers in the ugly room had reactions such as monotony, fatigue, headache, sleepiness, discontent, irritability, and hostility. The same researchers had feelings of comfort, pleasure, enjoyment, importance, and energy in the beautiful room (pp. 92–94).

Color seems to affect people's behavior. The color pink appears to have the effect of causing a loss of muscular strength in people, thus curbing aggressive behavior. Accordingly, it is being used for holding cells for violent criminals and in schools for hyperactive children. Green also appears to be a tranquilizing color and has the effect of speeding up time. Red and orange are known to stimulate appetites and appear to make time slow down. Red also tends to increase blood pressure and is the most arousing of all colors, followed by orange, yellow, violet, blue, and green. Blue seems to have a calming effect and reduces blood pressure (Birren, 1982; Mehrabian, 1976). There is a story of a rural tavern where the men spit tobacco in the dark corner of the floor. The owner painted the corner white, and the spitting stopped. The color white is pristine and had the desired effect.

Furniture can be deliberately designed to affect behavior. At the Copenhagen Café in Denmark, customers were lingering endlessly over coffee. The owners hired Henning Larsen, who developed a chair that exerts disagreeable pressure on the spine if occupied for over a few minutes. This chair was later marketed in America (Sommer, 1969, p. 121). Conversely, expensive restaurants and cocktail lounges have very comfortable seats. An industrial engineer said, "For a plush tavern, I design chairs that are tremendously comfortable, that encourage the patron to linger over drinks, and bring his friends back for leisurely meals" (O'Donnell & Kable, 1982, p. 100). Hotel lobbies and airports are designed for short waiting periods. It is hoped that those waiting will be uncomfortable enough to wander to the restaurant, fast-food centers, the bar, or shops, where the chances are good that they will spend some money.

Researchers continue to delve into the effects of the environment on behavior. There is a shifting of focus in research to study individuals behaving in the environment on a day-to-day basis, not as isolated and stable entities, but as a part of a complex composite of activities, places, and time. There is a persuasive, even propagandistic, connection between the environment and behavior. Changes that take place in individual and group behavior can be related to the influences of the built environment. Knowledge about the influence of the built environment offers people insight into their interactions with their physical surroundings and how their behavior is thereby influenced.

References

Appleyard, D. (1979). Environment as a social symbol: Within a theory of environmental action and perception. *American Planners Association Journal, 45*, 145–53.

Betts, K. (2004, October 4). Home shopping. *Time, 164*(14), 89.

Birren, F. (1982). *Light, color, and environment.* New York: Van Nostrand Reinhold.

Brennan, A., Chugh, J. S., & Kline, T. (2002). Traditional versus open office design: A longitudinal field study. *Environment & Behavior, 34*(3), 279–299.

Devlin, A. S., & Arneill, A. B. (2003). Health care environments and patient outcomes: A review of the literature. *Environment & Behavior, 35*(5), 665–694.

Franck, K. A. (1984). Exorcising the ghost of physical determinism. *Environment & Behavior, 16*(4), 411–435.

Hall, E. T. (1959). *Silent language.* Garden City, NY: Doubleday.

Harris, L. (1980). *The Steelcase National Study of Office Environments: No. II. Comfort and productivity in the office of the 80s.* Grand Rapids, MI: Steelcase.

Helmer, S. D. (1985). *Hitler's Berlin: The Speer plans for reshaping the central city.* Ann Arbor, MI: UMI Research Press.

Ittelson, W. H., Proshansky, H. M., Rivlin, L. G., & Winkel, G. H. (1976). *Environmental psychology.* New York: Holt, Rinehart, and Winston.

Kuo, F. E. & Sullivan, W. C. (2001, July). Aggression and violence in the inner-city: Effects of the environment via mental fatigue. *Environment and Behavior, 33*(4), 543–571.

Maass, A., Merici, I., Villafranca, E., Furlani, R., Gaburro, E., Getrevi, A., et al. (2000). Intimidating building: Can courthouse architecture affect perceived likelihood of conviction? *Environment & Behavior, 32*(5), 674–683.

Maslow, A., & Mintz, N. (1956). Effects of aesthetic surroundings. *Journal of Psychology, 51,* 247–254.

Mehrabian, A. (1976). *Public places and private spaces: The psychology of work, play and living.* New York: Basic Books.

O'Donnell, V., & Kable, J. (1982). *Persuasion: An interactive dependency approach.* New York: Random House.

Personal space: An inside look at five fabulous offices. (1984, July). *Savvy,* pp. 29–36.

Pinkney, D. (1958). *Napoleon III and the rebuilding of Paris.* Princeton, NJ: Princeton University Press.

Rapoport, A. (1982). *The meaning of the built environment.* Beverly Hills, CA: Sage.

Ritzer, G. (2004). *Enchanting a disenchanted world: Revolutionizing the means of consumption* (2nd ed.). Thousand Oaks, CA: Sage.

Seamon, D. (1979). *A geography of the lifeworld: Movement, rest, and encounter.* New York: St. Martin's.

Sommer, R. (1969). *Personal space.* Englewood Cliffs, NJ: Prentice Hall.

Steele, F. I. (1973). *Physical settings and organizational development.* Reading, MA: Addison-Wesley.

Stuart, C. (1973). Architecture in Nazi Germany: A rhetorical perspective. *Western Speech, 37,* 253–263.

Tuan, Yi-Fu. (1990). *Topophilia: A study of environmental perception, attitudes, and values.* New York: Columbia University Press.

12

U.S. Public Diplomacy

Its History, Problems, and Promise

Nancy Snow

The U.S. reputation has become tarnished during recent years. Public attitudes toward our country are now reported to be at a fifty-year low. Fewer people abroad consider the United States as their best friend. Fewer people believe that our nation shares a mutuality of interests with them. And fewer have trust and confidence in the ability of the United States to provide wise and steady leadership in the current world upheaval. Simultaneously, the negative aspects of America's image have gained new prominence. The mental picture that many foreigners have of our nation is increasingly that of a violent, lawless, overbearing, even a sick society. According to one recent survey, one-fourth of Italians and British, three of ten Japanese, and four of ten of the French and Germans say that their opinion of the United States has fallen appreciably during the past two years.[1]

One might think that such a statement was made in the twenty-first century. In fact, this is from the summary report of expert witness testimony before a House subcommittee that sponsored a one-day symposium on July 22, 1968, called "The Future of United States Public Diplomacy." At the time, three factors were linked to the rise of such a poor mental picture of the United States: Vietnam, race relations in the United States, and crime and lawlessness, presented so vividly to the world by the 1968 assassinations of Rev. Martin Luther King Jr. and Senator Robert Kennedy. While the words of those experts are equally applicable to today's environment, what three factors might we link now to such a dismal picture of the image of the United States: Iraq, preemptive strikes, and unilateralism?

U.S. public diplomacy addresses ongoing questions of a nation's image and credibility in the world as well as tracks, monitors, and builds upon the government and nongovernmental contacts, transactions, and influences that shape the opinions, attitudes, and behaviors of global publics. As a concept, it is closely linked to U.S. foreign policy and communication outcomes from elites to influential and street-level foreign publics as opposed to just traditional elite-elite communication common in official diplomatic communiqués. Public diplomacy was first coined in 1965 by former U.S. Foreign Service Officer Edmund Gillion, then Dean of the Fletcher School of Law and Diplomacy at Tufts University, at the establishment of the Edward R. Murrow Center for Public Diplomacy. Murrow, a broadcasting legend at CBS News, directed the U.S. government's independent public diplomacy agency, the United States Information Agency, from 1961 to 1963. At the time, the Murrow Center brochure explained public diplomacy as "including the cultivation by governments of public opinion in other countries; the interaction of private groups and interests in one country with those of another . . . (and) the transnational flow of information and ideas."[2]

Dante Fascell, chairman of that 1968 subcommittee overseeing its future, said then that "by 'public diplomacy' we mean the cultivation by governments of public opinion in other countries; the interaction, outside the framework of government channels, of groups and interests in one country with those in others; communication between those whose job is communications; and the result of these processes for the formulation of foreign policy and the conduct of foreign affairs."[3] Some thirty-three years later after September 11, 2001, public diplomacy once again came to the forefront in the American public's minds and in U.S. foreign policy circles, particularly in response to troubling anti-American sentiment in the Arab and Muslim world. The 2003 war in Iraq only amplified those negative feelings toward the United States, and not only in the Middle East. As the Pew Research Center reported in 2004, "A year after the war in Iraq, discontent with America and its policies has intensified rather than diminished. . . . Perceptions of American unilateralism remain widespread in European and Muslim nations, and the war in Iraq has undermined America's credibility abroad."[4] U.S. public diplomacy programs were initiated post-9/11 to inform, engage, and influence people around the globe and included multimedia assets such as international radio broadcasting as well as government-sponsored exchanges to the United States to help explain American culture and society to VIP visitors. Altogether, only about $600 million was spent by the U.S. State Department in 2003 on public diplomacy efforts, nearly half in educational exchanges and about $150 million to the target audience outreach in the Arab and Muslim world, an amount considered "absurd and dangerous" by the U.S. Advisory Group for the Arab and Muslim world, led by former U.S. Ambassador Edward Djerejian.[5]

Public diplomacy today is as difficult to implement and measure for effectiveness as it is to define. Placing an emphasis on diplomacy, its history suggests an official government process designed to enhance national security interests:

> Public Diplomacy seeks to promote the national interest of the United States through understanding, informing and influencing foreign audiences.[6]

> Public diplomacy is as important to the national interests as military preparedness.[7]

At other times, the U.S. Information Agency (USIA) defined public diplomacy as a two-track process, both one-way informational and declaratory in purpose and two-way educational and mutual in outcome:

> promoting the national interest and the national security of the United States through understanding, informing, and influencing foreign publics and broadening the dialogue between American citizens and institutions and their counterparts abroad.[8]

The Smith-Mundt Act, also known as the U.S. Information and Educational Exchange Act of 1948, is one of the linchpins of U.S. public diplomacy. It has two-way communication strategies in its language: "The objectives of this Act are to enable the Government of the United States to correct the misunderstandings about the United States in other countries, which constituted obstacles to peace, and to promote mutual understanding between the peoples of the United States and other countries, which is one of the essential foundations of peace."[9] One of its authors, Karl Mundt, clearly viewed the act more as a one-way informational counter to Soviet propaganda. He wrote, "Immediately following the close of World War II when we realized that we were leaving a hot war only to enter a cold war, many of us recognized the importance of fashioning programs to meet effectively the non-military challenge confronting us. It was out of this era that the Smith-Mundt Act emerged." These Cold War weapons of words were needed because the United States faced "an alien force which seeks our total destruction."[10]

The other U.S. public diplomacy linchpin, the Fulbright Hays Act of 1961, incorporated provisions of Senator Fulbright's amendment in 1946 and the

Smith-Mundt Act to establish a new educational and cultural exchange policy:

> to increase mutual understanding between the people of the United States and the people of other countries by means of educational and cultural exchange; to strengthen the ties which unite us with other nations by demonstrating the educational and cultural interests, developments, and achievements of the people of the United States and other nations, and the contributions being made toward a peaceful and more fruitful life for people throughout the world; to promote international cooperation for educational and cultural advancement; and thus to assist in the development of friendly, sympathetic, and peaceful relations between the United States and the other countries of the world.[11]

This view of mutual understanding and mutuality in public diplomacy would likely emphasize very different approaches and measures of effectiveness than one placing public diplomacy squarely in the midst of a national crisis. Over the past fifty years, however, no single consensus has emerged to define the direction of U.S. public diplomacy aside from the goals and whims of the incumbent executive branch of the U.S. government. As Michael Holtzman observed in the *New York Times*,

> United States public diplomacy is neither public nor diplomatic. First, the government—not the broader American public, has been the main messenger to a world that is mightily suspicious of it. Further, the State Department, which oversees most efforts, seems to view public diplomacy not as a dialogue but as a one-sided exercise . . . America speaking to the world.[12]

Holtzman belongs to a school of thought on U.S. public diplomacy advanced by Senator J. William Fulbright and Edward R. Murrow that suggests a far wider array of participants, practitioners, and perspectives than just those seen or heard in the armed forces, foreign service, or inside the beltway of Washington. As Murrow defined the field when appointed director of the USIA in 1963,

> Public diplomacy differs from traditional diplomacy in that it involves interaction not only with governments but primarily with non-governmental individuals and organizations. Furthermore, public diplomacy activities often present many differing views represented by private American individuals and organizations in addition to official government views.[13]

Murrow's definition suggests that public diplomacy in practice is as much at home in corporate boardrooms, pop concerts, and peace rallies as it is inside the halls of Congress. Nevertheless, U.S. public diplomacy is still often assumed to be linked in some way, peripherally or dead center, with traditional diplomatic goals of national governments. As Christopher Ross, U.S. State Department special coordinator for public diplomacy and public affairs, writes,

> The practitioners of traditional diplomacy engage the representatives of foreign governments in order to advance the national interests articulated in their own government's strategic goals in international affairs. Public diplomacy, by contrast, engages carefully targeted sectors of foreign publics in order to develop support for those same strategic goals.[14]

Whenever public diplomacy definitions are overtly linked to official outcomes of national governments, this tends to connote a more negative interpretation linked to propaganda outcomes. Public diplomacy is then perceived, rightly or wrongly, as a set of mostly mass communication techniques that use emotional appeals over rational facts to change attitudes; conceals information that does not favor the sender; and spreads messages promoting a certain ideology such as the social, economic, or military goals of the state. As British scholar J. A. C. Brown says, with propaganda, "answers are determined in advance."[15] American sociologist and propaganda scholar, Leonard Doob, argues the same. What separates propaganda from other forms of communication (education) is the power of suggestion that he defines as the "predetermined conclusion."[16] It uses strategic communications to lead a person to a specific conclusion as determined by the propaganda sponsor.

The hybrid nature of public diplomacy and propaganda outcomes and definitions makes it difficult in some circles to separate the two. Heritage Foundation analysts Johnson and Dale argue that propaganda, in contrast to public diplomacy,

> is information deliberately propagated to help or harm a person, group, or institution, regardless of whether the information is true or false. To many not aware of its exact meaning, propaganda suggests disinformation. Public diplomacy and public affairs officers have always maintained that any information they convey must be truthful. Propaganda or not, it must deal with the facts.[17]

Johnson and Dale adopt a "meat and potatoes" approach to American public diplomacy that involves a whole menu of communication interactions to encourage mutual understanding and cooperation between nations and their publics. These include foreign media briefings, publishing materials such as books and pamphlets that explain the United States and its values, sponsoring educational and cultural exchanges, and international broadcasting.

Internationally, public diplomacy is often seen as a both/and equation, both helpful to governmental purposes and useful to private organizations or companies that are involved in all aspects of international persuasion. Consider the words of Sir Michael Butler, former British permanent representative to the European Union:

> The purpose of public diplomacy is to influence opinion in target countries to make it easier for the British Government, British companies, or other British organizations to achieve their aims. The overall image of Britain in the country concerned is of great importance—but this is not to say that it is the only factor. The most important factor will usually be the actual policies of the British Government and the terms in which they are announced and explained by the Ministers. A narrow and open pursuit of national interests at the expense of others will be negative.[18]

This British definition of public diplomacy contrasts with American versions that are often associated with appeals made during national crisis or wartime that are put to rest at conflict's end. A distinct historical pattern in U.S. public diplomacy has emerged over the past century: (1) conflict arises that requires a public diplomacy/propaganda response, (2) new resources are allocated to alleviate the conflict/national crisis, and (3) at the end of the conflict, either congressional or executive action is taken to dissolve the public diplomacy agency. Woodrow Wilson's Creel Committee was shut down by Congress within months of World War I's end. Truman's Office of War Information (OWI) was abolished at the end of World War II. At the end of the Cold War, the USIA came under congressional scrutiny as a relic of a bygone ideological era and was finally abolished in 1999, with its remnants transferred to the State Department.

Today, public diplomacy, both nationally and globally, is viewed as more important than even during the Cold War era due to changes in global communications that have given rise to the global audience:

> It is the end of the Cold War which has made public diplomacy more important: the spread of democracy, the media explosion and the rise of global NGOs [nongovernmental organizations] and protest movements have changed the nature of power and put ever greater restraints on the freedom of action of national governments. This means that—even more than during the Cold War—we need to invest as much in communicating with foreign publics as with the governments that represent them if we are to achieve our objectives.[19]

The post–Cold War Information Age has forever altered the public face of public diplomacy. Behind-closed-doors traditional diplomacy has given way to a swinging door answerable to global publics and global media. As the Center for Strategic and International Studies points out in its study of the post–Cold War diplomatic ethos, "The public dimension receives less attention, yet it may be the most significant of the changes that affect the conduct of diplomacy. Virtually no major foreign affairs or domestic initiative is taken today without first testing public opinion."[20]

U.S. public diplomacy's legacy goes back to the early to mid-twentieth century. For two decades (1930s to 1950s), one paradigm dominated American scientific research in communication: persuasive communication—specifically, attitude change from mass media effects. Radio and then later television were thought to have effects that could "enlighten" the population, while government and military were concerned more with war propaganda efforts to challenge totalitarian ideologies. During this period, diplomacy was shaped by elites in the foreign service of their respective governments; the public had very little role to play, except as passive observers of democracy and media. The kingpin of mass communications research at this time was Harold Lasswell, who saw himself and others such as Walter Lippmann becoming witnesses to a worldwide growth of an agitated public aroused by mass persuasion. As a result, the study of public opinion formation and propaganda processes in a democratic society had to become a major concern of American social scientists. The goal of the propagandist was the "manipulation of collective attitudes," and questions associated with propaganda were not about morality or ethics but always efficiency: (1) How may hate be mobilized against an enemy? (2) How may the enemy be demoralized by astute manipulation? (3) How is it possible to cement the friendship of neutral and allied peoples? Propaganda represented total information warfare and the "mobilization of the civilian mind." Democracies achieve unity not by "regimentation of muscles" but "by a repetition of ideas rather than movements. The civilian mind is standardized by news and not by drills."[21]

By the end of the Cold War, scholars began to note a shift from traditional diplomacy and government-to-government relations toward public diplomacy public-to-public relations:

> The actors in public diplomacy can no longer be confined to the profession of diplomats but include various individuals, groups, and institutions who engage in international and intercultural communication activities which do have a bearing on the political relationship between two or more countries.[22]

Furthermore, Signitzer and Coombs in 1992 noted a distinction in public diplomacy between the so-called "tough-minded" school, which holds "that the purpose of public diplomacy is to exert an influence on attitudes of foreign audiences using persuasion and propaganda," and the "tender-minded" school, which "argues that information and cultural programs must bypass current foreign policy goals to concentrate on the highest long-range national objectives. The goal is to create a climate of mutual understanding."[23] Neither school of thought can stand entirely on its own but must be synthesized. A further breakdown from tough and tender is what practitioners in public diplomacy engage in on two tracks—political communication that is administered by a section of the foreign ministry, embassy, or State Department (in the U.S. context) and cultural communication that may be administered by a cultural section of the foreign ministry, embassy, or State Department but also by a quasi-governmental or nongovernmental body (e.g., the British Council, Sister Cities International, National Council of International Visitors). They further distinguish between two types of cultural communication: (1) cultural diplomacy, which aims to present a favorable national image abroad, and (2) cultural relations, which have mutual information exchange and no unilateral objective in mind, just "an honest picture of each country rather than a beautified one."[24]

A fascinating empirical measurement study of the nexus between the changing face of public diplomacy and international communication was completed by W. Phillips Davison almost thirty years ago, in which he interviewed both diplomats and diplomatic correspondents—those journalists who write about international affairs, regularly interact with diplomats, and attend and write about international conferences. These correspondents, Davison argues, belong to the foreign affairs community, and their observations are respected among foreign service officials. A State Department official explained, "They [the correspondents] can give you more information than you can give them. Their job is to know everybody; and some of them keep excellent files."[25]

Davison describes the existence of a "diplomatic reporting network," a network of mutually dependent relationships that puts both diplomat and correspondent into an elite category of foreign affairs specialists. To what extent such a network is in existence today is called into some question with the end of the Cold War, the decline in international bureaus of major news media outlets, and the wide availability of electronic information that precludes international travel and face-to-face contact between these two interdependent communities. A useful study might be to survey foreign corres- pondents and foreign nationals about the most respected diplomatic correspondents in their communities and how much influence these correspondents have on cultural relations. Davison's scholarship puts a kibosh on using public diplomacy campaigns to influence attitudes:

When it comes to influencing attitudes, we know that information is a very weak reed to lean on. When a predisposition already exists, communications can sometimes whip up greater enthusiasm. Communications can occasionally affect weak attitudes. But when important attitudes on subjects we and they really care about are concerned, one can blast away twenty-four hours a day and still achieve very little. We repeat: this is one of the best documented findings of communication research that information or propaganda is not an effective instrument for influencing strongly held attitudes.[26]

Davison suggests that public diplomacy campaigns be measured for effectiveness the way a candidate for high public office (who is well funded of course!) monitors public opinion on a systematic basis. "If the USIA could spend for research at the same rate as U.S. political candidates spend, we would have a very much larger overseas research program, the Agency's output would be more on target, and U.S. foreign policy would be in better shape."[27]

Not until the events of September 11, 2001, did U.S. public diplomacy become seen again as a critical component to winning a war as had the nearly fifty-year battle of imagery and words between the United States and Soviet Union. Defined as the promotion of national interest through informing, engaging, and influencing global publics, at the end of the Cold War, interest in public diplomacy withered as Clinton administration priorities shifted away from ideological battlegrounds to commercial engagement and expanding markets. The executive branch responsible for explaining and supporting U.S. foreign policy, influence, and values overseas, the USIA, had no domestic constituency to lobby for its survival, in part due to a 1948 congressional mandate, the Smith-Mundt Act, that prohibits the domestic propagandizing of the American people. Furthermore, the USIA in the early 1990s was particularly vulnerable to partisan one-upmanship as the Democratic White House battled with Republicans in Congress such as Senator Jesse Helms (R–NC), chair of the Foreign Relations Committee, who saw an opportunity to streamline foreign affairs and put an independent agency on the chopping block. On October 1, 1999, USIA's days of independence were over, and the leftovers were shifted to the U.S. Department of State with barely a whisper in the national press.

Almost two years later to the day, the U.S. government and the American people awakened to the reality that the world was not fully embracing either American policies or values. In a series of horror-filled images captured live during the East Coast morning rush hour, Osama bin Laden and Al Qaeda became names linked instantaneously not only with global terrorism but with global communications. On October 4, 2001, just days before the United

States attacked bin Laden's hideout in Afghanistan, the London-based *Economist* wrote that

> another sort of war is already under way, one in which journalists are already playing an important role as a conduit or filter, though not just the scribblers and broadcasters from the West. It is the propaganda war. That word has come to have a derogatory meaning, of the dissemination of untruths. In this case, America's task is (in truth) to disseminate truths, about its motives, about its intentions, about its current and past actions in Israel and Iraq, about its views of Islam. For all that, however, this part of the war promises to be no easier to win than the many other elements of the effort.[28]

To counter bin Laden and Saddam Hussein, the United States pulled out all the stops in its propaganda war. The Pentagon initiated Orwellian-sounding entities like Total Information Awareness and Office of Strategic Influence, which were designed to use covert, anything-but-the-truth information campaigns to track and monitor enemies, potential and real. The public outcry quickly shuttered both. The U.S. military deployed food and leaflet drops and initiated short-wave radio broadcasts from the Air Force C-130 Commando Solo, the only airborne radio and television military aircraft engaged in psychological operations such as warning civilian populations not to collaborate with enemy targets. The U.S. State Department tasked a Madison Avenue veteran in advertising, Charlotte Beers, who formerly sung the praises of Uncle Ben's Rice, to now do the same for Uncle Sam. As the undersecretary for public diplomacy and public affairs, Beers's brainchild of her eighteen-month tenure was the $15 million paid media ad campaign, Shared Values. Presented as a series of mini-documentaries to the Muslim world in December 2002 during the Muslim Holy month of Ramadan, the goal was to illustrate how happy and well treated Muslim Americans were after 9/11: "The thing I value most living here is the freedom and dignity I enjoy as a human being," says Abdul-Raouf Tawfik Hammuda, a bakery store owner from Toledo, Ohio. He, along with a journalist, schoolteacher, renowned scientist, and rescue worker, represent archetypes of American Muslims who illustrate U.S. "universal" values of free speech, education, entrepreneurial enterprise, science and technology, and public service. Accompanied by a State Department–sponsored front group, the Council of American Muslims for Understanding (CAMU), Shared Values was shut down permanently in the weeks before the outbreak of war with Iraq in March 2003. Many governments rejected the mini-docs as paid political ads of the U.S. government, which are banned on most state-run television broadcast outlets. The one formal press conference Beers gave to roll out the Shared Values campaign was interrupted by six American protesters who chanted a "You're selling war, we're not buying" slogan of their own.

"For someone who scorned modernity and globalization, and who took refuge in an Islamic state [Afghanistan] that banned television, bin Laden proved remarkably adept at public diplomacy," wrote Internews Network president David Hoffman in the pages of *Foreign Affairs* magazine.[29] His words were echoed by the perplexed thinking-out-loud rhetoric of Representative Henry Hyde (R–IL), who wondered, "How is it that the country that invented Hollywood and Madison Avenue has allowed such a destructive and parodied image of itself to become the intellectual coin of the realm overseas?"[30] The United States has offered its own communications response, but so far few are listening, and they counter with cries of no more information, let's talk policy.

In January 2003, the White House announced the formation of the Office of Global Communications (OGC), an offspring of the Coalition-Information Centers that were used to coordinate messages from Kabul to London to Washington during the Afghanistan war. The first publication of OGC was "Apparatus of Lies: Saddam's Disinformation and Propaganda 1999–2003," designed to build public support for a U.S.-led war against Iraq. "In the weeks ahead, as the international community seeks to enforce UN Security Council resolutions and disarm the Iraqi regime, governments, the media, and the public are urged to consider the regime's words, deeds, and images in light of this brutal record of deceit."[31] One year later, the Western regimes of George W. Bush of the United States and Tony Blair of Great Britain would be accused of using their own misinformation and disinformation campaigns to change public sentiment from ambivalence to decisively pro-war. Against the backdrop of a prisoner-of-war abuse scandal, U.S. public diplomacy has become an unmitigated disaster. The converse of the proverbial "success has a thousand mothers while defeat is an orphan," U.S. public diplomacy's failure has a thousand mothers in the form of critical domestic and international editorials, *Nightline* specials, Council on Foreign Relations conferences, special task forces, and reports such as "Changing Minds, Winning Peace" that wax negative about the United States being out-communicated by primitive, roving bands of terrorists who want to kill everything connected to the West.

To combat anti-Americanism, the United States sent out a broadcast signal version of a Valentine's Day greeting card on February 14, 2004, to win Arab hearts and minds. No Hallmark sentimentality like, "I'm thinking of you," but rather this greeting came in the form of a U.S. government-funded Arabic-language network with the very propagandistic moniker of "The Free One." President Bush has said that Al Hurra will help combat "the hateful propaganda that fills the airwaves in the Muslim world and tell people the truth about the values and policies of the United States." It seems to be doing so from a safe distance. Al Hurra is based not in the Middle East, but in Springfield, Virginia, just fifteen miles from downtown Washington, D.C. So far, the Arab-speaking public is not fully embracing the "free one" version, despite financing of $62 million in congressional funding for the first year alone. Al Jazeera still holds the comparative advantage, and Arab newspaper editorials have been universally thumbs down on the U.S.-based broadcast alternative, with the not unexpected negative reaction of "it's all American propaganda, anyway."

In American-led global communications, the phone is, more often than not, off the hook. First, there exists a disconnect in the official propaganda campaign coming out of Washington, D.C., between how the administration shapes its motives in the world and how others see U.S. actions in the world play out. In part, the Washington "dialogue of the deaf" is due to the reality that American values are incongruous with American interests. U.S. interests that emerge from Washington and New York are largely about economic access and advantage and using our global military presence to protect our economic interests. U.S. values are more political, cultural, and social. This battle, between interests and values, is a battle between Realpolitik (might makes right) and Soft Power (right makes might). So far, Realpolitik has always won because a sole superpower can change the rules of the game at will. The United States is so powerful that it can be inconsistent in its foreign policy applications and get away with it. More than any other reason, this is why America is hated today. Second, in true Hollywood fashion, U.S. national security goals and interests and American power in the world come across as the triumph of good over evil. Any ambiguity or dissenting points of view from a truly complex world are dismissed. Instead, America's propagandists hand down the Manichean dichotomy—"us and them," "good and bad," "those who are for us and those who are against." In that context, the world dialogue becomes one of "a clash of civilizations," as Samuel Huntington claims, but even more, a clash of propagandas and perceptions between what is perceived as "America's Imperial War" and "Operation Iraqi Freedom."[32] U.S. public diplomacy efforts are marred by a lack of global consensus about how to wage a battle against global terrorism. As the White House has so often made clear, what happened on September 11, 2001, was immediately declared by the president as an act of war, not treated as a law enforcement issue. Such a war declaration shifted thinking toward a public diplomacy mired in war rhetoric and crisis communications and away from a public diplomacy led by exchanges, relationship building, active listening, and efforts to promote mutual understanding and peace. As Rumsfeld told the 9/11 Commission investigating the terrorist attacks, "When our nation was attacked on September 11th, the President recognized that what had happened was an act of war and must be treated as such—not as a law enforcement matter. He knew that weakness would only invite aggression; and that the only way to defeat the terrorists was to take the war to them—to go after them where they live and plan and hide, and to make clear to states that sponsor and harbor them that such actions will have consequences."[33]

Toward a New U.S. Public Diplomacy

U.S. public diplomacy should not be viewed by global publics as directed exclusively by the U.S. government or any official source of information. We are misunderstood and increasingly resented by the world *precisely* because it is our president and our top government officials whose images predominate in explaining U.S. public policy. Furthermore, U.S. foreign policymakers are criticized for being intransigent on core policies such as unfailing support for Israel, with no evidence that dialogue about policy is even possible. While the U.S. policy of supporting Israel is not going to change, there is certainly room for U.S. policymakers to show more sympathy for Palestinian deaths as often as the United States condemns the killing of Israelis. One of the avenues by which goodwill and dialogue can be strengthened is through citizen diplomacy and international exchanges. While the penultimate purpose of official U.S. public diplomacy is a government marketing campaign to foreign publics in order to present U.S. foreign policy and national security objectives in the best light, an important secondary source for America's public diplomacy campaign is citizen diplomacy. This calls on the American public to play its part and not watch foreign policymaking from the sidelines. Mike McCarry of the Alliance for International Educational and Cultural Exchange writes,

> A globally literate and internationally engaged American public should be one of the strongest links in our national security. Mutual understanding and respect have never been more essential to our country's well-being, as the threat of terrorism demonstrates. There is no better way to address the dangerous two-way knowledge deficit than by enlisting the American public in advancing U.S. foreign relations through citizen exchange.[34]

U.S. public diplomacy's vision and energy must be drawn directly from the American people generally and in private, voluntary organizations in particular. It is the private citizens of the United States who are more comfortable acknowledging, with some degree of humility, that the United States has made mistakes in its past. Government officials seem to have a hard time with that one. Open criticism of a country's policies tends to embarrass government leaders. Over time, it can be the trump card in the deck of negotiating a peaceful (and lasting) settlement of international conflicts. The American people can better illustrate that we are a people willing to learn from our mistakes and can redirect our dealings with other nations to mutually beneficial ends, not just purposes that serve official Washington. The American people can better initiate direct contact with people in other countries whose support and understanding we need on the stage of world opinion. The American public is the best ad campaign going for the world. We have the greatest diversity in people and culture, and it shows in our receptiveness to learning, our generosity, and our creativity. We need to magnify these qualities to the world but, in the same spirit, listen more, talk less.

Over the long term, we need to build a global public diplomacy for peace. Ours is an age of propaganda, an age of manipulation to this cause or that cause. People are joiners; they choose sides, so why not make peace a side to choose? If so, then nations, both their governments and private citizens, need to keep advocating for peace, and not the peace that it is just something that is not war. Peace is coexistence, mutual interdependence. Peace is a requirement of the nuclear age. How might we establish a public diplomacy for peace? To begin, like a public policy version of the Hippocratic oath, we need to first do no harm. Why not reflect upon every public diplomacy program on its value to furthering not strictly national interests but, in addition, global security interests? This would require a stronger emphasis on cultural mediation and mutual understanding initiatives such as cultural diplomacy, cultural and educational exchanges, and strengthening sister city partnerships and civic and neighborhood organizations.

We need to continue to tell our stories to one another and support people-to-people dialogue and exchange, efforts that are based on mutual learning and mutual understanding. What this means is a Marshall Plan for International Exchange, a ten-fold increase in programs such as the Fulbright, International Visitor Program, and Arts exchanges. For too long, and perhaps in part due to our incredible comparative advantage in communications technology, the United States has emphasized amplification over active listening, telling America's story to the world over promoting international dialogue. Anti-Americanism and general ill will toward the United States are driven more by the perception that we talk first before we listen. For a change, it would not take much for the United States to listen first, talk second. It certainly would not make things worse if we tried harder to be citizen diplomats in our relations with our overseas counterparts. This is what international educational and cultural exchanges expect from those who travel across national boundaries. Why haven't we tapped these alumni as citizen ambassadors? We are simply not doing as much as we could.

Edward Djerejian, chair of the Advisory Group on the Arab and Muslim World, responded to the 9/11 Commission Report with a similar charge:

> I use the Woody Allen adage that, you know, 90 percent of life is just showing up. And we are not showing up in a significant manner in the Muslim world in a daily debate and discussion about US values and US policies. And basically one of the best instruments we have is this traditional public diplomacy, which are educational exchanges, getting students over here that have been seriously hindered.[35]

That hindrance refers to the U.S. visa restrictions following September 11 and the U.S. Patriot Act, which have made life more difficult for international students to enter the United States. Despite these new security restraints, international educational exchange numbers remain strong.

There is so much we still do not know, and we need to unite partnerships among government, the private sector, and universities to study social influence, changes in mind-sets, how to teach tolerance and mutual respect, and methodologies that will measure current public diplomacy programs in an effort to find best practices. We could start by undertaking efforts to identify the best practices used by other countries. Some of the world's leaders in soft power diplomacy include the Scandinavian countries such as Denmark and Norway, as well as the Netherlands, Japan, and the United Kingdom.

Finally, to have a lasting and effective public diplomacy, the United States must consider its legacy of strategies of truth. The short-lived and ill-conceived Office of Strategic Influence (OSI) was a here-today, gone-tomorrow debacle, but there remains plenty of public concern that some within the Department of Defense would just as soon continue to use such strategies of deception under the "whatever works" rubric. It is one thing to use deception against the enemy, but the OSI sought to use deception to plant false stories in reputable overseas news markets. Any approach based on falsehoods and deception will not have long-lasting, enduring outcomes but only short-term, tactical advantages. My public diplomacy experience at the USIA and my propaganda research has convinced me that the more transparent and genuine U.S. public diplomacy strategies are, the better off our national security and long-term strategic interests will be. As John Arquilla and David Ronfeldt write, "Truth must be the polestar of American strategic public diplomacy."[36]

Notes

1. "The Future of United States Public Diplomacy," Report No. 91–130, 91st Congress, Dante Fascell, Chairman. Reprinted in *The Case for Reappraisal of U.S. Overseas Information Policies and Programs,* ed. Edward L. Bernays and Burnet Hershey (New York: Praeger, 1970), 107.

2. Quoted from the United States Agency Alumni Association Web site, "What Is Public Diplomacy?" http://www.publicdiplomacy.org/1.htm.

3. Bernays and Hershey, 121.

4. "A Year after Iraq War: Mistrust of America in Europe Ever Higher, Muslim Anger Persists," The Pew Research Center for the People and the Press, Washington, D.C., March 16, 2004, 1.

5. As quoted in the Report of the Advisory Group on Public Diplomacy for the Arab and Muslim World, October 1, 2003 (Washington, D.C.: Department of State), http://www.state.gov/documents/organization/24882.pdf.

6. As quoted in a U.S. government planning report for integration of USIA into the State Department, June 20, 1997 (Washington, D.C.: United States Advisory Commission on Public Diplomacy). Report of the United States Advisory Commission on Public Diplomacy, 1990.

7. Report of the United States Advisory Commission on Public Diplomacy, 1990. As quoted in Michael Kunczik, *Images of Nations and International Public Relations* (Mahwah, NJ: Lawrence Erlbaum, 1997), 228.

8. "What Is Public Diplomacy?" U.S. Information Agency Alumni Association (USIAAA), September 1, 2002, at www.publicdiplomacy.org.

9. U.S. Congress, House Committee on Foreign Affairs, United States Information and Educational Exchange Act of 1947 (Washington, D.C.: Government Printing Office), 3.

10. Timothy Glander, *Origins of Mass Communications Research during the American Cold War: Educational Effects, Contemporary Implications* (Mahwah, NJ: Lawrence Erlbaum, 2000), 61.

11. Philip H. Coombs, *The Fourth Dimension of Foreign Policy: Education and Cultural Affairs* (New York: Harper & Row, 1964).

12. Michael Holtzman, *New York Times,* October 4, 2003.

13. Edward R. Murrow, speaking as USIA director, 1963.

14. Christopher Ross, "Public Diplomacy Comes of Age," *The Washington Quarterly* 25, no. 2 (2002): 75.

15. J. A. C. Brown, *Techniques of Persuasion: From Propaganda to Brainwashing* (Baltimore: Penguin, 1963), 13.

16. Leonard W. Doob, *Propaganda: Its Psychology and Techniques* (New York: Barnes & Noble Books), 1935.

17. Stephen Johnson and Helle Dale, "How to Reinvigorate Public Diplomacy," The Heritage Foundation Backgrounder No. 1645, April 23, 2003, 3. Available in its entirety at www.heritage.org/research/nationalsecurity/bg1645.cfm.

18. Sir Michael Butler, quoted in Mark Leonard, *Public Diplomacy* (London: Foreign Policy Centre, 2002), 1.

19. Leonard, *Public Diplomacy*, 3.

20. Center for Strategic & International Studies, "Diplomacy in the Information Age," A Report of the CSIS Advisory Panel, Washington, D.C., draft, October 9, 1998, 9.

21. Brett Gary, *The Nervous Liberals: Propaganda Anxieties from World War I to the Cold War* (New York: Columbia University Press, 1999), 62–3.

22. B. Signitzer and T. Coombs, "Public Relations and Public Diplomacy: Conceptual Convergences," *Public Relations Review* 18 (1992): 139.

23. Ibid., 140.

24. Ibid.

25. W. Phillips Davison, "Diplomatic Reporting: Rules of the Game," *Journal of Communication* 25 (1975): 141. See also W. P. Davison, "News Media and International Negotiation," *Public Opinion Quarterly* 38 (1975).

26. W. Phillips Davison, "The Case for Reappraisal," in *The Case for Reappraisal of U.S. Overseas Information Policies and Programs*, ed. E. L. Bernays and B. Hershey (New York: Praeger, 1970), 87–8.

27. Ibid., 90.

28. "The Propaganda War," *The Economist*, October 4, 2001.

29. David Hoffman, "Beyond Public Diplomacy," *Foreign Affairs*, March/April 2002.

30. Henry Hyde, "Speaking to Our Silent Allies: The Role of Public Diplomacy in U.S. Foreign Policy," Council on Foreign Relations, June 17, 2002.

31. http://www.whitehouse.gov/ogc/apparatus/apparatus-of-lies.pdf, p. 4 from Executive Summary.

32. Samuel Huntington, "The Clash of Civilizations?" *Foreign Affairs*, Summer 1993.

33. Donald H. Rumsfeld, testimony prepared for delivery to the National Commission on Terrorist Attacks upon the United States, March 23, 2004.

34. Coalition for Citizen Diplomacy, "Planning a Summit on Citizen Diplomacy: A Leadership Conference Report," Johnson Foundation Wingspread Conference Center, March 2004, p. 8. http://www.sister-cities.org/sci/pdf/CoalitionCitizenDip.pdf

35. Edward Djerejian, "Review of U.S. Foreign Policy Urged," Michele Kelemen, reporter. July 26, 2004. Available online at http://www.npr.org/templates/story/story.php? story Id = 3617213.

36. John Arquilla and David Ronfeldt, *The Emergence of Noopolitik: Toward an American Information Strategy* (Santa Monica, CA: RAND, 1991), 65.

13

Visualizing Absence

The Function of Visual Metaphors in the Effort to Make a Fitting Response to 9/11

Stuart J. Kaplan

The official effort to restore the World Trade Center facilities began shortly after the attacks of September 11, 2001. The speed with which a design process was established is, in itself, noteworthy given the high vacancy rate in Manhattan office buildings at the time. Political and emotional motivations, rather than practical economic considerations, may explain the accelerated pace of the program to replace the buildings that were destroyed in the attack. The need to have a swift and bold response to fill the void left by the attack had attained significant symbolic value in the months immediately after September 11. One commentator has suggested that the haste to rebuild on the WTC site and to memorialize that loss of lives and property was motivated, at least in part, on the Bush administration's desire to build public support for all-out "war on terror" (Edkins, 2003).

In addition to their physical presence as landmarks on the Manhattan skyline, the Twin Towers also had enormous symbolic importance as modernist icons. Immanuel Wallerstein (2002) argues that the World Trade

SOURCE: This was presented at the 17th annual Visual Communication conference in 2003.

243

Center towers were a metaphor for American economic success and technological skill. Thus, the September 11 attack was an attack on American capitalism and its associated values and achievements. Both the buildings and the thousands of lives that were lost in a shocking and devastating act of terrorism needed to be commemorated in a substantial way. To their credit, the public officials who were given the responsibility of facilitating a process for reimagining the World Trade Center have involved the public to an unprecedented extent. Since the first formal public hearings in July 2002, more than 100,000 people have attended community meetings or visited the various displays of architectural models. The public has been invited to submit comments in writing or via e-mail on numerous occasions. The outcome of this elaborate consultation process is a rich dialogue among citizens, public officials, architectural critics, and professional designers concerning the future of "Ground Zero."

In an earlier paper, I reported on the process of designing signature buildings for the WTC site (Kaplan, 2003). This essay will provide some background on the overall rebuilding effort, but the primary focus will be on the design process for a permanent memorial at the site. For the factual background, I have relied on transcripts of public hearings, testimony by public officials, the architects' own statements about their design concepts for the memorial, and commentary by leading architectural critics. With this background as context, I examined the memorial design as an example of using architecture for political persuasion. I will argue that a small set of very powerful and evocative visual metaphors started to take shape in the early stages of public consultation and then became sharpened and refined during the design proposal and competition phases. These visual metaphors significantly influenced the design work for the memorial to the tragic events of September 11, 2001, as well as the buildings that would constitute a restored WTC site. They were also a key element in the rhetorical effort to gain acceptance for the designs among the general public and the families of victims of the attack on the World Trade Center. Before applying metaphor analysis to the winning designs, I first briefly describe the process leading up to their selection, then review the basic elements of metaphor theory that seem relevant to that analysis. The chapter concludes with a discussion of various implications of this project for metaphor theory and for future research on persuasive uses of visual metaphors.

The Planning Process for the WTC Site and the Signature Buildings

Shortly after the September 11 attacks, the governor of New York created a new public agency, the Lower Manhattan Development Corporation

(LMDC), to oversee the rebuilding task. The LMDC commissioned initial concept plans, six of which were selected for presentation to the public in July 2002. More than 4,000 people attended the public meetings at which the initial designs for rebuilding at Ground Zero were presented and discussed. Their reaction to the proposals was overwhelmingly negative, in large part because the buildings seemed to simply replicate the boxy form of the buildings that were destroyed and distribute roughly the same amount of office space over multiple structures that were lower than the original Twin Towers but lacked their distinctive presence on the skyline. The negative comments by participants in the first public hearing were picked up by the press and amplified in subsequent contributions by members of the public and architects to form a surprisingly unified message: The replacement buildings needed to be more innovative in their design, and they had to serve both memorial and practical functions (Lower Manhattan Development Corporation, 2003).

In response to the overwhelmingly negative response to the first proposals, the LMDC launched a competition for new design proposals that attracted more than 400 submissions from design teams all over the world. A judging panel commissioned by the LMDC selected seven of the submissions for further development. This phase of the competition resulted in nine design concepts that were presented to the public in December 2002. An extensive public outreach campaign was instituted for the purpose of soliciting comments on the nine design concepts. More than 13,000 comments regarding the nine design concepts were received and read by the LMDC (Lower Manhattan Development Corporation, 2003). In March 2003, Daniel Libeskind's master plan for the site and "Freedom Tower" building design were selected.

The Competition for the WTC Memorial

The Lower Manhattan Development Corporation launched a design competition for a permanent memorial at the World Trade Center site in April 2003. The program guidelines were based on recommendations from family members of the World Trade Center attack victims, architects, and the general public. More than 5,000 entries were received and reviewed by a selection committee that included Maya Lin, the designer of the Vietnam Veterans Memorial in Washington, D.C. The design proposal "Reflecting Absence," by architect Michael Arad and landscape architect Peter Walker, was chosen from a group of eight finalists (Lower Manhattan Development Corporation, 2004).

Figure 13.1   "Reflecting Absence" pools within the footprints

SOURCE: From the Lower Manhattan Development Corporation.

"Reflecting Absence" creates a ground-level memorial plaza in which a grove of trees is punctuated by two large openings marking the "footprints" of the two Trade Center Towers that were destroyed on September 11, 2001. Reflecting pools are recessed within each of the two footprints (Figure 13.1). At the center of each pool is an additional void created by a water cascade. Visitors can descend ramps at the edges of the footprints, where they will be able to read the names of people who were killed in the September 11 attack.

Metaphor Studies Background

A substantial body of scholarship regarding metaphor phenomena has developed during the past three decades. In addition to the many essays that are concerned primarily with developing metaphor theory (for a recent example, see Engstrøm, 1999), numerous researchers have investigated the nature and function of actual metaphors used in particular situations or types of discourse. Topics covered in these studies include, for example, the role of metaphors in public opinion theory (Back, 1988), metaphorical thinking in organizational change (Smith & Eisenberg, 1987), figures of speech in the text accompanying advertising images (Leigh, 1994), metaphors in judicial discourse (Bosmajian, 1992), and the explanatory function of metaphors in news reports about corporate mergers (Koller, 2002).

Nonlinguistic metaphors have also been a focus of this effort. Two primary emphases in the literature on visual metaphors pertain to those used in artistic presentations and metaphors used for rhetorical purposes. Examples in the first category include metaphors in painting, sculpture, and graphic design (Aldrich, 1971; Hausman, 1989; Johns, 1984) and metaphors in movies (Whittock, 1990). Studies of visual metaphors used for rhetorical purposes generally concentrate on advertising. A familiar example is the technique of juxtaposing a picture of a sports car (in an ad for that type of vehicle) with the image of a panther, suggesting that the product has comparable qualities of speed, power, and endurance. A variation on this common technique is to merge elements of the car and the wild animal, creating a composite image. Kaplan (1990, 1993) investigated images of technology in commercial advertising and metaphors used in public service ads that promote civil liberties. Meister's (1997) study of advertising for a popular sports utility vehicle contextualizes a visual metaphor in those ads within contemporary political discourse regarding environmental policy. Other studies have examined visual metaphors in a broad range of advertising for products and services and classified them according to their formal features (Forceville, 1998; Kaplan, 1992a; Leigh, 1994).

The effort to develop and test theories of visual metaphor has been an interdisciplinary one, engaging the participation of scholars in a broad range of fields, including cognitive psychology, linguistics, communication, and the fine arts. The practical benefit of gaining a better understanding of the rhetorical functions of visual metaphors has also attracted the attention of academic researchers in advertising and marketing. This broad participation in visual metaphor studies represents a convergence of interest in nonverbal language and rhetoric. Of special note is the issue on "Metaphor and Visual Rhetoric," published by the influential journal *Metaphor and Symbolic Activity* (Kennedy & Kennedy, 1993).

Linguistic and Visual Metaphors: Similarities and Differences

Metaphors present two ideas or terms in relationship to one another such that one is used to organize or conceptualize the other (see Kittay, 1987; Lakoff & Johnson, 1980). For example, the statement "Encyclopedias are gold mines" uses the idea of gold mines to clarify or modify the reader's conception of encyclopedias. Various names have been given to the two terms that are combined in a metaphor. In the example just given, the subject of the metaphor, encyclopedias, is often called the topic or target. The idea that is used to transfer new meaning to the topic (e.g., that encyclopedias store riches) is often called the vehicle or metaphor source. These two essential components of metaphors apply to both the linguistic and nonlinguistic type. However, the task of identifying the two metaphor terms may be more difficult when they are presented in pictorial form.

For a metaphor to accomplish its work, two additional conditions must be met. First, the two terms must share some properties, and those common properties need to be at least minimally relevant to the claim made by the metaphor (i.e., A is B). Otherwise, the attempt at creating an analogy will seem implausible to the reader. Some metaphor theorists refer to the process of transferring the properties of the source to the target (for the sake of consistency, the terms *source* and *target* will be used to refer to the two components of a metaphor) as one of "mapping" relevant aspects of the source onto the target (Lakoff & Johnson, 1980). In this view of metaphor effects, the source transfers both some of its properties to the target and a structure for articulating the relationships among those properties. A somewhat different theoretical perspective is called "conceptual blending" (Turner & Fauconnier, 1995; Veale, 1998). There, the metaphor is said to create a unique conceptual structure in which selected aspects of the source and target are combined.

The second essential condition for a metaphor to work is that the attempt to combine properties of the source and target must seem at least mildly incongruous or initially nonsensical to the reader or viewer. That is, the proposition that A is B cannot be literally true. McQuarrie and Mick (1999) refer to this phenomenon in the context of advertising as an "artful deviation." An effective metaphor creates tension by intentionally violating norms of language use or the reader's beliefs about the world. Nilsen (1986) identifies three types of metaphoric tension: linguistic, pragmatic, and hermeneutic. In the context of visual metaphors, linguistic tension might result from a violation of conventions regarding the medium's syntax (e.g., not following the rules for framing a shot). Pragmatic tension might result when objects in a picture are distorted or greatly exaggerated. Hermeneutic tension results from a challenge to the viewer's beliefs about the true abstract qualities of the target of a metaphor.

The interplay of simultaneous similarity and incongruity in an effective metaphor stimulates a problem-solving response in the reader or viewer (Phillips, 1997). Brown (1976) emphasizes the literal absurdity of a good metaphor:

> The logical, empirical, or psychological absurdity of metaphor thus has a specifically cognitive function: it makes us stop in our tracks and examine it. It offers us a new awareness. The arresting vividness and tensions set off by the conjunction of contraries forces us to make our own interpretation, to see for ourselves. (p. 173)

Empirical evidence for the psychological response suggested by metaphor theories comes from a study by Tourangeau and Sternberg (1981), in which the participants were presented with metaphors that varied as to the proportion of shared and incongruous features and asked to rate the appeal of each example. The researchers found, for example, that the metaphor "A wildcat is an ICBM among mammals" received a higher rating than "A wildcat is a hawk among mammals," presumably because it possessed a substantial amount of incongruity in combination with sufficient similarity of features (both wildcats and ICBMs can be considered aggressors within their respective semantic domains) as to make the combination comprehensible. The assumption that using metaphors in rhetorical texts can facilitate persuasion receives support from a variety of sources. For example, McQuarrie and Mick (1999) found that subjects in their experiments who viewed ads containing figures of speech paid more attention to those ads, produced a more elaborate interpretation of their meaning, and reported a more positive opinion about the ad. The widespread belief in the persuasive power of metaphor is reflected in Leiss, Kline, and Jhally's (1986) assertion that "metaphor is the very heart of the basic communication form used in modern advertising" (p. 181). Phillips (2003) reviews research on the characteristics and effects of visual metaphors in advertisements.

Metaphor form will also affect the amount of tension or perceived incongruity in a metaphorical statement. The major formal distinction in this regard is between metaphors and similes. The proposition that "encyclopedias are *like* gold mines" (a simile) is a plausible analogy, whereas the metaphor "encyclopedias *are* gold mines" cannot be literally true. Thus, one would expect metaphors to stimulate greater engagement and problem-solving activity than might be the case with the equivalent simile. Support for this prediction is found in an experiment by Verbrugge (1980), in which the subjects gave more imaginative and fanciful written interpretations to sentences such as "sky-scrapers are giraffes" than to the equivalent simile "skyscrapers are like giraffes." In a test of this effect involving visual metaphors, Kaplan (1992b) found that subjects judged the metaphor version to be more imaginative than its simile equivalent and also attributed greater tension to the former.

Many metaphor theorists consider linguistic and visual metaphors to be essentially similar in most respects (see Dent & Rosenberg, 1990). Both types are based on two interacting terms, the source and the target, and a transfer of properties takes place either because the combination invites a direct analogy (i.e., in the case of similes) or because the presence of incongruity stimulates the reader or viewer to posit a provisional explanation or interpretation based on known or depicted similarities.

Other theorists call attention to the differences between words and images. For example, Whittock (1990) posits that visual images are inherently more specific than words because the underlying meaning category is made manifest through the artist's choice of a particular image. In Gibson's (1971) theory of pictorial perception, information is conveyed through an "informative structure of ambient light that is richer and more inexhaustible than the informative structure of language" (p. 34). Thus, to Gibson, "visual thinking is freer and less stereotyped than verbal thinking" (p. 34). These observations on the symbols used to create linguistic and visual metaphors suggest that the latter type may allow for greater range of treatments and variations.

Although the perspectives and theoretical arguments of scholars in this field differ on some points, there is widespread agreement on the fundamental role that metaphors play in thinking, behavior, and a range of aesthetic activities. Once considered little more than stylistic embellishment, metaphors are now broadly viewed as basic interpretive frameworks for organizing information about the world and making sense of experience:

> Accordingly, metaphor is neither an unusual use of language nor a special type of mental construction; rather, it is a form of resonating to the world, which is the source and the goal of metaphors. Thus, individual metaphors, and metaphors as such, come from perceiving the world, and they change one's perceiving of the world. (Dent-Read & Szokolszky, 1993, p. 240)

As basic interpretive frameworks, metaphors can possess considerable creative power, shaping how people come to understand unfamiliar or new ideas, products, and political issues (Gozzi, 1999). Schon (1979) notes the generative power of metaphors for suggesting novel solutions to difficult problems. He gives a number of actual examples of this phenomenon, including one where the metaphor of a paintbrush was the key to solving a difficult engineering problem in the design of a new pump. In the following sections, I describe the generative power of a few dominant metaphors that emerged during the initial public discussion regarding the World Trade Center rebuild, was continued in the discourse regarding the WTC memorial, and subsequently found material expression in the memorial design that was selected.

Initial Rhetorical Themes

As I noted above, the LMDC's public outreach effort was highly effective, as measured by the number of people who participated in public hearings and the quantity of comments submitted orally, in writing, and via e-mail. In an editorial published shortly before the final design proposal was selected, *The New York Times* lauded "a process that was far more democratic than history would have led us to expect. That alone is a fine memorial" ("The Future at Ground Zero," 2003).

Opinions about desirable qualities of the replacement structures coalesced around a few key themes. The two most often mentioned were preserving the footprints of the Twin Towers as a type of memorial (or for memorial functions) and the need to restore an important symbol on the Lower Manhattan skyline (Lower Manhattan Development Corporation, 2003). The LMDC reported that restoring the skyline by adding a major new symbol was considered highly important by 60% of attendees at the first couple of large public hearings, and preserving the footprints of the original towers was endorsed by 40% (Lower Manhattan Development Corporation, 2002).

The public consensus around a few rhetorical themes (I refer to these as rhetorical themes because the public process was, on its face, an attempt to influence the design of the replacement structures) was reinforced by the contributions of columnists and architecture critics. The idea of an empty space in the skyline is picked up in this example from *The New York Times:*

> In their absence, the World Trade Center towers are more a monument than ever. The physical void they leave is itself a poignant memorial, an aching emptiness that is the architectural counterpart to a human loss. (Lewis, 2001, p. 4)

How one of these rhetorical themes—preserving the "footprints" of the Twin Towers—found material expression in the design of the memorial that was approved for construction is the subject of the next section.

Voids as Containers for Memories

All buildings are made up of positive space and negative space. Architecture theorists refer to the various functions of "solids" and "hollows" (Arnheim, 1977) for defining activity areas and communicating symbolic values that the designers wish to project. The idea that defined empty space, such as the footprints of the original towers, could make a potent commemorative statement, emerged early in the discussion and planning process for the replacement buildings (Wyatt, 2002) and continued in discourse about the design for the memorial.

Daniel Libeskind's winning proposal made the most emotional use of the footprints by leaving the excavation where the foundations of the Twin Towers once stood in a fairly raw state (Campbell, 2003; Johnson, 2003). The directness of Libeskind's plan for preserving the footprints created a powerful container metaphor that was widely praised by journalists as this quote reflects:

> An open pit, the crucible when the fires burned for weeks after September 11, and the ground that held most of the bodies of the dead, will stand as the centerpiece of the city's effort to memorialize and rebuild after the terrorist attack. (Wyatt, 2003, p. A1)

Libeskind analogized the portion of the remaining building foundations (in the footprint void) as symbols for American democracy: "The memorial site exposes ground zero all the way down to the bedrock foundations revealing the heroic foundations of democracy for all to see" (Trachtenberg, 2003). The concrete sides of the footprint-container also acquired symbolic significance because they were built to protect the Twin Towers from the nearby river. The term *bathtub* caught on as a way to describe this property of the footprints:

> The bathtub is the inanimate hero of the disaster. It not only caught the incalculable power of the collapse, but managed—under the assault—to prevent the Hudson's waters from flooding Lower Manhattan. (Meyerowitz, 2003, p. A31)

The memorial design by Arad and Walker makes explicit use of the void metaphor in a number of significant ways. At ground level, the concrete berms mark out the perimeters of the Twin Towers, thus serving as afterimages of the destroyed towers. These persistent reminders of the missing towers will be visible to the inhabitants of the new buildings that are to be constructed, as well as visitors to many areas of the rebuilt WTC site, not only those who enter the site for the express purpose of visiting the memorial itself. Below ground, the memorial will provide access to the bedrock foundation referred to in the above quote, a retaining wall that encircles large portions of the overall WTC area and that served to protect Lower Manhattan from flooding immediately after the September 11 attack. Daniel Libeskind gave the label "memory foundations" to this structure in his master plan for rebuilding the WTC site. The memorial structure will open up to bedrock, thus embedding the footprint voids within a larger void.

A third metaphorical extension of the footprint voids is their symbolic value as containers for the memory of those lost in the attack. This function finds material expression in the names of victims that will be inscribed in below-ground viewing areas. Read more abstractly, however, the footprints provide a visual field with defined boundaries for containing memories of a tragic event that cannot be easily grasped. In their theory of ontological metaphors, Lakoff and Johnson (1980, pp. 25–32) propose that humans try to associate their experiences with bounded physical spaces as a way to reason about them.

Discussion

Memorials serve a variety of social and political purposes. They have been used to commemorate loss or celebrate victory, build community, and facilitate reconciliation in the aftermath of a highly divisive war (Carney, 1993). Thus, memorials are rhetorical texts, used for propaganda and persuasion. Memorials make moral arguments (Ehrenhaus, 1988). Because the most prominent memorials are typically financed and built by governments, they should be viewed as an expression of institutional authority, the authority of political institutions to explain the significance of past events (Ehrenhaus, 1988, pp. 56–57). With this context in mind, it may be instructive to consider the role of government in shaping the World Trade Center memorial project.

Earlier, I noted the haste with which the WTC rebuilding effort was initiated. A considerable amount of public money from New York state and the federal government was pledged to this effort very shortly after the September 11 attacks. This is an obvious break with tradition because memorials are typically constructed many years after the event that is being remembered or celebrated. Edkins (2003) argues that the speed with which the WTC rebuilding project was initiated, especially the memorial elements, might be explained by the Bush administration's foreign policy goals related to the war on terror:

In the case of September 11, it seems that by co-opting and accelerating or preempting the processes of grief, the US federal government laid the foundations for its resumption of authority and in particular put in place, in advance, the justification for its own use of violence. (p. 232)

A few powerful images, such as the footprints of the Twin Towers, played a key rhetorical role in the discourse about rebuilding on Ground Zero. Through a metaphorical process, those images became significant features in the work of architects who were selected to design replacement structures and the official WTC memorial. Thus, visual metaphors helped frame the discourse, inform the design work of the architects, and provide criteria for evaluating and comparing the design proposals. It is probably not coincidental that the winning design for the signature building and for the memorial made the most evocative use of the footprint metaphor.

Most of the work on visual metaphors has been done with advertising images. Advertising is a text with an obvious rhetorical intent and well-established norms and interpretative practices for making sense of the pictorial signs that are typically presented. Little attention has been given to persuasive functions of visual metaphor in architecture, although some scholars have examined the use of specific forms and design elements. For example, Schroeder (2003) studied the rhetorical impact of using classical columns in a contemporary building. Memorials, in particular, are rich texts for examining the uses of visual metaphors for persuasion and propaganda.

References

Aldrich, V. C. (1971). Form in the visual arts. *British Journal of Aesthetics, 11,* 215–226.

Arnheim, R. (1977). *The dynamics of architectural form.* Berkeley: University of California Press.

Back, K. W. (1988). Metaphors for public opinion. *Public Opinion Quarterly, 52,* 278–288.

Bosmajian, H. (1992). *Metaphor and reason in judicial opinions.* Carbondale: Southern Illinois University Press.

Brown, R. H. (1976). Social theory as metaphor: On the logic of discovery for the sciences of conduct. *Theory and Society, 3,* 169–197.

Campbell, R. (2003). Critique. *Architectural Record, 2,* 75–76.

Carney, L. S. (1993). Not telling us what to think: The Vietnam Veterans Memorial. *Metaphor and Symbolic Activity, 8,* 211–219.

Dent, C., & Rosenberg, L. (1990). Visual and verbal metaphors: Developmental interactions. *Child Development, 61,* 983–994.

Dent-Read, C. H., & Szokolszky, A. (1993). Where do metaphors come from? *Metaphor and Symbolic Activity, 8,* 227–242.

Edkins, J. (2003). The rush to memory and rhetoric of war. *Journal of Political and Military Sociology, 31,* 231–250.

Ehrenhaus, P. (1988). The Vietnam Veterans Memorial: An invitation to argument. *Journal of the American Forensic Association, 25,* 54–64.

Engstrøm, A. (1999). The contemporary theory of metaphor revisited. *Metaphor and Symbol, 14,* 53–61.

Forceville, C. (1998). *Pictorial metaphor in advertising.* New York: Routledge.

The future at Ground Zero. (2003, February 24). *The New York Times,* p. 29.

Gibson, J. J. (1971). The information available in pictures. *Leonardo, 4,* 27–35.

Gozzi, R. (1999). The power of metaphor: In the age of electronic media. *ETC: A Review of General Semantics, 56,* 380–389.

Hausman, C. R. (1989). *Metaphor and art.* Cambridge, UK: Cambridge University Press.

Johns, B. (1984). Visual metaphor: Lost and found. *Semiotica, 52,* 291–333.

Johnson, K. (2003, March 2). The very image of loss at Ground Zero. *The New York Times.*

Kaplan, S. J. (1990). Visual metaphors in the representation of communication technology. *Critical Studies in Mass Communication, 7,* 37–47.

Kaplan, S. J. (1992a). A conceptual analysis of form and content in visual metaphors. *Communication, 13,* 197–209.

Kaplan, S. J. (1992b, June). *An empirical investigation of tension in visual metaphors.* Paper presented at the Sixth Annual Visual Communication Conference, Flagstaff, AZ.

Kaplan, S. J. (1993, June). *Visualizing a civil liberty: Graphic representations of censorship and free expression.* Paper presented at the Seventh Annual Visual Communication Conference, Jackson Hole, WY.

Kaplan, S. J. (2003, June). *Footprints, shadows, and gardens in the sky: The role of visual metaphors in the effort to re-envision the World Trade Center.* Paper presented at the Seventeenth Annual Visual Communication Conference, Sandpoint, ID.

Kennedy, V., & Kennedy, J. (1993). A special issue: Metaphor and visual rhetoric. *Metaphor and Symbolic Activity, 8,* 149–151.

Kittay, E. F. (1987). *Metaphor: Its cognitive force and linguistic structure.* New York: Oxford University Press.

Koller, V. (2002). "A shotgun wedding": Co-occurrence of war and marriage metaphors in mergers and acquisitions discourse. *Metaphor and Symbolic Activity, 17,* 179–203.

Lakoff, G., & Johnson, M. (1980). *Metaphors we live by.* Chicago: University of Chicago Press.

Leigh, J. H. (1994). The use of figures of speech in print ad headlines. *Journal of Advertising, 23,* 17–33.

Leiss, W., Kline, S., & Jhally, S. (1986). *Social communication in advertising.* Toronto: Methuen.

Lewis, M. (2001, September 16). In a changing skyline, a sudden, glaring void. *The New York Times,* p. 4.

Lower Manhattan Development Corporation. (2002, October 24). *The public dialogue: Phase I.* New York: Author.

Lower Manhattan Development Corporation. (2003, February 27). *The public dialogue: Innovative design study.* New York: Author.

Lower Manhattan Development Corporation. (2004, January 14). *Architect Michael Arad and landscape architect Peter Walker unveil winning design for World Trade Center Site Memorial: Reflecting absence.* New York: Author.

McQuarrie, E. F., & Mick, D. G. (1999). Visual rhetoric in advertising: Text-interpretive, experimental, and reader-response analyses. *Journal of Consumer Research, 26,* 37–54.

Meister, M. (1997). "Sustainable development" in visual imagery: Rhetorical function in the Jeep Cherokee. *Communication Quarterly, 45,* 223–234.

Meyerowitz, J. (2003, February 27). Saving the wall that saved New York. *The New York Times,* p. A31.

Nilsen, D. L. F. (1986). The nature of ground in farfetched metaphors. *Metaphor and Symbolic Activity, 1,* 127–138.

Phillips, B. J. (1997). Thinking into it: Consumer interpretation of complex advertising images. *Journal of Advertising, 26,* 77–87.

Phillips, B. J. (2003). Understanding visual metaphors in advertising. In L. M. Scott & R. Batra (Eds.), *Persuasive imagery: A consumer response perspective* (pp. 298–310). Mahwah, NJ: Lawrence Erlbaum.

Schon, D. A. (1979). Generative metaphor: A perspective on problem-setting in social policy. In A. Ortony (Ed.), *Metaphor and thought* (pp. 254–283). Cambridge, UK: Cambridge University Press.

Schroeder, J. E. (2003). Building brands: Architectural expression in the electronic age. In L. M. Scott & R. Batra (Eds.), *Persuasive imagery: A consumer response perspective* (pp. 298–310). Mahwah, NJ: Lawrence Erlbaum.

Smith, R. C., & Eisenberg, E. M. (1987). Conflict at Disneyland: A root-metaphor analysis. *Communication Monographs, 54,* 367–380.

Tourangeau, R., & Sternberg, R. (1981). Aptness in metaphor. *Cognitive Psychology, 13,* 27–55.

Trachtenberg, M. (2003, February 23). A new vision for Ground Zero beyond mainstream modernism. *The New York Times.*

Turner, M., & Fauconnier, G. (1995). Conceptual integration and formal expression. *Metaphor and Symbolic Activity, 10,* 83–204.

Veale, T. (1998, April). *Pragmatic forces in metaphor appreciation: The mechanics of blend recruitment in visual metaphor.* Paper presented at CMA2, An International Workshop on Computation for Metaphors, Agents and Analogy, Aizu, Japan.

Verbrugge, R. R. (1980). Transformations in knowing: A realist view of metaphor. In R. P. Honeck & R. R. Hoffman (Eds.), *Cognition and figurative language* (pp. 87–125). Hillsdale, NJ: Lawrence Erlbaum.

Wallerstein, I. (2002). America and the world: The Twin Towers as metaphor. In C. Calhoun, P. Price, & A. Timmer (Eds.), *Understanding September 11* (pp. 345–360). New York: The New Press.

Whittock, T. (1990). *Metaphor and film.* Cambridge, UK: Cambridge University Press.

Wyatt, E. (2002, October 10). Fewer offices, more options in planning for Ground Zero. *The New York Times,* p. A1.

Wyatt, E. (2003, February 27). Design chosen for rebuilding at Ground Zero. *The New York Times,* p. A1.

14

Evening Gowns to Burqas

The Propaganda of Fame

Margaret Cavin

What is the biggest thing I could bring to the table for these women to get their situation known to the world and be a voice for the people whose voice has been stolen? My husband's fame. (M. N. Leno, personal communication, August 2, 2001)

Figure 14.1   Mavis Leno, wife of the *Tonight Show* host, Jay Leno

259

B efore most citizens of the United States were even aware of this ancient crossroad nation, Soviet troops invaded Afghanistan and installed a puppet regime in Kabul in 1979. The United States, China, Iran, Pakistan, and Saudi Arabia then offered support to the *mujahideen* "freedom fighters" who began a guerrilla war against the Soviets. Once these *mujahideen* forces removed the Soviet-backed government from power, rival militias fought for control. One of these rival militias was the Taliban, a group of young men usually under the age of 30 who adhered to a very conservative form of Islam. With the help of America's CIA, there to help the Afghan people fight Soviet expansionism, the Taliban formed a military force. The Soviets left Afghanistan in 1989, and 7 years later, the Taliban seized military control of the country. Immediately after doing so, they implemented two decisions that led to their country's contribution to the terror narrative. The Taliban offered Osama bin Laden refuge soon after they took power, and they immediately and drastically changed the conditions and rights for women in that country, motivated by their strict interpretation of Islamic law.

Before 1996 and since the 1960s, Afghan women held professional jobs in all the major professions such as teachers, physicians, and lawyers; they also held political office and were free to go out in public places. While many wore the traditional burqa, this was a reflection of their Islamic religious practice and was, to a large extent, practiced by individual choice. Once the Taliban took control of the country, they installed a fundamentalist form of Islamic religion as the law of the land. Among some of the changes in conditions for women were a moratorium on work for women and very strict guidelines inhibiting a woman's ability to step outside her home; for example, they were only allowed to beg in the streets for food if they did not have a male relative or a male child older than 6 years who could beg for them. The windows on homes were blackened so that no one could see women inside; women were forced to wear burqas at all times when they were in public, and if any part of their skin showed, severe punishment in the form of beatings or death were exacted. Women were also required to wear soft-soled shoes so that their presence would be quiet. In addition, women and female children were not allowed to be educated or to even be allowed to read a book. Also, because women physicians were not allowed to practice medicine and male doctors could not see the nakedness of women, many females died from childbirth and other preventable traumas and illnesses. Eventually, the Taliban allowed a few locations with the most primitive tools and conditions to provide female physicians for the care of women and female children, but concessions to the human dignity of females were tiny and very slow in coming; thus, depression and suicide became serious problems among women in the country.

Journalists were not allowed to enter the country so examples of abuse were "smuggled" out by women who risked their lives to communicate the abuse to the outside world. Later, it was learned that a journalist, Saira Shah, and an organization of Arab women (RAWA [Revolutionary Association Women in Afghanistan]) were at the time surreptitiously filming the conditions, dangers, and punishments of women and female children. Their efforts culminated in the award-winning documentary *Beneath the Veil* (June 2001). There were also women who secretly worked to educate the female children in their homes, and they were helped by RAWA, which clandestinely provided educational materials. However, their efforts were very limited because of the danger of exposure.

In 1998, the United States launched missiles at an alleged terrorist training camp and Osama bin Laden, in retribution for the bombing of embassies in Africa. Later, in 1999, the United Nations (UN) placed an air embargo and froze Taliban assets in order to force them to turn over bin Laden for trial. In 2001, the UN added an arms embargo against the Taliban, and also by this time, a record drought, cold, and civil war forced an estimated 200,000 more Afghans into refugee camps.

In March 2001, disregarding a public and international outcry, the Taliban destroyed two 2,000-year-old Buddhist statues in the cliffs above Bamian. Religious minorities were ordered to wear tags identifying them as non-Muslims, and Hindu women were forced to veil themselves like other Afghan women. Also, the Taliban banned the use of movies, playing cards, computer disks, Internet, satellite TV, musical instruments, and chessboards, saying they were against Islamic law.

On September 11, 2001, Al Qaeda terrorists attacked the U.S. World Trade Center and the Pentagon. Afraid of U.S. revenge, more than 4,000 Afghans began to flee each day across the border into Pakistan. At the same time, the U.S. demanded that the Taliban turn over bin Laden and Al Qaeda members, but the Taliban leaders responded that they would give bin Laden to the United States only if they were given evidence of his guilt. By the end of September, the Taliban called for a *jihad* against America if the U.S. forces entered Afghanistan. On October 7, the United States began to bomb strategic Taliban sites in Afghanistan. Osama bin Laden issued a statement calling on all Muslims to wage a holy war against the United States. Soon the United States began a ground assault against the Taliban and sent in special operations forces to hunt for bin Laden. In December 2001, the Taliban surrendered power, and the United States asserted that Al Qaeda had been destroyed in Afghanistan even though bin Laden was never located. Also during this time, Afghanistan agreed in principle to a UN peacekeeping force. By May 2003, Defense Secretary Donald Rumsfeld said that most of Afghanistan is secure and stabilized, but pro-Taliban insurgents continue to regularly attack government buildings, aid workers, and U.S. bases as "war lords" profit from the illegal cultivation of poppies.

The Ideology and Purpose of the Propaganda Campaign

Feminists were some of the first to communicate the Taliban's repression of women in Afghanistan. In particular, the Feminist Majority Foundation (FMF), located in Beverly Hills, California, quickly became involved. Fighting against the clear violation of women's rights, safety, and health occurring under Taliban rule was in keeping with the purpose of the organization. The foundation states on its Web site that it is "dedicated to women's equality, reproductive health, and non-violence. In all spheres, FMF utilizes research and action to empower women economically, socially, and politically. Our organization believes that feminists—both women and men, girls and boys— are the majority, but this majority must be empowered." Furthermore, the specific purpose of FMF's campaign for Afghan women and girls is communicated on its Web site as well: It "is a public education and grassroots effort that has brought the human rights catastrophe to national and international attention" (http://www.feminist.org/welcome/index.html).

The first part of the rhetorical campaign included agitating for global awareness and discovering methods of giving aid to these women in the form of money, food, educational materials, and so on. However, after September 11, 2001, when the United States was clearly headed for war with Afghanistan, FMF's language changed, predominantly demonstrated by its spokesperson, Mavis Leno. Her demands still included aid for the women and female children, but she added a call for the removal of the Taliban, the stated source of the repression of women and girls in Afghanistan. She also wanted to bring to light the plight of Afghan women by making it a part of the world's reporting on the war once it began and to emphatically state that women's rights would be a nonnegotiable part of a post-Taliban Afghanistan.

The Context in Which the Propaganda Occurs

The following analysis focuses on the rhetorical narratives created by Mavis Leno and how they were used in the media, starting with her involvement as chair of FMF early in 1997 and culminating with her rhetoric immediately before and after September 11, 2001. The importance of September 11,

2001, for this analysis is that it represents a turning point in her work and marks a specific change in the media characterization of Leno's identity. These changes represent a specific shift in focus and a move toward a use of entertainment forms as methods of white propaganda. The rhetorical documents used for this examination include all of the media events involving Ms. Leno that were provided to me by FMF, dating from October 21, 1998, to October 6, 2001. They are entertainment talk shows, news broadcasts, a press conference, and a town hall meeting. In addition, I interviewed Mavis Leno twice at the FMF headquarters (the first in Los Angeles and the second in its new facility in Beverly Hills). The first interview was conducted August 2, 2001, the month before September 11, 2001, and the second was January 15, 2004.

Identification of the Propagandist and the Structure of the Propaganda Organization

Since my early childhood I have been especially obsessed by things that aren't fair; I can't stand things that aren't fair. I'm really demented on that. And also, I have a very strong impulse to rescue people, to ride to the aid of somebody. I can't stand to see people frightened. If I see someone frightened, I have to take fear away from them, if I can. So I guess, all of those things played a role. (M. N. Leno, personal communication, January 15, 2004)

Mavis Nicholson Leno is the chair of the Feminist Majority Foundation's Campaign to Stop Gender Apartheid in Afghanistan and has been one of the most outspoken rhetors on its behalf. Leno joined the Board of Directors of the FMF in 1997 after playing a role in the attempt to defeat Proposition 209, the anti-affirmative action initiative on the 1996 California ballot.

Also in her role as chair, she testified on gender apartheid in March 1998 before Senator Diane Feinstein of the U.S. Senate Foreign Relations Committee and worked to persuade the Clinton and Bush administrations as well as the U.S. Congress to restore women's rights in Afghanistan. She was successful in defeating the energy company UNOCAL's determination to construct an oil pipeline across Afghanistan that would have provided the Taliban with more than $100 million and significantly increased their control in the region.

She is presently a leader in the attempt to make the reestablishment of women's rights a nonnegotiable part of a post-Taliban Afghanistan, and she has consistently been a vanguard to ensure that the terrible predicament of the Afghanistan women is communicated by the media when they report the war and postwar Afghanistan. Leno has appeared on many interview and talk shows such as *Larry King Live, The Today Show, The Tonight Show, The View, CNN With Paula Zahn, Hardball With Chris Mathews, Hannity & Colmes, CNN Morning News, FOX News,* and *MSNBC Nightly News;* she has appeared in popular entertainment shows such as *Extra, E! News Daily, Access Hollywood, Entertainment Tonight,* and *Entertainment Weekly* and has been interviewed for articles in *Newsweek, Time, Vanity Fair, US Magazine, People Magazine, Washington Post,* and the *Los Angeles Times.*

When Leno first became involved with FMF, as she has explained in many interviews (including mine), she had been unaware of the plight of the women of Afghanistan. She was surprised that she had been unaware because she reads a lot of books (approximately 10 per week), and she clearly thought that the American press had been negligent in their omission of the story. She explained to me in our second interview that she has always felt passionate about injustice, and when someone is a victim, she is eager to help. Leno had been involved in women's rights for many years and historically was involved on the level of stamping envelopes and working behind the scenes to contribute. But this time, she felt it was her "turn" and needed to "step up to the plate" (M. N. Leno, personal communication, January 15, 2004). She explained that she wanted to help but initially felt inadequate and focused on her weaknesses rather than her strengths. She believed herself to be shy and uncomfortable in speaking situations or situations where attention was placed on her. However, the cause was compelling, so she ignored her natural reticence and proceeded to become a central player in the unfolding drama.

In the campaign to end "gender apartheid" in Afghanistan, Leno acted as chair and was the visible leader in most media situations. The FMF has many goals with regard to the Campaign for Afghan Women and Girls. Before the terrorist attacks on American soil, the goals were to bring awareness to Americans on a grassroots level and then encourage Americans to write and call political leaders to put pressure on them to not acknowledge the Taliban as a legitimate government in Afghanistan. They also sought to raise funds to provide food, medical care, and educational resources for the women. Their message was urgent because women and female children were living in repressive conditions and dying in large numbers. Their campaign worked on the grassroots level, but FMF was also highly sophisticated in various forms of mass media such as print journalism, television, and the Internet. After the terrorist attacks in New York City, FMF's goals were to (a) increase peacekeeping forces, (b) support the Afghan Ministry for Women's Affairs, (c) support the Independent Human Rights Commission and Afghan women-led nongovernmental organizations (NGOs), (d) instigate leadership of women in post-Taliban Afghanistan, and (e) expand and monitor the provision of emergency and reconstruction assistance to women and girls (http://www .feminist.org/afghan/intro.asp). The organization requested on its Web site that individuals choose to help them achieve these goals by doing one of the following: "Urge the Bush Administration to immediately expand troops in Afghanistan," "Tell 10 friends," "Donate $25," "Form an action team," and "Buy Afghan crafts" (http://www.feminist.org/afghan/intro.asp). Individuals who donate money for the campaign are given a subscription to *Ms Magazine*, T-shirts, and Afghan crafts such as pillow cases, silk shawls, dolls, and holiday ornaments (http://www.feminist.org/afghan/intro.asp).

The Target Audience

Considering the urgency of the problem, sophisticated use of the media became a crucial part of the strategy to reach the largest American audience possible. The goal was to persuade people to write and call political leaders, pressuring them to avoid doing business with the Taliban and advocating that they continue to refuse to recognize the Taliban as the legitimate leadership of Afghanistan. Leno made clear on many occasions to the press the fear that the Bush administration was considering changing the status of the Taliban to one of legitimacy.

The target audience included specific politicians. Leno met with both the Clinton and the Bush administrations, as well as testifying before the U.S. Congress to encourage them toward greater involvement. Business leaders were also specifically targeted. When the energy company UNOCAL planned to build an oil pipeline across Afghanistan, as part of an ongoing campaign by FMF, Leno convinced one of the shareholders to let her take his seat at one of UNOCAL's meetings, and in the session, she attempted to persuade the company to withdraw its plans. Soon after, it did halt efforts.

Leno also planned several fund-raisers targeting Hollywood celebrities. This served two main purposes in that it provided the Hollywood community an opportunity to add its voices to the campaign and gave them an opportunity to give financial support.

In addition, Leno targeted media reporters, newscasters, and interviewers. Once they became aware of the situation, they were in a position to contribute to the "narrative" and reach a greater audience. After 9/11, the target audiences remained the same, but the goals shifted as the story took a more immediate and intimate turn.

Justification of Rhetorical Methodology to Analyze Propaganda

Rhetoric is an art form where artisans craft a definable product, an artifact, available to all for consideration, acceptance, or critique. Sonja K. Foss (2004, pp. 4–6) defines rhetoric as "the human use of symbols" in an effort to communicate and possibly to persuade others toward change. Rhetoric crosses many paths of study: semiotics, semantics, linguistics, performance, literature, oratory, and more. Any study of the symbols used in the act of propaganda can be enriched by a critical analysis steeped in the theories and perspectives offered by the rhetorical critical tradition. Rhetors seek, first of all, to construct a group of people of shared values and contextualities who are willing to be inspired into action based on the realities communicated in the speech act. Rhetorical critics attempt to understand and identify the realities that are created by the speaker, the audience, and the context within which the symbolic transaction takes place. Rhetorical critics then relate to their readers the total effect of the symbolic framing that exists within the world of the whole speech act. Words are "symbolic acts" of power (Burke, 1945/1969, pp. 38–42; Burke, 1989, pp. 77–85) that may lead us to act out in physical actions that may lead to further symbolic acts. To study important rhetors, particularly ones as visible as Leno in the feminist movement, and examine their language is not only useful but also compelling. The speech act is an artifact that, when properly contextualized, can shed light on potential effective language-based systems of persuasion and propaganda.

The particular rhetorical methodology used in this study is narrative criticism. Foss (2004) summons dramatic structure when she states that "a narrative generally is recognized to be a way of ordering and presenting a view of the world through a description of a situation involving characters, actions, and settings" (p. 400). She goes on to explain, "A narrative, as a frame upon experience, functions as an argument to view and understand the world in a particular way, and by analyzing that narrative, the critic can understand the argument being made and the likelihood that it will be successful in gaining adherence for the perspective it presents" (p. 400). Furthermore, narrative criticism can provide "the opportunity to analyze not simply the content of a worldview [such as pentadic criticism or fantasy-theme], but the form and structure of that worldview" (p. 401).

Walter Fisher (1987) sees the narrative paradigm as being the way humans "establish a meaningful life-world" (p. 62). For him, the hearers of stories are affected on a number of important levels simultaneously. The structure of the story appeals to a listener's sense of reason, emotion, intellect, imagination, sense of truth, and assessment of value (p. 75). Because of this multiple effect and because of the ubiquitous presence of storytelling throughout human history, Fisher believes that use of the narrative is a "reliable, trustworthy, and desirable guide to belief and action" (p. 95). If we accept Fisher's understanding of narrative potency, it is clear to see the potential benefits offered to propagandists who structure their message into a story. The narrative structure is a ready-made devise for delivering a message that is partly accepted simply because of its familiar form. This allows the propagandist to use strategic ellipses (remaining silent on issues that might complicate and thereby dissuade acceptance) and to communicate with simplicity in a limited amount of time. There seems to be a clear justification for using narrative rhetorical analysis when examining the story artifacts of propagandists. This method allows us to more carefully examine the strategies employed by the rhetor, and it allows the critic a greater opportunity to posit the effects of those strategies on the intended audience as it considers the text of the narrative, its context, method of dissemination, and impact.

Stewart, Smith, and Denton (2001, pp. 249–272) explained that argument from a narrative vision is a compelling persuasive structure used by social movements. In fact, they stated, "Finally, because narratives help us to interpret events, and because events help us to validate our choice of narrative, political history is a series of struggles for narrative dominance" (p. 270). Narratives are fluid and exist primarily among an exchange of adaptive strategies played out on and determined by popular media's reaction/construction of dramatic events around the stories of Mavis Leno, and those stories are, in turn, used by her as a form of white propaganda. White propaganda is defined by Jowett and O'Donnell (1999) as coming "from a source that is identified correctly, and the information in the message tends to be accurate" (p. 12), as opposed to black propaganda, which is "credited to a false source and spreads lies, fabrications, and deceptions" (p. 13). Leno engages in a white propaganda in an attempt to move a broad audience toward a recognition of the tragic human drama developing in Afghanistan.

Media Utilization Techniques

Mavis Leno, married to television personality and star Jay Leno, knew how to use the resources of glamour and drama of Hollywood, and she immediately called on these as strategies to use for her compelling mission to help the women of Afghanistan. She had never used them before but felt it necessary to do so in this situation. She explained in our second interview,

It took a long time for me to stop focusing on what I felt I was inadequate at, which when I began the traditional thing to do something about a human rights abuse would be to go to get money in the form of grants and to go to the serious press; get the issue into *Time,* blah, blah, blah . . . But I think that it is not uncommon for women to focus on what they don't know rather than what they do know because this is exactly what I was doing. And one day, the dime dropped, I realized, "Wait a minute, I don't know anything about these things, but I do know everything about how you make something famous in Hollywood." (M. N. Leno, personal communication, January 15, 2004)

The strategic use of celebrity power is of course not unique to FMF. It is useful to examine the effectiveness and power of celebrities within various persuasion and propaganda campaigns because it points to a greater understanding of the propagandist, the audience, and the reality surrounding the two.

It all began when Leno decided to use the strengths she had. She contacted her husband's publicists and asked them to help her plan two press conferences, one in New York (October 21, 1998) and one in Los Angeles (October 22, 1998), where she would announce that she and her husband were donating $100,000 to the cause. She claimed that this was the only way she knew to put an immediate end to the "silence" surrounding the plight of Afghan women. Once Mavis and Jay Leno held the press conferences, holding up a large billboard check with $100,000 written on it, there was indeed an immediate reaction by the popular media. They began to regularly appear together on local news shows, and within a day of the press conferences, they were invited on *Larry King Live* while other popular entertainment shows soon had them as guests.

The first media attention (October 22, 1998) came immediately after the Lenos held their press conference. The second cluster of media focus (March 29, 1999) came immediately before and after a Hollywood fundraiser that Mavis Leno created to involve stars in the cause. The crafting of this fund-raiser became part of the narrative. Linda Bloodworth Thomason, a television producer and creator of *Designing Women* and *Evening Shade,* strategically created the event. She had, along with her husband, been responsible for producing two inaugural celebrations for President Bill Clinton and is perceived as a powerful woman in both Hollywood and Washington, D.C. She came on board to help develop positive press around the fund-raiser with Mavis Leno at the center. "She would choreograph a high profile Hollywood event, marking Mavis Leno's debut as a humanitarian, mover, and shaker" (*CNN Entertainment Weekly,* May 6, 1999). Leno explained in my interview that many agents and publicists are women; thus, when she and Bloodworth called them, they were eager and passionate to help and would ask, "Who do you want to be there?" and then they made it happen (M. N. Leno, personal communication, January 15, 2004). She believed that Hollywood had as much right to speak as anyone else with the power to do so. She stated in my interview with her,

> First of all, I don't know why fame would disenfranchise you. You have as much right to your opinion as any other American and if it's more listened to because you're famous, it's your opinion, why wouldn't you want it to be more listened to? But what I really find hypocritical about it, since it mostly shows up in the news (regular people don't seem to be irritated by it, you know), the people that own the media, the people that own the newspapers, the magazines, the you know, television shows and networks; they don't own them because they're so incredibly well up on current affairs and political interactions. They own them because they're rich. Why is it okay for them to have a hugely disproportionate voice in American and international politics, and not all right for celebrities? (M. N. Leno, personal communication, January 15, 2004)

During both events, a consistent narrative emerged communicating the story of the rich and famous caring for abused and neglected women half a world away. The narrative was forged out of the materials of popular media, fame, and an awful truth.

The third cluster of media events surrounding Mavis Leno's campaign was immediately following the tragic terrorist attacks in New York City on 9/11. Leno explains this time period by stating,

> I was in Europe when it happened . . . Suzie Gilligan of FMF and Kathy were calling me every minute, this person wants an article, that person wants an article, "When you get back, would you do this interview?" I swear, as soon as I got back, I had 3 seconds to get over jet lag, because then it was just news, news, news. This was the chance we had been waiting for and we were not going to fluff it if possible. (M. N. Leno, personal communication, January 15, 2004)

Leno explained to me in the second interview that she was in Italy when the terrorist tragedy occurred at the World Trade Center. Once she returned home, the media bombarded her. Suddenly, everyone wanted her to appear on his or her show (M. N. Leno, personal communication, January 15, 2004). This cluster of media events was different from the two before in that it now included news as well as entertainment shows. Leno was invited to appear on *The Today Show, CNN News, FOX News,* and *Hardball.* Entertainment and news heavyweights in the industry such as Paula Zann, Chris Matthews, Lisa Givvens, and Katie Couric interviewed her. During this period, the story shifted and allowed the inclusion of the arch-villain Al Qaeda terrorist network, which had the effect of moving the narrative closer to melodrama and, perhaps, caused it to be ultimately subsumed into the larger melodrama—the war on terrorism.

Special Techniques to Maximize Effect

Narrative Prior to 9/11

Source credibility was initially an issue for Ms. Leno in that she was not well known by her intended audience, and no one considered her to be an expert in the area of international politics, religious extremism, or even basic Islamic traditions. But source credibility is thought to be a major contributing factor to the overall effectiveness of the propaganda event (Jowett & O'Donnell, 1999, p. 291). To compensate for the lack of initial source credibility, the narrative was constructed by Leno and others to draw upon the Hollywood star power of her husband, Jay Leno. I asked her if she felt it was a contradiction to use the star power of her husband for a feminist cause, and she replied,

> In this situation, he's doing it for me, and you know, when I said that the first thing you need to do, if you do this kind of thing, is get your ego out of it. That would be about my ego. Do I look like a hypocrite? Do I look like . . . ? What is the biggest thing I could bring to the table for these women to get their situation known to the world and be a voice for the people whose voice has been stolen? My husband's fame. If I am not willing to use it because people might think I was being less than a feminist, then my ego isn't out of it enough, is it? (M. N. Leno, personal communication, August 2, 2001)

The Lenos understood that once they agreed to be interviewed together, they would be giving up valued privacy to their personal lives, but according to Leno, they were willing to do so to help relieve the plight of Afghan women, and she knew that she lacked the credibility of star power to accomplish her goal (M. N. Leno, personal communication, August 2, 2001). Later, when media accounts focused on the Hollywood fund-raiser, referential source credibility was established when segments portrayed other celebrities present at the event. Reports began with comments about the "star-studded event" and "Hollywood turns out tonight" as well as "Big movie stars were out in force tonight to call attention to the plight of the women and girls in Afghanistan" (KCAL, March 29, 1999). A reporter on KCAL stated, "The glitz and glamour of Hollywood is literally a world away from the troubled streets of Afghanistan. But the women of Tinseltown are speaking out for their sisters across the globe" (KCAL, March 29, 1999). Lists of stars present at the event were given (KCAL, *Access Hollywood, Entertainment Tonight,*

E!, News Daily, CNN Entertainment Weekly, March 29, 1999). In some of the accounts, interviews occurred with some of the stars, and they consistently communicated agreement with Leno's cause and called attention to her heroism. Juliette Lewis said, "The fact that she's taken on this cause so strongly shows that that's an incredible woman right there" (*Access Hollywood,* March 30, 1999). Lionel Ritchie claimed, "One call from Mavis did it" (*CNN Entertainment Weekly,* May 6, 1999). While *E! News Daily* told the story of the fund-raiser, it had the words continually on the screen, "Mavis Message" (March 29, 1999). In addition, Jay Leno addressed his wife's reluctant heroism when he concluded the fund-raiser by tearfully stating, "I am so proud of her. The only one crying was the guy" (*Access Hollywood,* March 30, 1999). The weight of 1,000 celebrities present at the event, combined with that of her husband's, endowed Leno with a referential credibility all her own and provided a substantial opening between her and her intended mass audience.

Visual symbols of power, also a propaganda technique (Jowett & O'Donnell, 1999, pp. 293–294), were present in the media accounts. In many televised segments, images were shown repetitively of the Lenos attending Hollywood parties and awards ceremonies, attractively dressed in fashionable clothing, getting in and out of limousines, and filmed walking in slow motion, capturing the mystery and splendor of their lives. They were awash in the typical symbols of power, wealth, beauty, and glamour that entertainment television craves.

According to Jowett and O'Donnell (1999), "Messages have greater impact when they are in line with existing opinions, beliefs, and dispositions" (p. 290). Stewart et al. (2001) argue that the use of narrative in persuasive appeal "hinges less on changing beliefs, attitudes, or values than on integrating beliefs and behaviors into a story regarded by the audience as coherent, relevant, compatible, promising, and proper" (p. 250). For audiences, the personal narrative created by the media and Mavis and Jay Leno reinforced American values such as romance, traditional marriage and marriage roles, popularity, and success.

In the personal narrative, Mavis and Jay Leno live a glamorous life in Hollywood and are a happily married couple in a culture where that is unusual. One reporter said they are an "endangered species in Hollywood, a couple happily married for eighteen years in spite of the pressures of wealth and fame" (*Extra,* October 28, 1998). Sometimes, part of the narrative included how they met and fell in love. One reporter said, "They met twenty-two years ago at a L.A. Comedy Club. She was a struggling screenwriter sitting in the audience. Jay was performing and she caught his eye. And the rest is history" (*Extra,* January 16, 1999). When Jay introduced Mavis on

The Tonight Show, he stated, "My next guest, my best friend in the whole world, who I love more than anything" (March 23, 1999). During the show, they discussed how they met, how Jay proposed, and whether Jay was romantic or not. They are a successful, attractive, and wealthy couple who love each other and are living a fairy-tale life. There were several times when after crafting the narrative for the audience, a reporter would conclude, "That's sweet" and "They seem really happy" (*Extra,* March 24, 1999).

Their life appears to be one of romance as well as sexual pleasure. When Jay introduced Mavis on *The Tonight Show,* he stated, "She's the only guest I've slept with." During the interview, he discussed the car they first had sex in and explained that they still have the car and created an entire humorous scenario around the situation (March 23, 1999). Also, after Mavis appeared on *The Tonight Show* for the first time, an *Inside Edition* reporter interviewed the Lenos; Jay commented about what the situation of her appearance on his show had been like for the two of them, and he said, "It's like our first date together" (March 24, 1999). He then went on to make a sexual innuendo about the "first time" when he said, "Like first dates, we didn't know what was going to happen, but we know what is going to happen afterwards" (*Access Hollywood,* March 24, 1999).

Not only did the narrative emphasize Mavis's shyness but also the couple's attempts to be very private about their personal lives until the FMF campaign to help Afghan women. One commentator stated on the entertainment show, *Inside Edition,* "Jay is kind of opening up to us at home, showing us his family and showing us a little bit of himself. Before, he was just trying very hard to entertain, entertain, entertain. Now he's setting back and we're getting to know Jay a little better" (March 24, 1999). Mavis, more than her spouse Jay, values privacy. One reporter explained, "Mavis prefers to keep her private life private, but now is shedding her anonymity for women's rights" (*Extra,* January 16, 1999).

Mavis Leno's narrative before 9/11 perfectly reflected the grand narrative of contemporary fame. Her story was set to the defining attributes of the American mythology where everyone can be young, beautiful, well connected, virtual, and terribly rich. Leno tapped into this narrative context of fame because her story involved money, television, sex, and the titillating thrill of getting to know the Lenos, who were in the past private and mysterious. Her story also contained the essential ingredient of all dramas—conflict (kept at a safe distance), laced with bits of the exotica of a dark and mysterious eastern culture. Taken together, Leno's narrative reflected American fame and, in so doing, appropriated some of its mass potency.

As with anyone wishing to tap into the mass appeal that fame offers, Leno was restricted to performing within a set of constraints. One such constraint was time. She had to briefly communicate the details of her message and her preferred billboard-like statement "gender apartheid" (*KCET Life and Times Tonight,* November 19, 1998). Whenever she was given an opportunity, she briefly stated that women were allowed equality before the Taliban and that after the Taliban took power, their basic rights were removed, but her message was usually well seasoned with the two-word phrase that alluded to another historical narrative that included elements of a world behind a just cause and success. Usually, she gave the example of women being forced to wear burqas. She concluded several times, "Every other thing that constitutes human life has been stripped from them [the women]" (*KCET Life and Times Tonight,* November 19, 1998). Many times, she would display a burqa as a symbol of repression and point out the piece of one she wore on her clothing as a reminder of the women in Afghanistan (*Howie Mandel Show,* February 10, 1999). Some entertainment shows would show pictures of women wearing burqas in Afghanistan or neighboring Pakistan. The women would be shown walking in slow motion with mysterious yet upbeat music playing in the background (*Extra, Access Hollywood, Inside Edition,* 1998–1999).

When Leno described the situation, she creatively incorporated a strategy commonly used by propagandists; she built her argument on the structure of American group norms and values. According to Jowett and O'Donnell (1999), "Conforming tendencies are also used to create a 'herd instinct' in crowds" (p. 293). In one of the first interviews the Lenos gave, on *Larry King Live,* Mavis explained, "This is such a profound egregious violation of human rights, this is so far over the line." Jay Leno then stated, "As bizarre as this sounds, I don't want people to think this has anything to do with Muslim or Islamic faith. This is to the Muslim-Islamic faith what the Jerry Springer clan guy is to Christianity" (October 22, 1998). When Larry King interviewed the Lenos, Jay explained, "You see, there is no other side to this issue, I mean, there is no one else saying, 'Let's go to the opposition and see how they feel,' because there is no other side" (October 22, 1998). Several times, he compared the Taliban to Hitler's power in Germany. He said that no one in America believed people were being exterminated because it seemed too extreme to them. Both Lenos repetitively made the point that the Taliban are isolated from the rest of reasonable human beings, and if the audience is reasonable versus extreme, they too will want to be a part of the group that has nothing to do with the Taliban. Therefore, the audience must get involved and give money, contact Congress, and so on.

Prior to 9/11, reporters and interviewers typically communicated a warm interest in the Lenos' personal narrative but maintained a distance from the Afghanistan part of the story. Their take on the story was Mavis as reluctant heroine and Jay supporting her cause. One reporter ended the story after the

Afghan part was told with a dismissive "hmm" and then concluded with an update on Jay being a new columnist for *Popular Mechanic* (*Access Hollywood,* January 27, 1999). Many times after a brief discussion with Leno about Afghanistan, reporters asked her questions about her husband's comic material, why she has not had children, her travels, and so on. The sad tale of Afghanistan women was far away and did not involve U.S. politics (no pointing fingers at American political leaders) or religion. After the attacks of September 11, 2001, a new chapter was written in the narrative.

Narrative After 9/11

Leno understood the importance of the events on 9/11 to her rhetorical message. In our interview, she stated,

> Dealing with the events, I mean, one of the good things that came out of the hideous unspeakable situation obviously was huge visibility for what had happened to these women and for the profoundly villainous nature of the Taliban, which it was hard to actually persuade people prior to that, especially in the first couple of years we got doubted a lot by journalists. All of a sudden, it was a complete turn around. (M.N. Leno, personal communication, January 15, 2004)

Leno understood that a strategic rhetorical response was necessary to maximize the opportunity given to FMF in this situation. In some ways, her message remained the same after 9/11. The story had strong continuity in terms of the polarization between the people of Afghanistan (particularly women) and the Taliban. She stated, "They [the Afghan people] not only don't side with the Taliban. They hate them, they loathe them, they fear them, and they spend a huge amount of time escaping from them" (*Entertainment Tonight,* September 27, 2001). Here Leno's purpose was to create identification between the Afghan women and American audiences, so that Americans would want to provide help and safety for these people. Also, her focus on the Taliban was a staple of her message after 9/11 as well as before (KABC, September 27, 2001). Again, this emphasized the freedoms that had been taken away from the Afghan women as well as the idea that the women are the "invisible enemies" of the Taliban (News conference, September 30, 2001).

Source credibility continued to be a key strategy after 9/11—not from referential power, but rather from expertise and authority now granted to Mavis Leno. The narrative constructed after 9/11 had Leno as its central character, and there was only a tangential association with the celebrity of her husband. There were no longer discussions of the Lenos' marriage, Jay's comedy routines, or Mavis's shyness and desire for privacy. No longer did the media capitalize on the romance of the Lenos, detached from the plight of the women in Afghanistan.

Leno was still identified in most media accounts as the wife of Jay Leno, and there were still several glamorous images of the pair initially shown to establish context, but then full attention was directed at Leno. She was now characterized as a "prophet," one who knew the evil of the Taliban from almost the beginning, and the media were passionately engaged in her story. For example, the *KTLA Morning News* interviewer began his interview with Leno by saying, "When you came back in '99 we looked at you like 'What are you talking about?' Now we know what you are talking about." Later, in the interview, he said to her, "Somehow a lot of us are saying that we wished we had listened to you in '99" (September 26, 2001). Chris Matthews, on *Hardball,* began his interview with Leno by stating, "A couple of years ago I saw you and your husband, Jay, on television, the *Larry King Show.* And you were making a very strong case on this and like most Americans, I said, 'Of course,' and ignored it and said, 'What else is new? That's terrible but I don't care.' Now we care" (October 5, 2001). *Inside Edition* (September 27, 2001) began its show with, "Jay Leno's wife warned America about the evils of the Taliban. She knew what they were capable of." Finally, Jay also communicated the idea that Mavis knew and said we must listen to her. When he introduced her visit to his show for the second time, he said, "I'm very proud of my next guest, my wife, Mavis. You know she was very involved in this Taliban thing a couple of years ago and she brought it to my attention, and she met with the president and she met with a lot of people long before people even knew what it was to help the women of Afghanistan, and she is somewhat of an expert on this, as much as anybody in the country, and she's here to talk to us tonight, my wife, Mavis Leno" (*The Tonight Show,* October 3, 2001).

The media after 9/11 spent much more time crafting the drama of Afghanistan and many times would present this before Mavis was introduced. Reporters were shown in neighboring Pakistan, walking among women in burqas and menacing-looking men. Because of the availability of the film *Beneath the Veil* (2001), images of women being beaten, even killed by the Taliban, were repeatedly shown. These images were juxtaposed with images of people working at the FMF headquarters, images of the attacks on the World Trade Center in New York City, and images of American soldiers driving in Humvees in Afghanistan. Phrases on the screen were repeatedly shown, such as "War on Terrorism" (*FOX News,* KTLA, October 4, 2001), "America on Alert" (*KCAL News,* September 2, 2001), and "America's New War" (*Larry King Live,* September 2, 2001).

The drama became much larger, more menacing, and Americans were becoming a part of its structure. The narrative explained that Leno was a prophet among us who warned us of the evil in a far-away place called Afghanistan. She and the other brave individuals at FMF were hard at work on this issue long before we were victimized by the same evil. Now America must go to war and rid the world of the evil in Afghanistan that had come to our own country to commit atrocities. The Taliban as villain was the focal point of what was now taking shape as a melodrama, rather than Jay as the celebrity who was at the heart of the earlier story. Stewart et al. (2001) discuss strategies used by social movements, and one that is particularly effective is Kenneth Burke's rhetoric of polarization, which can include the identification of a devil that creates a common enemy worthy of destruction, therefore providing a source of unification for the audience (Burke, 1969, pp. 161–162). The media, with their passionately intense voices, used a rhetoric of polarization that included the following words to describe the Taliban: *tyrannical, militant, radical, violent, sickening, horrific, vicious, brutal, insane, abominable,* and *disgraceful* (*Hardball,* October 5, 2001; *Extra,* September 2, 2001; *FOX News With Hannity & Colmes,* October 4, 2001; *CNN News,* September 28, 2001; *Today Show,* October 2, 2001). Leno, too, engaged in this intense and passionate denouncement of the Taliban with words such as *insane, control freaks, ominous,* and *religious fanatics* (news conference, September 30, 2001; *CNN News,* September 28, 2001; *Today Show,* October 2, 2001).

In the narrative she created with the media, Leno communicated the evil of the Taliban and the urgency needed to remove them so that the women and children would not starve and die. She made a direct link between two villains, the Taliban and Osama bin Laden, when she said, "There's no question in my mind that Osama bin Laden and the Taliban are one and the same" (news conference, September 30, 2001), and she maintained in a different interview, "The only thing about that day [9/11/01], and everything that happened that was not shocking to the point of being almost incomprehensible, was that the Taliban, in the form of Osama bin Laden and his supporters, were direct suspects because there are 8–10 terrorist training camps that we know of in Afghanistan. They've been there right along since they took in bin Laden" (*KTLA Morning News,* September 26, 2001). The audience already has an enemy, Osama bin Laden, and Leno creatively links the villain of the audience with the villain she is denouncing.

Leno also created powerful identification by using metaphor to build her case. According to Foss (2004),

> We do not perceive reality and then interpret or give it meaning. Rather, we experience reality through the language by which we describe it; it is whatever we describe it *as.* Metaphor is a basic way by which the process of using

symbols to construct reality occurs. It serves as a structuring principle, focusing on particular aspects of a phenomenon and hiding others; thus, each metaphor produces a different description of the "same" reality. (p. 300)

If an audience accepts this "reality," the metaphor can then signify specific courses of action for listeners or readers. Not only is metaphor argument, according to Kenneth Burke (1945/1969, pp. 503–504), but it is also a marker delineating the user's "perspective." If we take Burke's position, it then follows that an analysis of the key symbolic constructs used by a given speaker enables the critic to understand point of view and to draw certain conclusions about motive, function, and effectiveness of the propagandist.

Leno maintained often, "They [women of Afghanistan] have been hijacked as surely as those people on the airliners were hijacked," and "When the Taliban took over, they took away every kind of weapon. Believe me, no one there has a box cutter" (*Larry King Live,* September 26, 2001). She extended the terrorist metaphor to create identification between the United States and the Taliban when she said,

The United States created the Taliban. Obviously we didn't foresee what would happen. The reason that we owe Afghanistan big time, is that when the Soviets gave up and the Afghanistan people won the war, we just left. We didn't oversee the peace. The country was semi-annihilated and was sown from end to end with landmines and you now had all these 17-year-old boys who were religious fanatics wandering the country armed to the teeth with nothing to do with themselves. You fill in the blank. What did we think would happen? We really dropped the ball on this one. We created a terrible humanitarian disaster for the people of this country, especially the women, and we created a landmine for ourselves which very sadly exploded in New York. (News conference, September 30, 2001)

So because of the United States's complicity with the Taliban coming into power, the United States suffered as well as the Afghan people have suffered at the hands of the evil Taliban; both had been "hijacked." As a result, the United States must rescue the Afghanistan people from the evil that was created by the United States, since the United States was guilty of the existence of the Taliban. Then, in her narrative, "The Taliban will collapse and be forced to release the country. And I do mean release, because the Taliban has essentially hijacked the Afghan people" (*KTLA Morning News,* September 27, 2001). She identified the victimization of Americans and terrorism with the victimization of Afghan women and terrorism. They also could identify the same evil villain and must remove that villain in order that they might live in peace, freedom, and justice. This strategic use of a terrorist metaphor has the potential to arouse great emotion in the audience considering the context of 9/11.

Audience Reaction to Various Techniques

There is evidence that there was favorable response by American audiences to Leno's rhetoric because some individuals called in to ask questions on talk shows when Leno wrote a letter in "Dear Abby" (*Entertainment Weekly*, May 1999); according to Eleanor Smeal, president of FMF, the telephone systems crashed at headquarters with responses from readers. Also, there was a very positive and large celebrity audience that attended the Hollywood fund-raiser and lent their support with money, voice, and presence. This was highly publicized in multiple media venues. After 9/11, Leno's narrative kept America focused on the plight of the women and female children in Afghanistan so that no one could forget the importance of including them in any solution found there during and after the war.

Effects and Evaluation

Kenneth Burke's (1945/1969, p. 42) appropriation of the melodramatic form as a means of critique is interesting in that he finds the hero-against-villain struggle useful in describing perpetual conflict arising from polar symbolic constructs. In this frame, Burke points to a kind of critical blindness that can obscure the exchange of symbols in a communication event when participants engage in reducing their perceptions to melodramatic dimensions. A reading of Burke would suggest that the positions of villain victimizer and heroic avenger—with their attributes of the demonized other, pure self, good and evil intent—tend to define or prescribe future acts. Once the melodrama has taken shape, there is little hope of escaping its terminal velocity.

Prior to the destruction of the World Trade Center Towers, Mavis Leno designed an entry onto the news entertainment platform by casting her story, with the Taliban as villain, the Afghan women as victims, and the good people of the United States as potential heroes. So the media turned their attention to an inside look at a giant celebrity. The tragic melodrama of Afghanistan became an exercise in voyeurism about the home life of a comedian. FMF's story was relegated to a side issue that lacked obvious mass appeal and might even be considered a downer. There was something missing in the melodramatic construct created by Mavis Leno and the FMF, and the story was languishing after its brief time in the spotlight.

Before the attacks on September 11, 2001, Mavis Leno was presented as a celebrity with a cause who traded her husband's fame for a little attention to suffering women half a world away. After the attacks, she was a prophet who had foretold of the villainous evildoers and the innocent hapless victims. And this time the hero was defined: It was the U.S. military.

The strategies taken by the feminists of the FMF have adapted media-constructed realities by fitting their message into a form most recognizable to producers of popular entertainment. It is perhaps too early to determine whether this adaptive maneuver signals a shift away from traditional forms of feminist social agitation, but the phenomena surrounding the Mavis Leno story suggest that new understandings of feminist power may be merging in a way that complements a tactical choice to use the primordial frame of melodrama in the virtual world of mass entertainment. As Leno explained to me when she was considering what had been the most effective choice looking back at her campaign, "And right now that would be one of the biggest things I would advise anyone trying to spread the word about anything to do. Forget the serious news, go to the popular press" (M. N. Leno, personal communication, January 15, 2004). With Leno and the FMF, there has been a conscious choice to enter a highly crafted narrative into the virtual world of entertainment. Popular entertainers have never shied away from speaking their mind on an issue, but what is new here is the use of the tools of commercial entertainment to communicate a message of counterhegemonic dissent. Leno commented on the effectiveness of this strategy when she told me about the hours after the September attacks. She stated, "And I do think the tremendous visibility we were able to get for this issue, even before 9/11, and then we were able to build on that after 9/11. I think it had some impact on our government's decision to make the restoration of women's civil and human rights in Afghanistan a nonnegotiable part of the new government" (M. N. Leno, personal communication, January 15, 2004).

Foss's (2004) narrative frame here is doubled. There is the frame of the story of oppressed women, and the frame of melodrama necessitated by the commercial nature of the media. Leno was offered a role in the melodrama that emerged out of the events of September 11. She was cast in the story because she was, at the time, producing her own related narrative. Because of the timing, she was able to use the larger melodrama to her advantage, but this involvement in the larger cast soon led to her disappearance from the stage. The media's ever-ravenous appetite for neater and more dramatic stories soon left Afghanistan and moved on to Iraq. But the effect of the Leno propaganda, in the given moment, seems to have been great. The country's familiarity with Islamic fundamentalism and the condition of life for the women within that system was obviously expanded.

As with using celebrity, using melodrama as a propaganda narrative construct has certainly been a part of public discourse for a very long time. But there is something more interesting about the recent use of the form, as it is here combined with the virtual world of popular entertainment; it seems to point to a new method of dissent, and it has one additional outcome. Mavis Leno was not a victim accusing her oppressor. She was not a hero figure saving the helpless masses. Instead, Mavis Leno placed the treatment of women onto the global stage, using Afghanistan as both real cause and metaphor, and by doing that, she circumvented the normal barriers that would offer resistance to her message. Because she spoke of a foreign melodrama, she could cast the whole world as heroes and thereby create a watershed of support for fair and just treatment of women worldwide. So, in the end, the over-reaching narrative produced propaganda that attempted to align the thoughts of the audience on several fronts: the situation of the oppressed women in Afghanistan, the "war on terror," and the more general problem of patriarchy. When I asked Leno what she believed to be the difference that she and the FMF made to the plight of the women in Afghanistan, she responded, "Women are always the chip that gets traded off when people are trying to make a deal at the table, when men are trying to make a deal at the table, and I think the difference is, we made this a chip that couldn't be traded off" (M. N. Leno, personal communication, January 15, 2004).

References

Beneath the veil [Film]. (2001). London: Hardcash Production.

Burke, K. (1969). *A grammar of motives*. Berkeley: University of California Press. (Original work published 1945)

Burke, K. (1989). *On symbols and society*. Chicago: University of Chicago Press.

Fisher, W. R. (1987). *Human communication as narration: Toward a philosophy of reason, value, and action*. Columbia: University of South Carolina Press.

Foss, S. K. (2004). *Rhetorical criticism: Exploration and practice* (3rd ed.). Long Grove, IL: Waveland.

Jowett, G. S., & O'Donnell, V. (1999). *Propaganda and persuasion* (3rd ed.). Thousand Oaks, CA: Sage.

Simons, H. W. (2000). Requirements, problems, and strategies: A theory of persuasion for social movements. In C. R. Burgchardt (Ed.), *Readings in rhetorical criticism* (pp. 369–389). State College, PA: Strate.

Stewart, C. J., Smith, C. A., & Denton, R. E. (2001). *Persuasion and social movements* (4th ed.). Prospect Heights, IL: Waveland.

Turner, V. (1982). *From ritual to theatre: The human seriousness of play*. New York: Performing Arts Journal Publications.

Media Artifacts

Access Hollywood, Internet Broadcasting Systems, Inc., October 22, 1998
Access Hollywood, Internet Broadcasting Systems, Inc., January 2, 1999
Access Hollywood, Internet Broadcasting Systems, March 24, 1999
Access Hollywood, Internet Broadcasting Systems, March 30, 1999
E! News Daily, E! Entertainment Television, October 22, 1998
E! News Daily, E! Entertainment Television, March 30, 1999
Entertainment Tonight, Paramount Television Group, March 30, 1999
Entertainment Tonight, Paramount Television Group, September 27, 2001
Entertainment Weekly, Entertainment Weekly and Time, Inc., May 6, 1999
Extra, Time Telepictures Television, October 22, 1998
Extra, Time Telepictures Television, January 1, 1999
Extra, Time Telepictures Television, March 24, 1999
Extra, Time Telepictures Television, September 27, 2001
Hardball, MSNBC, October 5, 2001
Howie Mandel Show, Paramount Domestic Television, February 10, 1999
Inside Edition, King World Production, March 24, 1999
Inside Edition, King World Production, September 27, 2001
Larry King Live, CNN, October 22, 1998
Larry King Live, CNN, September 26, 2001
Life & Times Tonight, KCET Community Television of Southern California,
    November 19, 1998
Life & Times Town Hall, KCET Community Television of Southern California,
    October 6, 2001
Morning News, CNN, October 21, 1998
Morning News, KTLA, January 13, 1999
News, FOX, March 8, 1999
News, KABC (Four Interviews), October 22, 1998
News, KABC (Seven Interviews), September 27, 2001
News, KCAL (Two Interviews), March 29, 1999
News, KCAL (Nine Interviews), September 27, 2001
News, KNBC, March 29, 1999
News, KNBC (Four Interviews), September 26, 2001
News, KTLA, March 29, 1999
News, KTLA (Five Interviews), September 26, 2001
News, KTLA (Five Interviews), September 27, 2001
News With Hannity & Colmes, FOX, October 4, 2001
News With Paula Zahn, CNN, September 28, 2001
News conference, Feminist Majority Foundation (Four Interviews), September 30, 2001
The View, ABC, March 9, 1999
Today Show, MSNBC, October 2, 2001
Tonight Show, NBC, March 23, 1999
Tonight Show, NBC, October 3, 2001

About the Editors

Garth S. Jowett is Professor of Communication at the University of Houston. He obtained his Ph.D. in communications history from the University of Pennsylvania. He has served as Director for Social Research for the Canadian government's Department of Communication and has been a consultant to various international communication agencies. He was appointed a Gannett Center Fellow in 1987–1988 and has published widely in the area of popular culture and the history of communication. His book *Film: The Democratic Art* (1976) was an important benchmark in film history. His volume in Sage's Commtext series, *Movies as Mass Communication* (with James M. Linton), is a unique and widely appreciated study. His most recent publication, *Children and the Movies: Media Influences and the Payne Fund Studies* (with Ian C. Jarvie & Kathryn H. Fuller), is a detailed account of an important rediscovery of a hitherto lost episode in mass communication history in the United States. He is also on the boards of several communication and film journals. He is currently working on a social history of television in the United States.

Victoria O'Donnell is Professor Emeritus and former Director of the University Honors Program and Professor of Communication at Montana State University–Bozeman. Previously, she was the Chair of the Department of Speech Communication at Oregon State University and Chair of the Department of Communication and Public Address at the University of North Texas. In 1988, she taught for the American Institute of Foreign Studies at the University of London. She received her Ph.D. from the Pennsylvania State University. She has published articles and chapters in a wide range of journals and books on topics concerning persuasion, the social effects of media, women in film and television, British politics, Nazi propaganda, collective memory, cultural studies theory, and science fiction films of the 1950s. She is also the author (with June Kable) of *Persuasion: An Interactive-Dependency Approach, Propaganda and Persuasion* (with Garth

Jowett), and *Speech Communication.* She is currently writing a book on television criticism. She made a film, *Women, War, and Work: Shaping Space for Productivity in the Shipyards During World War II,* for PBS through KUSM Public Television at Montana State University. She has also written television scripts for environmental films and has done voice-overs for several PBS films. She served on editorial boards of several journals. The recipient of numerous research grants, honors, and teaching awards, including being awarded the Honor Professorship at North Texas State University and the Montana State University Alumni Association and Bozeman Chamber of Commerce Award of Excellence, she has been a Danforth Foundation Associate and a Summer Scholar of the National Endowment for the Humanities. She has taught in Germany and has been a visiting lecturer at universities in Denmark, Norway, Sweden, and Wales. She has also served as a private consultant to the U.S. government, a state senator, the tobacco litigation plaintiffs, and many American corporations.

About the Contributors

Beth S. Bennett is an Associate Professor at the University of Alabama, where she is acting Chair of the Communication Department and Graduate Program Director. She teaches undergraduate and graduate courses in rhetorical studies. Her Ph.D. is from the University of Iowa. She has published articles about medieval rhetoric in several rhetoric journals, books, and an encyclopedia. She also writes about the application of rhetorical principles to contemporary issues. She received the Board of Visitors Excellence in Teaching Award and the Knox Hagood Outstanding Faculty Award.

Kenneth Burke (1897–1993), literary critic, poet, and rhetorician, taught at various colleges and universities, mainly at Bennington College in Vermont. He is best known for his philosophy of language and for contributing new ideas to rhetorical theory. He wrote many seminal books, including *Language as Symbolic Action, A Rhetoric of Motives,* and *The Grammar of Motives.* He was the first serious rhetorical critic to analyze Nazi propaganda.

Margaret Cavin is an Associate Professor of communication at Florida Gulf Coast University, where she teaches rhetoric and communication classes. She has also taught at California State University–Long Beach, the University of Tennessee–Chattanooga, Biola University, and Oklahoma Baptist University. She received her Ph.D. from the University of North Texas. She has published articles in *Peace and Change* and several book chapters in which she examined the rhetorical constructs of peace and social justice used by various orators such as William Sloane Coffin, Helen Caldicott, Sis Levin, Glenn Smiley, Greg Dell, and Elise Boulding.

David Culbert is Professor of History at Louisiana State University, Baton Rogue, and the editor of the *Historical Journal of Film, Radio and Television.* Among his wide range of publications are *News for Everyone: Radio and Foreign Affairs in Thirties America* (1976) and *Mission to Moscow* (1980), and he is one of the editors (with David Welch and Nicholas Cull) of the major reference source for propaganda studies, *Propaganda and Mass Persuasion: A Historical Encyclopedia, 1500–Present* (2003).

Jacques Ellul (1912–1994), French Protestant theologian and social critic, was a member of the French Resistance during World War II and later served as Professor of History and Sociology at the University of Bordeaux from 1946 to 1980. A prolific author, he wrote more than 30 books on ethics, biblical scholarship, and argued against total faith in technology. His book *Propaganda* (1965) is a classic in many languages.

Stuart J. Kaplan is Associate Professor of Communication at Lewis and Clark College in Portland, Oregon. He received his Ph.D. from the University of Oregon. He has published articles on communication policy, Internet free speech, and visual communication in *Communication Monographs, Quarterly Journal of Speech, Journalism Quarterly, Critical Studies in Mass Communication,* and *Idaho Law Review.*

Paul M. A. Linebarger was Professor of Asiatic Studies at Johns Hopkins University, School of Advanced International Studies. He was born in Milwaukee in 1913 and grew up and was educated in China and Japan, as well as attending school in Germany. He knew six languages and served in World War II as an army second lieutenant. He was involved in the formation of the Office of War Information and helped to organize the U.S. Army's first psychological warfare section. He was also well known as a writer of science fiction under the name Cordwainer Smith. He died in 1966.

Sean Patrick O'Rourke is Associate Professor of Rhetoric at Furman University. He also taught at Vanderbilt University and Oregon State University. He received his J.D. and Ph.D. from the University of Oregon. He writes on the rhetorical aspects of deliberative democracy, and his works have appeared in both scholarly and popular publications. He has been recognized by several outstanding teaching awards, including the Meehan Award for Teaching Excellence at Oregon State University, the Ingalls Award at Vanderbilt University, and the Furman Award for Meritorious Teaching at Furman University.

Nancy Snow is Associate Professor in the College of Communications at California State University, Fullerton, and a lecturer at the USC Annenberg School for Communication. She received her Ph.D. in International Relations from the School of International Service at The American University in Washington, D.C., and from 1992–1994 she worked for the U.S. Information Agency. She is one of the leading experts on the issue of diplomacy as propaganda, and the author of several major articles and books on this subject, including *Propaganda, Inc.: Selling America's Culture to the World* (2002), and *Information War: American Propaganda, Free Speech and Opinion Control Since 9/11* (2003).

Thomas C. Sorenson graduated from the University of Nebraska, Lincoln, in 1947, and after working as a radio and newspaper journalist, he joined the U.S. Information Agency in 1951. Following assignments in Beirut, Cairo, and Washington, he was appointed deputy director of the agency. He later became a vice president at the University of California, and in the last years of his life, he worked in private industry as a specialist in Middle Eastern affairs. He died in 1997 at age 71.

Philip Taylor is one of the leading historians and analysts of propaganda and is a Professor of International Communications at the University of Leeds. His many publications include *War and the Media: Propaganda and Persuasion in the Gulf War* (1998) and *Munitions of the Mind: A History of Propaganda From the Ancient World to the Present Day* (1990).

Gladys Thum began her career as a public relations writer for the Air Transport Command in World War II and later worked for several governmental agencies before becoming a faculty member at Florissant Valley Community College in St. Louis. **Marcella Thum** was an advertising copywriter with the Army Public Information Office in Okinawa and had a position with the Historical Division in Germany before becoming a librarian; she also was an Air Force librarian for many years and later worked in the school systems of St. Louis. The Thum sisters wrote several books together, including *Exploring Military America* (1982) and *Airlift: Story of Military Airlift Command* (1986).

David A. Welch is Professor of Modern European History and Director of the Centre for the Study of Propaganda and War at the University of Kent, Canterbury, England. He is the author of several major works examining the history of Nazi propaganda, most notably *The Third Reich: Politics and Propaganda* (2002). He is currently at work on a history of propaganda.